# LEVITICUS

WISDOM COMMENTARY

Volume 3

# Leviticus

S. Tamar Kamionkowski

Lauress Wilkins Lawrence
*Volume Editor*

Barbara E. Reid, OP
*General Editor*

A Michael Glazier Book

LITURGICAL PRESS
Collegeville, Minnesota

www.litpress.org

A Michael Glazier Book published by Liturgical Press

Cover design by Ann Blattner. *Chapter Letter 'W', Acts of the Apostles, Chapter 4,* Donald Jackson, Copyright 2002, *The Saint John's Bible,* Saint John's University, Collegeville, Minnesota USA. Used by permission. All rights reserved.

1    2    3    4    5    6    7    8    9

Library of Congress Control Number: 2018943823

ISBN 978-0-8146-8102-2    ISBN 978-0-8146-8127-5 (e-book)

*For my mother Leah, the strongest woman I have ever known.*

# Contents

# *Abbreviations*

| | |
|---|---|
| AB | Anchor Bible |
| *ABD* | *Anchor Bible Dictionary* |
| ABRL | Anchor Bible Reference Library |
| *AJSR* | *Association for Jewish Studies Review* |
| AOTC | Abingdon Old Testament Commentaries |
| ApOTC | Apollos Old Testament Commentary |
| ASOR | American Schools of Oriental Research |
| b. Ar | b. Arachin |
| b. Hul | b. Hullin |
| b. Kid | b. Kiddushin |
| b. Meg | b. Megillah |
| b. Pes | b. Pesachim |
| b. Sanh | b. Sanhedrin |
| BDB | F. Brown, S.R. Driver, and C.A. Briggs, *Hebrew and English Lexicon of the Old Testament* |
| BETL | Bibliotheca Ephemeridum Theologicarum Lovaniensium |
| *Bib* | *Biblica* |
| BibInt | Biblical Interpretation Series |

| BR | Biblical Research |
| BWANT | Beiträge zur Wissenschaft vom Alten und Neuen Testament |
| BZAR | Beihefte zur Zeitschrift für Altorientalische und Biblische Rechtsgeschichte |
| CAD | The Assyrian Dictionary of the Oriental Institute of the University of Chicago |
| CBQ | Catholic Biblical Quarterly |
| ETR | Etudes théologiques et religieuses |
| EvQ | Evangelical Quarterly |
| FAT | Forschungen Zum Alten Testament |
| FCB | Feminist Companion to the Bible |
| GBS | Guides to Biblical Scholarship |
| HALOT | L. Koehler and W. Baumgartner, The Hebrew and Aramaic Lexicon of the Old Testament |
| HAR | Hebrew Annual Review |
| HAT | Handbuch zum Alten Testament |
| HBM | Hebrew Bible Monographs |
| HCOT | Historical Commentary on the Old Testament |
| HS | Hebrew Studies |
| HTR | Harvard Theological Review |
| HUCA | Hebrew Union College Annual |
| IFT | Introductions to Feminist Theology |
| Int | Interpretation |
| IVP | InterVarsity Press |
| JAAR | Journal of the American Academy of Religion |
| JANER | The Journal of Ancient Near Eastern Religions |
| JAOS | Journal of the American Oriental Society |
| JBL | Journal of Biblical Literature |
| JBQ | Jewish Bible Quarterly |
| JFSR | Journal of Feminist Studies in Religion |

| | |
|---|---|
| *JHebS* | *Journal of Hebrew Scriptures* |
| *JNES* | *Journal for Near Eastern Studies* |
| JPS | Jewish Publication Society |
| *JQR* | *Jewish Quarterly Review* |
| JSB | Jewish Study Bible |
| *JSOT* | *Journal for the Study of the Old Testament* |
| JSOTSup | Journal for the Study of the Old Testament Supplementary Series |
| LHB/OTS | The Library of Hebrew Bible/ Old Testament Studies |
| *JSQ* | *Jewish Studies Quarterly* |
| LAI | Library of Ancient Israel |
| LCL | Loeb Classical Library |
| m. Ker | m. Keritot |
| m. Mid | m. Middot |
| m. Qidd | m. Qiddushin |
| NJPS | New Jewish Publication Society |
| NRSV | New Revised Standard Version |
| OTL | Old Testament Library |
| *PEQ* | *Palestine Exploration Quarterly* |
| PL | Patrologia Latina |
| *PMLA* | *Proceedings of the Modern Language Association of America* |
| *RB* | *Revue Biblique* |
| SPCK | Society for Promoting Christian Knowledge |
| SBL | Society of Biblical Literature |
| SJLA | Studies in Judaism in Late Antiquity |
| *ST* | *Studia Theologica* |
| StBibLit | Studies in Biblical Literature (Lang) |
| SymS | Symposium Series |
| *TDOT* | *Theological Dictionary of the Old Testament*, ed. G. J. Botterweck and H. Ringgren |
| *TWOT* | *Theological Wordbook of the Old Testament* |

| | |
|---|---|
| *UF* | *Ugarit-Forschungen* |
| URJ | Union of Reform Judaism |
| *VT* | *Vetus Testamentum* |
| VTSup | Supplements to *Vetus Testamentum* |
| WBC | Word Biblical Commentary |
| WMANT | Wissenschaftliche Monografien zum Alten und Neuen Testament |
| *ZA* | *Zeitschrift für Assyriologie und Vorderasiatische Archäologie* |
| *ZAW* | *Zeitschrift für die Alttestamentliche Wissenschaft* |

# Contributors

Solomon Olusola Ademiluka (PhD, MA, BA Ed.), a graduate of University of Ilorin, Nigeria, is an associate professor of the Old Testament at Kogi State University, Anyigba, Nigeria. He is also a research fellow of University of South Africa (Unisa).

Rabbi Kerry Chaplin was ordained in 2015 from the Ziegler School of Rabbinic Studies. At the core of her rabbinate is relationship, which inspires her to work toward a world in which truth and empathy shall kiss and justice and peace shall meet (Ps 85:11). That work is anchored by a Jewish practice in which our greatest socio-political inequities not only shape who we are but also help us reveal the Divine among and within one another and compel us to shape a more whole world.

Susan K. Roll is associate professor of liturgy and sacraments in the Faculty of Theology, Saint Paul University, Ottawa, Canada, since 2003. Her publications include *Toward the Origins of Christmas* (1995) as well as two edited books and numerous publications on the liturgical year, the sacraments of initiation, and the feminist liturgical movement.

Kathleen Rushton of Otautahi Christchurch, Aotearoa, New Zealand, is an independent scholar whose doctoral research and publications are on Johannine birth imagery. Her current project is on social and ecological justice in the Gospel according to John to enable readings that hear both the cry of the earth and the cry of the poor.

David Seidenberg is director and creator of neohasid.org and the author of *Kabbalah and Ecology: God's Image in the More-Than-Human World* (Cambridge University Press, 2015). He holds a doctorate from the Jewish Theological Seminary (JTS) and was ordained by both JTS and Rabbi Zalman Schachter-Shalomi.

Jane Via, PhD (Marquette University 1976), JD, is a former professor of biblical studies, a retired attorney, and an ordained Roman Catholic Womanpriest and bishop. She serves as pastor emerita at the independent Roman Catholic parish she founded in 2005 in San Diego, California.

Alex Weissman received rabbinic ordination from the Reconstructionist Rabbinical College in Pennsylvania and currently serves as the Senior Jewish Educator at Brown RISD Hillel.

Sonia Kwok Wong is a lecturer in Hebrew Bible at the Chinese University of Hong Kong. She holds a PhD in religious studies from Vanderbilt University. She has written essays on postcolonial biblical interpretation and cross-textual hermeneutics.

# Foreword

# "Tell It on the Mountain"—or, "And You Shall Tell Your Daughter [as Well]"

*Athalya Brenner-Idan*

*Universiteit van Amsterdam/Tel Aviv University*

What can Wisdom Commentary do to help, and for whom? The commentary genre has always been privileged in biblical studies. Traditionally acclaimed commentary series, such as the International Critical Commentary, Old Testament and New Testament Library, Hermeneia, Anchor Bible, Eerdmans, and Word—to name but several— enjoy nearly automatic prestige, and the number of women authors who participate in those is relatively small by comparison to their growing number in the scholarly guild. There certainly are some volumes written by women in them, especially in recent decades. At this time, however, this does not reflect the situation on the ground. Further, size matters. In that sense, the sheer size of the Wisdom Commentary is essential. This also represents a considerable investment and the possibility of reaching a wider audience than those already "converted."

Expecting women scholars to deal especially or only with what are considered strictly "female" matters seems unwarranted. According to Audre Lorde, "The master's tools will never dismantle the master's house."[1] But this maxim is not relevant to our case. The point of this commentary is not to destroy but to attain greater participation in the interpretive dialogue about biblical texts. Women scholars may bring additional questions to the readerly agenda as well as fresh angles to existing issues. To assume that their questions are designed only to topple a certain male hegemony is not convincing.

At first I did ask myself: is this commentary series an addition to calm raw nerves, an embellishment to make upholding the old hierarchy palatable? Or is it indeed about becoming the Master? On second and third thoughts, however, I understood that becoming the Master is not what this is about. Knowledge is power. Since Foucault at the very least, this cannot be in dispute. Writing commentaries for biblical texts by feminist women and men for women and for men, of confessional as well as non-confessional convictions, will sabotage (hopefully) the established hierarchy but will not topple it. This is about an attempt to integrate more fully, to introduce another viewpoint, to become. What excites me about the Wisdom Commentary is that it is not offered as just an alternative supplanting or substituting for the dominant discourse.

These commentaries on biblical books will retain nonauthoritative, pluralistic viewpoints. And yes, once again, the weight of a dedicated series, to distinguish from collections of stand-alone volumes, will prove weightier.

That such an approach is especially important in the case of the Hebrew Bible/Old Testament is beyond doubt. Women of Judaism, Christianity, and also Islam have struggled to make it their own for centuries, even more than they have fought for the New Testament and the Qur'an. Every Hebrew Bible/Old Testament volume in this project is evidence that the day has arrived: it is now possible to read *all* the Jewish canonical books as a collection, for a collection they are, with guidance conceived of with the needs of women readers (not only men) as an integral inspiration and part thereof.

In my Jewish tradition, the main motivation for reciting the Haggadah, the ritual text recited yearly on Passover, the festival of liberation from

---

1. Audre Lorde, "The Master's Tools Will Never Dismantle the Master's House," in *Sister Outsider: Essays and Speeches* (Berkeley, CA: Crossing Press, 1984, 2007), 110–14. First delivered in the Second Sex Conference in New York, 1979.

bondage, is given as "And you shall tell your son" (from Exod 13:8). The knowledge and experience of past generations is thus transferred to the next, for constructing the present and the future. The ancient maxim is, literally, limited to a male audience. This series remolds the maxim into a new inclusive shape, which is of the utmost consequence: "And you shall tell your son" is extended to "And you shall tell your daughter [as well as your son]." Or, if you want, "Tell it on the mountain," for all to hear.

This is what it's all about.

# Editor's Introduction to Wisdom Commentary

## "She Is a Breath of the Power of God" (Wis 7:25)

### Barbara E. Reid, OP

*General Editor*

Wisdom Commentary is the first series to offer detailed feminist interpretation of every book of the Bible. The fruit of collaborative work by an ecumenical and interreligious team of scholars, the volumes provide serious, scholarly engagement with the whole biblical text, not only those texts that explicitly mention women. The series is intended for clergy, teachers, ministers, and all serious students of the Bible. Designed to be both accessible and informed by the various approaches of biblical scholarship, it pays particular attention to the world in front of the text, that is, how the text is heard and appropriated. At the same time, this series aims to be faithful to the ancient text and its earliest audiences; thus the volumes also explicate the worlds behind the text and within it. While issues of gender are primary in this project, the volumes also address the intersecting issues of power, authority, ethnicity, race, class, and religious belief and practice. The fifty-eight volumes include the books regarded as canonical by Jews (i.e., the Tanakh); Protestants (the "Hebrew Bible" and the New Testament); and Roman Catholic, Anglican, and Eastern Orthodox

Communions (i.e., Tobit, Judith, 1 and 2 Maccabees, Wisdom of Solomon, Sirach/Ecclesiasticus, Baruch, including the Letter of Jeremiah, the additions to Esther, and Susanna and Bel and the Dragon in Daniel).

## A Symphony of Diverse Voices

Included in the Wisdom Commentary series are voices from scholars of many different religious traditions, of diverse ages, differing sexual identities, and varying cultural, racial, ethnic, and social contexts. Some have been pioneers in feminist biblical interpretation; others are newer contributors from a younger generation. A further distinctive feature of this series is that each volume incorporates voices other than that of the lead author(s). These voices appear alongside the commentary of the lead author(s), in the grayscale inserts. At times, a contributor may offer an alternative interpretation or a critique of the position taken by the lead author(s). At other times, she or he may offer a complementary interpretation from a different cultural context or subject position. Occasionally, portions of previously published material bring in other views. The diverse voices are not intended to be contestants in a debate or a cacophony of discordant notes. The multiple voices reflect that there is no single definitive feminist interpretation of a text. In addition, they show the importance of subject position in the process of interpretation. In this regard, the Wisdom Commentary series takes inspiration from the Talmud and from *The Torah: A Women's Commentary* (ed. Tamara Cohn Eskenazi and Andrea L. Weiss; New York: Women of Reform Judaism, Federation of Temple Sisterhood, 2008), in which many voices, even conflicting ones, are included and not harmonized.

Contributors include biblical scholars, theologians, and readers of Scripture from outside the scholarly and religious guilds. At times, their comments pertain to a particular text. In some instances they address a theme or topic that arises from the text.

Another feature that highlights the collaborative nature of feminist biblical interpretation is that a number of the volumes have two lead authors who have worked in tandem from the inception of the project and whose voices interweave throughout the commentary.

## Woman Wisdom

The title, Wisdom Commentary, reflects both the importance to feminists of the figure of Woman Wisdom in the Scriptures and the distinct wisdom that feminist women and men bring to the interpretive process. In the Scriptures, Woman Wisdom appears as "a breath of the power of God, and a pure emanation of the glory of the Almighty" (Wis 7:25), who was present and active in fashioning all that exists (Prov 8:22-31; Wis 8:6). She is a spirit who pervades and penetrates all things (Wis 7:22-23), and she provides guidance and nourishment at her all-inclusive table (Prov 9:1-5). In both postexilic biblical and nonbiblical Jewish sources, Woman Wisdom is often equated with Torah, e.g., Sirach 24:23-34; Baruch 3:9–4:4; 38:2; 46:4-5; 2 Baruch 48:33, 36; 4 Ezra 5:9-10; 13:55; 14:40; 1 Enoch 42.

The New Testament frequently portrays Jesus as Wisdom incarnate. He invites his followers, "take my yoke upon you and learn from me" (Matt 11:29), just as Ben Sira advises, "put your neck under her [Wisdom's] yoke and let your souls receive instruction" (Sir 51:26). Just as Wisdom experiences rejection (Prov 1:23-25; Sir 15:7-8; Wis 10:3; Bar 3:12), so too does Jesus (Mark 8:31; John 1:10-11). Only some accept his invitation to his all-inclusive banquet (Matt 22:1-14; Luke 14:15-24; compare Prov 1:20-21; 9:3-5). Yet, "wisdom is vindicated by her deeds" (Matt 11:19, speaking of Jesus and John the Baptist; in the Lucan parallel at 7:35 they are called "wisdom's children"). There are numerous parallels between what is said of Wisdom and of the *Logos* in the Prologue of the Fourth Gospel (John 1:1-18). These are only a few of many examples. This female embodiment of divine presence and power is an apt image to guide the work of this series.

## Feminism

There are many different understandings of the term "feminism." The various meanings, aims, and methods have developed exponentially in recent decades. Feminism is a perspective and a movement that springs from a recognition of inequities toward women, and it advocates for changes in whatever structures prevent full human flourishing. Three waves of feminism in the United States are commonly recognized. The first, arising in the mid-nineteenth century and lasting into the early twentieth, was sparked by women's efforts to be involved in the public sphere and to win the right to vote. In the 1960s and 1970s, the second wave focused on civil rights and equality for women. With the third wave, from the 1980s forward, came global feminism and the emphasis on the contextual nature of interpretation. Now a fourth wave may be emerging, with a stronger emphasis on the intersectionality of women's concerns with those of other marginalized groups and the increased use of the internet as a platform for discussion and activism.[1] As feminism has matured, it has recognized that inequities based on gender are interwoven with power imbalances based on race, class, ethnicity, religion, sexual identity, physical ability, and a host of other social markers.

### Feminist Women and Men

Men who choose to identify with and partner with feminist women in the work of deconstructing systems of domination and building structures of equality are rightly regarded as feminists. Some men readily identify with experiences of women who are discriminated against on the basis of sex/gender, having themselves had comparable experiences; others who may not have faced direct discrimination or stereotyping recognize that inequity and problematic characterization still occur, and they seek correction. This series is pleased to include feminist men both as lead authors and as contributing voices.

### Feminist Biblical Interpretation

Women interpreting the Bible from the lenses of their own experience is nothing new. Throughout the ages women have recounted the biblical stories, teaching them to their children and others, all the while interpreting them afresh for their time and circumstances.[2] Following is a very brief sketch of select foremothers who laid the groundwork for contemporary feminist biblical interpretation.

One of the earliest known Christian women who challenged patriarchal interpretations of Scripture was a consecrated virgin named Helie, who lived in the second century CE. When she refused to marry, her

---

1. See Martha Rampton, "Four Waves of Feminism" (October 25, 2015), at http://www.pacificu.edu/about-us/news-events/four-waves-feminism; and Ealasaid Munro, "Feminism: A Fourth Wave?," https://www.psa.ac.uk/insight-plus/feminism-fourth-wave.

2. For fuller treatments of this history, see chap. 7, "One Thousand Years of Feminist Bible Criticism," in Gerda Lerner, *Creation of Feminist Consciousness: From the Middle Ages to Eighteen-Seventy* (New York: Oxford University Press, 1993), 138–66; Susanne Scholz, "From the 'Woman's Bible' to the 'Women's Bible,' The History of Feminist Approaches to the Hebrew Bible," in *Introducing the Women's Hebrew Bible*, IFT 13 (New York: T&T Clark, 2007), 12–32; Marion Ann Taylor and Agnes Choi, eds., *Handbook of Women Biblical Interpreters: A Historical and Biographical Guide* (Grand Rapids: Baker Academic, 2012).

parents brought her before a judge, who quoted to her Paul's admonition, "It is better to marry than to be aflame with passion" (1 Cor 7:9). In response, Helie first acknowledges that this is what Scripture says, but then she retorts, "but not for everyone, that is, not for holy virgins."[3] She is one of the first to question the notion that a text has one meaning that is applicable in all situations.

A Jewish woman who also lived in the second century CE, Beruriah, is said to have had "profound knowledge of biblical exegesis and outstanding intelligence."[4] One story preserved in the Talmud (b. Berakot 10a) tells of how she challenged her husband, Rabbi Meir, when he prayed for the destruction of a sinner. Proffering an alternate interpretation, she argued that Psalm 104:35 advocated praying for the destruction of sin, not the sinner.

In medieval times the first written commentaries on Scripture from a critical feminist point of view emerge. While others may have been produced and passed on orally, they are for the most part lost to us now. Among the earliest preserved feminist writings are those of Hildegard of Bingen (1098–1179), German writer, mystic, and abbess of a Benedictine monastery. She reinterpreted the Genesis narratives in a way that presented women and men as complementary and interdependent. She frequently wrote about feminine aspects of the Divine.[5] Along with other women mystics of the time, such as Julian of Norwich (1342–ca. 1416), she spoke authoritatively from her personal experiences of God's revelation in prayer.

In this era, women were also among the scribes who copied biblical manuscripts. Notable among them is Paula Dei Mansi of Verona, from a distinguished family of Jewish scribes. In 1288, she translated from Hebrew into Italian a collection of Bible commentaries written by her father and added her own explanations.[6]

Another pioneer, Christine de Pizan (1365–ca. 1430), was a French court writer and prolific poet. She used allegory and common sense

3. Madrid, Escorial MS, a II 9, f. 90 v., as cited in Lerner, *Feminist Consciousness*, 140.

4. See Judith R. Baskin, "Women and Post-Biblical Commentary," in *The Torah: A Women's Commentary*, ed. Tamara Cohn Eskenazi and Andrea L. Weiss (New York: Women of Reform Judaism, Federation of Temple Sisterhood, 2008), xlix–lv, at lii.

5. Hildegard of Bingen, *De Operatione Dei*, 1.4.100; PL 197:885bc, as cited in Lerner, *Feminist Consciousness*, 142–43. See also Barbara Newman, *Sister of Wisdom: St. Hildegard's Theology of the Feminine* (Berkeley: University of California Press, 1987).

6. Emily Taitz, Sondra Henry, Cheryl Tallan, eds., *JPS Guide to Jewish Women 600 B.C.E.–1900 C.E.* (Philadelphia: Jewish Publication Society of America, 2003), 110–11.

to subvert misogynist readings of Scripture and celebrated the accomplishments of female biblical figures to argue for women's active roles in building society.[7]

By the seventeenth century, there were women who asserted that the biblical text needs to be understood and interpreted in its historical context. For example, Rachel Speght (1597–ca. 1630), a Calvinist English poet, elaborates on the historical situation in first-century Corinth that prompted Paul to say, "It is well for a man not to touch a woman" (1 Cor 7:1). Her aim was to show that the biblical texts should not be applied in a literal fashion to all times and circumstances. Similarly, Margaret Fell (1614–1702), one of the founders of the Religious Society of Friends (Quakers) in Britain, addressed the Pauline prohibitions against women speaking in church by insisting that they do not have universal validity. Rather, they need to be understood in their historical context, as addressed to a local church in particular time-bound circumstances.[8]

Along with analyzing the historical context of the biblical writings, women in the eighteenth and nineteenth centuries began to attend to misogynistic interpretations based on faulty translations. One of the first to do so was British feminist Mary Astell (1666–1731).[9] In the United States, the Grimké sisters, Sarah (1792–1873) and Angelina (1805–1879), Quaker women from a slaveholding family in South Carolina, learned biblical Greek and Hebrew so that they could interpret the Bible for themselves. They were prompted to do so after men sought to silence them from speaking out against slavery and for women's rights by claiming that the Bible (e.g., 1 Cor 14:34) prevented women from speaking in public.[10] Another prominent abolitionist, Sojourner Truth (ca. 1797–1883), a former slave, quoted the Bible liberally in her speeches[11] and in so doing challenged cultural assumptions and biblical interpretations that undergird gender inequities.

---

7. See further Taylor and Choi, *Handbook of Women Biblical Interpreters*, 127–32.

8. Her major work, *Women's Speaking Justified, Proved and Allowed by the Scriptures*, published in London in 1667, gave a systematic feminist reading of all biblical texts pertaining to women.

9. Mary Astell, *Some Reflections upon Marriage* (New York: Source Book Press, 1970, reprint of the 1730 edition; earliest edition of this work is 1700), 103–4.

10. See further Sarah Grimké, *Letters on the Equality of the Sexes and the Condition of Woman* (Boston: Isaac Knapp, 1838).

11. See, for example, her most famous speech, "Ain't I a Woman?," delivered in 1851 at the Ohio Women's Rights Convention in Akron, OH; http://www.fordham.edu/halsall/mod/sojtruth-woman.asp.

Another monumental work that emerged in nineteenth-century England was that of Jewish theologian Grace Aguilar (1816–1847), *The Women of Israel*,[12] published in 1845. Aguilar's approach was to make connections between the biblical women and contemporary Jewish women's concerns. She aimed to counter the widespread notion that women were degraded in Jewish law and that only in Christianity were women's dignity and value upheld. Her intent was to help Jewish women find strength and encouragement by seeing the evidence of God's compassionate love in the history of every woman in the Bible. While not a full commentary on the Bible, Aguilar's work stands out for its comprehensive treatment of every female biblical character, including even the most obscure references.[13]

The first person to produce a full-blown feminist commentary on the Bible was Elizabeth Cady Stanton (1815–1902). A leading proponent in the United States for women's right to vote, she found that whenever women tried to make inroads into politics, education, or the work world, the Bible was quoted against them. Along with a team of like-minded women, she produced her own commentary on every text of the Bible that concerned women. Her pioneering two-volume project, *The Woman's Bible*, published in 1895 and 1898, urges women to recognize that texts that degrade women come from the men who wrote the texts, not from God, and to use their common sense to rethink what has been presented to them as sacred.

Nearly a century later, *The Women's Bible Commentary*, edited by Carol Newsom and Sharon Ringe (Louisville: Westminster John Knox, 1992), appeared. This one-volume commentary features North American feminist scholarship on each book of the Protestant canon. Like Cady Stanton's commentary, it does not contain comments on every section of the biblical text but only on those passages deemed relevant to women. It was revised and expanded in 1998 to include the Apocrypha/Deuterocanonical books, and the contributors to this new volume reflect the global face of contemporary feminist scholarship. The revisions made in the third edition, which appeared in 2012, represent the profound advances in feminist biblical scholarship and include newer voices. In both the second and third editions, *The* has been dropped from the title.

---

12. The full title is *The Women of Israel or Characters and Sketches from the Holy Scriptures and Jewish History Illustrative of the Past History, Present Duty, and Future Destiny of the Hebrew Females, as Based on the Word of God.*

13. See further Eskenazi and Weiss, *The Torah: A Women's Commentary*, xxxviii; Taylor and Choi, *Handbook of Women Biblical Interpreters*, 31–37.

Also appearing at the centennial of Cady Stanton's *The Woman's Bible* were two volumes edited by Elisabeth Schüssler Fiorenza with the assistance of Shelly Matthews. The first, *Searching the Scriptures: A Feminist Introduction* (New York: Crossroad, 1993), charts a comprehensive approach to feminist interpretation from ecumenical, interreligious, and multicultural perspectives. The second volume, published in 1994, provides critical feminist commentary on each book of the New Testament as well as on three books of Jewish Pseudepigrapha and eleven other early Christian writings.

In Europe, similar endeavors have been undertaken, such as the one-volume *Kompendium Feministische Bibelauslegung*, edited by Luise Schottroff and Marie-Theres Wacker (Gütersloh: Gütersloher Verlagshaus, 2007), featuring German feminist biblical interpretation of each book of the Bible, along with apocryphal books, and several extrabiblical writings. This work, now in its third edition, has recently been translated into English.[14] A multivolume project, *The Bible and Women: An Encylopaedia of Exegesis and Cultural History*, edited by Irmtraud Fischer, Adriana Valerio, Mercedes Navarro Puerto, and Christiana de Groot, is currently in production. This project presents a history of the reception of the Bible as embedded in Western cultural history and focuses particularly on gender-relevant biblical themes, biblical female characters, and women recipients of the Bible. The volumes are published in English, Spanish, Italian, and German.[15]

Another groundbreaking work is the collection The Feminist Companion to the Bible Series, edited by Athalya Brenner (Sheffield: Sheffield Academic, 1993–2015), which comprises twenty volumes of commentaries on the Old Testament. The parallel series, Feminist Companion

14. *Feminist Biblical Interpretation: A Compendium of Critical Commentary on the Books of the Bible and Related Literature*, trans. Lisa E. Dahill, Everett R. Kalin, Nancy Lukens, Linda M. Maloney, Barbara Rumscheidt, Martin Rumscheidt, and Tina Steiner (Grand Rapids: Eerdmans, 2012). Another notable collection is the three volumes edited by Susanne Scholz, *Feminist Interpretation of the Hebrew Bible in Retrospect*, Recent Research in Biblical Studies 7, 8, 9 (Sheffield: Sheffield Phoenix, 2013, 2014, 2016).

15. The first volume, on the Torah, appeared in Spanish in 2009, in German and Italian in 2010, and in English in 2011 (Atlanta: SBL Press). Five more volumes are now available: *Feminist Biblical Studies in the Twentieth Century*, ed. Elisabeth Schüssler Fiorenza (2014); *The Writings and Later Wisdom Books*, ed. Christl M. Maier and Nuria Calduch-Benages (2014); *Gospels: Narrative and History*, ed. Mercedes Navarro Puerto and Marinella Perroni; English translation ed. Amy-Jill Levine (2015); *The High Middle Ages*, ed. Kari Elisabeth Børresen and Adriana Valerio (2015); and *Early Jewish Writings*, ed. Eileen Schuller and Marie-Theres Wacker (2017). For further information, see http://www.bibleandwomen.org.

to the New Testament and Early Christian Writings, edited by Amy-Jill Levine with Marianne Blickenstaff and Maria Mayo Robbins (Sheffield: Sheffield Academic, 2001–2009), contains thirteen volumes with one more planned. These two series are not full commentaries on the biblical books but comprise collected essays on discrete biblical texts.

Works by individual feminist biblical scholars in all parts of the world abound, and they are now too numerous to list in this introduction. Feminist biblical interpretation has reached a level of maturity that now makes possible a commentary series on every book of the Bible. In recent decades, women have had greater access to formal theological education, have been able to learn critical analytical tools, have put their own interpretations into writing, and have developed new methods of biblical interpretation. Until recent decades the work of feminist biblical interpreters was largely unknown, both to other women and to their brothers in the synagogue, church, and academy. Feminists now have taken their place in the professional world of biblical scholars, where they build on the work of their foremothers and connect with one another across the globe in ways not previously possible. In a few short decades, feminist biblical criticism has become an integral part of the academy.

## Methodologies

Feminist biblical scholars use a variety of methods and often employ a number of them together.[16] In the Wisdom Commentary series, the authors will explain their understanding of feminism and the feminist reading strategies used in their commentary. Each volume treats the biblical text in blocks of material, not an analysis verse by verse. The entire text is considered, not only those passages that feature female characters or that speak specifically about women. When women are not apparent in the narrative, feminist lenses are used to analyze the dynamics in the text between male characters, the models of power, binary ways of thinking, and the dynamics of imperialism. Attention is given to how the whole text functions and how it was and is heard, both in its original context and today. Issues of particular concern to women—e.g., poverty, food, health, the environment, water—come to the fore.

---

16. See the seventeen essays in Caroline Vander Stichele and Todd Penner, eds., *Her Master's Tools? Feminist and Postcolonial Engagements of Historical-Critical Discourse* (Atlanta: SBL Press, 2005), which show the complementarity of various approaches.

One of the approaches used by early feminists and still popular today is to lift up the overlooked and forgotten stories of women in the Bible. Studies of women in each of the Testaments have been done, and there are also studies on women in particular biblical books.[17] Feminists recognize that the examples of biblical characters can be both empowering and problematic. The point of the feminist enterprise is not to serve as an apologetic for women; it is rather, in part, to recover women's history and literary roles in all their complexity and to learn from that recovery.

Retrieving the submerged history of biblical women is a crucial step for constructing the story of the past so as to lead to liberative possibilities for the present and future. There are, however, some pitfalls to this approach. Sometimes depictions of biblical women have been naïve and romantic. Some commentators exalt the virtues of both biblical and contemporary women and paint women as superior to men. Such reverse discrimination inhibits movement toward equality for all. In addition, some feminists challenge the idea that one can "pluck positive images out of an admittedly androcentric text, separating literary characterizations from the androcentric interests they were created to serve."[18] Still other feminists find these images to have enormous value.

One other danger with seeking the submerged history of women is the tendency for Christian feminists to paint Jesus and even Paul as liberators of women in a way that demonizes Judaism.[19] Wisdom Commentary aims to enhance understanding of Jesus as well as Paul as Jews of their day and to forge solidarity among Jewish and Christian feminists.

---

17. See, e.g., Alice Bach, ed., *Women in the Hebrew Bible: A Reader* (New York: Routledge, 1998); Tikva Frymer-Kensky, *Reading the Women of the Bible* (New York: Schocken Books, 2002); Carol Meyers, Toni Craven, and Ross S. Kraemer, *Women in Scripture* (Grand Rapids: Eerdmans, 2000); Irene Nowell, *Women in the Old Testament* (Collegeville, MN: Liturgical Press, 1997); Katharine Doob Sakenfeld, *Just Wives? Stories of Power and Survival in the Old Testament and Today* (Louisville: Westminster John Knox, 2003); Mary Ann Getty-Sullivan, *Women in the New Testament* (Collegeville, MN: Liturgical Press, 2001); Bonnie Thurston, *Women in the New Testament: Questions and Commentary*, Companions to the New Testament (New York: Crossroad, 1998).

18. Cheryl Exum, "Second Thoughts about Secondary Characters: Women in Exodus 1.8–2.10," in *A Feminist Companion to Exodus to Deuteronomy*, FCB 6, ed. Athalya Brenner (Sheffield: Sheffield Academic, 1994), 75–97, at 76.

19. See Judith Plaskow, "Anti-Judaism in Feminist Christian Interpretation," in *Searching the Scriptures: A Feminist Introduction*, ed. Elisabeth Schüssler Fiorenza (New York: Crossroad, 1993), 1:117–29; Amy-Jill Levine, "The New Testament and Anti-Judaism," in *The Misunderstood Jew: The Church and the Scandal of the Jewish Jesus* (San Francisco: HarperSanFrancisco, 2006), 87–117.

Feminist scholars who use historical-critical methods analyze the world behind the text; they seek to understand the historical context from which the text emerged and the circumstances of the communities to whom it was addressed. In bringing feminist lenses to this approach, the aim is not to impose modern expectations on ancient cultures but to unmask the ways that ideologically problematic mind-sets that produced the ancient texts are still promulgated through the text. Feminist biblical scholars aim not only to deconstruct but also to reclaim and reconstruct biblical history as women's history, in which women were central and active agents in creating religious heritage.[20] A further step is to construct meaning for contemporary women and men in a liberative movement toward transformation of social, political, economic, and religious structures.[21] In recent years, some feminists have embraced new historicism, which accents the creative role of the interpreter in any construction of history and exposes the power struggles to which the text witnesses.[22]

Literary critics analyze the world of the text: its form, language patterns, and rhetorical function.[23] They do not attempt to separate layers of tradition and redaction but focus on the text holistically, as it is in

---

20. See, for example, Phyllis A. Bird, *Missing Persons and Mistaken Identities: Women and Gender in Ancient Israel* (Minneapolis: Fortress, 1997); Elisabeth Schüssler Fiorenza, *In Memory of Her: A Feminist Theological Reconstruction of Christian Origins* (New York: Crossroad, 1984); Ross Shepard Kraemer and Mary Rose D'Angelo, eds., *Women and Christian Origins* (New York: Oxford University Press, 1999).

21. See, e.g., Sandra M. Schneiders, *The Revelatory Text: Interpreting the New Testament as Sacred Scripture*, rev. ed. (Collegeville, MN: Liturgical Press, 1999), whose aim is to engage in biblical interpretation not only for intellectual enlightenment but, even more important, for personal and communal transformation. Elisabeth Schüssler Fiorenza (*Wisdom Ways: Introducing Feminist Biblical Interpretation* [Maryknoll, NY: Orbis Books, 2001]) envisions the work of feminist biblical interpretation as a dance of Wisdom that consists of seven steps that interweave in spiral movements toward liberation, the final one being transformative action for change.

22. See Gina Hens-Piazza, *The New Historicism*, GBS, Old Testament Series (Minneapolis: Fortress, 2002).

23. Phyllis Trible was among the first to employ this method with texts from Genesis and Ruth in her groundbreaking book *God and the Rhetoric of Sexuality*, OBT (Philadelphia: Fortress, 1978). Another pioneer in feminist literary criticism is Mieke Bal (*Lethal Love: Feminist Literary Readings of Biblical Love Stories* [Bloomington: Indiana University Press, 1987]). For surveys of recent developments in literary methods, see Terry Eagleton, *Literary Theory: An Introduction*, 3rd ed. (Minneapolis: University of Minnesota Press, 2008); Janice Capel Anderson and Stephen D. Moore, eds., *Mark and Method: New Approaches in Biblical Studies*, 2nd ed. (Minneapolis: Fortress, 2008).

its present form. They examine how meaning is created in the interaction between the text and its reader in multiple contexts. Within the arena of literary approaches are reader-oriented approaches, narrative, rhetorical, structuralist, post-structuralist, deconstructive, ideological, autobiographical, and performance criticism.[24] Narrative critics study the interrelation among author, text, and audience through investigation of settings, both spatial and temporal; characters; plot; and narrative techniques (e.g., irony, parody, intertextual allusions). Reader-response critics attend to the impact that the text has on the reader or hearer. They recognize that when a text is detrimental toward women there is the choice either to affirm the text or to read against the grain toward a liberative end. Rhetorical criticism analyzes the style of argumentation and attends to how the author is attempting to shape the thinking or actions of the hearer. Structuralist critics analyze the complex patterns of binary oppositions in the text to derive its meaning.[25] Post-structuralist approaches challenge the notion that there are fixed meanings to any biblical text or that there is one universal truth. They engage in close readings of the text and often engage in intertextual analysis.[26] Within this approach is deconstructionist criticism, which views the text as a site of conflict, with competing narratives. The interpreter aims to expose the fault lines and overturn and reconfigure binaries by elevating the underling of a pair and foregrounding it.[27] Feminists also use other postmodern approaches, such as ideological and autobiographical criticism. The former analyzes the system of ideas that underlies the power and

24. See, e.g., J. Cheryl Exum and David J. A. Clines, eds., *The New Literary Criticism and the Hebrew Bible* (Valley Forge, PA: Trinity Press International, 1993); Edgar V. McKnight and Elizabeth Struthers Malbon, eds., *The New Literary Criticism and the New Testament* (Valley Forge, PA: Trinity Press International, 1994).

25. See, e.g., David Jobling, *The Sense of Biblical Narrative: Three Structural Analyses in the Old Testament*, JSOTSup 7 (Sheffield: University of Sheffield, 1978).

26. See, e.g., Stephen D. Moore, *Poststructuralism and the New Testament: Derrida and Foucault at the Foot of the Cross* (Minneapolis: Fortress, 1994); *The Bible in Theory: Critical and Postcritical Essays* (Atlanta: SBL Press, 2010); Yvonne Sherwood, *A Biblical Text and Its Afterlives: The Survival of Jonah in Western Culture* (Cambridge: Cambridge University Press, 2000).

27. David Penchansky, "Deconstruction," in *The Oxford Encyclopedia of Biblical Interpretation*, ed. Steven McKenzie (New York: Oxford University Press, 2013), 196–205. See, for example, Danna Nolan Fewell and David M. Gunn, *Gender, Power, and Promise: The Subject of the Bible's First Story* (Nashville: Abingdon, 1993); David Rutledge, *Reading Marginally: Feminism, Deconstruction and the Bible*, BibInt 21 (Leiden: Brill, 1996).

values concealed in the text as well as that of the interpreter.[28] The latter involves deliberate self-disclosure while reading the text as a critical exegete.[29] Performance criticism attends to how the text was passed on orally, usually in communal settings, and to the verbal and nonverbal interactions between the performer and the audience.[30]

From the beginning, feminists have understood that interpreting the Bible is an act of power. In recent decades, feminist biblical scholars have developed hermeneutical theories of the ethics and politics of biblical interpretation to challenge the claims to value neutrality of most academic biblical scholarship. Feminist biblical scholars have also turned their attention to how some biblical writings were shaped by the power of empire and how this still shapes readers' self-understandings today. They have developed hermeneutical approaches that reveal, critique, and evaluate the interactions depicted in the text against the context of empire, and they consider implications for contemporary contexts.[31] Feminists also analyze the dynamics of colonization and the mentalities of colonized peoples in the exercise of biblical interpretation. As Kwok Pui-lan explains, "A postcolonial feminist interpretation of the Bible needs to investigate the deployment of gender in the narration of identity, the negotiation of power differentials between the colonizers and the colonized, and the reinforcement of patriarchal control over spheres where these elites could exercise control."[32] Methods and models from sociology and cultural anthropology are used by feminists to investigate

28. See Tina Pippin, ed., *Ideological Criticism of Biblical Texts: Semeia* 59 (1992); Terry Eagleton, *Ideology: An Introduction* (London: Verso, 2007).

29. See, e.g., Ingrid Rosa Kitzberger, ed., *Autobiographical Biblical Interpretation: Between Text and Self* (Leiden: Deo, 2002); P. J. W. Schutte, "When *They*, *We*, and the Passive Become *I*—Introducing Autobiographical Biblical Criticism," *HTS Teologiese Studies / Theological Studies* 61 (2005): 401–16.

30. See, e.g., Holly Hearon and Philip Ruge-Jones, eds., *The Bible in Ancient and Modern Media: Story and Performance* (Eugene, OR: Cascade, 2009).

31. E.g., Gale Yee, ed., *Judges and Method: New Approaches in Biblical Studies* (Minneapolis: Fortress, 1995); Warren Carter, *The Gospel of Matthew in Its Roman Imperial Context* (London: T&T Clark, 2005); *The Roman Empire and the New Testament: An Essential Guide* (Nashville: Abingdon, 2006); Elisabeth Schüssler Fiorenza, *The Power of the Word: Scripture and the Rhetoric of Empire* (Minneapolis: Fortress, 2007); Judith E. McKinlay, *Reframing Her: Biblical Women in Postcolonial Focus* (Sheffield: Sheffield Phoenix, 2004).

32. Kwok Pui-lan, *Postcolonial Imagination and Feminist Theology* (Louisville: Westminster John Knox, 2005), 9. See also Musa W. Dube, ed., *Postcolonial Feminist Interpretation of the Bible* (St. Louis: Chalice, 2000); Cristl M. Maier and Carolyn J. Sharp,

women's everyday lives, their experiences of marriage, childrearing, labor, money, illness, etc.[33]

As feminists have examined the construction of gender from varying cultural perspectives, they have become ever more cognizant that the way gender roles are defined within differing cultures varies radically. As Mary Ann Tolbert observes, "Attempts to isolate some universal role that cross-culturally defines 'woman' have run into contradictory evidence at every turn."[34] Some women have coined new terms to highlight the particularities of their socio-cultural context. Many African American feminists, for example, call themselves *womanists* to draw attention to the double oppression of racism and sexism they experience.[35] Similarly, many US Hispanic feminists speak of themselves as *mujeristas* (*mujer* is Spanish for "woman").[36] Others prefer to be called "Latina feminists."[37] Both groups emphasize that the context for their theologizing is *mestizaje* and *mulatez* (racial and cultural mixture), done *en conjunto* (in community), with *lo cotidiano* (everyday lived experience) of Hispanic women as starting points for theological reflection and the encounter with the divine. Intercultural analysis has become an indispensable tool for working toward justice for women at the global level.[38]

---

*Prophecy and Power: Jeremiah in Feminist and Postcolonial Perspective* (London: Bloomsbury, 2013).

33. See, for example, Carol Meyers, *Discovering Eve: Ancient Israelite Women in Context* (New York: Oxford University Press, 1991); Luise Schottroff, *Lydia's Impatient Sisters: A Feminist Social History of Early Christianity*, trans. Barbara and Martin Rumscheidt (Louisville: Westminster John Knox, 1995); Susan Niditch, *"My Brother Esau Is a Hairy Man": Hair and Identity in Ancient Israel* (Oxford: Oxford University Press, 2008).

34. Mary Ann Tolbert, "Social, Sociological, and Anthropological Methods," in *Searching the Scriptures*, 1:255–71, at 265.

35. Alice Walker coined the term (*In Search of Our Mothers' Gardens: Womanist Prose* [New York: Harcourt Brace Jovanovich, 1967, 1983]). See also Katie G. Cannon, "The Emergence of Black Feminist Consciousness," in *Feminist Interpretation of the Bible*, ed. Letty M. Russell (Philadelphia: Westminster, 1985), 30–40; Renita Weems, *Just a Sister Away: A Womanist Vision of Women's Relationships in the Bible* (San Diego: Lura Media, 1988); Nyasha Junior, *An Introduction to Womanist Biblical Interpretation* (Louisville: Westminster John Knox, 2015).

36. Ada María Isasi-Díaz (*Mujerista Theology: A Theology for the Twenty-First Century* [Maryknoll, NY: Orbis Books, 1996]) is credited with coining the term.

37. E.g., María Pilar Aquino, Daisy L. Machado, and Jeanette Rodríguez, eds., *A Reader in Latina Feminist Theology* (Austin: University of Texas Press, 2002).

38. See, e.g., María Pilar Aquino and María José Rosado-Nunes, eds., *Feminist Intercultural Theology: Latina Explorations for a Just World*, Studies in Latino/a Catholicism (Maryknoll, NY: Orbis Books, 2007).

Some feminists are among those who have developed lesbian, gay, bisexual, and transgender (LGBT) interpretation. This approach focuses on issues of sexual identity and uses various reading strategies. Some point out the ways in which categories that emerged in recent centuries are applied anachronistically to biblical texts to make modern-day judgments. Others show how the Bible is silent on contemporary issues about sexual identity. Still others examine same-sex relationships in the Bible by figures such as Ruth and Naomi or David and Jonathan. In recent years, queer theory has emerged; it emphasizes the blurriness of boundaries not just of sexual identity but also of gender roles. Queer critics often focus on texts in which figures transgress what is traditionally considered proper gender behavior.[39]

Feminists also recognize that the struggle for women's equality and dignity is intimately connected with the struggle for respect for Earth and for the whole of the cosmos. Ecofeminists interpret Scripture in ways that highlight the link between human domination of nature and male subjugation of women. They show how anthropocentric ways of interpreting the Bible have overlooked or dismissed Earth and Earth community. They invite readers to identify not only with human characters in the biblical narrative but also with other Earth creatures and domains of nature, especially those that are the object of injustice. Some use creative imagination to retrieve the interests of Earth implicit in the narrative and enable Earth to speak.[40]

## Biblical Authority

By the late nineteenth century, some feminists, such as Elizabeth Cady Stanton, began to question openly whether the Bible could continue to be regarded as authoritative for women. They viewed the Bible itself as

39. See, e.g., Bernadette J. Brooten, *Love between Women: Early Christian Responses to Female Homoeroticism* (Chicago and London: University of Chicago Press, 1996); Mary Rose D'Angelo, "Women Partners in the New Testament," *JFSR* 6 (1990): 65–86; Deirdre J. Good, "Reading Strategies for Biblical Passages on Same-Sex Relations," *Theology and Sexuality* 7 (1997): 70–82; Deryn Guest, *When Deborah Met Jael: Lesbian Feminist Hermeneutics* (London: SCM, 2011); Teresa Hornsby and Ken Stone, eds., *Bible Trouble: Queer Readings at the Boundaries of Biblical Scholarship* (Atlanta: SBL Press, 2011).

40. E.g., Norman C. Habel and Peter Trudinger, *Exploring Ecological Hermeneutics*, SymS 46 (Atlanta: SBL Press, 2008); Mary Judith Ress, *Ecofeminism in Latin America*, Women from the Margins (Maryknoll, NY: Orbis Books, 2006).

the source of women's oppression, and some rejected its sacred origin and saving claims. Some decided that the Bible and the religious traditions that enshrine it are too thoroughly saturated with androcentrism and patriarchy to be redeemable.[41]

In the Wisdom Commentary series, questions such as these may be raised, but the aim of this series is not to lead readers to reject the authority of the biblical text. Rather, the aim is to promote better understanding of the contexts from which the text arose and of the rhetorical effects it has on women and men in contemporary contexts. Such understanding can lead to a deepening of faith, with the Bible serving as an aid to bring flourishing of life.

## Language for God

Because of the ways in which the term "God" has been used to symbolize the divine in predominantly male, patriarchal, and monarchical modes, feminists have designed new ways of speaking of the divine. Some have called attention to the inadequacy of the term *God* by trying to visually destabilize our ways of thinking and speaking of the divine. Rosemary Radford Ruether proposed *God/ess*, as an unpronounceable term pointing to the unnameable understanding of the divine that transcends patriarchal limitations.[42] Some have followed traditional Jewish practice, writing *G-d*. Elisabeth Schüssler Fiorenza has adopted *G\*d*.[43] Others draw on the biblical tradition to mine female and non-gender-specific metaphors and symbols.[44] In Wisdom Commentary, there is not one standard way of expressing the divine; each author will use her or his preferred ways. The one exception is that when the tetragrammaton, YHWH, the name revealed to Moses in Exodus 3:14, is used, it will be without vowels, respecting the Jewish custom of avoiding pronouncing the divine name out of reverence.

---

41. E.g., Mary Daly, *Beyond God the Father: A Philosophy of Women's Liberation* (Boston: Beacon, 1973).

42. Rosemary Radford Ruether, *Sexism and God-Talk: Toward a Feminist Theology* (Boston: Beacon, 1983).

43. Elisabeth Schüssler Fiorenza, *Jesus: Miriam's Child, Sophia's Prophet; Critical Issues in Feminist Christology* (New York: Continuum, 1994), 191 n. 3.

44. E.g., Sallie McFague, *Models of God: Theology for an Ecological, Nuclear Age* (Philadelphia: Fortress, 1987); Catherine LaCugna, *God for Us: The Trinity and Christian Life* (San Francisco: Harper Collins, 1991); Elizabeth A. Johnson, *She Who Is: The Mystery of God in Feminist Theological Discourse* (New York: Crossroad, 1992). See further Elizabeth A. Johnson, "God," in *Dictionary of Feminist Theologies*, 128–30.

## Nomenclature for the Two Testaments

In recent decades, some biblical scholars have begun to call the two Testaments of the Bible by names other than the traditional nomenclature: Old and New Testament. Some regard "Old" as derogatory, implying that it is no longer relevant or that it has been superseded. Consequently, terms like Hebrew Bible, First Testament, and Jewish Scriptures and, correspondingly, Christian Scriptures or Second Testament have come into use. There are a number of difficulties with these designations. The term "Hebrew Bible" does not take into account that parts of the Old Testament are written not in Hebrew but in Aramaic.[45] Moreover, for Roman Catholics and Eastern Orthodox believers, the Old Testament includes books written in Greek—the Deuterocanonical books, considered Apocrypha by Protestants.[46] The term "Jewish Scriptures" is inadequate because these books are also sacred to Christians. Conversely, "Christian Scriptures" is not an accurate designation for the New Testament, since the Old Testament is also part of the Christian Scriptures. Using "First and Second Testament" also has difficulties, in that it can imply a hierarchy and a value judgment.[47] Jews generally use the term Tanakh, an acronym for Torah (Pentateuch), Nevi'im (Prophets), and Ketuvim (Writings).

In Wisdom Commentary, if authors choose to use a designation other than Tanakh, Old Testament, and New Testament, they will explain how they mean the term.

## Translation

Modern feminist scholars recognize the complexities connected with biblical translation, as they have delved into questions about philosophy of language, how meanings are produced, and how they are culturally situated. Today it is evident that simply translating into gender-neutral formulations cannot address all the challenges presented by androcentric texts. Efforts at feminist translation must also deal with issues around authority and canonicity.[48]

---

45. Gen 31:47; Jer 10:11; Ezra 4:7–6:18; 7:12-26; Dan 2:4–7:28.

46. Representing the *via media* between Catholic and reformed, Anglicans generally consider the Apocrypha to be profitable, if not canonical, and utilize select Wisdom texts liturgically.

47. See Levine, *The Misunderstood Jew*, 193–99.

48. Elizabeth Castelli, "*Les Belles Infidèles*/Fidelity or Feminism? The Meanings of Feminist Biblical Translation," in *Searching the Scriptures*, 1:189–204, here 190.

Because of these complexities, the editors of the Wisdom Commentary series have chosen to use an existing translation, the New Revised Standard Version (NRSV), which is provided for easy reference at the top of each page of commentary. The NRSV was produced by a team of ecumenical and interreligious scholars, is a fairly literal translation, and uses inclusive language for human beings. Brief discussions about problematic translations appear in the inserts labeled "Translation Matters." When more detailed discussions are available, these will be indicated in footnotes. In the commentary, wherever Hebrew or Greek words are used, English translation is provided. In cases where a wordplay is involved, transliteration is provided to enable understanding.

## Art and Poetry

Artistic expression in poetry, music, sculpture, painting, and various other modes is very important to feminist interpretation. Where possible, art and poetry are included in the print volumes of the series. In a number of instances, these are original works created for this project. Regrettably, copyright and production costs prohibit the inclusion of color photographs and other artistic work. It is our hope that the web version will allow a greater collection of such resources.

## Glossary

Because there are a number of excellent readily available resources that provide definitions and concise explanations of terms used in feminist theological and biblical studies, this series will not include a glossary. We refer you to works such as *Dictionary of Feminist Theologies*, edited by Letty M. Russell with J. Shannon Clarkson (Louisville: Westminster John Knox, 1996), and volume 1 of *Searching the Scriptures*, edited by Elisabeth Schüssler Fiorenza with the assistance of Shelly Matthews (New York: Crossroad, 1992). Individual authors in the Wisdom Commentary series will define the way they are using terms that may be unfamiliar.

## Bibliography

Because bibliographies are quickly outdated and because the space is limited, only a list of Works Cited is included in the print volumes. A comprehensive bibliography for each volume is posted on a dedicated website and is updated regularly. The link for this volume can be found at wisdomcommentary.org.

## A Concluding Word

In just a few short decades, feminist biblical studies has grown exponentially, both in the methods that have been developed and in the number of scholars who have embraced it. We realize that this series is limited and will soon need to be revised and updated. It is our hope that Wisdom Commentary, by making the best of current feminist biblical scholarship available in an accessible format to ministers, preachers, teachers, scholars, and students, will aid all readers in their advancement toward God's vision of dignity, equality, and justice for all.

## Acknowledgments

There are a great many people who have made this series possible: first, Peter Dwyer, director of Liturgical Press, and Hans Christoffersen, publisher of the academic market at Liturgical Press, who have believed in this project and have shepherded it since it was conceived in 2008. Editorial consultants Athalya Brenner-Idan and Elisabeth Schüssler Fiorenza have not only been an inspiration with their pioneering work but have encouraged us all along the way with their personal involvement. Volume editors Mary Ann Beavis, Carol J. Dempsey, Amy-Jill Levine, Linda M. Maloney, Ahida Pilarski, Sarah Tanzer, Lauress Wilkins Lawrence, and Seung Ai Yang have lent their extraordinary wisdom to the shaping of the series, have used their extensive networks of relationships to secure authors and contributors, and have worked tirelessly to guide their work to completion. Two others who contributed greatly to the shaping of the project at the outset were Linda M. Day and Mignon Jacobs, as well as Barbara E. Bowe of blessed memory (d. 2010). Editorial and research assistant Susan M. Hickman has provided invaluable support with administrative details and arrangements. I am grateful to Brian Eisenschenk and Christine Henderson who have assisted Susan Hickman with the Wiki. I am especially thankful to Lauren L. Murphy and Justin Howell for their work in copyediting and to the staff at Liturgical Press, especially Colleen Stiller, production manager; Stephanie Nix, production assistant; and Tara Durheim, associate publisher.

# *Acknowledgments*

I am indebted to numerous individuals who have served as conversation partners during the course of this project. My research assistants, Rabbi Maurice Harris, Mackenzie Reynolds, and Nora Woods, asked challenging and pertinent questions that helped open my eyes to new interpretive possibilities. I am grateful for the faculty research grants of the Reconstructionist Rabbinical College that enabled me to hire such wonderful thinking partners. Rabbi Alan Lapayover at the library of RRC patiently tracked down obscure resources for me. There are too many colleagues to name, whose wisdom and insights have influenced this volume. I hope that they see the influence of their work in my own.

Back in 2012, I received an invitation from Barbara Reid to participate in this groundbreaking project. My appreciation for Barbara has only deepened over the years as I have witnessed the tremendous amount of work that goes into the publication of a new Bible commentary series, especially one that breaks the mold! My volume editor, Lauress Wilkins Lawrence, has helped to strengthen and clarify almost every page of this commentary. I am deeply grateful for her careful readings and probing questions. I have acquired not only an editor but also a wise friend.

Finally, I thank my family for their patience and understanding and I apologize for the many evenings during which they did not receive my full attention. I thank them for their willingness to put up with piles of books in almost every room of the house on sacrifices, blood, genital discharges, incest, skin afflictions, and more blood! To Jennifer and Tali who teasingly asked why another book titled *Leviticus* is necessary, I hope that the content of this commentary speaks for itself.

# Author's Introduction

# *Reading Leviticus with a Feminist Lens*

*The Adoration of Innana of Ur*[1]
Knowing Wise, Queen of all the Lands,
Who Multiplies (all) living creatures (and) peoples—
I have uttered your Holy Song.
Life-Giving Goddess, fit for the ME,
Whose acclamation is exalted,
Merciful, Life-Giving, Woman, Radiant of Heart,
I have uttered it before You in accordance with the ME.
I have entered before You in my holy gipar,[2]
*I, the En, Enheduanna,*
*Carry the masab-basket, I uttered a joyous chant . . .*

This commentary reflects my interactions with the book of Leviticus and the community of scholarship that enfolds it from the perspective of a female Jewish feminist biblicist. I write about Leviticus because I love it—I find it endlessly fascinating. It is a part of my people's

1. Betty de Shong Meader, *Inanna, Lady of the Largest Heart: Poems of the Sumerian High Priestess Enheduanna* (Austin: University of Texas Press, 2000).
2. The *gipar* was the sacred space for the priestess. The last known Mesopotamian *gipar* was built by Nabonidus for his daughter around 590 BCE, attesting to the longevity of this holy space for over two thousand years. Enheduanna's *gipar* had a sacred washing room and food preparation areas for the ceremonial meals. "Its principal occupants were the moon-goddess Ningal and the en-priestess who so intimately assumed the goddess's role on earth. All the activity in the gipar focused on maintaining the link between these two" (ibid., 65).

tradition and thus a part of me. Unfortunately, within the history of biblical scholarship, Leviticus has been a site for conscious and unconscious anti-Semitism. Therefore, in full disclosure, I cannot read the text without some degree of defensiveness, and it is my hope that I will be successful in uncovering and exposing the gems in the text as I also call the text to account where it promotes oppressive or potentially harmful positions.

## Ritual or Text?

Perhaps the greatest challenge in exploring the book of Leviticus is identifying the genre of the material, which, as John Barton explains, is important for understanding a text. For example, when we hear "Not Guilty!" we know that the context is a criminal trial.[3] Regarding Leviticus, however, we cannot easily identify its genre, its context, or its earliest purposes. If we consider the first seven chapters of Leviticus, we encounter instructions regarding ritual offerings to the deity. Do these first chapters of Leviticus constitute a manual for priests, or a work of fictional literature, or perhaps an ideologically rich political platform? The uncertainty of genre constrains our ability to understand the text.

While there are many theories regarding the nature of this biblical book, a comparison between two specific approaches is illuminating. Baruch Levine, in his commentary on Leviticus,[4] states that his approach to the material is via realism; he assumes that the texts accurately portray some of the practices of ancient Israel and that, while the book may have taken its final shape in the early postexilic world, it was composed of a collection of earlier works that reflect actual rituals. Simultaneously, he acknowledges that the Aaronide priesthood seems to be a late construction because there is no mention of an Aaronide line from Judges through Kings and Ezekiel. Levine also asserts that while late Second Temple Judaism makes many references to an elaborate cult in Jerusalem, we cannot determine the degree to which the temple relied on the book of Leviticus.[5] Thus, while the final composition of Leviticus projects back

3. John Barton, *Reading the Old Testament: Method in Biblical Study*, rev. and enl. ed. (Louisville: Westminster John Knox Press, 1996), 32.

4. Baruch Levine, *Leviticus: A JPS Torah Commentary* (Philadelphia: Jewish Publication Society of America, 1989).

5. The significant corpus of Qumran scrolls interprets and leverages Leviticus for the various needs of early Jewish sectarianism and has helped scholars to better understand the world of Second Temple Judaism(s). While this body of literature is essential for understanding the reception history of Leviticus, the focus of this commentary is on the theology and ideology of the book of Leviticus itself.

into early Israel, the Aaronides and the tabernacle narrative, the building blocks of the book, are likely rooted in actual ancient practices. Levine's ultimate goal is therefore to reconstruct as much as possible the realia of the ancient biblical cult.

Jacob Milgrom engaged a lifetime of research on Leviticus and priestly (P) literature with the assumption that Leviticus reflects the actual practices of ancient Israel. His focus, however, was less on a reconstruction of those ancient practices (although he does do a lot of this) than on uncovering the rationale behind the priestly laws. Milgrom believes that the ritual law reflects a coherent and consistent belief system. He argues that the sacrificial system is the manifestation of a profound theological worldview and that a close study of the regulations and rituals can reveal the underlying system of thought. As Stephen Geller has expressed it, the priestly writers do not present systematic theologies; they embed their theology into the fabric of the ritual descriptions:

> The intellectual problem represented by P has nothing to do with the embarrassment he may cause to belief or to taste—both outside the realm of scholarly inquiry—but with the puzzling contrast between the clearly extensive ideational process implied by his massive editorial-compositional activity as creator of the Pentateuch and his reticence to verbalize his underlying concepts. P certainly has ideas but he rarely presents them openly. His motto seems to be, "Never explain!"[6]

In recent years, anthropologists and other scholars from intersecting fields have questioned to what degree rituals actually communicate coherent systems of meaning. Critics have proven that different participants in the same ritual understand the significance of the ritual differently and that, in many cases, participants cannot provide a consistent rationale for their activities. The functions of rituals change over time. The description of a ritual is not the same thing as an experience of a ritual.[7]

Many years ago, a friend told me a story of a synagogue that had an interesting custom. During Torah services on Sabbath morning, when the Torah was carried around the sanctuary in a procession, whoever was carrying the scroll would bend down at a particular point in the sanctuary and then rise up and continue the procession. A curious visitor began asking around to determine the meaning of this ritual act, but nobody

---

6. Stephen A. Geller, "Blood Cult: Toward a Literary Theology of the Priestly Work of the Pentatuch," *Prooftexts* 12 (1992): 99.

7. For a recent and comprehensive review of different interpretations of rituals and their influence on Leviticus studies, see James W. Watts, *Ritual and Rhetoric in Leviticus: From Sacrifice to Scripture* (Cambridge: Cambridge University Press, 2007), 1–26.

could give a reason: "That's just what we do" was a typical response. The visitor finally found one of the oldest members of the congregation and asked her about the ritual. The elderly woman remembered that before the sanctuary had been remodeled there was a low beam at that spot in the sanctuary, so people would have to bend down to avoid hitting the beam! How many times might we, as interpreters, develop complex explanations because we don't know that there was once a low beam? While this may be an extreme example, it mandates caution in reading rituals as logical and coherent.

Another important factor to consider is that rituals reflect and reinforce social structure and priestly privilege. As Saul Olyan has written, "Ritual, in my view, is not simply a reproductive activity in which social distinctions are mirrored, but also a productive operation in which social difference is realized. Rites shape reality for participants; they do not simply reflect some preexisting set of social arrangements brought into being elsewhere."[8] This commentary will pay particular attention to the interplay between rituals and power dynamics.

In addition, somewhat influenced by our access to new documents from the Second Temple period and a dissolution of the boundaries between Hebrew Bible scholars and scholars of the Second Temple period, more recent research shows that, as the biblical books began to take their final shape, readers of Leviticus were already interpreting the texts actively and creatively. Gary Anderson refers to this phenomenon as the "scripturalization of the cult."[9] Textual witnesses such as the Temple Document, the Book of Jubilees, and portions of the Mishnah "seek to reconstruct a model of sacrifice that is not simply reflective of actual practice, but results from learned exegesis of the Bible in its final canonical form."[10] In fact, in the aftermath of the destruction of the temple, the study of the text replaced the cult; b. Menachot 110a reads: "Whoever engages in the study of Torah portion on *olah*, is as if he sacrificed an *olah*, the portion on *mincha*, as if he offered a *mincha*, the portion on *hattat*, as if he sacrificed a *hattat*." The study and interpretation of the text becomes the ritual activity itself.

In recent years, many scholars have shifted from thinking about Leviticus as a book of rituals to Leviticus as text that uses ritual language.

---

8. Saul Olyan, *Rites and Rank: Hierarchy in Biblical Representations of Cult* (Princeton: Princeton University Press, 2000), 4.

9. Gary A. Anderson, "Sacrifice and Sacrificial Offerings (OT)," *ABD* (1992), 5:882.

10. Ibid., 5:873.

Wes Bergen has pointed out that texts about ritual probably arise from the absence of ritual. He likens Milgrom's approach to that of the rabbis who wrote after the destruction of the Second Temple. With the absence of ritual came the rise of the text. "So it would not be surprising for the rabbis to highlight the interior motivation (guilt) rather than the exterior action (bringing offering) of the one performing the ritual, given that the exterior action is no longer performed. This is the use Milgrom makes of them, in corroborating his own preference for the interior."[11]

The most eloquent proponent of the view that we ought to read Leviticus as text, and more specifically as text that has a rhetorical function, is James Watts. In response to scholars who believe that P's descriptions reflect actual practice, Watts states that "the setting of these ritual instructions in the Tent of Meeting, which no longer existed when P was written, gives the entire composition a utopian and even nostalgic cast." He further claims that just because the texts became authoritative does not mean that P's intended interpretations became authoritative.[12] Watts, therefore, advocates for a reading of Leviticus that asks about the rhetorical message of the text.

Watts rightly critiques Jacob Milgrom for reading this material strictly as ritual and not as literature.[13] Nevertheless, even Watts, for whom this work is rhetorical, delves into the detailed philological and exegetical work of identifying obscure references that are not necessarily central to the rhetoric of the literature. Part of the challenge lies in the likelihood that Leviticus contains embedded in it materials from different periods of the priestly authors. Some of this material may have originated as priestly instructional materials, but we know that by the post–Second Temple period it served as sacred literature. Thus, this literature is probably based on a complex combination of "realia" and "fantasy," that is, references to specific ritual practices packaged in rhetorical wrapping. The topics must be familiar enough for the early audiences of these texts to accept them; however, it is not simply a descriptive document. Therefore, I choose to adopt an eclectic approach to Leviticus, one that seeks to understand the material as recorded ritual and as a sacred, written document.

---

11. Wesley J. Bergen, *Reading Ritual: Leviticus in Postmodern Culture*, LHB/OTS 417 (London: T&T Clark, 2005), 7.

12. Watts, *Ritual and Rhetoric*, 27–29.

13. Ibid., 50–54.

As we engage in exegesis, therefore, we will focus on the rhetorical features that the texts employed, and we will try to discern theological components of the writers of these texts. We will often need to engage in philological and historical discussions, but not for the purpose of locating these texts in a particular historical period or for the purpose of imagining any realia behind them. We are seeking to understand what messages they were conveying, not what actions they were prescribing.

## The Gross Factor

Another challenge in reading the first parts of Leviticus is that the topic feels alienating, if not downright offensive, to many modern Westerners. Leviticus confronts us with slaughter, butchery, and blood manipulation. It is no surprise that both Jewish and Christian clergy tend to flounder for good sermonic material in this part of the Bible. We tend to read the text as reflecting primitive thought, an aspect of our past for which we must produce apologetics. Rabbi Maurice Harris shares a story about teaching this part of the Bible to a group of thirteen-year-old kids in Hebrew school. As usual, the kids described the text as gross and barbaric. Then one of his students exclaimed in response to the claim that animal sacrifices are gross:

> Well which do you think is more moral? Doing a sacred ritual and dealing with God every time you kill an animal for its meat, or anonymously shoving millions of animals into crowded pens and cages so that they're growing up in their own feces on factory farms, and filling the animals up with drugs . . . and then cutting up their body parts, shrink wrapping them in plastic and lining the walls of grocery store refrigerator cases with a horror show of dead animal parts from factory farms while you and your parents stand there talking about soccer?[14]

Perhaps it is not the fact of animal sacrifices that has put off generations of interpreters but the experience of having those Levitical practices placed at front and center.

## Leviticus and Feminist Studies

In the *IVP Women's Commentary*, Susan M. Pigott asks:

---

14. Maurice D. Harris, *Leviticus: You Have No Idea* (Eugene, OR: Cascade Books, 2013), 36.

What has Leviticus to do with women? On first glance it might seem little, if anything. The regulations are placed in the mouth of a man, Moses, and are directed primarily to men. No women play prominent roles in Leviticus as they do in Genesis, Exodus or even Numbers. The book focuses heavily on the role and responsibilities of the Aaron priests, none of whom were women. Laws about women focus on childbirth and menstruation, the two most intimate and unique aspects of sexuality that set women apart from men, both of which resulted in the epithet unclean. And when women vowed themselves to Yahweh, they were valued less than men were.[15]

Few feminists run to the book of Leviticus for inspiration! There have been, however, an increasing number of studies on Leviticus written by women and reflecting feminist values. Ironically, gender-sensitive readings of Leviticus came to the fore as (male) scholars began challenging the normative interpretation of the so-called ban on homosexuality in Leviticus 18:22 and 20:13.[16] In the past decade, a number of women in the field of biblical studies have produced monographs on Leviticus and gender. These studies focus mainly on the purity/impurity laws, especially as related to the parturient, menstruation, and sexual taboos. These studies include the work of Liz Goldstein,[17] Tarja Philip,[18] Deborah Ellens,[19] Eve

---

15. Susan M. Pigott, "Leviticus," in *The IVP Women's Bible Commentary*, ed. Catherine Clark Kroeger and Mary J. Evans (Downer's Grove, IL: InterVarsity Press, 2002), 50.

16. One notable exception is Mayer I. Gruber, who was one of the first male writers to note the important role of women in the Israelite cult ("Women in the Cult According to the Priestly Code," in *Judaic Perspectives on Ancient Israel*, ed. Jacob Neusner, Baruch A. Levine, and Ernest S. Frerichs [Philadelphia: Fortress, 1987], 35–48).

17. Elizabeth W. Goldstein, *Impurity and Gender in the Hebrew Bible* (Lanham, MD: Rowman & Littlefield, 2015).

18. Tarja S. Philip, *Menstruation and Childbirth in the Bible: Fertility and Impurity* StBibLit 88 (New York: Lang, 2006); "Gender Matters: Priestly Writing on Impurity," in *Embroidered Garments: Priests and Gender in Biblical Israel*, ed. Deborah W. Rooke (Sheffield: Sheffield Phoenix, 2009), 40–59.

19. Deborah L. Ellens, "Leviticus 15: Contrasting Conceptual Associations regarding Women," in *Reading the Hebrew Bible for a New Millennium*, ed. W. Kim et al. (Harrisburg, PA: Trinity Press International, 2000), 2:131–36, 138–41; "Menstrual Impurity and Innovation in Leviticus 15," in *Wholly Woman, Holy Blood: A Feminist Critique of Purity and Impurity*, ed. Judith A. Herbert, Judith Ann Johnson, and Anne-Marie Korte (Harrisburg, PA: Trinity Press International, 2003), 29–44; *Women in the Sex Texts of Leviticus and Deuteronomy: A Comparative Conceptual Analysis*, LHB/OTS 458 (London: T&T Clark, 2008).

Levavi Feinstein,[20] Sarah Shechtman,[21] Dorothea Erbele-Küster,[22] and Hilary Lipka.[23] Nicole Ruane's study on how gender hierarchy is reflected and reinforced in the biblical laws of sacrifice is groundbreaking.[24] It is a pleasure to foreground these scholars in a Leviticus commentary.

This feminist commentary on Leviticus seeks to accomplish several goals. One goal is to pay attention to ignored, overlooked aspects of the text and to ask questions that have not yet been asked of the text. For example, who is behind the production of the grain offerings, whether cooked or offered raw, given that women were the primary producers of breads? Another goal is to name the problematic and oppressive aspects of the text and to expose the ideologies of power that stand behind them. An obvious example is the fact that only men born of a certain family may gain access to the most holy spaces and objects. As we will note, this has ramifications for class distinctions between Aaronide and non-Aaronide women. A third goal, and perhaps the most challenging, is to uncover the ideologies and practices that actually undermine our assumptions about what we expect to find in a patriarchal system. Several recent monographs have addressed this question by differentiating between the patriarchal environment in which the writers lived and reflected, on the one hand, and the more egalitarian theologies and ideologies of the priestly writers, on the other hand. A fourth goal emerges from feminist scholarship of the 1980s—attempting to fill in the gaps and the silences and sometimes using what I like to call informed imagination, somewhat akin to the Jewish textual practice of midrash. For example, Athalya Brenner reflects:

> How does the priest's daughter's case differ from that of other daughters in a similar situation of presumably independent sexual behavior?
> . . . This harshness toward the priest's daughter is highly suspect, decidedly gratuitous—unless, unless, once upon a time, a priest's

---

20. Eve Levavi Feinstein, *Sexual Pollution in the Hebrew Bible* (New York: Oxford University Press, 2014).

21. Sarah Shechtman, "The Social Status of Priestly and Levite Women," in *Levites and Priests in Biblical History and Tradition*, ed. Mark A. Leuchter and Jeremy M. Hutton (Atlanta: SBL Press, 2011), 83–99; *Women in the Pentateuch: A Feminist and Source-Critical Analysis*, HBM 23 (Sheffield: Sheffield Phoenix, 2009).

22. Dorothea Erbele-Küster, *Körper und Geschlecht: Studien zur Anthropologie von Leviticus 12 und 15*, WMANT 121 (Neukirchen-Vluyn: Neukirchener Verlag, 2008).

23. Hilary B. Lipka, *Sexual Transgression in the Hebrew Bible* (Sheffield: Sheffield Phoenix, 2006).

24. Nicole J. Ruane, *Sacrifice and Gender in Biblical Law* (Cambridge: Cambridge University Press, 2013).

daughter belonged to the succession line, somehow, together with her brothers. Other explanations are of course possible, but why not also consider this one?[25]

In other words, a feminist commentary acknowledges that a significant part of biblical interpretation is based on patriarchal assumptions about how things must have been for the lives of the writers of the texts. I am not condoning assumptions and informed suppositions; our sources are so limited that informed conjecture is a necessity of the field of biblical interpretation. If we do need to fill in the blanks with our best guesses, however, then why use patriarchal assumptions? In this commentary I will, from time to time, use a feminist informed imagination as Athalya Brenner boldly proposes.

## Translation Matters

There are particular challenges in rendering the book of Leviticus into English, so while the primary translation provided is from the NRSV, I will often suggest alternative translations. Levine points to translation challenges in the introduction to his commentary when he cites Leviticus 1:4 and then remarks that to understand this verse, one must understand what an עלה is; identify what the verb סמך means in this particular context; comprehend the concept of נרצה and appreciate what כפר signifies when it appears with the preposition על.[26] Levine is pointing to the fact that the language of Leviticus is highly technical and specific. It is not enough to look up the Hebrew words in a lexicon because P may assign a very particular use to a word that appears elsewhere in more general terms.

Another challenge in translating Leviticus emerges from the tension between translating certain terms to best convey their meaning versus translating terms to best represent their rhetorical effect. For example, Milgrom translates the חטאת as a purification offering because he believes that the primary function of this offering was to purify the sancta. Watts points out that by translating חטאת as purification offering, Milgrom obstructs the rhetorical power of the repeated root, which is that חטאת as an offering is connected to the verb חטא and that the terms are used in interesting configurations. In a case like this one, there is significant

---

25. Athalya Brenner, "Gender in Prophecy, Magic and Priesthood: From Sumer to Ancient Israel," in *Embroidered Garments: Priests and Gender in Biblical Israel*, ed. Deborah W. Rooke (Sheffield: Sheffield Phoenix, 2009), 9.

26. Levine, *Leviticus*, xviii.

tension between capturing the meaning of the text and representing the literary form of the text.

Furthermore, Franziska Bark notes that we often have the context of narrative that assists us in determining the nuance of a word in translating biblical texts. Bark writes,

> It relieves her [the translator] of having to distinguish a thematic argument of the keywords, precisely because they do not form the complimentary or contrasting backdrop for some narrative. In fact, in Leviticus one often feels provided with hardly anything but keywords. The interdependence between what the text communicates and how this is signified, between its semantic and its structural make-up, is exceedingly dense. Here the keywords not only enforce the development of the thematic argument, but actually constitute it.[27]

## Organization and Structure of the Book

While the P source is interwoven throughout the first four books of the Pentateuch,[28] there is a priestly block of material that extends from Exodus 25:1 through Numbers 10:10. A commentary on the book of Leviticus must investigate the integrity of the book, but to understand its contents, we must consider the material in Exodus and Numbers from time to time.

Most commentators agree that Leviticus 1–16 constitutes the first section of the book and chapters 17–27 represent the work of another priestly school. From this starting point, commentators break down the book in different ways. Gordon Wenham sees four sections in Leviticus (chaps. 1–7, 8–10, 11–16, and 17–27), while John E. Hartley breaks the book into six sections (chaps. 1–7, 8–10, 11–15, 16, 17–26, and 27). For Hartley, chapter 16 sets the transition from a priesthood and community that needs to be cleansed and forgiven to a people who are ready to live by the laws prescribed in chapter 17 onward.[29]

---

27. Franziska Bark, " 'Listen Your Way in with Your Mouth': A Reading of Leviticus," *Judaism* 48 (1999): 201.

28. I use the term P to designate the priestly writings in the Pentateuch. In this commentary, I will not differentiate between various redactions of the priestly material. For the most part, I am interested in the final form of P texts. In this work I will use "priestly" to refer to a modality of thinking or worldview.

29. John E. Hartley, *Leviticus*, WBC 4 (Waco, TX: Word Books, 1992), xxxv. For a detailed study of the compositional history of Leviticus 17–26 in particular, see Henry T. C. Sun, *An Investigation of the Compositional History of the So-Called Holiness School: Leviticus 17–26* (PhD diss., Claremont Graduate School, Claremont, CA, 1990).

In recent years, several scholars have approached the question of the book's organization through a more complex lens. Mary Douglas has argued that the book of Leviticus is constructed with a series of ring structures, or set of sequences with a reversal midpoint through the ring, and that these rings are combined to form larger, more complex rings. The final composition of Leviticus is thus composed of three concentric rings with the sanctity of the tabernacle at the center. The outer ring represents the outer court, the middle ring represents the inner sanctuary space, and the inner ring corresponds to the holy of holies. She calls this kind of organization "analogical" and conceptually premodern. In short, she argues that the entire book is an intentionally crafted complex of concentric circles that were meant to correspond to priestly theology.[30]

More recently, Moshe Kline, building on Douglas's work, has argued that Leviticus is composed of "prime pericopes" that are then organized into rows of dyads or triads and then brought together into a three-by-three "table of prime pericopes," which Kline calls "units." Each of the nine pericopes that make up a single unit is connected vertically and horizontally. Kline identifies twenty-two units in Leviticus, which are arranged into larger units or structural elements. The structural elements are arranged in a complex chiastic construction. Ultimately, Kline sees an extraordinarily complex structure in the book that is very difficult to describe without recourse to diagrams and tables. He suggests that the author of Leviticus created this complex structure in order to create "an experience for the reader that bears a resemblance to the experience of the high priest on the Day of Purification. This would imply that the author was in possession of a way to re-create the highest order of religious experience and that this was somehow embedded in the book. Leviticus could then be viewed as a manual for arriving at this experience."[31]

The approaches of Douglas and Kline assume a single author who crafted a brilliantly complex edifice in order to offer the reader a particular experience. Kline, in particular, seems to imagine the book as a

30. Mary Douglas, *Leviticus as Literature* (Oxford: Oxford University Press, 1999). See also Bryan D. Bibb, *Ritual Words and Narrative Worlds in the Book of Leviticus*, LHB/OTS 480 (London: T&T Clark, 2009).

31. Moshe Kline, "Structure Is Theology: The Composition of Leviticus," *Current Issues in Priestly and Related Literature: The Legacy of Jacob Milgrom and Beyond*, ed. Roy Gane and Ada Taggar-Cohen (Atlanta: SBL Press, 2015), 255.

guided meditation, beckoning the reader to enter into the high priest's shoes on the Day of Purification. As a feminist, this nonlinear approach to the book, an approach that invites the reader not just to receive information and to analyze but also to engage emotionally and creatively, is appealing. Nevertheless, a few important questions bear consideration. If Douglas and Kline are correct in their general conclusions, can a modern reader share the experience of earlier generations of readers? If nobody else has detected these structures before, are they truly embedded in the text or have these structures been imposed on the text? A number of the smaller building blocks that they each identify feel forced. Still, this approach to Leviticus is bound to yield interesting new investigations into Leviticus and into ancient methods of composition.

## Authorship and Date

Assigning a date to the P texts continues to be the source of much disagreement among biblicists. Julius Wellhausen's theory set the stage for the debate. He understood the history of the religion of the Israelites as one that began with spontaneous simple worship (reflected in the J/E sources), then reached its apex as a religion rooted in ethics and right behavior (reflected in the prophets and in the D source), and finally took an unfortunate turn with the highly legalistic work of the priests in the postexilic period (reflected in P source). He argued that in the postexilic period, in the absence of kings, the priests rose to power and systematized worship. The P source was thus the latest of the sources of Torah and reflected an emergent Judaism characterized by ritual legalism.[32]

Alternatively, Yehezkel Kaufmann's view was that P predates Deuteronomy (D) and betrays its antiquity in a number of ways. He argued that many terms and rituals contained in P were not readily understood in the postexilic period, so they must be older in origin. He also posited that D refers to P, but not the other way around.[33] Menahem Haran used comparative studies with ancient Near Eastern materials to show that similar cult practices as those described in Leviticus existed at earlier times in

---

32. Julius Wellhausen, *Prolegomena to the History of Israel*, trans. J. S. Black and A. Menzies (Eugene, OR: Wipf and Stock, 2003). Originally published as *Prolegomena zur Geschichte Israels* (Berlin: Druck und Verlag von G. Reimer, 1882).

33. Yehezkel Kaufmann, *The Religion of Israel: From Its Beginnings to the Babylonian Exile*, trans. Moshe Greenberg (Chicago: University of Chicago Press, 1960).

the ancient Near East.[34] Avi Hurvitz generally followed Kaufmann with linguistic analyses of P material,[35] noting that the language predates the language of Ezekiel. Chronicles, Ezra, Nehemiah, and even Ezekiel share a common vocabulary and language for the cult, but P does not, so P material must be from an earlier time. These studies were in part provoked by Wellhausen's assumption that ritual legalism was the immediate forerunner to Judaism, while Christianity promoted the visions of the prophets. In recent years, scholars vary significantly in their dating of the P materials, although the current trend is to view P against the backdrop of the Persian Empire and the politics of repatriation.[36]

In recent decades, the dating of P has been interwoven with the dating of Holiness Legislation (H).[37] Scholars have long recognized that chapters 17–26[38] had a distinctive voice and perspective. For centuries this body of material was dated as a pre-P text that was absorbed into P in its final form. These chapters were titled the "Holiness Code" because of the central admonition to the people to be holy. Israel Knohl's study effected a significant change in perspective. He argued for an early preexilic date for P material and a later (but still preexilic) date for H. Knohl convincingly showed that H is a complement or supplement to P

---

34. Menahem Haran, "Behind the Scenes of History: Determining the Date of the Priestly Source," *JBL* 100 (1981): 321–33. See, more recently, Ziony Zevit, "Converging Lines of Evidence Bearing on the Date of P," *ZAW* 94 (2013): 263–75.

35. See, for example, Avi Hurvitz, "On the Usage of the Priestly term עדה in Biblical Literature," *Tarbiz* 40 (1970–1971): 261–67 (Hebrew); "The Evidence of Language in Dating the Priestly Code: A Linguistic Study in Technical Idioms and Terminology," *RB* 81 (1974): 24–56; and "Dating the Priestly Source in Light of the Historical Study of Biblical Hebrew: A Century of Wellhausen," *ZAW* 100 (1988): 88–100. Joseph Blenkinsopp's "An Assessment of the Alleged Pre-Exilic Date of the Priestly Material in the Pentateuch," *ZAW* 108 (1996): 495–518, ought to be taken more as a corrective than as a flat-out rejection of the possibility of a preexilic date for much of P.

36. See, for example, Mark Leuchter, "The Politics of Ritual Rhetoric: A Proposed Sociopolitical Context for the Redaction of Leviticus 1–16," *VT* 60 (2010): 345–65. Leuchter argues that Leviticus 16 was written to counter Nehemiah's appointment of Levites and teachers to positions of religious leadership.

37. In this commentary, H indicates Holiness Legislation instead of Holiness Code, following Baruch Schwartz's observation that H materials are found outside of this cluster of chapters and that calling the material a Code makes assertions about the composition, function, and style of the material. See Baruch J. Schwartz, *The Holiness Legislation: Studies in the Priestly Code* (Jerusalem: Magnes Press, 1999), 17–24 (Hebrew).

38. The origins of chapter 27 remain a matter of great debate, as will be discussed below.

written by priestly schools who heeded the words of Isaiah and that ethics must be a part of the priestly vision.[39] Milgrom,[40] Baruch Schwartz,[41] and David P. Wright[42] have followed Knohl's model with some modifications. Other scholars agree that H postdates P but argue that both works are postexilic. In other words, the dating of these materials continues to be a contentious issue.

For the purposes of this commentary, I believe that most of the P material existed in some raw form in the preexilic period and that the work took its final shape in the postexilic era. I follow Knohl, Milgrom, Schwartz, and Wright in believing that there is a distinct body of literature produced by a priestly group that is differentiated from the works of P by literary style, philological variation, worldview, and theology, and that is chronologically later than most of the P writings. I believe that H is a polemical response and supplement to P thinking. I find Avi Hurvitz's linguistic evidence to be compelling, and I am sympathetic to the sophisticated theological observations made by Milgrom and Knohl in considering H as a priestly revision of preexilic P cultic writings. I am convinced by the positions of Milgrom and Knohl[43] regarding the following points:

H is a polemical rejoinder to and theological revision of earlier P cultic material.

39. Israel Knohl, *The Sanctuary of Silence: The Priestly Torah and the Holiness School* (Winona Lake, IN: Eisenbrauns, 2007). Knohl has identified the work of H in other Pentateuchal passages besides Lev 17–26, such as Lev 7:22-36; 10:6-11; 11:43-45; 15:31; and 16:29b-33. He also identifies H interpolations in the book of Numbers.

40. Jacob Milgrom, *Leviticus 1–16*, AB 3 (New York: Doubleday, 1991), *Leviticus 17–22*, AB 3A (New York: Doubleday, 2000), and *Leviticus 23–27*, AB 3B (New York: Doubleday, 2001).

41. Schwartz, *The Holiness Legislation*; as argued similarly in his article, " 'Profane' Slaughter and the Integrity of the Priestly Code," *HUCA* 67 (1996): 15–42, esp. 16 n. 2.

42. David P. Wright, "Holiness in Leviticus and Beyond: Differing Perspectives," *Int* 53 (1999): 351–64.

43. Knohl, *Sanctuary of Silence*; and Jacob Milgrom, "The Changing Concept of Holiness in the Pentateuchal Codes with Emphasis on Leviticus 19," in *Reading Leviticus: A Conversation with Mary Douglas*, ed. John F. A. Sawyer (Sheffield: Sheffield Academic, 1996), 71. See also Baruch J. Schwartz, "Israel's Holiness: The Torah Traditions," in *Purity and Holiness: The Heritage of Leviticus*, ed. Marcel Poorthius and Joshua Schwartz, Jewish and Christian Perspectives 2 (Leiden: Brill, 2000), 47–59; and Wright, "Holiness in Leviticus and Beyond."

H represents a priestly response to prophetic critiques regarding the needs of ordinary Israelites.

H democratizes P's holiness, extending it beyond the priests to all of Israel and beyond the sanctuary to the entire land of Israel.

H uses anthropomorphic language to describe a God invested in the affairs of human beings.

H expands proper conduct beyond the realm of the purely cultic to include ethical behavior as well.[44]

## Theology in Leviticus

### Purity and Impurity

Anyone who encounters Leviticus, or works of interpretation about this book, invariably comes across the word טמאה, which is most often translated as "uncleanness" or "impurity."[45] Jewish practices and complex Christian theologies have been deeply informed by interpretations of this Hebrew word. Yet there is no single English word that best captures the meaning of this elusive term. We know that the counterpart to טמאה is טהרה and that the concept of holiness, קדושה, is interrelated with these two terms. Leviticus presents two sets of dualities: pure versus impure and holy versus common. God is holy and pure and therefore cannot tolerate impurity. People are generally not holy but can live in a state of purity or impurity. According to P, the community of Israel must keep itself pure to ensure God's continued presence in the tabernacle. As David Wright has defined it, impurity is "that which is a threat to or opposes holiness, and hence must be kept separate from that sphere."[46] Therefore, in this commentary I translate the term טמאה as "impurity" or "ritual impurity."

The central question that has plagued biblical scholars is the relationship between impurity and sin.[47] Jonathan Klawans detects two categories

---

44. These last two points are argued specifically by Knohl, *Sanctuary of Silence*, 225–30, contra Milgrom (*Leviticus 1–16*, 13–35) who believes there are ethical underpinnings in the priestly law.

45. The appearance of this root in non-priestly texts (e.g., Deut 12:22; 14:4; 24:4; Isa 6:5; 52:1; Jer 2:23; Hos 6:10) does not connote the same technical meaning that P uses.

46. David P. Wright "Unclean and Clean (OT)," *ABD* 6:729.

47. For a concise, yet thorough presentation of the priestly views on impurity and purity, see Tikva Frymer-Kensky, "Pollution, Purification, and Purgation in Biblical

of impurity in the Bible: ritual impurity and moral impurity. He argues that ritual impurity is not sinful, that there is usually a contact-contagion factor, and that it is an impermanent condition; moral impurity, however, is a consequence of grave sin and places a permanent stain on the individual. Moral impurities include idolatry, incest, and murder.[48] David Wright also recognizes two primary categories of impurity, which he labels "tolerated" and "prohibited." Tolerated impurities include the ritual impurities that Klawans discusses, but he further breaks down those impurities by severity. The prohibited impurities are broken down into two subcategories, intentional and unintentional. The unintentional prohibited impurities overlap both tolerated impurities and intentional prohibited impurities.[49]

My approach is somewhat different because I do not think that P and H material contribute to a systemic whole.[50] In this commentary I separate the theology of P and H and, by extension, their views on impurity or sin. For P, the impurities are those that Klawans and Wright describe as ritual or tolerated except for two cases: unintentional moral impurities and willful neglect of the ritual impurities. In other words, P's central concern is with ritual impurity and a handful of very specific unintentional wrong behaviors. H, on the other hand, addresses three grave sins: incest, murder, and idolatry. The two systems are independent of one another, and reading Leviticus 1–16 through a lens of the moral judgments in Leviticus 17–27 is an error that has generated much confusion.

Milgrom's approach is most useful to me in that he focuses on the relationship between the holy and the ritually impure rather than different categories of impurity. Milgrom suggests that the primary concern in priestly texts is between the holy and the impure—both of which are dynamic and communicable (contagious). By contrast, the profane is

---

Israel," in *The Word of the Lord Shall Go Forth: Essays in Honor of David Noel Freedman in Celebration of His Sixtieth Birthday*, ed. Carol L. Meyers and M. O'Connor, ASOR (Winona Lake, IN: Eisenbrauns, 1983): 399–414; reprinted in Tikva Frymer-Kensky, *Studies in Biblical and Feminist Criticism* (Philadelphia: Jewish Publication Society of America, 2006), 329–50.

48. Jonathan Klawans, *Impurity and Sin in Ancient Judaism* (Oxford: Oxford University Press, 2000), 22–31.

49. David P. Wright, "The Spectrum of Priestly Impurity," in *Priesthood and Cult in Ancient Israel*, ed. Gary A. Anderson and Saul M. Olyan, JSOTSup 125 (Sheffield: JSOT Press, 1991), 150–81.

50. It is useful for Klawans to bring different sources together because his primary interest is in reception of impurity laws in early Judaism.

essentially the absence of holiness, but it is a static condition as is the category of purity. Mary Douglas offers:

> Biblical impurity is of no use in demarcating advantaged social classes or ranks (except for a little protection for the privileges of the priests). It does not either recognize hereditary defiling categories. Leviticus does not draw social distinctions. Idolatry covers all kinds of moral as well as bodily imperfection, but all are capable of purification if the will to repent is there. In effect, biblical defilement is a cerebral creation, it has no philosophical uses, it does not accuse.[51]

In more recent years, Thomas Kazen has approached impurity and sin from a very different perspective. He suggests that impurity derives from primal feelings of disgust, negative reactions to threatening stimuli, and both morality and purity may originate with emotional bodily reactions.[52] Kazen points to studies wherein disgust first develops as a primary reaction to protect an organism from oral incorporation of harmful substances but then memory ties in the association of disgust with new experiences, when that immediate stimulus is no longer present.[53]

## God and Bodies

In order to understand P's obsession with the sacrificial cult, with blood, with blemishes, with genital discharges, with dietary restrictions, with skin conditions, and with which bodies come into sexual contact with other bodies, we must understand how P imagined God. I believe that Leviticus 1–16 is primarily about solving a problem that P theology creates. P's understanding of God is unique among the voices of the Hebrew Bible.

The J source assumes that God has a body. God regularly appears to individuals, and those individuals never respond with shock at actually seeing God. God manifests as a human (or three humans!) while approaching Abraham and Sarah in the heat of the day (Gen 18). When

---

51. Mary Douglas, *In the Wilderness: The Doctrine of Defilement in the Book of Numbers*, JSOTSup 158 (Sheffield: JSOT Press, 1993), 51.

52. Thomas Kazen, "Dirt and Disgust: Body and Morality in Biblical Purity Laws," *Perspectives on Purity and Purification in the Bible*, ed. Baruch S. Schwartz, Naftali S. Meshel, Jeffrey Stackert, David P. Wright, LHB/OTS 474 (New York: T&T Clark, 2008), 45.

53. Influenced by William Ian Miller, *The Anatomy of Disgust* (Cambridge, MA: Harvard University Press, 1997).

Jacob sees God standing next to him in his dream of the heavenly ladder (Gen 32), Jacob's surprise is not that God appeared but that God appeared to him in that place! The D school rejects this kind of theology, reworking the Sinai narrative so that the people never see any manifestation of the deity; the community only hears the word of God (see Deut 4:11-12; 36). Moses seeks to view God, and while he is not granted permission to see all of God, he does get to view a glimpse of part of God's body. For D, God has a body, but something about its nature and size is unknowable to human beings. In addition, while D does not believe that God's body is anything like human bodies, D's God has a robust personality with which people can interact.

P's God is utterly different in nature. The God of Leviticus 1–16 is obscure, nonanthropomorphic, profoundly Other. This God does not get angry or jealous. This God does not speak of a loving relationship with Israel. Stephen Geller describes the God of P as a "tremendous force . . . essentially mechanical."[54] P's God is immanent, residing among the people, but whatever it is that resides in the holy of holies is completely unknowable to people. Israel Knohl has argued that P's God comes to full expression when God reveals God's name to Moses:

> The revelation of the name of Yahweh results in a Copernican revo-
> lution. Moses and, following him, Israel learn to recognize the divine
> nature, which is unrelated to creation, or to humanity and its needs. This
> dimension cannot be fully comprehended by humans and surpasses
> the limits of morality and reason, since morality and its laws are only
> meaningful in relation to human society and human understanding. The
> aspect of the divine essence that surpasses reason and morality—the
> "numinous" element—is represented in PT [Priestly Torah] by the name
> of Yahweh . . . the impersonal, nonanthropomorphic language of the
> period of Moses expresses the majesty of the holy and its awesomeness.[55]

Scholars still debate whether P's understanding of God attributes morality to God (which is a human characteristic), but the general nature of P's God, as a nonanthropomorphic, force-like God who is physically immanent but dangerously other, is generally agreed. This view of God

---

54. Stephen A. Geller, "The God of the Covenant," in *One God or Many? Concepts of Divinity in the Ancient World,* ed. Barbara Nevling Porter, Transactions of the Casco Bay Assyriological Institute 1; (Chebeague, ME: Casco Bay Assyriological Institute, 2000), 278. See also Geller's detailed study, *Sacred Enigmas: Literary Religion in the Hebrew Bible* (London: Routledge, 1996), chap. 4.

55. Knohl, *Sanctuary of Silence,* 146–47.

is radically different from other biblical theologies and thus presents unique challenges.

P asserts that God created human beings in the image of God but also that human beings must procreate and reproduce. God created humanity to live through cycles of birth, growth, aging, and death. Given the extraordinarily abstract, "otherly" understanding of P's God, one of the central challenges that Leviticus undertakes to reconcile is the enormous gulf between "being God-like" and having a body that is constantly in flux. This creates a problem, as Aviva Zornberg has written: "Man's greatness, therefore, his creation in the image of God, his dominating the sensual swarming landscape, locks in an inescapable tension with his participation in that world of proliferation and change, of waxing and waning. He is attached to two mutually exclusive ways of being."[56] Howard Eilberg-Schwartz focuses more on body issues when he writes that "God has 'nobody,' neither others with whom to interact nor a body, with which to do it. Thus the dual expectation of being like God and being obligated to reproduce pulled in opposite directions. There was no escape from the body. Pressed between these conflicting impulses, the body became an object of cultural elaboration."[57]

In its many discussions of human bodies, Leviticus will talk about male bodies and female bodies, but never as separate ontological categories. Both male and female bodies become impure as a matter of course, and both male and female bodies have the same access to the Divine. (The exclusively male priesthood is a different issue that I will address elsewhere.) In other words, male and female anatomy is conceptually equal!

I am aware that this perspective stands at odds with many other readings of Leviticus, which I believe may be overly influenced by the ongoing power of Western dualistic thinking. I am attempting, insofar as it is possible, to read the text through the lens of predualistic philosophy. I believe it just as probable that P's thinking emerged from other earlier systems of thought in the ancient Near East. For example, while Sumerian culture preceded P's world by hundreds, if not thousands, of years, early Mesopotamian literature and art present a different model as articulated by Julia M. Asher-Greve:

56. Aviva Gottlieb Zornberg, *Genesis: The Beginning of Desire* (Lincoln: University of Nebraska Press, 1995), 16.

57. Howard Eilberg-Schwartz, "The Problem of the Body for the People of the Book," in *Reading Bibles, Writing Bodies: Identity and the Book*, ed. Timothy K. Beal and David M. Gunn (London: Routledge, 1997), 39.

> The Mesopotamian holistic concept of the human being was based on a physical system, with the body as fundamental point of reference. The body was the total self, the essence of humanity, equally matter and spirit, emotion and reason, both temporal and eternal. Gender was the interpretation of anatomical differences and imperfections. The inscription of gender on the body was one option to structure society.[58]

I am not suggesting any direct line of influence from Sumerian reasoning to biblical priestly thinking; however, we must be aware of the contexts from which we read and that Hellenistic dualistic thinking is not helpful in analyzing priestly thought.

P attempts to bridge the divide by regulating *when* human bodies and *in what conditions* human beings can approach the Divine. We tend to think about the conditions that limit access to God and then interrogate the role of gender in those conditions, but it is important to remember that, in truth, bodies with penises and bodies with vaginas are welcome to participate equally among the lay community. Pregnant bodies, new bodies, old bodies, feverish bodies, bodies with green eyes, bodies with grey hairs—all these kinds of bodies are equally welcome. Our culture denies privilege to many more types of bodies than those of P's world. We deny privilege to obese bodies, to bodies of color, to diseased bodies, to old bodies. . . . Before we critique the priestly limitations, we might critique those of our own societies.

## God and Relationship

H's God is more anthropomorphic and is in a partnership with the people of Israel. The dissimilar view of God is only one factor in two very different theological outlooks. The research of Israel Knohl, Jacob Milgrom, Jan Joosten, and Baruch Schwartz has shown that while P holiness is static, H holiness is dynamic, or, to use my own terminology, H holiness is pliable and malleable. According to Milgrom, "The dynamic catalyst that turns H's view of the Lord's covenant from a static picture into one of flux is its concept of holiness. For H, the ideal of holiness is not only embodied in a limited group (priests), animals (sacrifices), and space (sanctuary) but affects all who live on God's land: persons and

---

58. Julia M. Asher-Greve, "Mesopotamian Concepts of the Gendered Body," in *Gender and the Body in the Ancient Mediterranean*, ed. Maria Wyke (Oxford: Blackwell, 1998), 29.

animals, Israel and the גר."[59] For Milgrom, the idea of dynamic holiness means that Israel can enhance its collective holiness in proportion to its observance of God's commandments. Milgrom does not consider the opposite dynamic—that God might also be affected in this dynamic relationship.

To date, the many studies on holiness in the priestly works have focused on holiness as that which is designated for God or set apart as God-related. Thus, scholars of priestly thought have studied, in detail, the holiness and profanation of people, objects, and places. There is, however, relative silence on the question of what it means to desecrate God's name, another common object of desecration, along with people, objects, and places.

The H theologians were calling for a radically new understanding of the relationship between God and Israel. I believe that H's theology has a feminist twist to it. To the extent that P distances God from the life of Israel, H brings God into a profound intimacy. The knot that binds God and Israel is holiness, and the term that expresses this aspect of the divine, in intimate relationship with Israel, is שם ("name"). Scholars tend to focus on the ways in which the community of Israel is impacted by its observance or disregard of God's laws, but interpreters pay little attention to the ways in which God is affected. This reticence to consider how Israel's actions may affect God may be a symptom of a patriarchal worldview in which the powerful cannot be touched—the hegemony of the boss. The truth is, however, that the God of the Hebrew Bible is neither omnipotent nor omniscient. As a feminist, I am interested in both sides of the relationship between God and the people of Israel.

H understands holiness as the central relational principle between God and Israel. God identifies God's self as holy and the one who makes holy. People, places, and things can also be holy and can make holy. Concurrently, people, places, and things can have their holiness diminished, and God can have God's name diminished. H is centered in holiness as relationship between God and Israel, with both partners able to impact the other profoundly. While H absolutely maintains a hierarchical relationship between God and Israel, H also espouses a relationship in which both partners are vulnerable and interdependent. God is not Other; God models relationships of mutual interdependence, and the people are commanded to emulate God in all relationships.

---

59. Milgrom, "The Changing Concept of Holiness," 71.

H never mentions God's כבוד ("glory" in NRSV); rather, H is theologically interested in one particular aspect of God and designates that aspect as שם. In the כבוד system of P, טמאה ("impurity" in NRSV; but see discussion above) can drive God out of the sanctuary as a matter of chemistry. For H, people's moral actions can also have an impact on God but not on God's כבוד. Unethical behavior or certain wrongdoings can desecrate the שם of God. Humanity can directly affect this aspect of God. The כבוד cannot be directly desecrated. The שם is that part of God that has a more intimate relationship with humanity. The inclusion of the שם of God acknowledges God not just as a force residing within the sanctuary but also as a God in dynamic relationship with the people of Israel. In H, the relationship between God and Israel is still hierarchical, but God is not "Other," rather a partner.

## Leviticus and Theology Today

Part of the task of a commentator is to make a case for the value of a book. As a feminist commentator, I suggest seven compelling messages that emerge for the modern reader of Leviticus. These teachings, or perhaps more accurately values, can speak to readers from different faith traditions and to secular readers as well.

(1) The nature of human bodies is that they are constantly in flux. P notes that bodies can become damaged, diseased, and gender-elusive and that human bodies are permeable, allowing substances in to and out of the body. P's theology imagines a God of stability and perfection, which naturally results in a tension between God's static nature and humanity's constantly changing nature. P believes that placing some controls on the changing nature of human bodies can bring humanity closer to God. In its attempt to legislate control of bodies, however, P actually brings to light the many ways in which human bodies change from moment to moment. As readers of Leviticus we might find an affirmation of the diversity of bodies and their constantly changing natures and choose to celebrate this fact, despite P's notion that it creates a chasm between God and us.

(2) Within Leviticus, P's understanding of atonement and forgiveness places the full weight of responsibility on the individual who has done wrong. Leviticus argues for a model that includes no intermediaries—people are responsible for their own actions, and those who neglect to take the appropriate actions necessary to remedy the wrong bring harm to themselves and to the entire community.

(3) P offers compelling views of community and the careful balance between the needs of individuals and the needs of the community. P emphasizes that the private seeps into the public and that an individual wrong can have consequences for the greater community. Leviticus offers a counter to "me generation" attitudes.

(4) P emphasizes the absolute value of life even as it makes accommodations for the carnivorous nature of humans. It places a series of checks to ensure that no life is taken without a conscious acknowledgment of the loss of life.

(5) Leviticus teaches us to note the holy in everyday actions. What we eat from day to day matters. How we interact with others around us matters. How we conduct business matters. How we engage in family affairs matters. Each moment provides the opportunity for a holy moment, for a shift toward God's holiness.

(6) Given the realities of unequal distribution of power and resources, Leviticus orients us toward generosity and compassion. While framed within a patriarchal worldview, H especially does not deny the existence of privilege and inequality, nor does H idealize it.

(7) Leviticus reminds us that, despite our claims to land ownership, the land does not belong to human beings at all. The assumption that people own land is a human construct, but it is not self-evident. The land and all the resources that emerge from the land belong to God, and we are tenants. If we abuse access to the land, the land will spit us out (see Lev 18:28; 20:22).

# Leviticus 1:1–3:17

# *Offerings, Offerers, and Considerations of Gender*

The first seven chapters of Leviticus describe five types of offerings that an Israelite could bring to the tabernacle: עלה (burnt offering), מנחה (grain offering), שלמים (well-being offering), חטאת (purification/sin offering), and אשם (guilt offering). The burnt, grain, and well-being offerings appear frequently in other biblical texts while the purification and guilt offerings appear only in P texts. It is important to remember that the description of the sacrificial system in these chapters does not necessarily correlate with the actual practices of the people of ancient Israel; nor do P's ritual descriptions correlate with other biblical texts. The first three chapters of Leviticus assume that the reader is familiar with the purpose of the burnt, grain, and well-being offerings so the writer focuses on how the offerer and the priest are to perform the ritual.

## Bringing the Community into the Tabernacle (1:1)

The book of Exodus ends with a description of the intensity of YHVH's[1] presence in the inner sanctum of the tabernacle. The book of Leviticus

---

1. The Bible refers to God with a variety of names and epithets, but two terms stand out as the most common. The first is אלהים, translated as "God," and refers to

*Lev 1:1*

¹:¹The Lᴏʀᴅ summoned Moses and
spoke to him from the tent of meeting,
saying:

opens with a divine summons to Moses from that same inner sanctum.
This is the only narrative in which YHVH speaks to Moses from the tent
of meeting. At other times, we note that Moses is permitted to enter into
the inner sanctum, to stand before the curtain to the ark (see Exod 25:22;
30:6, 36; Num 7:89; 17:19) and to hear God's words emanating from the
holy of holies. By starting Leviticus with Moses outside the inner sanctum, the writer creates a smooth flow from the end of one book to the
beginning of the next.

The tent of meeting (Lev 1:1) refers to the inner portion of the tabernacle or מִשְׁכָּן, inside the curtain that divides the tabernacle into two equal
parts and before the veil that separates the ark, the holy of holies, from
the inner courtyard. The term "tent of meeting" appears in two different
sources of the Bible, P and E. The priestly tent of meeting stands within
the tabernacle, which in turn is stationed at the center of the Israelite
camp. Moses enters the tent of meeting to communicate with God, and
the priests, on rare occasions, enter the space in order to fulfill the laws
of cultic worship. Given the fact that only priests could enter the inner
sanctum, it is safe to conclude that, according to the priestly tradition,
women never would have had access to this holy space. E does not,
however, exclude women from the sacred space. In the E tradition, the
tent of meeting stands at the outskirts of the camp, at the liminal place

---

the biblical God of Israel who is later associated with the one God of Judaism, Christianity, and Islam. The Bible also uses God's personal name, rendered יהוה in Hebrew
and often translated as "Lᴏʀᴅ." (In some progressive Jewish communities, the term
"Lᴏʀᴅ" is replaced with other less hierarchical epithets like "Holy One.") In Jewish
tradition, the divine name is never pronounced so among many Jewish (and some
non-Jewish) scholars, the divine name is represented by its four consonants as YHWH.
The third consonant was originally pronounced like a "w" and the name of the letter
is called "waw" in academic circles; however, in modern Hebrew the consonant is
pronounced like a "v" and the letter is called a "vav." I have adopted the convention
of rendering the divine name as YHVH, which both acknowledges the divine name
as presented in the Bible and acknowledges my identity as a modern Jew who reads
Hebrew with a "vav" and not a "waw."

between the ordered world of the Israelite camp and the chaos and danger of the wilderness. When Miriam challenges Moses's authority along with her brother Aaron, God calls all three of them to the tent of meeting. God speaks directly to Miriam and Aaron about the special status of Moses (Num 12).

Before a single sacrifice is mentioned, Leviticus makes it clear that this information is to be shared with all of Israel. Jacob Milgrom reads this instruction as indicating "a gaping chasm that separates Israel from its neighbors," citing a Mesopotamian ritual text that permits only the *mudu* to lead the ritual and to see the actual text. In addition, he cites the Book of the Dead, which forbids anyone from looking at its content.[2] Based on this evidence, he adduces that publicizing these ritual texts democratizes information. Milgrom's argument assumes that Leviticus 1–9 was written primarily for priests about actual practices. If, however, a reader follows James Watts's view that references in Leviticus are more rhetorical and literary than referential of actual events, then providing everyone with access to this information would have been just the point! The formulation of the book's opening verse is poetic in its profundity: the deepest point inside will be exposed publicly; the public has literary, if not physical, access to the most holy of spaces.

## Who Is Sacrificing? (1:2)

The legislation begins in verse 2 with the statement: "an אדם when s/he offers from among you (m. pl.) an offering." Readers of the Bible will usually think of אדם (*'adam*) as the first human created by God, the human who was male and female at the beginning. Most often, אדם refers generically to a person. Several translations choose to translate אדם as "man." NRSV avoids making a gender reference by translating "when any of you" from the Hebrew phrase אדם כי, which is very rare (see Lev 13:2 in connection with skin disease and Num 19:14 in connection with the handling of a corpse).

John E. Hartley believes that the use of אדם indicates the universal nature of ritual offerings; i.e., a Gentile could bring an offering.[3] Nobuyoshi Kiuchi argues that אדם here must mean "male" and that the term cannot be inclusive because the animal represents the offerer and, regarding

---

2. Jacob Milgrom, *Leviticus 1–16*, AB 3 (New York: Doubleday, 1991), 143–44.
3. John E. Hartley, *Leviticus*, WBC 4 (Waco, TX: Word Books, 1992), 11.

[2]Speak to the people of Israel and say to them: When any of you bring an offering of livestock to the LORD, you shall bring your offering from the herd or from the flock.

the burnt offering, the animal must be male.[4] This argumentation would suggest that those rituals for which a female animal is prescribed were for female offerers only, and yet a female animal is prescribed for one of the purification offerings (Lev 4:28) and we know that men offered these sacrifices.[5] According to the Sotah ritual prescribed in Numbers 5, the suspected adulteress is brought into the tabernacle with a grain offering on her behalf. The text does not suggest that there is anything unusual or that special provisions must be made to accommodate the presence of a woman. In Proverbs 7, a woman reports that she must bring an offering to God as part of a vow that she has fulfilled. Her husband has left town without leaving any money, so she intends to seduce a man in order to make money for the offering. Outside of the central cultic system, the necromancer of Endor sacrifices a calf for Saul following the death of Samuel. Even as she stands outside of the state-sponsored cultic system, the text expresses no judgment on, or surprise by, her actions (1 Sam 28:24). Leviticus itself mandates that a parturient or a woman after menstruation or other blood-based genital emission must bring an offering to YHVH. Therefore, there is no compelling reason to believe that Leviticus 1:2 addresses only males. Both men and women could bring offerings to the tabernacle. The gender or biological sex of the offerer is not a relevant category in this material! In fact, Dvora E. Weisberg reports that the rabbis approved of both men and women slaughtering animals and that late medieval historical documents reveal that women routinely served as slaughterers for kosher meat in parts of Europe.[6]

4. Nobuyoshi Kiuchi, *Leviticus*, ApOTC 3 (Nottingham: Inter-Varsity Press, 2007), 55.

5. Jacob Milgrom argues that males were used more often than females because they were more expendable, the females being the ones who bear offspring and provide milk (*Leviticus 1–16*, 147).

6. Dvora E. Weisberg, "Post-biblical Interpretations: VaYikra," in *The Torah: A Women's Commentary*, ed. Tamara Cohn Eskenazi and Andrea L. Weiss (New York: URJ Press, 2008), 588–59.

### Women in the Shit

The first time I practiced slaughtering chickens, the wife of the chicken farmer walked in, and, in Hebrew, she asked: "You want to do this? You know there are better professions for women." My Hebrew language skills and American sense of politeness prevented me from responding: But we women are always in the shit—sometimes literally. Why should this be any different? My grandmother used to gut the chickens herself—the revolting smell of partially and fully digested feed was her normal. My sister-in-law is usually covered in poop or baby cheese. We are always doing the messiest work.

Halakhah didn't explicitly forbid women from becoming *shochetot* until the *acheronim* (read: sixteenth century and later). Prior to their rulings, women were permitted to do this work "just like men" (Ramban, the Rosh, the Tur). I won't enter an academic argument about what changed, but I will say the reasons given to deny women access to *shechitah* are offensive: even a woman who is an expert should not be given a certificate of *shechitah* because, as you well know, women faint (the Rama, the Rashal, Simlah Hadashah). Um, no.

Now I didn't learn this skill for the sake of bucking halakhah, though even as an observant Jew, I do celebrate righteous subversiveness. I wanted to learn to slaughter chickens so I knew that I could. I had to know where my meat came from—real living creatures, different from me only by DNA and, depending who you ask, soulfulness. I had to know that I could pick up the knife, pick up the animal, slit its throat, drain it of lifeblood, and, after all of that mess, still eat it. Just in case it's not obvious: looking a living creature in the eye, sensing its fear, and killing it, is really, really hard. The animal knows, and you know, and you do it anyway. What does that say about the slaughterer? About humans?

When you make your own decisions about meat, and kosher slaughter, remember this: in our time of disconnection and distant connection, kosher slaughter connects us to our gross, visceral selves, our insides and the insides of the creatures around us. It's messy work, necessary not only for the immediate product—meat— but for our own spiritual and moral accountability in eating that meat. Get to know kosher slaughter as the messy work it is.

*Kerry Chaplin*

The term קָרְבָּן appears only in P and twice in Ezekiel (2:28; 40:43). The term is best translated as "offering" because the Hebrew root means "nearness," whether as an adjective that means "near" or a *hiphil* verb that describes the act of bringing something near or close, or a nominal form like קָרְבָּן that is used in cultic contexts to describe something that is brought close to the Divine. This word reflects specialized P terminology for any offering including animals, grains and precious metals (Num 7:13; 31:50). In other non-P texts, we find the term זֶבַח most commonly used. It is possible that P uses a unique term in order to indicate that its system should not be confused with the more popular practices that are referred to in the non-P Torah texts, Deuteronomic narratives, and prophetic literature.

To summarize, the opening of Leviticus ties itself to the end of Exodus and indicates that the teachings about the most holy space are for the entire community, that anyone might bring an offering, and that the use of the new word קָרְבָּן communicates that what follows is a unique system. For a system that will restrict access only to priests, the opening verses of the book do not make reference to or assumptions about gender.

## The Burnt Offering (1:3-13)

The remaining verses of Leviticus 1 (vv. 3-17) describe the procedures for three types of burnt offerings: those from the herd, those from the flock, and those from the birds.[7] The text does not provide any information about the function of this ritual offering or guidance regarding the use of these three categories of animals. The chapter is simply about the mechanics: if you bring a burnt offering, here is how it should be done. A person should bring the offering to the entrance of the tent of meeting (v. 3), that is, to the outer court, which contained the altar and laver. The person should then lay a hand on the animal and slaughter it (vv. 4-5). The priest should capture the blood and sprinkle it on the altar (v. 5). In the next stage, the offerer should skin and cut up the animal and the priest should get a fire started on the altar (v. 6). The priest should arrange

---

7. Leviticus prescribes specific types of quadrupeds for specific offerings. These offerings may be bovines, ovines (sheep), or caprines (goat). There are a number of different subcategories within these three classes. For a presentation of the various classifications, see Naphtali S. Meshel, *The "Grammar" of Sacrifice: A Generativist Study of the Israelite Sacrificial System in the Priestly Writings* (Oxford: Oxford University Press, 2014), esp. 33–62.

³If the offering is a burnt offering from the herd, you shall offer a male without blemish; you shall bring it to the entrance of the tent of meeting, for acceptance in your behalf before the LORD. ⁴You shall lay your hand on the head of the burnt offering, and it shall be acceptable in your behalf as atonement for you. ⁵The bull shall be slaughtered before the LORD; and Aaron's sons the priests shall offer the blood, dashing the blood against all sides of the altar that is the entrance of the tent of meeting. ⁶The burnt offering shall be flayed and cut up into its parts. ⁷The sons of the priest Aaron shall put fire on the altar and arrange wood on the fire. ⁸Aaron's sons the priests shall arrange the parts, with the head and the suet, on the wood that is on the fire on the altar; ⁹but its entrails and its legs shall be washed with water. Then the priest shall turn the whole into smoke on the altar as a burnt offering, an offering by fire of pleasing odor to the LORD.

¹⁰If your gift for a burnt offering is from the flock, from the sheep or goats, your offering shall be a male without blemish. ¹¹It shall be slaughtered on the north side of the altar before the LORD, and Aaron's sons the priests shall dash its blood against all sides of the altar. ¹²It shall be cut up into its parts, with its head and its suet, and the priest shall arrange them on the wood that is on the fire on the altar; ¹³but the entrails and the legs shall be washed with water. Then the priest shall offer the whole and turn it into smoke on the altar; it is a burnt offering, an offering by fire of pleasing odor to the LORD.

the body parts on top of the wood fire (vv. 7-8). The offerer should wash out the intestines and hind legs before the priest sets them on the fire (v. 9). The ritual description ends here. If words were spoken, formally or informally, they are not mentioned in this text. The concern is with the ritual actions involved in a burnt offering.

References to the עלה ("burnt offering") appear both in P and throughout the Hebrew Bible. The עלה is often paired with זבח (e.g., Exod 10:25; Deut 12:6, 11; Josh 22:26; 1 Sam 6:15; 2 Kgs 5:17; 10:24; Isa 43:23; Jer 6:20). We should keep in mind that P's prescription for the burnt offerings' procedures does not necessarily reflect or align with the functions of the burnt offerings mentioned in other texts of the Bible. In Genesis, the burnt offerings seem to be spontaneous offerings that are not connected to the tabernacle or the priesthood. Historical narratives have the kings offering up burnt offerings and well-being offerings in celebration (1 Sam 6:14; 2 Sam 6:17-18; 1 Kgs 9:25; see also Gen 8:20; Exod 10:25; Judg 6:26). Abraham is commanded to sacrifice his son Isaac as a burnt offering

(Gen 22:2, 7, 8, 13), and the Moabites offer up burnt offerings (2 Kgs 3:27). The prophets refer to the burnt offering as a general all-purpose offering. The עלה seems to have been the most common kind of offering, and rituals combined this sacrifice with other types of offerings in many contexts. In Leviticus, it is the only offering that is completely burnt up (excluding the skin, which goes to the priest; see Lev 7:8) on the altar; that is to say, no part of the meat is set aside for the priests or the offerer.

## Unblemished Male

This first instruction contains a number of code words or terminology that we will encounter throughout these initial chapters. The text indicates that when presenting an animal from the herd for the burnt offering, it must be an unblemished male. While male animals are required predominantly, the חטאת offering for an individual's sin must be a female goat and the שלמים offerings can be either male or female animals (Lev 3:1, 6; 4:28, 32; 5:6). The text never provides any rationale for the use of a male or female animal, but this is not surprising because the material in these opening chapters of Leviticus does not address the "whys."[8] (See commentary on Lev 4 for a more detailed discussion of gender and offerings.)

In addition to being a male animal, the offering must also be תמים. The Hebrew term תמים is usually translated as "without blemish," but the Hebrew word has the sense of "wholeness." A more accurate translation is therefore "a whole male animal." The tendency to translate the positive word תמים in the negative "unblemished" is overly specific. Unfortunately, the P source never defines what it means to be "whole." The H source defines P's use of תמים by listing a series of defects (מום), which disqualify an animal from use as an offering. According to Leviticus 22:22-24, defects include any animal that is blind, injured, maimed, oozing, scarred, or scabbed or whose testicles are bruised, crushed, torn, or cut. In addition, all offerings except for a free-will offering cannot have extended or contracted limbs. In Numbers 19:2 the red heifer ritual requires a female animal that is "whole" and "in which there is no defect [מום]." Since the list of defects does not refer to female anatomy, we have to wonder whether any variations in female genitalia were of issue to the writers. Many scholars have noted that the defects are all visible

8. Meshel observes that all sacrificial animals are identified via three categories: zoological class, sex, and age (ibid., 33).

conditions on the exterior of the animal and that the issue has more to do with appearance than health. Setting aside the point that a careful examination of a female animal may show some anomalies with regard to the animal's femaleness (e.g., genital disfigurement or deformities of the udders), what becomes clear is that regarding biological sex, a whole male is one whose genitalia conform to the idealized male and that a whole female is essentially a non-male. The Temple Scroll (11QT 52:5-7) ironically gives more attention to female animals by arguing that pregnant animals are considered to be defective as well.[9]

Charlotte Elisheva Fonrobert suggests that while we usually translate זכר תמים as "male and unblemished," we can also understand it as "unblemished with regard to its maleness." In other words, the ritual requirement may be for a male animal that is unambiguously male—a biologically "complete" male with no damage to its testicles. Fonrobert points to a rabbinic text that addresses the types of defects that would prohibit an animal from sacrificial use. As the rabbis attempt to make sense of the biblical list of defects regarding testicles, they conclude that the issue concerns sex ambiguity and androgyny.[10]

> For the following they do not slaughter—neither in the Temple nor outside the Temple: If it had non-persistent white spots in its eye, or non-persistent tearing or if its inner gums are missing a piece but not uprooted, or if it had eczema, a wart or boils or if it was old or sick or smelled bad, or if a sin [of bestiality] was committed with it or if it killed a man [as determined] by the word of one witness or by the owner's admission, a *tumtum* [an animal with recessed sexual organs whose sex is therefore impossible to determine] or an *androginos* [an animal with both male and female sexual organs], neither in the Temple nor outside it. Rabbi Yishmael says, there is no blemish greater than this [i.e., being an *androginos*]; but the Sages say it is not a first-born and can be sheared and worked. (m. Bechorot 6:7)[11]

9. Cited in Nicole J. Ruane, *Sacrifice and Gender in Biblical Law* (Cambridge: Cambridge University Press, 2013), 69 n. 107 from Joseph M. Baumgarten, "A Fragment on Fetal Life and Pregnancy in 4Q270," in *Pomegranates and Golden Bells: Studies in Biblical, Jewish, and Near Eastern Ritual, Law, and Literature in Honor of Jacob Milgrom*, ed. David P. Wright et al. (Winona Lake, IN: Eisenbrauns, 1995), 445.

10. Charlotte Elisheva Fonrobert, "Bodily Perfection in the Sanctuary," in *Torah Queeries: Weekly Commentaries on the Hebrew Bible*, ed. Gregg Drinkwater, Joshua Lesser, and David Schneer (New York: New York University Press, 2009), 123–28.

11. Fonrobert notes that the rabbis extend disqualifications for immoral behavior as well.

Fonrobert summarizes:

> The discussion concerns the identity of the doubly sexed animal, whether it is to be treated as a first-born of doubtful gender identity or whether it should be regarded as a male animal with a blemish (Mishnah Bekhorot 6:12, Bekhorot 41a–43b, Tosafot Bekhorot 42a *almah*), or, as the medieval commentator Rashi glosses this minority opinion, "because the place of femininity (*makom nekevut*, i.e., the female genitalia) is like a blemish" (Rashi, ad loc., 41a). This tannaitic opinion engenders considerable disagreement in the talmudic discourse. However, it reinforces a semiotic system in which the male organ has greater signifying force than the female organ. Discussions in the United States about the practice of surgical gender assignment for babies born with ambiguous genitalia demonstrate a similar practice of privileging anatomical maleness over femaleness.[12]

In other words, a male sacrificial animal must be uncontestably male.

## Hand-Leaning

Leviticus 1:4 instructs the offerer to lay a hand (or "hand pressing")[13] on the head of the animal so that the offering will be acceptable to atone for the offerer. In other words, in order for the offering to fulfill its function, the offerer must lay a hand on the head of the animal before slaughtering it. The meaning of the laying on of a hand is contested among scholars. Debates regarding this custom have included explanations such as the following: transference of sin from person to animal; identification or vicarious substitution; declaration of one's sins or purpose in bringing the offering; and demonstration of the offerer's ownership of the animal.[14] Leviticus 16:21 provides the most detailed description of the laying on of hands or hand-leaning ritual and so has influenced our understanding of this act in other texts. Leviticus 16 provides the only case, however, in which both hands are to be set upon the animal. In all other cases, the offerer places one hand upon the animal's head. Milgrom notes that the laying on of hands is not required when bringing a bird or a grain offering or for the guilt offering. He argues the difference is that the offerer is hold-

---

12. Charlotte Elisheva Fonrobert, "Gender Identity in Halakhic Discourse," *Jewish Women: A Comprehensive Historical Encyclopedia*, March 1, 2009, *Jewish Women's Archive*, http://jwa.org/encyclopedia/article/gender-identity-in-halakhic-discourse.

13. James W. Watts, *Leviticus 1–10*, HCOT (Leuven: Peeters, 2013), 189.

14. See Kiuchi, *Leviticus*, 56 for an argument that favors identification of the self with the animal, representing a version of vicarious punishment.

ing the meal offering or the bird with his hands already and that with the guilt offering, the offerer may bring money in place of an animal offering. He concludes that the purpose of the hand-leaning is to designate ownership of the animal, to ensure that the offerer gets credit for the offering.[15]

## Coordination of Priest and Laity

An important key to understanding the ritual description is taking note of the participants in the ritual. Most English translations of the Hebrew obscure the role of the offerer in the ritual by translating the third-person masculine singular verbs as general passives rather than 3ms active verbs in which the subject must be the offerer. When we translate the verbs as general passives, we diminish the role of the offerer, if not excise the offerer altogether. The text reads very differently if we stay true to the Hebrew and translate the 3ms verbs as active. Compare the following (my translation) to the NRSV:

> The offerer shall slaughter the bull before YHVH. Aaron's sons the priests shall offer the blood. . . . The offerer shall flay the burnt offering and cut it up into pieces. The sons of Aaron the priest shall put fire on the altar. . . . Aaron's sons shall arrange the parts, with the head and suet on the wood. . . . The offerer shall wash its entrails and its legs with water. Then the priest shall turn the whole into smoke on the altar as a burnt offering.

The Hebrew text gives the layperson a significant role in the ritual and places both the priest and the layperson within the outer court of the tabernacle working together. The priest manages the altar while the layperson does the rest. Ezekiel 44:10-11 attempts to remove the layperson's role altogether, assigning slaughter to the Levites; nonetheless, Leviticus is clear on the central role of the offerer.

In postbiblical interpretation, the focus is always on the role of the priests, but the text prescribes the ritual offering as a joint project. Viewed through James Watts's lens, the priests may have presented robust participation of the layperson in order to make it more likely that the people would accept the priestly torah. Conversely, it could be that priests from a later period projected themselves into earlier practices conducted primarily by laity. By commanding that blood be sprinkled on the altar, and by limiting access to the altar to the priests alone, P makes the inclusion of priests necessary.

15. Milgrom, *Leviticus 1–16*, 151–53.

Finally, it is important to remember that sacrificing animals—that is, the slaughtering and butchering—is extremely physically demanding. If both men and women offered sacrifices, then both men and women were engaged in intense physical labor.

Regarding the use of an animal from the flock, the procedure is the same except for the manner of slaughter. Here the slaughter is on the north side of the altar before YHVH. It is important to note that this second section is less detailed than the description of the herd animals, not because there were fewer steps, but because the P writer assumes that the reader carries forward information already given.

## A Sliding Scale (1:14-17)

Leviticus 1:2 does not mention birds in the introduction to the עלה unit, and this has led some scholars to suggest that the section on birds was added later to make provision for the poor in the community.[16] This is likely given that the instructions for skin conditions and the parturient are explicit about the use of a bird if the person cannot afford a sheep (see Lev 5:7-10; 12:8; 14:21-22). The procedure for the bird offering is different from that of the offering from the herd or flock. The bird is not "slaughtered," but, rather, the priest nips off the bird's head and drains the blood of the animal down along the side of the altar. Ironically, the procedure for offering the bird does not give the layperson a role in its slaughter. This may be due to the size of a bird; regardless, instruction on this offering confers a less active role on the part of the offerer. Those who can afford the ideally required animal get a more significant role in the ritual.

This highlights the tensions that often arise between aiding the impoverished and maintaining their dignity. This difference in the manner of slaughter highlights some of the same socio-economic dynamics we experience today. On the one hand, the text recognizes that not everyone is able to give equally, so it offers alternatives to enable the poor to participate. On the other hand, the poor do not have an equal role in the ritual; the person with more financial assets is the one who gets to participate most fully in the ritual. Is the inclusion of the birds an example of faux inclusion or an earnest attempt at maximal participation?[17]

16. Ibid., 166–67.

17. The Mishnah relates a story about the prohibitively high price of birds for sacrifice in the late Second Temple period. According to the story, Rabban Simeon ben Gamaliel, noticing the high price for birds, adjusted laws regarding women's impurity so that fewer sacrifices would be needed, and indeed, the price for sacrificial birds dropped dramatically (m. Ker 1:7).

¹⁴If your offering to the Lord is a burnt offering of birds, you shall choose your offering from turtledoves or pigeons. ¹⁵The priest shall bring it to the altar and wring off its head, and turn it into smoke on the altar; and its blood shall be drained out against the side of the altar. ¹⁶He shall remove its crop with its contents and throw it at the east side of the altar, in the place for ashes. ¹⁷He shall tear it open by its wings without severing it. Then the priest shall turn it into smoke on the altar, on the wood that is on the fire; it is a burnt offering, an offering by fire of pleasing odor to the Lord.

---

**TRANSLATION MATTERS**

Interpreters usually translate the last segment of verse 9 as "an offering by fire of pleasing odor to the Lord" (NRSV). Rendering the Hebrew אשה as "by fire" assumes that this word is related to the word אש ("fire"). Milgrom notes, however, that this word is used in connection with the wine libation (Num 15:10) and the showbread (Lev 24:7, 9), neither of which is associated with fire. In addition, other offerings that are burned on the altar are not called אשה. This evidence calls the general translation "by fire" into doubt. Milgrom argues that the root may be connected to the Ugaritic word *iṯṯ*, which means "gift," and that we should translate אשה as "food gift."[18] Watts helpfully points out that we should "not ignore the apparent etymological connection between the offering name and the common noun אש ('fire') when the P writers use them in close juxtaposition with every indication that they were conscious of the link."[19]

---

## The Grain Offering (2:1-10)

The מנחה ("grain offering," NRSV) is well attested in biblical texts outside of P. The term מנחה was not restricted to grain offerings. In fact, מנחה simply means a present or a gift. Most often, in non-P texts, the grain offering accompanied other offerings and was presented to God in the form of smoke (e.g., Judg 13:19; 1 Kgs 8:64; 2 Kgs 16:13, 15; Isa 19:21; Jer 14:12; Amos 5:22). There are biblical and extrabiblical sources that describe the offering of loaves to a variety of gods. In these cases, the grain is completely burnt up. It is possible that P restricted the מנחה usage to specific types of grain offerings in order to curb the use of the

---

18. Milgrom, *Leviticus 1–16*, 162. See Hartley, *Leviticus*, 22–23 for a brief discussion of the power of scent and smell in ritual.

19. Watts, *Leviticus 1–10*, 210.

*Lev 2:1-10*

2:1When anyone presents a grain offering to the Lord, the offering shall be of choice flour; the worshiper shall pour oil on it, and put frankincense on it, 2and bring it to Aaron's sons the priests. After taking from it a handful of the choice flour and oil, with all its frankincense, the priest shall turn this token portion into smoke on the altar, an offering by fire of pleasing odor to the Lord. 3And what is left of the grain offering shall be for Aaron and his sons, a most holy part of the offerings by fire to the Lord.

4When you present a grain offering baked in the oven, it shall be of choice flour: unleavened cakes mixed with oil, or unleavened wafers spread with oil.

5If your offering is grain prepared on a griddle, it shall be of choice flour mixed with oil, unleavened; 6break it in pieces, and pour oil on it; it is a grain offering. 7If your offering is grain prepared in a pan, it shall be made of choice flour in oil. 8You shall bring to the Lord the grain offering that is prepared in any of these ways; and when it is presented to the priest, he shall take it to the altar. 9The priest shall remove from the grain offering its token portion and turn this into smoke on the altar, an offering by fire of pleasing odor to the Lord. 10And what is left of the grain offering shall be for Aaron and his sons; it is a most holy part of the offerings by fire to the Lord.

מנחה in popular Israelite worship. P also mandates that the grain offering not be burnt up entirely but that only a token portion goes on the altar, while most of the grain goes to the priests. In P texts, the grain offering can serve as a standalone offering[20] or as an offering that accompanies a burnt offering or a well-being offering.

Leviticus 1 names the offerer of a burnt offering an אדם, which indicates any person regardless of gender. Leviticus 2 identifies the offerer as נפש ("anyone," NRSV). In this context, נפש signifies any person, but since the word itself is grammatically feminine, it requires the verb to take the feminine form. Thus, the first chapter begins with יקריב (masc. sg. "brings," in 1:2, NRSV), while the second chapter begins with תקריב (fem. sg. "presents" in 2:1, NRSV). The interchange of grammatically feminine and masculine forms within the discourse on sacrificial animals and their offerers helps to raise the question of gender inclusivity for feminist readers today.

20. For example, bread loaves are prepared as the showbread (Lev 24:5-9), grain is brought as a purification offering if one cannot afford to bring an animal (Lev 5:11), and the high priest's daily offering takes the form of a grain offering (Lev 6:12-16).

*Grain on the Altar*

The instruction begins with a description of an uncooked grain of-fering. The offerer brings a high-quality grain (סלת), pours oil on it, and places frankincense on it. The priest scoops up a handful of the mixture along with the entirety of the frankincense and offers it up on the altar. The portion that is burned on the altar is called the אזכרה. There is no agreement as to the meaning of this word. The term also appears in Numbers 5, where a man who suspects his wife of adultery brings the woman to the priest along with a grain offering of barley flour without any oil or frankincense. During the Sotah ritual, the priest places the grain offering in the woman's hand and then later takes a portion for burning on the altar; this portion is called the אזכרה. While the ingredients for the two rituals are different, in both cases a portion of the offering is placed on the fire of the altar as an אזכרה. The root of the word is זכר, which evokes the concept of memory or notice.[21] While there is not suf-ficient evidence to make sense of this term accurately, some suggest a memorial of some sort or perhaps an invocation (from the *hiphil* form, which can mean "to pronounce"). Milgrom suggests that the term may be related to remembrance, "referring to the fact that the entire cereal offering should really go up in smoke, and that the portion that does is *pars pro totus*: it stands for the remainder; in other words, it is a 'token portion.'"[22] To this day, before challah is braided and baked, a token portion of the dough is thrown directly into the oven accompanied by a blessing. This token portion may be similar to the biblical אזכרה.

After the portion is offered up on the altar, the remaining grain goes to the priests for their sustenance. This food source is called "a holy part" to indicate that it must be eaten only by the priests in a holy space. In other words, the offering is made to YHVH, and the priests partake of the sanctified meal. Leviticus 22 enumerates who from the priest's household may eat the sacred food.

Leviticus 2:4 shifts from third person to second. The text calls directly to the offerer, thereby bringing the reader more fully into the role of par-ticipant. This is the first time in Leviticus that the offerer is addressed directly. This verse also introduces toasted/fried/baked grain. Three forms of preparation are permitted: grain and oil baked in an oven, grain and oil prepared on a griddle and crumbled into pieces, and grain

---

21. The same three Hebrew letters also signify "male."
22. Milgrom, *Leviticus 1–16*, 182.

and oil prepared in a pan. In contrast to instructions for raw grain (Lev 2:1-3), frankincense is not designated for the cooked grain offerings; it is likely that frankincense would have been prohibitively expensive for the poor. Again, a portion is offered up to God and the rest is given to priests as holy sustenance.

## Women and Grain

The preparation of the meal offering situates the offerer's labor outside of the tabernacle precincts. Animal sacrifices would have required the slaughter to take place in close proximity to the priests, but the preparation of unleavened breads could have taken place anywhere. Biblical texts never indicate a specific location for the preparation of the grain offerings. It is possible that the grain offerings were prepared in domestic quarters, and if this was the case, then it is likely that women prepared the breads. The task of preparing bread was usually assigned to women (Gen 18:6; Lev 26:26; 1 Sam 8:13). The association of women with baking affirms women's participation in the cult.

Jeremiah 44 highlights the important role that women played by baking bread used in cultic practices. In a rare instance of hearing directly from women in opposition to a prophet, the women proudly own their role in preparing cakes, and they describe the role that their husbands and sons have in gathering the wood for the fires. As described in Jeremiah 44, everyone in the family has a role in the preparation of grain offerings. In the Jeremiah passage, the women are baking cakes to the queen of heaven. We can only wonder whether the priestly writers associated women's baking with pagan practices.

In postbiblical Jewish texts, the responsibility for baking bread was assigned as women's work. Naftali Cohn cites many rabbinic texts that set a scene with a woman baking bread, borrowing utensils, and grinding grain. m. Ketubbot 5:5 reads: "The following are the tasks a woman does for her husband: She grinds flour, bakes, launders, cooks." Notice how baking is set apart from the other tasks of cooking. m. Hallot 4:1 addresses what portion of bread is to be set aside for God. The text distinguishes between the case of personal, domestic baking and professional baking in large quantities, and it lists both men and women as bakers in the public arena.[23] Eventually baking challah with the ritual separation

23. Cynthia M. Baker, *Rebuilding the House of Israel: Architectures of Gender in Jewish Antiquity* (Stanford, CA: Stanford University Press, 2002), 80–82; and Naftali S.

of a portion of the dough for God landed in the domain of women in traditional Jewish practice.

## Salty, not Sweet! (2:11-16)

Leviticus 2:11-13 has two miscellaneous rules related to the category of grain offerings. The first law prohibits the accompaniment of leaven or honey with grain offerings. Such breads may be brought to the tabernacle as gifts of the first fruit offerings, but no portion of the dough can be offered on the altar. Leaven is forbidden for the grain offering (Lev 2:11) and for the bread that accompanies sacrificial meats (Lev 6:17). In Leviticus 23:17 the people offer loaves to the priests during the festival of Weeks, and Leviticus 7:13 commands that people should bring loaves of bread for the priests when they bring their offerings of thanksgiving. In both of these latter cases, the bread does not end up on the altar; the priests receive it as food.

The second law mandates that salt must be included with grain offerings. The NRSV suggests that there are two components to this verse: first, you shall not omit from your grain offerings the salt of the covenant with your God, and second, with all your offerings you shall offer salt. But there are three verbal clauses in the verse: first, you must salt your grain offerings; second, do not omit the salt of the covenant with your God; and third, offer salt with all your offerings. Obviously, this threefold repetition of salt emphasizes the importance of salt with the grain offerings. Watts argues that verses 11-13 stand apart from the rest of the chapter because of shifts in grammatical structures and the use of repeated terms. Watts suggests that verse 13 builds on verses 11-12 but also shifts to the singular address so that, rhetorically, this "highlights the individual's obligation to prepare offerings with salt."[24]

Most commentators believe that salt was required on all offerings in P's system, perhaps as a preservative to counter the risk of leavening. This assertion is based on verse 13 and supported by only one other biblical text, Ezekiel 43:23, which mandates the sprinkling of salt on meat

---

Cohn, "Domestic Women: Constructing and Deconstructing a Gender Stereotype in the Mishnah," in *From Antiquity to the Postmodern World: Contemporary Jewish Studies in Canada*, ed. Daniel Maoz and Andrea Gondos (Newcastle upon Tyne: Cambridge Scholars Publishing, 2011), 38–61, esp. 45, which notes that the man is given a professional title while the woman is simply called a "woman."

24. Watts, *Leviticus 1–10*, 263.

*Lev 2:11-16*

[11]No grain offering that you bring to the LORD shall be made with leaven, for you must not turn any leaven or honey into smoke as an offering by fire to the LORD. [12]You may bring them to the LORD as an offering of choice products, but they shall not be offered on the altar for a pleasing odor. [13]You shall not omit from your grain offerings the salt of the covenant with your God; with all your offerings you shall offer salt.

[14]If you bring a grain offering of first fruits to the LORD, you shall bring as the grain offering of your first fruits coarse new grain from fresh ears, parched with fire. [15]You shall add oil to it and lay frankincense on it; it is a grain offering. [16]And the priest shall turn a token portion of it into smoke—some of the coarse grain and oil with all its frankincense; it is an offering by fire to the LORD.

for a purification offering. While Ezra 6:9 and 7:22 describe the need for massive amounts of salt to be delivered to the temple, the text does not specify the purpose for the salt. The only evidence for the use of salt on all sacrifices, both animal and grain, is Leviticus 2:13. If in fact this verse commands salting all offerings, its placement in the text is quite unusual because the mandate of salt should appear in the instructions for meat offerings. One could argue that verse 13 applies only to grain offerings and not to animal sacrifices.

In Numbers 18:19, the requirement of offering salt with sacred gifts for YHVH is followed by the phrase ברית מלח עולם, "an everlasting covenant of salt." The coupling of "salt" with "covenant" has led to investigations regarding the role of salt in ancient Near Eastern treaties and other texts. While salt clearly had many practical and symbolic uses, it is not clear that our text has anything to do with these. Salting practices likely had apotropaic functions as well. Salt functions as a healing agent in Ezekiel 47:11, and it is used by Elisha to make a spring in Jericho wholesome (2 Kgs 2:19-22). A number of Semitic birth rituals include sprinkling salt around the baby or the home to avert the evil eye.[25]

The last verses of Leviticus 2 introduce two additional offerings: the first processed offering קרבן ראשית, which was baked leavened bread

---

25. A. M. Honeyman, "The Salting of Shechem," *VT* 3 (1953): 192–95 also suggests an apotropaic function for salt. Note also the Sumerian "Incantation against Gall," which mentions the use of salt in conjunction with an incantation to counter an illness: "When you take a lump of salt in your hand, When you cast the spell, When you place (the salt) in his mouth, then . . . " (Piotr Michalowski, "Carminative Magic: Towards an Understanding of Sumerian Poetics," *ZA* 71 (1981): 4.

that did not go upon the altar (vv. 11-12), and the grain offering of first fruits (מנחת בכורים) described in verses 14-16. The first fruit meal offering consisted of coarse corn grain with roasted sheaves, or as my colleague Rabbi Vivie Mayer has said, "Popcorn!" In Leviticus 2:14-16, the coarse grain is mixed with oil and frankincense and then offered up to YHVH. This text is a part of a larger amalgam of texts that prescribe "first fruits" to be offered to YHVH through the medium of a priest.[26]

## The Well-Being Offering (3:1-17)

> Leviticus 3 has not played a big role in subsequent biblical interpretation. Apart from worries among rabbinic interpreters about the practical implementation of the ban on consuming fat, Jewish and Christian readers have only occasionally tried to allegorize that ban. Modern historians have seized on the fact that amity slaughter offerings are shared meals between deity and worshippers to theorize about the origins of Israelite or human rituals, religion and culture. But that is precisely the aspect of this offering that Leviticus 3 ignores almost entirely. As a result, the chapter has for the most part lain fallow while interpreters cultivated other biblical ground.[27]

While commentary on Leviticus 3 has been sparse in comparison to other chapters, the use of the term שלמים ("well-being offering") appears regularly throughout the Bible. Most references to well-being offerings appear in Deuteronomic narratives that describe the kings offering burnt offerings along with well-being offerings. In Judges 20:26, the community offers burnt and well-being offerings after fasting in order to inquire of YHVH. During Solomon's prayer at the dedication of the temple in Jerusalem (1 Kgs 8), well-being offerings are sacrificed. In the view of some scholars, this statement, in the context of the dedication ceremony, establishes the meaning of the word שלמים as a sacrifice intended to reaffirm the covenant between God and the Israelite community.

Cognates of this root appear in Akkadian as *shulmānu*, "gift of greeting" from a vassal to his overlord.[28] Comparative evidence suggests that the term שלמים originally meant "tribute." Baruch Levine suggests

---

26. Israel Knohl (*The Sanctuary of Silence: The Priestly Torah and the Holiness School* [Winona Lake, IN: Eisenbrauns, 2007], 23–27) makes a compelling argument that these two offerings reflected popular religious practices that P and H incorporated into their festival calendars. See discussion on Leviticus 23 for more detail.

27. Watts, *Leviticus 1–10*, 207.

28. *CAD*, "Shin," 3:244–47.

that in the Israelite cult "the well-being assumed the form of an animal sacrifice offered to God when one came before Him to greet Him at a sacred meal. It was adopted as the name of a particular sacrifice because it expressed the fellowship experienced by the worshipers and priests in God's presence, as they greeted their divine guest."[29] Since P uses key words with precise technical meanings, we cannot know with certainty what the term שלמים meant in P's system. Neither cognates nor other biblical narratives shed light on this at present.

## The Mechanics of the Well-Being Offering (3:1-17)

Leviticus 3 is coherent and clearly organized and follows closely the form of chapter 1. Without stating a subject (e.g., אדם or נפש), Leviticus 3 begins: "if a well-being is his/her offering, then . . ." Given the gender inclusivity of Leviticus 1 and 2, I assume that the 3ms possessive suffix on קרבנו is not just masculine but rather a generic reference. It would be difficult to explain why burnt offerings and grain offerings would be offered by men and women while well-being offerings would be restricted only to men. This type of offering is similar to that of the burnt offering insofar as the offerer may use animals from the herd or the flock. The offerer places his hand on the animal and slaughters it, and then the priest dashes the blood on the altar. The primary difference between the two sacrifices is that the burnt offering is cut up and offered in its entirety on the altar while the well-being offerings provide God with the fat and vital organs. There is no mention as to the treatment of the rest of the animal in this chapter, but other references (e.g., Lev 7:15, 18, 20, 32; 10:14; 19:6-7) to the well-being offering indicate that the rest of the meat was eaten by the priests and the offerer.

### Sacrificial Animals and Gender

In Leviticus 1, we are taken back to P's creation account, which uses the term אדם to represent the whole of humanity (see Gen 1:26-28). Leviticus 3 evokes another part of that same creation text: distinction between "male" and "female." A feature of this chapter is that the text designates the use of either a male or a female animal, while the burnt offering must be male only. The phrase אם זכר אם נקבה is a part of the protatis (the "if" clause) of verse 1: "If the offering is a sacrifice of well-being" and "if you

---

29. Baruch Levine, *In the Presence of the Lord: A Study of Cult and Some Cultic Terms in Ancient Israel*, SJLA 5 (Leiden: Brill, 1974).

*Lev 3:1-17*

³:¹If the offering is a sacrifice of well-being, if you offer an animal of the herd, whether male or female, you shall offer one without blemish before the Lᴏʀᴅ. ²You shall lay your hand on the head of the offering and slaughter it at the entrance of the tent of meeting; and Aaron's sons the priests shall dash the blood against all sides of the altar. ³You shall offer from the sacrifice of well-being as an offering by fire to the Lᴏʀᴅ, the fat that covers the entrails; ⁴the two kidneys with the fat that is on them at the loins, and the appendage of the liver, which he shall remove with the kidneys. ⁵Then Aaron's sons shall turn these into smoke on the altar, with the burnt offering that is on the wood on the fire, as an offering by fire of pleasing odor to the Lᴏʀᴅ.

⁶If your offering for a sacrifice of well-being to the Lᴏʀᴅ is from the flock, male or female, you shall offer one without blemish. ⁷If you present a sheep as your offering, you shall bring it before the Lᴏʀᴅ ⁸and lay your hand on the head of the offering. It shall be slaughtered before the tent of meeting, and Aaron's sons shall dash its blood against all sides of the altar. ⁹You

offer an animal of the herd" and "whether male or female," then "you shall offer one without blemish before the Lᴏʀᴅ." Verse 1 (see also 3:6) does not designate a particular gender of animals sacrificed for שלמים but simply says that your offering must be an unambiguous female or unambiguous male. This presents a significant contrast, however, to P's other references to the well-being offering; outside of this prescriptive chapter, P mentions only male animals in well-being rituals.

Nicole Ruane has recently suggested that the gender of the sacrificial animal mirrors gender roles in sacrifice rituals. She writes, "Just as only male humans make public and communal sacrificial offerings, in the final form of the Pentateuch, all animal offerings made at any scheduled, regular time and during a public event should be males." She continues, "Males are the preferred victims not only for observances in the ritual calendars but also for most types of offerings."[30] This leads her to conclude:

> In the priestly legal texts, therefore, male animals appear to be the only offerings for regular sacrifices or public sacrifices, whereas female animals are only specifically required for the private sin offering of a commoner and are otherwise only permissible as well-being offerings. The distinction mirrors the gender pattern found among human participants in which males are required to attend and bring offerings to corporate and national public sacrificial rituals, whereas females are not so re-

---

30. Ruane, *Sacrifice and Gender*, 45.

*Lev 3:1-17 (cont.)*

shall present its fat from the sacrifice of well-being, as an offering by fire to the LORD: the whole broad tail, which shall be removed close to the backbone, the fat that covers the entrails, and all the fat that is around the entrails; [10]the two kidneys with the fat that is on them at the loins, and the appendage of the liver, which you shall remove with the kidneys. [11]Then the priest shall turn these into smoke on the altar as a food offering by fire to the LORD.

[12]If your offering is a goat, you shall bring it before the LORD [13]and lay your hand on its head; it shall be slaughtered before the tent of meeting; and the sons of Aaron shall dash its blood against all sides of the altar. [14]You shall present as your offering from it, as an offering by fire to the LORD, the fat that covers the entrails, and all the fat that is around the entrails; [15]the two kidneys with the fat that is on them at the loins, and the appendage of the liver, which you shall remove with the kidneys. [16]Then the priest shall turn these into smoke on the altar as a food offering by fire for a pleasing odor.

All fat is the LORD's. [17]It shall be a perpetual statute throughout your generations in all your settlements: you must not eat any fat or any blood.

quired (or where it is unclear). Just as women made personal offerings, so female animals are only required for the personal sacrifices of a private person, not a priest or lay leader. In this way, the male animal, like the male person, is related to the public, patrilineal, corporate body, whereas the female can at times represent the private individual.[31]

Baruch Levine and Jacob Milgrom have offered a more pragmatic suggestion, namely, that "most animal sacrifices consisted of males for the probable reason that fewer males than females were necessary to reproduce the herds and flocks."[32] Similarly, regarding the purification offering for the commoner, Milgrom asks why the female, the more valuable animal, would be required of the commoner while the chieftain only needed to bring a male animal, that of lesser worth. He concludes that a poor commoner would be likely to keep only female animals for sustenance while a richer person could afford to keep several males for breeding.[33] Yet another approach is presented by Hartley who suggests that "the general requirements for sacrifice under this category [of well-

---

31. Ibid., 46.

32. Baruch Levine, *Leviticus: A JPS Torah Commentary* (Philadelphia: Jewish Publication Society of America, 1989), 25.

33. Milgrom, *Leviticus 1–16*, 252.

being offering] are more lax since this is a praise offering that was offered more spontaneously."[34] Moreover, he claims, with regard to the חטאת ("purification offering"), "The higher the position of the person who has sinned, the more costly the animal required for sacrifice."[35]

Finally, the most common explanation for preference of males as sacrificial animals is based on the patriarchal assumption that the male (whether human or animal) is considered the more whole, the more complete, the higher-level being, while the female is incomplete, subordinate to the male, and therefore less desirable. If we approach Leviticus 3 as reflecting the realities of ancient farming practices, then it makes sense to consider issues of animal husbandry and the relative value of female and male domesticated animals. If we read the text symbolically, then we can posit a correlation between the gender of an animal and the relative societal values ascribed to gender in general.

When the text indicates that either a female or male animal may be used, the text pairs the words זכר and נקבה. The terms זכר and נקבה appear together remarkably few times and only in the Pentateuch; furthermore, all occurrences bar one (Deut 4:16) come from P's narrative of the primordial era. Therefore, the well-informed reader would immediately associate the paired terms in Leviticus 3:1 and 6 with their use in these other central passages (Gen 1:27; 5:2; 6:19; 7:3, 9, 16). The occurrences in Genesis stress the unity of these two genders, that humanity (and animals) exist by virtue of mingling male and female. Leviticus 3:1 introduces an element of that unity as it shifts from "and" to "or." Ironically, then, choosing one and not the other forms the basis for the well-being or "wholeness" offering.

I do not claim to have a more compelling explanation for the inclusion of male and female animals for the well-being category.[36] There is certainly nothing more lax about this sacrifice than any other category. In fact, one could argue that this category is the most complex because it requires the most careful and detailed dissection of the animal. The need to excise certain organs and tissue from the animal for a well-being offering would have required more intimate time with the body of the animal.

---

34. Hartley, *Leviticus*, 39.

35. Ibid., 59.

36. Ramban (a leading Jewish medieval scholar also known as Nachmanides) claims that a burnt offering is always male because it rises to the highest levels, that the well-being can be male or female because the word שלם means "whole," and that sin offerings are females (he provides no rationale for this).

Interestingly, nowadays, women are beginning to carve out for themselves new businesses as female butchers because of the increasing demand to eat local meats. Kari Underly, a butcher, author, and consultant, was hired by a company to determine how to make the most of a cow to boost profits. She has been credited with developing two new cuts of steak. Underly recognizes the difficulties that female butchers experience in a male-dominated business. A 2016 article on a conference for female butchers describes Underly's presentation:

> Underly moves on to the next animal: a tougher mutton that she slips her knife into with both brute force and finesse. In a male-dominated profession, the women who cut meat do so in a way that maintains a vibe of nurturing and care.
>
> She anchors her elbow, using her other arm to twist the animal's leg "where the saddle dips visually." Holding the sheep's leg in one pink-gloved hand, she mentally catches up to a joke she started earlier but never finished.
>
> "You know why I wear these pink gloves? Guys don't steal a pink glove," she says. The amused crowd erupts into laughter again. And Underly ends her demo right there, dropping the knife like a mic: "We're out!"[37]

When asked if she thought that women make better butchers she replied: "I do. It's about detail, nurturing, and grounding. Men tend to—there are some very good men butchers—but women have more finesse, make sure it looks pretty, with more nurturing care. Guys are more about production: How much can I get done? It's about might vs. finesse."[38]

37. Victoria Bouloubasis, "Women Butchers and Farmers Are Growing in Number, Especially in North Carolina," *Indy Week*, October 5, 2016, http://www.indyweek.com /indyweek/women-butchers-and-farmers-are-growing-in-number-especially-in -north-carolina/Content?oid=5072911.

38. Ruth Graham, "A Female Butcher on Beef, Death Threats, and Why Women Are Better at the Job," *The Grindstone*, May 14, 2012, http://www.thegrindstone.com /2012/05/14/office-politics/kari-underly-range-female-butcher-career-152/2 /#ixzz4aTbGlJ00.

# Leviticus 4:1–6:7

# Something New:
# Purification and Guilt

As we move into Leviticus 4 and 5, we find significant differences from the preceding chapters. The first three chapters seem to assume that the reader knows the purpose of various offerings (i.e., why someone would offer a grain offering, a burnt offering, or a well-being offering), and therefore they focus on how rituals should be performed. In contrast, each section of chapters 4 and 5 begins with a "why" and then a "how." Several scholars have suggested that the חטאת ("purification offering") and the אשם ("guilt offering") were the innovations of the priestly author(s) of this text. James Watts, in particular, argues that the writers of Leviticus intentionally began with commonly known offerings as a rhetorical device to get the buy-in of the audience. Once the readers trust the writer(s), they might be more willing to accept new mandates. In fact, while the terms עולה, מנחה, and שלמים appear throughout the Bible, the חטאת offering appears only in the priestly materials from the final chapters of Exodus, Leviticus, and Numbers, and then again in Ezekiel's temple vision (Ezek 40–48), in Ezra 8:35, and in 2 Chronicles 29. This suggests that the priestly schools created and promoted the חטאת.[1]

---

1. Christophe Nihan, *From Priestly Torah to Pentateuch: A Study in the Composition of the Book of Leviticus*, FAT 25 (Tübingen: Mohr Siebeck, 2007), 160–72 believes that Lev 4–5 as well as Lev 6–7 reflect a late addition to priestly material.

## Mistakes, Sins, and Guilt (4:1-2)

Apart from the mechanics of the חטאת offering, Leviticus 4–5 explores conditions under which the חטאת is necessary. Leviticus 12–15 illustrates the requirement for a חטאת in cases of major impurity (e.g., Lev 12:6-7; 14:19-20; 15:14-15). It is apparent that, according to the priestly literature, one who has intentionally committed a trespass cannot approach the cultic system to make things right. So apart from major ritual impurities, the purification offering is brought in cases where a sin has been committed unwittingly (שגגה). Nobuyoshi Kiuchi argues that שגגה refers to sins that have been committed unconsciously, without any awareness of the wrongdoing.[2] Baruch Levine specifies the scope to include cases in which the individual is ignorant of the law. Levine further points out that the rabbis understood שגגה to include two different aspects: "(1) inadvertence with respect to the facts of law; and (2) inadvertence with respect to the nature of the act."[3] For example, I may walk out of a bookshop with a newspaper because I assumed that there was no charge or I may have walked out without realizing that the newspaper was in my bag. In the first case, I would be ignorant with respect to the facts of law; in the second case, I would have been unaware of my actions.

Whatever the nature of the error, sin results in the person or community becoming guilty. The verb אשם has been the subject of much religious and academic debate. Interestingly, the Hebrew term אשם and the English word "guilt" share a common range of meanings. For example, one can feel guilty (as in ashamed or embarrassed) or, within the judicial system, one can be declared guilty (as opposed to innocent); in the latter case one's emotional state is not necessarily relevant. So one of the central questions is whether אשם in Leviticus 4–5 refers to an offerer who feels guilty and seeks an emotional absolution, or who is legally/cultically guilty and needs to make restitution. The objective meaning of אשם ("state of guilt") was the dominant reading in early biblical criticism until Milgrom argued for a subjective meaning ("feeling guilty"). The problem with both approaches is that no single approach works with every use of אשם in Leviticus 4 and 5. This led Kiuchi to suggest that אשם could have both an objective and a subjective meaning: "Since the

2. Nobuyoshi Kiuchi, *The Purification Offering in the Priestly Literature: Its Meaning and Function* (Sheffield: Sheffield Academic, 1987), 26.

3. Baruch Levine, *Leviticus: A JPS Torah Commentary* (Philadelphia: Jewish Publication Society of America, 1989), 19.

### Lev 4:1-2

4:1The LORD spoke to Moses, saying: 2Speak to the people of Israel, saying: When anyone sins unintentionally in any of the LORD's commandments about things not to be done, and does any one of them:

sinner is guilty, he feels guilty."[4] As John E. Hartley writes, "The legal dimension is stressed here; i.e., the sinners are culpable for their act. Yet the text also assumes the dynamic nature of guilt; their guilt will eventually lead to their becoming aware that they have committed a wrong."[5]

There are a number of technical terms introduced in Leviticus 4 and any interpretation of this chapter and what follows depends on how one understands these terms. As discussed in the introduction, the words כפר, נסלח, אשם, and חטאת have a rich and varied set of associations in the history of interpretation. To compound this confusion, we must also ask who or what has been offended and who or what needs restitution. To highlight some of these issues, note how differently two popular English translations render instructions on offerings to be made on behalf of a ruler (Lev 4:22-23) and on behalf of an individual (Lev 4:27-28):

> When a ruler sins, doing unintentionally any one of all the things that by commandments of the LORD his God ought not to be done and incurs guilt, once the sin that he has committed is made known to him, he shall bring . . . (Lev 4:22-23, NRSV)

> If anyone of the ordinary people among you sins unintentionally in doing any one of the things that by the LORD's commandments ought not to be done and incurs guilt, when the sin that you have committed is made known to you, you shall bring . . . (Lev 4:27-28, NRSV)

> In case it is a chieftain who incurs guilt by doing unwittingly any of the things which by the commandment of the LORD his God ought not to be done, and he realizes his guilt—or the sin of which he is guilty is brought to his knowledge—he shall bring . . . (Lev 4:22-23, NJPS)

> If any person from among the populace unwittingly incurs guilt by doing any of the things which by the LORD's commandments ought not to be done, and he realizes his guilt—or the sin of which he is guilty is brought to his knowledge—he shall bring . . . (Lev 4:27-28, NJPS)

---

4. Kiuchi, *The Purification Offering*, 34.
5. John E. Hartley, *Leviticus*, WBC 4 (Waco, TX: Word Books, 1992), 62.

The NRSV understands the text to mean that when one sins unintentionally, the sin automatically incurs guilt. When one is informed of his or her sin, a purification offering is required. The NJPS understands the text to communicate that a purification offering is either required when one incurs guilt unknowingly and then realizes one's guilt or when the offense is made known to the person. Part of the challenge with translation is that it is difficult to encompass the nuances of certain terms. אשם can have an objective meaning ("to incur guilt") or a subjective meaning ("to feel guilty"). Thus, translators have used a variety of wordings to capture their interpretation of the word: "become guilty," "feel guilty," "realize guilt."

Hartley presents a reading of the text that attempts to be all encompassing. He suggests, "The primary way that one learns about his unintentional sin then is through the dynamic of guilt. Even though a person sins unintentionally, he incurs guilt (אשם). This guilt eventually works its way into his conscience so that 'he feels guilty' (אשם). The belief here is that psychological guilt awakens one to an inadvertent sin."[6] Watts, on the other hand writes, "Interpreters' difficulties stem from demanding a level of technical precision from language that is instead being deployed impressionistically for rhetorical effect. When we recognize repeated word plays in chaps. 4–5, the interpretive question becomes what effect the writers were trying to achieve rather than what exact meaning the words carry."[7]

Levine approaches the challenge of understanding the relationship between guilt and sin by paying close attention to the context of the text:

> The laws of chapters 4–5 see an inherent connection between sinfulness and impurity, a connection that is apparent in a variety of situations. Many technical terms can mean both "sin" and "impurity." Since antiquity, there has been a tendency in many languages to juxtapose ritual and legal concepts. Even today, we use the word "fault" to connote both a physical or structural imperfection as well as a misdeed. In the context of ritual, one is perceived as either pure or impure, which implies a physical, or nearly physical, state. In the context of law, one is innocent or guilty, which relates primarily to behavior. In the Levitical codes of the Torah, as in many other ancient traditions, these two contexts have been blended, so that what is sinful is at the same time impure; conversely, the forgiven person is at the same time purified.[8]

---

6. Ibid., 67.
7. James W. Watts, *Leviticus 1–10*, HCOT (Leuven: Peeters, 2013), 342.
8. Levine, *Leviticus*, 19.

## Propitiation, Expiation, Mitigation, and Purification

The first verse in Leviticus 4–5 provides the reason for making a חטאת offering. If anyone transgresses unintentionally regarding YHVH's prohibitive commandments, they are required to bring a purification offering. The prohibitive commandments, also known as negative commandments, are essentially the "do nots" (as opposed to the positive commandments, which are the "dos"). The חטאת applies only when a prohibitive commandment is not followed by mistake or due to an accident.

Before looking at the specific cases for the חטאת it will be useful to pay attention to the ultimate goal of this offering. It is almost impossible to provide an English translation for Hebrew words that are associated with חטאת because there are no comparable words in English. For example, for centuries the Hebrew word כפר was translated as "atonement," but, as Watts has rightly noted, the English word "atonement" is laden with centuries of theological overtones. Watts notes that William Tyndale first translated כפר as "atonement" in 1526. While the translation was retained for many centuries, the English word "atonement" began to take on more complex Christian theological nuance, so critical translators have now shifted to words like "expiate" or "purify."

Similarly, it is difficult to provide an English translation for חטאת because no single English word encompasses the range of meanings for this Hebrew word. At the root of our confusion is that a חטאת is required both for inadvertent sins and for major ritual impurities. In the instructions in Leviticus 4, חטאת rituals end with a statement that the priest כפר for the person/community and the person/community is נסלח (usually rendered "forgiven"). In Leviticus 12–15, however, the result of the חטאת is טהר ("to be clean," Lev 12:7-8, NRSV). There has been a lot of literature devoted to the meaning of כפר and נסלח in the context of the חטאת. The root כפר may be connected to the Akkadian word *kuppuru* ("wipe off") or it might be a denominative form of the noun כפר, "ransom."[9]

---

9. Baruch Levine, *In the Presence of the Lord: A Study of Cult and Some Cultic Terms in Ancient Israel*, SJLA 5 (Leiden: Brill, 1974), 67–68, posits two verbs that appear to have the same root: כפר I, "purify," and כפר II, "make expiation" (related to ransom). For an overview of the possible meanings of כפר, see Jay Sklar, *Sin, Impurity, Sacrifice, Atonement: The Priestly Conceptions*, HBM 2 (Sheffield: Sheffield Academic, 2005), esp. 1–8. For a refutation of the connection between כפר and the Akkadian *kuppuru*, "wipe off," see Yitzhaq Feder, "On Kuppuru, Kipper and Etymological Sins That Cannot Be Wiped Away," *VT* 60 (2010): 535–45.

It may be that for inadvertent sins, the offering serves to propitiate God and that for ritual impurities, the same offering functions to purify the Sancta. Thus one debate is whether the verb means "expiate" or "propitiate." In other words, when the priest כפר, is he removing the wrongdoing (expiating) or is he appeasing God (propitiating)? Recently, Watts has offered a third possibility: "to mitigate." He writes, the word "mitigation" "describes the alleviation of negative consequences produced by various kinds of problems ranging from legal conflicts to environmental pollution. It can also refer to relieving both emotional and physical burdens and to assuaging someone's anger."[10]

Jacob Milgrom's approach has served as a catalyst for other theories. In the priestly literature, כפר seems to be about removing the wrongdoing, but from what or whom? Since P does not describe God as an angry or vengeful deity, why does the transgression need to be expiated? Milgrom argues that every time an individual in the community sins, the sin releases a negative force or miasma that attaches itself to the sanctuary. If too much of this impure energy contaminates any of the sacred objects or the sanctuary itself, God may remove God's self from the holy space. God requires a space that is completely holy and pure; any threat to those conditions makes the space incompatible with the Divine Presence.[11] With this view in mind, the blood of the sacrificial animal functions as ritual detergent, clearing away the pollution and ensuring that only purity is in the sacred space.

According to Milgrom, therefore, when the priest makes expiation for the offerer, the priest is essentially cleansing the sacred space on behalf of the offerer. Thus, the purification offering purifies the sanctuary, not the individual. By bringing an offering, the individual essentially acknowledges that she or he unintentionally has done something that negatively impacts the sanctuary, and he or she is taking responsibility to make it right so that God's presence remains among the community.

Scholars argue that blood has another purpose as well: to release the offerer from bearing further responsibility for the sin because the blood of the animal comes to represent vicariously the blood of the sinner.[12] Therefore, while the priest uses the blood to purge the sanctuary, the indi-

10. Watts, *Leviticus 1–10*, 345.

11. Jacob Milgrom, *Leviticus 1–16*, AB 3 (New York: Doubleday, 1991), 254–61; see also Milgrom's classic article, "Israel's Sanctuary-Priestly Picture of Dorian-Gray," *RB* 83 (1976): 390–99.

12. See Nihan, *From Priestly Torah to Pentateuch*, 177 n. 294 for a brief summary of this theory and its proponents.

vidual is forgiven directly by God. The priest does not mediate between God and the individual. Roy Gane, a student of Milgrom's, agrees that the חטאת purifies the sanctuary on the Day of Atonement and at the first dedication of the sanctuary. He differs from Milgrom, however, in his interpretation of day-to-day חטאת offerings as set out in Leviticus 4–5. Gane argues that usually the חטאת seems to remove sin or impurity from the offerer and that the חטאת does not impact the sanctuary in any way.[13] My position within these discussions is mostly influenced by Milgrom's work. I will translate the חטאת sacrifice as "purification offering," and I will translate כפר as "purify" or "expiate."

## The Case of the Anointed Priest (4:3-12)

The unit on the purification offering (Lev 4:1–5:13) is organized into five sections; the first four sections are organized by class and status while the last section presents more specific examples of transgressions that require the purification offering. The classes are the anointed priest, the assembly of all Israel, the ruler, and the lay individual. Each category has distinguishing characteristics.

Leviticus 4–5 anticipates the induction of Aaron and his sons at the tabernacle in chapter 8. The phrase הכהן המשחית (the anointed priest) occurs only in Leviticus 4:3, 5, and 16, and in Leviticus 6:15, which describes the special offering that is made at the time that Aaron or one of his descendants is ordained and anointed into office. Reference to "the anointed priest" is unexpected in Leviticus 4, since the prior chapters consistently refer to Aaron and his sons, or to the general designation of priest. Leviticus 4 explains that when the anointed priest inadvertently transgresses, he brings guilt upon the entire people. Only the anointed priest's transgressions affect the entire community.

The ritual slaughter of the bull follows the pattern of the other sacrifices; however, the use of the blood of the sacrifice plays the most central role in the offering. The burnt offering and the well-being offering have the blood poured onto the altar on which the animal would be offered. But in the purification offering, the anointed priest engages in an elaborate ritual of blood manipulation, first sprinkling blood seven times in front of the curtain, then dabbing blood on the horns of the incense offering, and then pouring out the remaining blood on the altar of burnt

---

13. Roy E. Gane, *Cult and Character: Purification Offerings, Day of Atonement, and Theodicy* (Winona Lake, IN: Eisenbrauns, 2005).

³If it is the anointed priest who sins, thus bringing guilt on the people, he shall offer for the sin that he has committed a bull of the herd without blemish as a sin offering to the LORD. ⁴He shall bring the bull to the entrance of the tent of meeting before the LORD and lay his hand on the head of the bull; the bull shall be slaughtered before the LORD. ⁵The anointed priest shall take some of the blood of the bull and bring it into the tent of meeting. ⁶The priest shall dip his finger in the blood and sprinkle some of the blood seven times before the LORD in front of the curtain of the sanctuary. ⁷The priest shall put some of the blood on the horns of the altar of fragrant incense that is in the tent of meeting before the LORD; and the rest of the blood of the bull he shall pour out at the base of the altar of burnt offering, which is at the entrance of the tent of meeting. ⁸He shall remove all the fat from the bull of sin offering: the fat that covers the entrails and all the fat that is around the entrails; ⁹the two kidneys with the fat that is on them at the loins; and the appendage of the liver, which he shall remove with the kidneys, ¹⁰just as these are removed from the ox of the sacrifice of well-being. The priest shall turn them into smoke upon the altar of burnt offering. ¹¹But the skin of the bull and all its flesh, as well as its head, its legs, its entrails, and its dung—¹²all the rest of the bull—he shall carry out to a clean place outside the camp, to the ash heap, and shall burn it on a wood fire; at the ash heap it shall be burned.

offerings. The priest is then to offer up the same parts of the animal, as one would do for the well-being offering. As we will see, Leviticus 4 refers back to the well-being offering and the burnt offering. Unlike the well-being offering, the remaining parts of the animal are taken outside the camp to be burned on the ash heap. This offering resembles the well-being offering insofar as the same parts of the animal are burnt on the altar, and it resembles the burnt offering insofar as no part of the animal is consumed. It thus falls into the familiar but introduces new elements by giving it unique actions like removing the rest of the animal to the ash heap and, more important, the elaborate use of the blood. This is the only purification offering in which the priests do not receive a portion of the meat as food.

## The Case of the Community (4:13-21)

The second case is more complicated and merits deeper investigation. The text indicates that when the entire עדה ("official body") has transgressed unintentionally and the קהל ("community") has not recognized

*Lev 4:13-21*

[13]If the whole congregation of Israel errs unintentionally and the matter escapes the notice of the assembly, and they do any one of the things that by the LORD's commandment ought not to be done and incur guilt; [14]when the sin that they have committed becomes known, the assembly shall offer a bull of the herd for a sin offering and bring it before the tent of meeting. [15]The elders of the congregation shall lay their hands on the head of the bull before the LORD, and the bull shall be slaughtered before the LORD. [16]The anointed priest shall bring some of the blood of the bull into the tent of meeting, [17]and the priest shall dip his finger in the blood and sprinkle it seven times before the LORD, in front of the curtain. [18]He shall put some of the blood on the horns of the altar that is before the LORD in the tent of meeting; and the rest of the blood he shall pour out at the base of the altar of burnt offering that is at the entrance of the tent of meeting. [19]He shall remove all its fat and turn it into smoke on the altar. [20]He shall do with the bull just as is done with the bull of sin offering; he shall do the same with this. The priest shall make atonement for them, and they shall be forgiven. [21]He shall carry the bull outside the camp, and burn it as he burned the first bull; it is the sin offering of the assembly.

it, they (uncertain referent) incur guilt (Lev 4:13). The קהל provides the sacrificial animal, and the elders of the עדה place their hands on the animal (Lev 4:14-15). It may be that the two terms "congregation" and "assembly" are used interchangeably in this section,[14] but it is more likely that these two bodies are not identical. In some cases, the term עדה refers to an officially constituted body,[15] while קהל refers to a community (see Exod 16:3; Num 15:15). As Tamara Eskenazi points out, Ezra 10:1 defines the קהל as "men, women, and children."[16]

The text uses masculine plural verbs for both עדה and קהל so it is not clear if the actions of the officials have misled the community to sin unwittingly or if the actions of the officials affect only the officials. The ritual slaughter and the blood manipulation follow the prior case; however, this section ends with an assertion that is absent in the first

14. Levine, *Leviticus*, 22–24. Milgrom, *Leviticus 1–16*, 241–43, argues that עדה was an older term that went out of use during the period of the monarchy. קהל became more common, but עדה was still retained in some texts out of respect for the text.

15. See BDB, 417 for "company assembled together by appointment."

16. Tamara Cohn Eskenazi, "VaYikra," in *The Torah: A Women's Commentary*, ed. Tamara Cohn Eskenazi and Andrea L. Weiss (New York: URJ Press, 2008), 580.

section. The anointed priest mitigates for them and they are forgiven. Again, the text does not indicate whether it is the officials or the community that needs mitigation and forgiveness. The text becomes even more confusing as it ends with a unique summary statement for this subsection: it is a purification offering of the קהל (Lev 4:21), that is, the entire assembly.[17]

Leviticus 4:13-21 thus raises interesting questions regarding culpability and liability between a community's leadership and the community itself. One scenario is that the leadership errs and therefore leads the community astray so that the community becomes guilty. Thus the community must atone for its communal errors and the elders of the official body present the offering. Another possible scenario runs as follows: the leadership errs and incurs guilt, while the general community does not know about it; but when the truth comes out, the community initiates the mechanism to rectify the situation. In this scenario, the community has a responsibility to call its leaders to account for their mistakes. It is called the purification offering of the community because it is the community that initiates the process. Commentators who read the terms עדה and קהל as general synonyms obscure the relationship between the actions of a community and the actions of its official leaders and the power of a community to call its leaders to account.

### The Case of the Chieftain (4:22-26)

The third case involves the inadvertent sins of the נשיא ("chieftain").[18] A male goat is to be offered rather than a bull, and the blood ritual is not as elaborate, restricted to the burnt offering altar with dabs on the horns of the offering and the rest poured at the base. Additionally, the well-being is referred to when describing the parts of the animal to be offered up. There is no indication about what happens to the rest of the animal, whether it is taken outside the camp or given to the priest. Presumably, some of the meat is taken by the priests as sacred food.

---

17. In Num 15:24-26, only the term עדה is used in reference to communal sin and communal restitution.

18. The word נשיא to indicate a leader is used in a variety of contexts to indicate tribal chieftains (e.g., Num 1:16), a prince (e.g., 1 Kgs 11:34), or special leaders of the congregation (e.g., Josh 9:15). Strategically, this enables the P writers to discuss the responsibilities of a leader without specifying the particular form of government.

*Lev 4:22-26*

²²When a ruler sins, doing unintentionally any one of the things that by commandments of the Lᴏʀᴅ his God ought not to be done and incurs guilt, ²³once the sin that he has committed is made known to him, he shall bring as his offering a male goat without blemish. ²⁴He shall lay his hand on the head of the goat; it shall be slaughtered at the spot where the burnt offering is slaughtered before the Lᴏʀᴅ; it is a sin offering. ²⁵The priest shall take some of the blood of the sin offering with his finger and put it on the horns of the altar of burnt offering, and pour out the rest of its blood at the base of the altar of burnt offering. ²⁶All its fat he shall turn into smoke on the altar, like the fat of the sacrifice of well-being. Thus the priest shall make atonement on his behalf for his sin, and he shall be forgiven.

## The Case of Individual Women and Men (4:27-35)

The final section of Leviticus 4 follows the same protocol as that of the נשיא ("chieftain"). The only difference is that an individual offers a female goat. Among the five general types of offerings, this is the only place where a female animal is specified: either a male or female can be offered as a well-being sacrifice.

Commentators have noted that the animals in Leviticus 4 reflect the status of the wrongdoer: the high priest offers a bull and brings the blood into the holy of holies, thus affording him access to the most interior region of holiness; the community offers a bull, but the blood is not taken into the inner sanctum; the ruler offers a male goat, while the individual offers a female goat. The priestly text accords the leaders a status below that of the community and the individual stands on the lowest rung of the priestly social ladder.

Nicole Ruane argues that the female animal is an inferior animal because those at the lowest end of the priestly hierarchy are required to offer the she-goat. "The law of the ḥaṭṭāt't thus uses the gender and species of its victims to make explicit the social status of its offerers."[19] In other words, it is not necessarily that the individual simply brings the animal of lower status, but that the gender and status of the animal itself reflect and define the offerer. "Having a female victim as one's symbol reveals that a common man is not only socially inferior but also that he

19. Nicole J. Ruane, *Sacrifice and Gender in Biblical Law* (Cambridge: Cambridge University Press, 2013), 52.

²⁷If anyone of the ordinary people among you sins unintentionally in doing any one of the things that by the Lᴏʀᴅ's commandments ought not to be done and incurs guilt, ²⁸when the sin that you have committed is made known to you, you shall bring a female goat without blemish as your offering, for the sin that you have committed. ²⁹You shall lay your hand on the head of the sin offering; and the sin offering shall be slaughtered at the place of the burnt offering. ³⁰The priest shall take some of its blood with his finger and put it on the horns of the altar of burnt offering, and he shall pour out the rest of its blood at the base of the altar. ³¹He shall remove all its fat, as the fat is removed from the offering of well-being, and the priest shall turn it into smoke on the altar for a pleasing odor to the Lᴏʀᴅ. Thus the priest shall make atonement on your behalf, and you shall be forgiven.

³²If the offering you bring as a sin offering is a sheep, you shall bring a female without blemish. ³³You shall lay your hand on the head of the sin offering; and it shall be slaughtered as a sin offering at the spot where the burnt offering is slaughtered. ³⁴The priest shall take some of the blood of the sin offering with his finger and put it on the horns of the altar of burnt offering, and pour out the rest of its blood at the base of the altar. ³⁵You shall remove all its fat, as the fat of the sheep is removed from the sacrifice of well-being and the priest shall turn it into smoke on the altar, with the offerings by fire to the Lᴏʀᴅ. Thus the priest shall make atonement on your behalf for the sin that you have committed, and you shall be forgiven.

is less 'male' than the man represented by a male animal."[20] Ruane notes that while female animals are of more value to farmers than their male counterparts (for reproduction and as a source of milk), there is evidence that infertile female animals were slaughtered. Thus, Ruane posits that a person would most likely offer up an aged or sterile female for the חטאת. This raises an interesting question about infertility and blemishes. Can a female domesticated animal be considered whole and without blemish if she infertile?

## Inadvertent Sins (5:1-5)

While Leviticus 4 begins by addressing the individual who mistakenly breaks a prohibitive ("do not") commandment, the first four cases in Leviticus 5 address scenarios in which an individual fails to act in ac-

20. Ibid., 53.

*Lev 5:1-5*

5:1When any of you sin in that you have heard a public adjuration to testify and—though able to testify as one who has seen or learned of the matter—do not speak up, you are subject to punishment. 2Or when any of you touch any unclean thing—whether the carcass of an unclean beast or the carcass of unclean livestock or the carcass of an unclean swarming thing—and are unaware of it, you have become unclean, and are guilty. 3Or when you touch human uncleanness— any uncleanness by which one can become unclean—and are unaware of it, when you come to know it, you shall be guilty. 4Or when any of you utter aloud a rash oath for a bad or a good purpose, whatever people utter in an oath, and are unaware of it, when you come to know it, you shall in any of these be guilty. 5When you realize your guilt in any of these, you shall confess the sin that you have committed.

cordance with a positive commandment. The four cases seem somewhat haphazard at first glance. The first statement indicates that anyone who has heard a public adjuration for witnesses with first- or secondhand information regarding a legal case, and who has neglected to come forward as a witness, will bear liability (will presumably be subject to the curse that was threatened in the public call). The text does not address why the witness does not step forward; what matters is that the person had relevant information and withheld it.

The healthy functioning of judicial systems was of central importance in the ancient Near East. The first three laws in the Code of Hammurabi address false or malicious testimony, and the Code assigns the death penalty in some cases. Within the Bible, Exodus 20:16 admonishes: "You shall not bear false witness against your neighbor." The same sentiment is expressed in the parallel text Deuteronomy 5:20 and in Exodus 23:1. Psalms and Proverbs routinely condemn false witness (see Ps 35:11; Prov 12:17; 14:5; 19:5; 21:28; 24:26; 25:18). The case in Leviticus 5:1 treats a person who fails to come forward at all as guilty![21]

While some ancient cultures prohibited women from serving as witnesses, the biblical texts do not. In Greek and Roman society, women were excluded from participation in any legal deliberations.[22] This practice was carried forward into medieval Europe. Unfortunately, prohibitions against women serving as witnesses developed in early Judaism as

---

21. Watts, *Leviticus 1–10*, 357, asserts that the curse is uttered by the victim and not by the court.

22. A. N. Sherwin-White, *Roman Citizenship* (Oxford: Oxford University Press, 1979).

well. *The Committee on Jewish Law and Standards of the Rabbinical Assembly* of the Conservative Movement on women serving as witnesses stated: "The prohibition of women's testimony was a hermeneutic development based on various passages of Scripture, but the Rabbis could reach no consensus in identifying the text which validated the ban. The prohibition confirmed, however, and provided legal force for the stereotype of women as outside the arena of commerce, unaware of legal protocol and inattentive to the normal transactions of economic engagement." It was not until 2001 that the *Committee on Jewish Law and Standards* developed a new ruling to allow women to serve as witnesses in Jewish courts.[23]

The next two cases describe scenarios in which an individual fails to bathe and launder clothes upon contracting minor ritual impurities. Verses 2-3 contain the protasis of the legal situation, setting out the facts of the case; the consequences are deferred until verse 4. Verse 2 hypothesizes a person who has come in contact with the carcass of an impure wild animal, an impure domesticated animal, or an impure swarming animal and who has forgotten or neglected to bathe and launder, but then she realizes that she is in fact impure and has failed to fulfill her obligations regarding the impurity and then feels guilty.[24] Verse 3 describes the case of a person coming into contact with human impurity, neglecting to engage in the proper rituals of purification, and then realizing his mistake and feeling guilty. Although Leviticus 5:3 fails to define human impurity, most scholars assume that the sources of impurity are those enumerated in Leviticus 12–13, such as contact with genital discharges or contact with something that may have been contaminated. The final case in verse 4 describes a situation in which a person makes an oath aloud without having thought it through, then forgets about the oath, and later feels guilty.

According to this chapter, whenever a person feels guilty regarding the four scenarios just specified, that is, acknowledges an awareness of the wrong committed, then the person must confess. There are only four P passages in which confession is required (Lev 5:1-4; 16:21; 26:40; Num 5:6-7). Milgrom posits that "confession must, then, play a vital role in the judicial process. Because it only occurs when deliberate sin is expi-

23. Myron S. Geller, "Woman Is Eligible to Testify," Committee on Jewish Law and Standards of the Rabbinical Assembly, HM 35:14.2001a. https://www.rabbinical assembly.org/sites/default/files/public/halakhah/teshuvot/19912000/geller _womenedut.pdf.

24. Lev 11:31-40 addresses in more detail the consequences and necessary rectifications of contact with impure animal carcasses.

ated by sacrifice, the conclusion is ineluctable: confession is the legal device fashioned by the Priestly legislators to convert deliberate sins into inadvertencies, thereby qualifying them for sacrificial expiation."[25] While Milgrom aligns confession closely with sacrificial expiation, Levine understands confession as more tightly connected to feeling or incurring guilt. Thus, confession is still part of the extended protasis. Levine also notes that, in each of these cases, the wrong is a private matter as opposed to the cases in Leviticus 4 in which someone brings the matter to the attention of the offender. Nobuyoshi Kiuchi notes that in Leviticus 4, sins are committed by accident while in Leviticus 5, the person נעלם ממנו ("he is unaware of it," NRSV). Kiuchi interprets this phrase as relating to the subconscious; in other words, these cases describe an existential problem wherein "an initial concrete act is obscured in his consciousness," so that the wrongdoing is no longer on the surface of consciousness but rather in the realm of subconscious knowing.[26]

The first and fourth cases address neglect with regard to taking speech seriously. In the first case, an individual fails to speak up, and in the fourth case, an individual speaks up recklessly. The second and third cases deal with failure to act. In all four cases, nobody except the offender may be aware of the wrong committed. Confession transforms a private matter into a public one with appropriate use of speech. Through proper speech (confession) and sacrifice (action), the offender is again right with God. It is worth noting that the remedies presented for guilt alleviation in Leviticus follow male tendencies over those of females. "As expected, individuals with a masculine gender role preferred more action-oriented strategies to alleviate guilt and shame feelings, whereas individuals with a feminine gender role relied more heavily on verbal responses."[27]

If we take a step back from the details of the text, interesting meta-questions emerge. In a premodern worldview, what would have driven an individual to come forward with a confession and purification offering? If it is accurate that a person who withholds knowledge about a legal case would never "get caught," then what drives that person to come forward? Only the first case of the four states that the person will bear their punishment, that is, that God will know of the wrongdoing even if

---

25. Milgrom, *Leviticus 1–16*, 301–2.

26. Nobuyoshi Kiuchi, *A Study of Ḥāṭā' and Ḥaṭṭā't in Leviticus 4–5*, FAT 2 (Tübingen: Mohr Siebeck, 2003).

27. Jessica Benetti-McQuoid and Krisanne Bursik, "Individual Differences in Experiences of and Responses to Guilt and Shame: Examining the Lenses of Gender and Gender Role," *Sex Roles* 53 (2005): 140.

it is hidden from the community. Is it fear of punishment then or a respect for the integrity of the system of communal governance? A pessimistic response would posit that the priestly leadership fueled the fear of divine retribution, which drove the guilty to come forward in order to maintain the flow of goods (meat, grains, and, later, money) into the sanctuary. This interpretation reflects a rather low level of moral development according to Lawrence Kohlberg's hierarchy, in which children do what is right because they fear punishment.[28] I suspect, however, that the motivation for participation is not based on fear of punishment. P's God is not a vengeful or authoritarian God because P's God is described as that unknowable, absolute Other. P's God resides in the holy of holies in a wholly nonanthropomorphic essence that people only see as a cloud or fire. So if this God has no human personality, as evidenced partially by P's lack of rhetoric regarding God's rage or jealousy, then a fear of punishment by the divine cannot be the motivating factor for bringing an offering.

Perhaps what lies behind P's assumption of compliance is a higher and more complex system of moral reasoning that is driven by a shared ideal: divine presence within the community. While Kohlberg's stage 4 of moral reasoning,[29] rooted in the concept of obedience to a social order, seems most appropriate for understanding the community compliance, I believe the work of Carol Gilligan helps to elucidate the situation. According to Gilligan, there is a "caring perspective" of moral development that is rooted in relationships and caring instead of just logic and justice.[30] In P's system, the priests wield the power to set the rules and societal expectations; however, what the community is really doing is collectively extending hospitality to God. For the system to work, everyone must choose to participate in this project of collective hospitality.

## Sliding Scales for Purification Offerings (5:6-13)

At this point in the chapter, the text shifts to the type of animals that should be brought for a purification offering. In Leviticus 4:28 and 32, a purification offering on behalf of an individual is to be a female goat or a female sheep. Leviticus 5:6 legislates the same animals for private

28. Lawrence Kohlberg, "Education, Moral Development and Faith," *Journal of Moral Education* 4 (1974): 5–16.

29. Lawrence Kohlberg, "The Claim to Moral Adequacy of a Highest Stage of Moral Judgment," *The Journal of Philosophy* 70 (1973): 630–46.

30. Carol Gilligan, *In a Different Voice: Psychological Theory and Women's Development* (Cambridge, MA: Harvard University Press, 1982).

[6]And you shall bring to the LORD, as your penalty for the sin that you have committed, a female from the flock, a sheep or a goat, as a sin offering; and the priest shall make atonement on your behalf for your sin.

[7]But if you cannot afford a sheep, you shall bring to the LORD, as your penalty for the sin that you have committed, two turtledoves or two pigeons, one for a sin offering and the other for a burnt offering. [8]You shall bring them to the priest, who shall offer first the one for the sin offering, wringing its head at the nape without severing it. [9]He shall sprinkle some of the blood of the sin offering on the side of the altar, while the rest of the blood shall be drained out at the base of the altar; it is a sin offering. [10]And the second he shall offer for a burnt offering according to the regulation. Thus the priest shall make atonement on your behalf for the sin that you have committed, and you shall be forgiven.

[11]But if you cannot afford two turtledoves or two pigeons, you shall bring as your offering for the sin that you have committed one-tenth of an ephah of choice flour for a sin offering; you shall not put oil on it or lay frankincense on it, for it is a sin offering. [12]You shall bring it to the priest, and the priest shall scoop up a handful of it as its memorial portion, and turn this into smoke on the altar, with the offerings by fire to the LORD; it is a sin offering. [13]Thus the priest shall make atonement on your behalf for whichever of these sins you have committed, and shall be forgiven. Like the grain offering, the rest shall be for the priest.

wrongdoings or failure to act. The next seven verses indicate alternative offerings for those who cannot afford to offer a goat or a sheep. An offerer may bring two birds in place of the flock animal, and for those who cannot even afford the two birds, he may bring a grain offering without frankincense or oil to serve as the purification offering.[31]

It is not clear if the graduated offerings apply only to the four cases enumerated at the outset of the chapter or if the individual offender in chapter 4 also had these options. It is certainly a possibility given the fact that we have encountered a "sliding scale" in earlier chapters of Leviticus.

31. The use of grain for a purification offering, in which no blood is placed on the altar, raises questions about the function of the purification offering in cases of sins of omission. For scholars who disagree with Milgrom's proposition that every purification offering serves to purify the tabernacle with blood "ritual detergent" (see especially Gane, *Cult and Character*), the case of the bloodless grain offering presents a significant challenge to Milgrom's theory. Milgrom's own explanation is highly speculative and conjectural (*Leviticus 1–16*, 315–16).

### Desecrating YHVH's Property (5:14-16)

The next section of chapter 5 addresses a very particular kind of wrongdoing: desecration of anything that has been deemed holy. The word מעל ("trespass," NRSV, or "desecrate") is quite rare, and its meaning can only be surmised by the context. מעל appears primarily in two contexts: an action by a member of Israel against God and an action by a wife against her husband. Usually trespass or treachery is used to describe this wrongdoing against God while unfaithfulness is used to describe the wrongdoing against a husband. (See Num 5, the case of the suspected adulteress.) Thus, a woman who may have sexual intercourse with another man may be "spoiling" her husband's property just as members of the community may "spoil" God's property.

This is the first time in Leviticus that we encounter monetary payments in place of or in addition to animal sacrifices, and these payments in silver are similar to the payments described in Leviticus 27 regarding votive offerings. Both offerings deal with items that shift from sacred to common. The reparation offering addresses those things that are desecrated by accident while the votive offers a method for reclaiming something that had been sanctified to YHVH. Levine points out that the term ערך ("convertible," NRSV, or "assessed value") appears in chapter 27 in connection to the אשם and to the votive offerings. Levine believes that the reparation offering may have begun as a votive offering, as a payment in silver, but then developed into an altar offering as well.[32]

### Potential Violations (5:17-19)

The use of the reparation offering becomes even more complicated in verses 17-19. Verse 17 reads, "If any of you sin without knowing it, doing any of the things that by the Lord's commandments ought not to be done, you have incurred guilt and are subject to punishment." Notice how close Leviticus 5:17 is to 4:27-28: "If anyone of the ordinary people among you sins unintentionally in doing any one of the things that by the Lord's commandments ought not to be done and incurs guilt, when that sin that you have committed is made known to you." The case in chapter 4 is straightforward: a person sins by accident and incurs guilt (objective guilt) and then has the wrongdoing pointed out. In 5:17-18, however, a person sins without knowing it and feels guilty (subjective)

---

32. Levine, *Leviticus*, 31.

¹⁴The LORD spoke to Moses, saying: ¹⁵When any of you commit a trespass and sin unintentionally in any of the holy things of the LORD, you shall bring, as your guilt offering to the LORD, a ram without blemish from the flock, convertible into silver by the sanctuary shekel; it is a guilt offering. ¹⁶And you shall make restitution for the holy thing in which you were remiss, and shall add one-fifth to it and give it to the priest. The priest shall make atonement on your behalf with the ram of the guilt offering, and you shall be forgiven.

¹⁷If any of you sin without knowing it, doing any of the things that by the LORD's commandments ought not to be done, you have incurred guilt, and are subject to punishment. ¹⁸You shall bring to the priest a ram without blemish from the flock, or the equivalent, as a guilt offering; and the priest shall make atonement on your behalf for the error that you committed unintentionally, and you shall be forgiven. ¹⁹It is a guilt offering; you have incurred guilt before the LORD.

and is then subject to punishment. How can a person make things right with YHVH if she does not know that she has committed a wrongdoing? The verse must be describing a situation in which someone feels guilty or is worried that he has erred but does not know it with certainty. The reparation is thus brought forward "just to be on the safe side!"[33]

## Acts of Deceit (6:1-7)

Leviticus 6:1-7 addresses the final category for which a reparation offering is required. The text goes into significant detail regarding the ways in which one might deceive a fellow human being for monetary gain: deposit, pledge, robbery, fraud, finding something that belongs to another and lying about it. While many of these criminal actions are addressed in other biblical books, Leviticus is concerned with a particular aspect of the crime: deception via lying. These crimes are an offense within the community (theft) and an offense against YHVH (swearing falsely). An offender who feels guilty can repair the damage by returning the stolen property plus an additional 20 percent of the value of the stolen goods.[34] Additionally, a reparation offering is required to alleviate the

33. This is the dominant interpretation in rabbinic literature and is followed by both Levine (*Leviticus*, 32) and Milgrom (*Leviticus 1–16*, 333–34).

34. Exod 21:37 and 22:3 assert that the offender must pay back double the value of the stolen goods.

*Lev 6:1-7*

⁶:¹The Lᴏʀᴅ spoke to Moses, saying: ²When any of you sin and commit a trespass against the Lᴏʀᴅ by deceiving a neighbor in a matter of a deposit or a pledge, or by robbery, or if you have defrauded a neighbor, ³or have found something lost and lied about it—if you swear falsely regarding any of the various things that one may do and sin thereby—⁴when you have sinned and realize your guilt, and would restore what you took by robbery or by fraud or the deposit that was committed to you, or the lost thing that you found, ⁵or anything else about which you have sworn falsely, you shall repay the principal amount and shall add one-fifth to it. You shall pay it to its owner when you realize your guilt. ⁶And you shall bring to the priest, as your guilt offering to the Lᴏʀᴅ, a ram without blemish from the flock, or its equivalent, for a guilt offering. ⁷The priest shall make atonement on your behalf before the Lᴏʀᴅ, and you shall be forgiven for any of the things that one may do and incur guilt thereby.

offense against God, since YHVH's name was invoked in false testimony. Numbers 5:5-10 provides a roughly similar text with a few differences. The text in Numbers requires the offender to make a confession prior to making restitution. Numbers 5:5-10 also provides instruction on how to make restitution if the wronged person is dead and has no living kin.

---

### The Questionable Legitimacy of the Ransoming Power of Purification and Reparation Offerings: A Chinese Cultural Perspective

Having grown up in the religiously pluralistic setting of colonial Hong Kong immersed in the polytheistic environment of ritual-based Chinese popular religion, I inevitably approach the biblical texts with a set of culturally conditioned assumptions stemming from the Chinese religious milieu. In my reading of the Levitical sacrificial rituals of purification (חטאת, "sin offering," NRSV) and reparation (אשם, "guilt offering," NRSV; see Lev 4:1–6:7[5:26]; 14:1–15:33), the associative ritual practices in Chinese popular religion naturally enter into dialogue and contestation. These two Levitical offerings are prescribed to those who seek divine forgiveness for certain expiable sins and ritual impurities (Lev 4:20, 26, 31, 35; 5:10, 13, 16, 18; 6:7 [5:26]). The offerings' ritual efficacy lies in their dual power of ransoming and purging (כפר *piel*).[35] Purification and reparation offerings are presented by the guilty party to Yhwh, the offended deity, in part as a ransom payment that aims to ward off or to mollify divine punishment. Even though the ransoming efficacy of these offerings is often taken for granted in the Levitical rituals, it must be noted that the substantive "ransom" (כפר) is elsewhere used to denote bribery or illegitimate payment (Num 35:31, 32; 1 Sam 12:3; Job 36:18; Amos 5:12).[36] Thus, its legitimacy is in no way self-evident. In fact, the ransoming component of *kipper* is likely to be found ethically problematic and even reprehensible under the Chinese popular religious worldview.

The Chinese pantheon is structured with an imperial metaphor.[37] Headed by Jade Emperor (Yuhuangdadi), the divine counterpart of the human emperor, Chinese deities are conferred with imperial, usually bureaucratic, titles comparable to their divine status in the imperial hierarchy and adorned in imperial garments. Their temples are typically modeled after a magistrate court. Each bureaucratic deity is appointed a ministerial post or assigned a terrestrial jurisdiction, along with its lower-ranking deities. Just like their human counterparts, Chinese deities are regarded as potentially fallible and corruptible, each with his or her unique temperament and moral inclinations, even if they are supposed to be the protectors of public morality and benefactors of humankind.[38] Their role as imperial officials requires them to be impartial in their dispensation of justice and punishment. Their verdicts are morally binding and can be overturned only with an appeal to a higher-ranking official. They do not, however, guarantee fair judgment, and they could be insulted personally. Because of the potential fallibility and corruptibility of deities, stories of deities inflicting harm in order to receive a ransom payment from a worshiper are not uncommon. Such an act would be considered extortion. In a similar vein, a devotee's attempt to evade

35. Jay Sklar, *Sin, Impurity, Sacrifice, and Atonement*.

36. Ibid., 56–61.

37. Robert P. Weller, *Unities and Diversities in Chinese Religion* (Seattle: University of Washington Press, 1987), 37–59; Stephan Feuchtwang, *Popular Religion in China: The Imperial Metaphor* (Richmond, Surrey: Curzon, 2001); Vincent Goossaert, "Chinese Religion: Popular Religion," in *Encyclopedia of Religion*, ed. L. Jones (Detroit: Macmillan Reference USA, 2005), 1619.

38. Arthur P. Wolf, "Gods, Ghosts, and Ancestors," in *Religion and Ritual in Chinese Society*, ed. A. P. Wolf (Stanford, CA: Stanford University Press, 1974), 168.

or mollify divine punishment with the presentation of gifts would be considered bribery. The only legitimate offerings in Chinese popular religion are those presented out of the devotees' volition, obeisance, and gratitude.

With the imperial metaphor of the Chinese pantheon in view, it is not difficult to understand why someone who grew up in the milieu of Chinese popular religion would find the ransoming efficacy of the purification and reparation offerings problematic. How could one make an offering to a deity in order to have faults forgiven and divine punishment averted? The ransom payment would have been considered extortion or bribery under the Chinese popular religious worldview. Nonetheless, it must be pointed out that the ransoming efficacy seems to be bolstered by some Levitical assumptions that are absent in the Chinese popular religion.

Unlike the Chinese deities, Yhwh is a punitive deity, infallible and incorruptible, who judges according to evaluative ethical standards and who, being self-sufficient, would not be subject to extortion by foodstuffs for his own gratification. Purification and reparation offerings are only prescribed for inadvertent, expiable moral faults and ritual impurities of lesser gravity and with the prerequisite of the genuine repentance of the guilty party (Lev 4:13, 22, 27; 5:2-5, 17; 6:4 [5:23]) and the compensation to the injured human party (Lev 5:16). All of these assumptions would have served to safeguard the legitimacy of their ransoming power within the Levitical ritual system. Nonetheless, to those who grew up in a different religious culture and are unaware of the Levitical assumptions, the ransoming efficacy is still likely to be incomprehensible and even reprehensible.[39]

*Sonia K. Wong*

---

39. See also Sonia K. Wong, "The Notion of כפר in the Book of Leviticus and Chinese Popular Religion," in *Leviticus and Numbers*, ed. Athalya Brenner and Archie Chi Chung Lee (Minneapolis: Fortress, 2013), 77–96.

# Leviticus 6:8–7:38

# *Another Perspective on Offerings, or What's in It for the Priests?*

L eviticus 6–7 returns to a discussion of the five offerings, but this set of instructions is addressed to Aaron and his sons, not to the congregation of Israel. Attention is focused on matters most relevant for the priests, such as the priestly prebends of meat and grains. The text introduces the instructions for each offering with the statement: this is the *torah*, the instruction regarding X. The chapter presents the offerings in the following order: עלה (burnt offering), מנחה (grain offering), חטאת (purification offering), אשם (guilt offering), and שלמים (well-being offerings).

Leviticus 6:2 mentions the first *torah* in what will be a series of ten *torot* for the priests. The first five *torot* address sacrifice, and the last five address impurity. The fact that the language of "instruction" appears for the first time in chapter 6 reinforces the notion that the first five chapters were intended for a more general audience.

## The Burnt Offering, Again (6:8-13)

The עלה of the first chapter addresses what ought to happen when someone brings a burnt offering, describing the role of the layperson

*Lev 6:8-13*

⁸The LORD spoke to Moses, saying: ⁹Command Aaron and his sons, saying: This is the ritual of the burnt offering. The burnt offering itself shall remain on the hearth upon the altar all night until the morning, while the fire on the altar shall be kept burning. ¹⁰The priest shall put on his linen vestments after putting on his linen undergarments next to his body; and he shall take up the ashes to which the fire has reduced the burnt offering on the altar, and place them beside the altar. ¹¹Then he shall take off his vestments and put on other garments, and carry the ashes out to a clean place outside the camp. ¹²The fire on the altar shall be kept burning; it shall not go out. Every morning the priest shall add wood to it, lay out the burnt offering on it, and turn into smoke the fat pieces of the offerings of well-being. ¹³A perpetual fire shall be kept burning on the altar; it shall not go out.

and bringing in the priest when a part of the ritual must be restricted to the priests. In the renewed description of the burnt offering, the point of entry is not the need of the layperson but the need of the sanctuary (Lev 6:6-13, NRSV). This burnt offering is immediately defined as the one that is to burn all through the night, each night. The layperson's perspective is limited to the moment of the ritual itself, but the priests are concerned with the establishment and maintenance of a larger system in which nightly offerings are required within the system. An additional new element here is time: the offering burns or smolders through the night with a fire on the altar that must be kept going. Housekeeping issues are also addressed and instructions regarding clothing inside and outside are prescribed. Housekeeping required the priests to clean off the ashes every morning, first by piling them next to the altar and then by changing clothes and removing them outside the camp. It is not altogether clear whether the removal of the ashes from the altar was considered simple housekeeping or whether it was a ritual; however, the rabbis understood הרים ("take up," NRSV) to mean not simply "remove" but rather "dedicate," and they referred to this ritual as תרומת דשן ("offering of the ashes").

The ritualization of housekeeping is common in many cultures. Alice Peck's collection considers the ways in which housekeeping intersects with spirituality and religion; for example:

> Unlike laundry—a job that has a start and a finish—sweeping is never quite finished. Once you've swept, there remain traces of the sweeping

to do away with, and no end to dust. Through the repetition of the task, we learn that there will always be more to sweep. From this perspective, we can immerse ourselves in the process, seeing beyond the back-and-forth movements of the broom into acts of service and lovingkindness.[1]

Janet Marder, a contributor to the *Women's Torah Commentary*, reflects on the words of her teacher Melila Hellner-Eshed who suggests that to some extent priests become " 'God's housewives'—feminized men who dress in skirts and busy themselves with the domestic work of cooking and cleaning in God's holy dwelling."[2]

Finally, the priests feed the fire with wood each morning. The final statement commands that there be an אש תמיד ("perpetual fire," NRSV) on the altar, first mentioned in Exodus 27:20-21. Jacob Milgrom suggests that the continual fire originates from the first fire on the altar, which was created when YHVH consumed the very first offering by divine fire (Lev 9:24).[3]

## The Grain and Anointing Offerings (6:14-23)

Discussion of the grain offering in this chapter (Lev 6:14-18, NRSV) supplements the earlier material (Lev 2:1-10) by focusing on the pro-hibition to consume the offering with any leavening agent, with the restriction that the grain be consumed only in the sacred space of the sanctuary and that the food which they are consuming is holy. (See below for more.) In verses 19-23 (NRSV), the text shifts to a more specific category of grain offerings. Each priest must bring a tenth of an *ephah* of grain offering to be offered daily, half in the morning and half at night. This offering must be prepared with oil. The text emphasizes that this is a חק עולם ("perpetual due," Lev 6:22, NRSV = Heb. Lev 6:15) for all descendants and that it all goes to God.

Milgrom explores how it would be possible for priests to offer so much semolina at their own cost or for the temple treasury to bear such costs, and he concludes that this obligation would be incumbent only on

---

1. Alice Peck, ed., *Godliness: Finding the Sacred in Housekeeping* (Woodstock, VT: Skylights Path Publishing, 2007), 35.

2. Janet Radner, "Contemporary Reflection on Vayikra," in *The Torah: A Women's Commentary*, ed. Tamara Cohn Eskenazi and Andrea L. Weiss (New York: URJ Press, 2008), 589.

3. Jacob Milgrom, *Leviticus 1–16*, AB 3 (New York: Doubleday, 1991), 389.

¹⁴This is the ritual of the grain offering: The sons of Aaron shall offer it before the Lord, in front of the altar. ¹⁵They shall take from it a handful of the choice flour and oil of the grain offering, with all the frankincense that is on the offering and they shall turn its memorial portion into smoke on the altar as a pleasing odor to the Lord. ¹⁶Aaron and his sons shall eat what is left of it; it shall be eaten as unleavened cakes in a holy place; in the court of the tent of meeting they shall eat it. ¹⁷It shall not be baked with leaven. I have given it as their portion of my offerings by fire; it is most holy, like the sin offering and the guilt offering. ¹⁸Every male among the descendants of Aaron shall eat of it, as their perpetual due throughout your generations, from the Lord's of-ferings by fire; anything that touches them shall become holy.

¹⁹The Lord spoke to Moses, say-ing: ²⁰This is the offering that Aaron and his sons shall offer to the Lord on the day when he is anointed: one-tenth of an ephah of choice flour as a regular offering, half of it in the morn-ing and half in the evening. ²¹It shall be made with oil on a griddle; you shall bring it well soaked, as a grain offering of baked pieces, and you shall present it as a pleasing odor to the Lord. ²²And so the priest, anointed from among Aaron's descendants as a successor, shall prepare it; it is the Lord's—a perpetual due—to be turned entirely into smoke. ²³Every grain offering of a priest shall be wholly burned; it shall not be eaten.

the high priest. If, however, we imagine these prescriptions to be texts ritually recited for the laity, rather than describing real rituals, then the rhetorical impact on early lay audiences might have conveyed the idea that the priests give so much from their own hands in comparison to what is asked of the laypeople. In fundraising campaigns, the leaders of the campaign will always signal that they have given generously in order to motivate others to do likewise.

## The Purification Offering, Again (6:24-30)

The section regarding the purification offering is the shortest, six verses in total (Lev 6:24-30, NRSV). This material adds a few points to the de-tailed information of Leviticus 4. Chapter 4 makes it clear that when a high priest or the community sins, the entire animal of the purification offering is disposed of, part on the altar and the rest outside the camp (Lev 4:11-12, 21). The purification offering an individual is directed to

*Lev 6:24-30*

²⁴The Lᴏʀᴅ spoke to Moses, saying: ²⁵Speak to Aaron and his sons, saying: This is the ritual of the sin offering. The sin offering shall be slaughtered before the Lᴏʀᴅ at the spot where the burnt offering is slaughtered; it is most holy. ²⁶The priest who offers it as a sin offering shall eat of it; it shall be eaten in a holy place, in the court of the tent of meeting. ²⁷Whatever touches its flesh shall become holy; and when any of its blood is spattered on a garment, you shall wash the bespattered part in a holy place. ²⁸An earthen vessel in which it was boiled shall be broken; but if it is boiled in a bronze vessel, that shall be scoured and rinsed in water. ²⁹Every male among the priests shall eat of it; it is most holy. ³⁰But no sin offering shall be eaten from which any blood is brought into the tent of meeting for atonement in the holy place; it shall be burned with fire.

bring does not include the instruction to take the animal outside of the camp. The absence of an explicit instruction suggests that the priests could consume an individual's purification offering, but Leviticus 6:26 makes it clear that the officiating priest does eat the meat in the tabernacle (בחצר אהל מועד).⁴

Conditions of holiness are absolute for these sacred meals—the meat, the place, and the consumers are all required to be in a state of holiness. Furthermore, Leviticus 6:27 stipulates that whatever touches the flesh of the meat יקדש ("becomes holy," NRSV). And so, clothing that comes in contact with the blood of the flesh must be washed in the holy place, clay vessels in which the meat has been cooked or served must be broken, and bronze vessels require scouring and rinsing in water. This idea of holiness contagion appears in Exodus 29:35-37 and 30:29 in discussing the consecration of the altar. The text indicates that once the altar is consecrated, anything that comes in contact with the altar becomes holy and can no longer be used outside of the sanctuary. Ezekiel 44:19 reflects the same idea of holiness contagion, describing why the priests may not take their holy vestments outside the sanctuary: contact with the vestments confers holiness (see also Ezek 46:20).

Baruch Levine argues that holiness is not contagious and that verse 27 should be translated as "Anyone who is to touch its flesh must be

---

4. This courtyard is first described in Exod 27:9-19; it is the place where the most holy foods are to be eaten by the priests.

in a holy state."[5] Levine's reading is in part a response to the fact that ordinarily, when impurity comes in contact with something sacred, the impurity defiles the sacred.[6] James Watts suggests that Ezekiel 44:19; 46:20; and Haggai 2:11-13 reflect a priestly debate regarding holiness contagion and that the P texts do not come down explicitly on one side of the debate or the other.[7] The possibility that some priests believed in holiness contagion may help us to understand the long restrictions of women from the sanctuary after childbirth and the phrase דמי טהרה ("blood purification," NRSV) in Leviticus 12.

## The Guilt Offering, Again (7:1-10)

The discussion of the guilt offering (Lev 7:1-6) provides the kind of information that we expect to find in Leviticus 1–5, that is, a description of *how* to enact the ritual.

Leviticus 7:6 repeats what we have seen regarding the grain offerings and the purification offerings: that only males from the priestly family may consume the meat from the offering and that the consumption can only take place in a holy place (במקום קדש) because the meat and the grain offerings are most holy (קדש קדשים הוא). The unambiguous declaration of males from the priestly line indicates that this "most holy" meat could not be shared with the women of the priest's family. Leviticus 22:12-14 will address what women from the priestly families could eat with their husbands and fathers, namely, well-being offerings and first fruits.

Verses 7-10 digress into a clarification regarding the consumption of sanctified foods. For guilt offerings and purification offerings, the priest who officiates receives the meat portion. In cases of the burnt offerings, the priest who presides receives the hide; for cooked grain offerings, the officiant receives a portion; and for dry grain offerings, all of the priests share the portion.

---

5. Baruch Levine, *Leviticus: A JPS Torah Commentary* (Philadelphia: Jewish Publication Society of America, 1989), 41.

6. See also Menahem Haran, "The Priestly Image of the Tabernacle," *HUCA* 36 (1965): 216; and his book *Temples and Temple-Service in Ancient Israel: An Inquiry into the Character of Cult Phenomena and the Historical Setting of the Priestly School* (Oxford: Oxford University Press, 1978), esp. 175–77. Gordon Wenham, *The Book of Leviticus* (Grand Rapids: Eerdmans, 1979), 121.

7. James W. Watts, *Leviticus 1–10*, HCOT (Leuven: Peeters, 2013), 398–402.

⁷:¹This is the ritual of the guilt offering. It is most holy; ²at the spot where the burnt offering is slaughtered, they shall slaughter the guilt offering, and its blood shall be dashed against all sides of the altar. ³All its fat shall be offered: the broad tail, the fat that covers the entrails, ⁴the two kidneys with the fat that is on them at the loins, and the appendage of the liver, which shall be removed with the kidneys. ⁵The priest shall turn them into smoke on the altar as an offering by fire to the LORD; it is a guilt offering. ⁶Every male among the priests shall eat of it; it shall be eaten in a holy place; it is most holy.

⁷The guilt offering is like the sin offering, there is the same ritual for them; the priest who makes atonement with it shall have it. ⁸So, too, the priest who offers anyone's burnt offering shall keep the skin of the burnt offering that he has offered. ⁹And every grain offering baked in the oven, and all that is prepared in a pan or on a griddle, shall belong to the priest who offers it. ¹⁰But every other grain offering, mixed with oil or dry, shall belong to all the sons of Aaron equally.

## The Well-Being Offering, Again (7:11-21)

Leviticus 7:11-18 addresses the well-being sacrifices. These verses address subcategories of well-being sacrifices and the ways in which they are and are not to be consumed. Because the well-being is the offering laity may eat, the addressees shift from priests to laity. The first subcategory is the תודה ("thanksgiving offering"), which the laity consumes along with leavened breads (not on altar), while giving one of each loaf to the officiating priest. The meat must be eaten by the next morning. People may consume the נדר ("votive") and נדבה ("free-will") offerings on the second day as well, but what remains until the third day is to be burned. The priests have less control of lay consumption of well-being meats, but the priestly work (v. 18) emphasizes that sacred meat that is eaten outside the prescribed time makes the well-being offering null and void, and that the offender is held guilty. Verses 19-21 emphasize the importance of eating the meat of the well-being offering only in a state of ritual purity. Anyone who eats sacred meat while impure will experience divine punishment.

## Supplemental Information Regarding the Well-Being (7:22-28)

The rest of Leviticus 7 provides additional information regarding eating and the well-being offering. First, the ban against eating the fatty portions of animals is reiterated (Lev 3:16-17) because the fat belongs to

¹¹This is the ritual of the sacrifice of the offering of well-being that one may offer to the LORD. ¹²If you offer it for thanksgiving, you shall offer with the thank offering unleavened cakes mixed with oil, unleavened wafers spread with oil, and cakes of choice flour well soaked in oil. ¹³With your thanksgiving sacrifice of well-being you shall bring your offering with cakes of leavened bread. ¹⁴From this you shall offer one cake from each offering, as a gift to the LORD; it shall belong to the priest who dashes the blood of the offering of well-being. ¹⁵And the flesh of your thanksgiving sacrifice of well-being shall be eaten on the day it is offered; you shall not leave any of it until morning. ¹⁶But if the sacrifice you offer is a votive offering or a freewill offering, it shall be eaten on the day that you offer your sacrifice, and what is left of it shall be eaten the next day; ¹⁷But what is left of the flesh of the sacrifice shall be burned up on the third day. ¹⁸If any of the flesh of your sacrifice of well-being is eaten on the third day, it shall not be acceptable, nor shall it be credited to the one who offers it; it shall be an abomination, and the one who eats of it shall incur guilt.

¹⁹Flesh that touches any unclean thing shall not be eaten; it shall be burned up. As for other flesh, all who are clean may eat such flesh. ²⁰But those who eat flesh from the LORD's sacrifice of well-being while in a state of uncleanness shall be cut off from their kin. ²¹When any one of you touches any unclean thing—human uncleanness or an unclean animal or any unclean creature—and then eats flesh from the LORD's sacrifice of well-being, you shall be cut off from your kin.

²²The LORD spoke to Moses, saying: ²³Speak to the people of Israel, saying: You shall eat no fat of ox or sheep or goat. ²⁴The fat of an animal that died or was torn by wild animals may be put to any other use, but you must not eat it. ²⁵If any of you eats the fat from

God and is offered up on the altar. Fat from dead animals may be used for other purposes, but not for consumption. The ban against eating blood is again mentioned. And finally, the unit concludes with information about the priest's portion of the meat of the well-being. The breast of the elevation offering and the right thigh of every well-being offering go to the priests.

The details regarding the priestly prebends in Leviticus 6 and 7 would have been of great importance to the priests. While P itself provides no narratives regarding priestly consumption of sacrificial meats, the priestly prebends became the object of great criticism during the Second Temple period. Jonathan Klawans quotes one rabbinic text:

an animal of which an offering by fire may be made to the Lᴏʀᴅ, you who eat it shall be cut off from your kin. ²⁶You must not eat any blood whatever, either of bird or of animal, in any of your settlements. ²⁷Any one of you who eats any blood shall be cut off from your kin.

²⁸The Lᴏʀᴅ spoke to Moses, saying: ²⁹Speak to the people of Israel, saying: Any one of you who would offer to the Lᴏʀᴅ your sacrifice of well-being must yourself bring to the Lᴏʀᴅ your offering from your sacrifice of well-being. ³⁰Your own hands shall bring the Lᴏʀᴅ's offering by fire; you shall bring the fat with the breast, so that the breast may be raised as an elevation offering before the Lᴏʀᴅ. ³¹The priest shall turn the fat into smoke on the altar, but the breast shall belong to Aaron and his sons. ³²And the right thigh from your sacrifices of well-being you shall give to the priest as an offering; ³³the one among the sons of Aaron who offers the blood and fat of the offering of well-being

shall have the right thigh for a portion. ³⁴For I have taken the breast of the elevation offering, and the thigh that is offered, from the people of Israel, from their sacrifices of well-being, and have given them to Aaron the priest and to his sons, as a perpetual due from the people of Israel. ³⁵This is the portion allotted to Aaron and to his sons from the offerings made by fire to the Lᴏʀᴅ, once they have been brought forward to serve the Lᴏʀᴅ as priests; ³⁶these the Lᴏʀᴅ commanded to be given them, when he anointed them, as a perpetual due from the people of Israel throughout their generations.

³⁷This is the ritual of the burnt offering, the grain offering, the sin offering, the guilt offering, the offering of ordination, and the sacrifice of well-being, ³⁸which the Lᴏʀᴅ commanded Moses on Mount Sinai, when he commanded the people of Israel to bring their offerings to the Lᴏʀᴅ, in the wilderness of Sinai.

"Lift up your heads, oh gates, (Ps 24:7) and let enter Yohanan ben Narbai, the disciple of Pinkai, and he will fill his stomach with sacred offerings." It was said of Yohanan ben Narbai that he would eat three hundred calves, and drink three hundred barrels of wine, and eat forty seahs of birds for dessert. They said that all the days of Yohanan ben Narbai there were never any sacrificial leftovers in the Temple.[8]

8. Jonathan Klawans, *Purity, Sacrifice, and the Temple: Symbolism and Supersessionism in the Study of Ancient Judaism* (Oxford: Oxford University Press, 2006), 181, citing b. Pes 57a. See also 175–211 for a compelling analysis of rabbinic perspectives on the Second Temple.

Klawans suggests that the call to the gates to lift up their heads refers to the priest's corpulence. It is clear from the many sources of the Second Temple period that the priesthood had become corrupt and that priests would buy their way into power. Priestly prebends became associated with material wealth and power. We know much less about the situation during the First Temple period and even less about what the P writers envisioned. In any case, the priests would have been the primary meat consumers of the community because every sacrifice except the burnt offering resulted in meat (or grain) allocations for the priests.

# Leviticus 8:1–10:20

# *Coming Into and Managing Power*

Chapter 8 introduces the principal narrative in Leviticus. For the first time the text describes Moses "doing" rather than "speaking." This new section, the only narrative in Leviticus 1–16,[1] seems to be the sequel to the narrative of Exodus 35–40; Leviticus 8–10 describes the investiture of Aaron and his sons, the consecration of the tabernacle, and the first misuse of the priestly privileges within the tabernacle.

A certain idiom stands out in Leviticus 8 and 9: "as YHVH commanded" appears in 8:4, 9, 13, 17, 21, 29, 31, 34, 35, 36; 9:6, 7, 10, and 21. Most scholars believe that these repeated references are linked to Exodus 29, where the description of the ordination of the priests is prescribed.

The ritual for the ordination of Aaron and his sons is set out in great detail; however, we cannot take the description of the inauguration of the Aaronides as a literal description of a ceremony. For example, the text as it stands would have Aaron's sons standing wet and naked for a significant period of time as Moses consecrated the tabernacle.[2]

---

1. There is one narrative in the H material in Leviticus 24.
2. The sons are washed in Lev 8:6, then Aaron is clothed (vv. 7-9), Moses anoints the tabernacle (vv. 10-12), and Moses dresses the sons (v. 13).

## Sanctifying with Oil and Holy Dressing (8:1-13)

Moses gathers Aaron and his sons, the priestly vestments, anointing oil, a bull for a purification offering, two rams, a basket of unleavened breads, and finally the community (vv. 2-4). Moses washes Aaron and his sons with water and then dresses Aaron with the holy vestments assigned to the high priest as instructed in Exodus 28. At verse 10, Moses takes the anointing oil and anoints the tabernacle and everything in it.[3] Moses sprinkles the altar seven times and then anoints the implements and the basin with the oil in order to consecrate (קדש) the space and its sacred items. Moses then pours the anointing oil over Aaron's head to consecrate him.[4] Finally, Moses dresses Aaron's sons in their priestly vestments.

Exodus 28:2 indicates that the command to make priestly vestments is addressed to those who have the requisite abilities (חכמי לב) and divinely endowed skills, and several biblical texts support the view that those vestments were probably made by women. Exodus 35:25 indicates that women have the skills (חכמת לב) to spin yarn and linens. Proverbs 31:10-31, an ode to "a capable wife" (NRSV, or "a woman of strength") devotes a full seven verses to a woman's role in weaving. According to this text, the ideal woman spins, provides her family with clothing, creates a business selling garments to merchants, and crafts such beautiful garments for herself and her husband that her husband has a seat of honor among men. In addition, in Judges 16:13-14 Delilah weaves Samson's hair with a loom, and in 2 Kings 23:7 the narrator describes the role of women in weaving for the goddess Asherah in a special room within the temple compounds. Lisbeth Fried describes women's graves at Susa (1000 BCE) that show women sitting on stools and spinning.[5] Thus, it is reasonable to imagine that women made the priestly vestments included in the ritual of ordination.

The inclusion of breeches or undergarments as part of the priestly garb has garnered attention because it is not altogether clear why breeches would have been required since the tunics were very long robes that would have provided for modesty. Most scholars assume that the breeches were required in order to cover one's genitalia while serving God. The commonly cited source text for this interpretation is Exodus 20:26, which

---

3. The formula for the anointing oil is provided in Exod 30:22-25.

4. The ritual of anointing has been the topic for much scholarly exploration. See Daniel E. Fleming, "The Biblical Tradition of Anointing Priests," *JBL* 117 (1998): 401–14.

5. Lisbeth S. Fried, "Another View on P'kudei," in *The Torah: A Women's Commentary*, ed. Tamara Cohn Eskenazi and Andrea L. Weiss (New York: URJ Press, 2008), 560. See also Carol Meyers, "In the Household and Beyond: The Social World of Israelite Women," *ST* 63 (2009): 19–41.

*Lev 8:1-13*

8:1The LORD spoke to Moses, saying; 2Take Aaron and his sons with him, the vestments, the anointing oil, the bull of sin offering, the two rams, and the basket of unleavened bread; 3and assemble the whole congregation at the entrance of the tent of meeting. 4And Moses did as the LORD commanded him. When the congregation was assembled at the entrance of the tent of meeting, 5Moses said to the congregation, "This is what the LORD has commanded to be done."

6Then Moses brought Aaron and his sons forward, and washed them with water. 7He put the tunic on him, fastened the sash around him, clothed him with the robe, and put the ephod on him. He then put the decorated band of the ephod around him, tying the ephod to him with it. 8He placed the breast-piece on him, and in the breastpiece he put the Urim and the Thummim. 9And he set the turban on his head, and on the turban, in front, he set the golden ornament, the holy crown, as the LORD commanded Moses.

10Then Moses took the anointing oil and anointed the tabernacle and all that was in it, and consecrated them. 11He sprinkled some of it on the altar seven times, and anointed the altar and all its utensils, and the basin and its base, to consecrate them. 12He poured some of the anointing oil on Aaron's head and anointed him, to consecrate him. 13And Moses brought forward Aaron's sons and clothed them with tunics, and fastened sashes around them, and tied headdresses on them, as the LORD commanded Moses.

forbids a person to ascend altars with steps lest nakedness be exposed. Another text that suggests modesty is 2 Samuel 6, where Michal is infuriated because David was exposing himself while dancing before the ark.

In a 2009 study, Deborah W. Rooke explored the priestly requirement for breeches.[6] She begins by noting that tunics were worn by both men and women (see 2 Sam 13:18; Song 5:3) and therefore did not mark gender, but that the addition of the headdress, belt, and breeches marked the body encompassed by such garb as male. In other words, priestly garments mark gender, status, and occupation. Claudia Bender argues that breeches are specified when the priests are active in a ceremony that requires them to change their clothing. The breeches provide modesty while changing from regular to ceremonial clothing.[7] Rooke, however,

---

6. Deborah W. Rooke, "Breeches of the Covenant: Gender, Garments and the Priesthood," in *Embroidered Garments: Priests and Gender in Biblical Israel*, ed. Deborah W. Rooke (Sheffield: Sheffield Phoenix, 2009), 19–37.

7. Claudia Bender, *Die Sprache des Textilen: Untersuchungen zu Kleidung und Textilien im Alten Testament*, BWANT 177 (Stuttgart: Kohlhammer, 2008). Cited by Rooke, "Breeches of the Covenant," 25–27. See Exod 20:26 and 2 Sam 6 for examples of such texts.

asserts that the priests would not have changed outside in public so modesty could not have been the purpose for the breeches. Instead, she suggests that breeches, as those required in Exodus 28:42-43 and Leviticus 16:4, were required to hide the priests' masculinity.

> Covering the male genitals by means of breeches when in the presence of the deity can be construed as an act of feminization that allows male priests to be devotees of a male God without threatening the normative heterosexuality which underpinned the ancient Israelite world order. The priests are real men, whole men, fully functional, but in relation to the male deity they are required to take on a "feminine" role of submissive obedience, and this is symbolized by them hiding their physical masculinity via the wearing of the breeches.[8]

While there is not sufficient evidence to fully accept Rooke's theory, she draws our attention to the ways in which the intimacy between a male god and male priests may manifest itself. Rooke rightly cites the groundbreaking work of Howard Eilberg-Schwartz, who explored the homoerotic dimensions of the relationship between a male deity and male devotees. My own work has explored this homoerotic dynamic in Psalms literature and in the writing of Ezekiel.[9] Since the priests reveal so little about their devotion and their interior religious lives (except, perhaps, for the narrative of Nadav and Avihu), it is difficult to document how the priests felt about their role vis-à-vis YHVH. Rooke's interpretation of the breeches as a symbolic feminization of priestly masculinity is intriguing.

## Purifying and Sanctifying with Blood (8:14-29)

The focus shifts in Leviticus 8:14 from anointing of priests to ritual offerings, beginning with a bull that Moses offers for purification. Aaron and his sons place their hands upon the bull, it is slaughtered, and Moses manipulates the blood on the horns and the base of the altar to purify

---

8. Rooke, "Breeches of the Covenant," 29–30.

9. S. Tamar Kamionkowski, "Breaking Through the Binaries: A Case Study of Ezekiel 16," in *The Feminist Companion to the Latter Prophets*, ed. Athalya Brenner, FCB 2, 2nd ser. (Sheffield: Sheffield Academic, 2002), 170–85; and "The Erotics of Pilgrimage: A Fresh Look at Psalms 84 and 63," in *Gazing on the Deep: Ancient Near Eastern, Biblical, and Jewish Studies in Honor of Tzvi Abusch*, ed. Jeffrey Stackert, Barbara Nevling Porter, and David P. Wright (Bethesda, MD: CDL Press, 2010), 467–78.

[14]He led forward the bull of sin offering; and Aaron and his sons laid their hands upon the head of the bull of sin offering, [15]and it was slaughtered. Moses took the blood and with his finger put some on each of the horns of the altar, purifying the altar; then he poured out the blood at the base of the altar. Thus he consecrated it, to make atonement for it. [16]Moses took all the fat that was around the entrails, and the appendage of the liver, and the two kidneys with their fat, and turned them into smoke on the altar. [17]But the bull itself, its skin and flesh and its dung, he burned with fire outside the camp, as the LORD commanded Moses.

[18]Then he brought forward the ram of burnt offering. Aaron and his sons laid their hands on the head of the ram, [19]and it was slaughtered. Moses dashed the blood against all sides of the altar. [20]The ram was cut into its parts, and Moses turned into smoke the head and the parts and the suet. [21]And after the entrails and the legs were washed with water, Moses turned into smoke the whole ram on the altar; it was a burnt offering for a pleasing odor, an offering by fire to the lord, as the LORD commanded Moses.

[22]Then he brought forward the second ram, the ram of ordination. Aaron and his sons laid their hands on the head of the ram, [23]and it was slaughtered. Moses took some of its blood and put it on the lobe of Aaron's right ear and on the thumb of his right hand

it (vv. 14-15). Then Moses consecrates the altar in order to make expiation upon it (vv. 16-17) as initially described in Leviticus 4:3-12.[10] A ram is offered as a burnt offering on behalf of the priests, and Moses again serves as the officiant (vv. 18-21). A second ram is offered as an ordination offering, with Moses daubing the priests instead of the altar with the blood. Moses places blood on Aaron's right earlobe, right thumb, and right big toe;[11] he repeats the action for Aaron's sons as well (vv. 22-24). Moses places portions of the animal fat and right thigh with grain offerings on the palms of the priests as an elevation offering (vv. 25-28). He then collects all the material and burns it on the offering for YHVH, retaining the breast as his portion (v. 29).

10. So Baruch Levine, *Leviticus: A JPS Torah Commentary* (Philadelphia: Jewish Publication Society of America, 1989), 52.

11. This specific ritual involving the right earlobe, thumb, and toe appears in only one other situation, the ritual for the reentry of one afflicted with a skin disease (Lev 14:14, 17, 25-26).

and on the big toe of his right foot. [24]After Aaron's sons were brought forward, Moses put some of the blood on the lobes of their right ears and on the thumbs of their right hands and on the big toes of their right feet; and Moses dashed the rest of the blood against all sides of the altar. [25]He took the fat—the broad tail, all the fat that was around the entrails, the appendage of the liver, and the two kidneys with their fat—and the right thigh. [26]From the basket of unleavened bread that was before the LORD, he took one cake of unleavened bread, one cake of bread with oil, and one wafer, and placed them on the fat and on the right thigh. [27]He placed all these on the palms of Aaron and on the palms of his sons, and raised them as an elevation offering before the LORD. [28]Then Moses took them from their hands and turned them into smoke on the altar with the burnt offering. This was an ordination offering for a pleasing odor, an offering by fire to the LORD. [29]Moses took the breast and raised it as an elevation offering before the LORD; it was Moses' portion of the ram of ordination, as the LORD commanded Moses.

## Final Steps of Ordination (8:30-36)

Moses takes the anointing oil and blood and sprinkles them on Aaron and his sons and on their vestments to consecrate them (Lev 8:30). Moses instructs the priests to boil his portion of the meat of the ordination offering and to partake of their first sacred meal. Moses commands them to remain within the holy structure for seven days, for this is the time necessary to complete their consecration and their expiation (8:31-36).

Among interpreters there is some disagreement regarding what happens during those seven days. Exodus 29:35-37 suggests that these offerings and sacred meals took place each day for seven days. Gerald Klingbeil argues that only the specified offerings of Leviticus 8 were required during this period.[12] Part of what is at stake in this debate is the relationship between Leviticus 8 and Exodus 29; the latter provides the instructions, and the former serves as the fulfillment of what God commanded. The texts are so similar that most scholars agree that they are in some kind of direct relationship with one another. Victor Hurowitz sets Exodus 29 and Leviticus 8 within the context of ancient Near Eastern temple building narratives.[13]

---

12. Gerald A. Klingbeil, "Ritual Time in Leviticus 8 with Special Reference to the Seven Day Period in the Old Testament," *ZAW* 109 (1997): 512.

13. Victor Hurowitz, "The Priestly Account of Building the Tabernacle," *JAOS* (1985): 21–30.

³⁰Then Moses took some of the anointing oil and some of the blood that was on the altar and sprinkled them on Aaron and his vestments, and also on his sons and their vestments. Thus he consecrated Aaron and his vestments, and also his sons and their vestments. ³¹And Moses said to Aaron and his sons, "Boil the flesh at the entrance of the tent of meeting, and eat it there with the bread that is in the basket of ordination offerings as I was commanded, 'Aaron and his sons shall eat it'; ³²and what remains of the flesh and the bread you shall burn with fire. ³³You shall not go outside the entrance of the tent of meeting for seven days, until the day when your period of ordination is completed. For it will take seven days to ordain you; ³⁴as has been done today, the Lord has commanded to be done to make atonement for you. ³⁵You shall remain at the entrance of the tent of meeting day and night for seven days, keeping the Lord's charge so that you do not die; for so I am commanded." ³⁶Aaron and his sons did all the things that the Lord commanded through Moses.

He points to the strong tendency to separate the instructions for building a temple from the narrative of building the temple as instructed.[14] James Watts argues that Leviticus 8–10 functions to legitimate the Aaronide line of priests as the sole legitimate priests, with the frequently repeated phrase "as God commanded" adding a sense of ancient authority. The story of Nadav and Avihu (Lev 10:1-3) demonstrates the danger of the work and the risks that priests take to fulfill their duties.[15]

*Power Dynamics and Ritual Roles*

Leviticus 8 reveals a number of interesting dynamics regarding the establishment of new power systems. Leviticus 1–7 describes the roles and responsibilities that the priest will have, but until Leviticus 8 and the actual ordination of the priest, the power resides with Moses. While Moses may be presenting YHVH's directives with accuracy, Moses is the only person with the authority and the legitimacy to set the norms for the community. Leviticus 8 reveals P's understanding of how the al-

14. Christophe Nihan, *From Priestly Torah to Pentateuch: A Study in the Composition of the Book of Leviticus*, FAT 25 (Tübingen: Mohr Siebeck, 2007), 127–34. Nihan convincingly argues that discrepancies between these two chapters can be attributed to minor redactions in both chapters.
15. James W. Watts, *Leviticus 1–10*, HCOT (Leuven: Peeters, 2013), 438.

location of power should take place. According to the narrative of this chapter, Moses enters a liminal state that enables him to exercise even more power than he generally holds. In order to establish a new authoritative body, Moses must temporarily inhabit the role and authority of a priest. This liminal state, in which Moses *plays the role* of a priest *without being* a priest, enables him to ready the priests for their new roles. It is only in this chapter that Moses is authorized to officiate over sacrifices and to manipulate the blood on the sancta in order to change the status of the priests and the sacred space from the ordinary to the holy. The community of Israel is called to witness the proceedings, but they do not play any active role (vv. 4-5). In fact, when the priests begin to go through their week-long process of status transformation, they are hidden from view. The priests are forbidden from leaving the tabernacle, so the rest of the community is completely cut off from the transfer of power.

The repetitive refrain "as YHVH commanded" stresses that the ritual of Leviticus 8 is legitimate and that the ordination of the priests is strictly by the book. Watts writes, "Leviticus 8 thus contributes to the characterization of the model rabbi or minister who hears God's commands, transmits and interprets them to the people, and scrupulously follows them himself."[16] The priests have full ritual authority because the ritual participants followed God's commandments exactly. In this model, authority comes directly from God as preserved in holy text. Therefore, to question priestly authority is to question the text (which most people could not access or read) and ultimately God.

A ritual text from Emar describes the installation of an *entu* (priestess).[17] The rituals are quite similar to those in Exodus 29 and Leviticus 8, so regardless of whether it is male or female leadership, the rituals serve to set up unquestionable power relations; some people, whether male or female, are accorded a fundamentally different status than the rest of the community. It is this group that has sole control over access to the divine. At issue is not just that men can be priests and that women are always excluded; it is that a small, distinct group of people has unique power, authority, and status that is immutable.

In contrast to the Levitical model for the establishment of ritual authority, we might compare an example of ritual authority that is rooted in women's experiences. Susan Starr Sered engaged in an anthropological

16. Ibid., 441.
17. Daniel E. Fleming, *Time at Emar: The Cultic Calendar and the Rituals from the Diviner's Archive* (Winona Lake, IN: Eisenbrauns, 2000).

study of Middle Eastern Jewish women and concluded that women engage in "relationship-oriented religiosity."[18] Sered observed, for example, that the women with whom she lived believed that while their rabbi might study the dietary laws, the women were the ones who really knew how to run a kosher kitchen. While a man might try to correct a woman's practice, the women tended to shrug off these comments, knowing that the true knowledge of sacred food preparation was passed on from mother to daughter: "The fact that women prepare for holidays means that it is the women who are ritual experts, the guardians of law and tradition, the ones with the power to make and create, not simply participate."[19] I bring this study into the discussion of Leviticus 8 because a broad comparison of these two systems highlights the particularly patriarchal nature of the initiation ritual. Women claim ritual authority through feeding others and running their kitchens, while priests claim authority as coming from God. Or said differently, women in this community exhibit "power to" serve while the priests of the P source exhibit "power over" others.

## Dedication of the Sanctuary (9:1-24)

Leviticus 9 describes Aaron's first day at work. On the eighth day (i.e., following the seven-day ordination ritual described in chapter 8), Moses instructs Aaron to offer a purification offering and a burnt offering on behalf of the priests and then to do the same on behalf of the community (Lev 9:1-17) in preparation for the appearance of the divine presence (v. 4). The ritual of offerings culminates with the first well-being offerings (vv. 18-21). Each step of the offering is described in detail to demonstrate that Aaron and his sons understand their duties.

Aaron then offers his first blessing for the community with uplifted arms (v. 22). Jewish traditions suggest that he pronounced the priestly benediction of Numbers 6:22-27.[20] Then Aaron and Moses reenter the holy space and again come out to bless the people. Immediately, YHVH's כבוד ("divine presence") appears before all the people in the form of fire, and they respond with joy and awe.

---

18. Susan Starr Sered, "Food and Holiness: Cooking as a Sacred Act among Middle Eastern Jewish Women," *Anthropological Quarterly* 61 (1988): 137. See also her fuller study, *Women as Ritual Experts: The Religious Lives of Elderly Jewish Women in Jerusalem* (Oxford: Oxford University Press, 1996).

19. Sered, "Food and Holiness," 135.

20. Suggested in the Sifra, a collection of halachic (legal) midrash on Leviticus.

⁹:¹On the eighth day Moses summoned Aaron and his sons and the elders of Israel. ²He said to Aaron, "Take a bull calf for a sin offering and a ram for a burnt offering, without blemish, and offer them before the Lord. ³And say to the people of Israel, 'Take a male goat for a sin offering; a calf and a lamb, yearlings without blemish, for a burnt offering; ⁴and an ox and a ram for an offering of well-being to sacrifice before the Lord; and a grain offering mixed with oil. For today the Lord will appear to you.'" ⁵They brought what Moses commanded to the front of the tent of meeting; and the whole congregation drew near and stood before the Lord. ⁶And Moses said, "This is the thing that the Lord commanded you to do, so that the glory of the Lord may appear to you." ⁷Then Moses said to Aaron, "Draw near to the altar and sacrifice your sin offering and your burnt offering, and make atonement for yourself and for the people; and sacrifice the offering of the people, and make atonement for them; as the Lord has commanded."

⁸Aaron drew near to the altar, and slaughtered the calf of the sin offering, which was for himself. ⁹The sons of Aaron presented the blood to him, and he dipped his finger in the blood and put it on the horns of the altar; and the rest of the blood he poured out at the base of the altar. ¹⁰But the fat, the kidneys, and the appendage of the liver from the sin offering he turned into smoke on the altar, as the Lord commanded Moses; ¹¹and the flesh and the skin he burned with fire outside the camp.

¹²Then he slaughtered the burnt offering. Aaron's sons brought him the blood, and he dashed it against all sides of the altar. ¹³And they brought him the

## TRANSLATION MATTERS

The Hebrew text in v. 4 states that YHVH נראה to them. The Masoretes pointed the text with a *kamatz* under the aleph, which can indicate two possible forms. The verb can be read as a masculine perfect or as a feminine participle. The first possibility would lead us to translate YHVH (m): "YHVH appeared to you." The second possibility would render YHVH in the feminine, "YHVH (f) is about to appear to you." As much as I would like to see YHVH marked as both masculine and feminine, neither reading works in context. The solution may be found at the end of the chapter where the community sees the fire of YHVH consume the offering. The Hebrew word for fire can be a feminine noun. It may be that an earlier form of the text read נראה with a *segol* under the aleph, which would indicate a masculine participle and that the Masoretes were uncomfortable with a statement that the community would actually see YHVH. By repointing the verb as a feminine, the Masoretes draw our attention to the fire (f) of YHVH—much more palatable to the rabbis.

burnt offering piece by piece, and the head, which he turned into smoke on the altar. [14]He washed the entrails and the legs and, with the burnt offering, turned them into smoke on the altar.

[15]Next he presented the people's offering. He took the goat of the sin offering that was for the people, and slaughtered it, and presented it as a sin offering like the first one. [16]He presented the burnt offering, and sacrificed it according to regulation. [17]He presented the grain offering, and, taking a handful of it, he turned it into smoke on the altar, in addition to the burnt offering of the morning.

[18]He slaughtered the ox and the ram as a sacrifice of well-being for the people. Aaron's sons brought him the blood, which he dashed against all sides of the altar, [19]and the fat of the ox and of the ram—the broad tail, the fat that covers the entrails, the two kidneys and the fat on them, and the appendage of the liver. [20]They first laid the fat on the breasts, and the fat was turned into smoke on the altar; [21]and the breast and the right thigh Aaron raised as an elevation offering before the Lord, as Moses had commanded.

[22]Aaron lifted his hands toward the people and blessed them; and he came down after sacrificing the sin offering, the burnt offering, and the offering of well-being. [23]Moses and Aaron entered the tent of meeting, and then came out and blessed the people; and the glory of the Lord appeared to all the people. [24]Fire came out from the Lord and consumed the burnt offering and the fat on the altar; and when all the people saw it, they shouted and fell on their faces.

Christophe Nihan notes that Leviticus 9 is a narrative culmination of a problem presented at the end of Exodus. Exodus ends with the presence of YHVH filling the tent and thus prohibiting Moses from entering (Exod 40:34-35). Thus, while YHVH finally has a tabernacle, no person can approach the deity; however, "Leviticus 1-10 recounts the gradual abolishment of this gap."[21] Nihan argues that the sacrificial cult functions primarily as a mode of communication between YHVH and Israel. A new relationship is thus enabled between the realm of the divine and the human. "This new relationship is highlighted by a double device: the leaders of the community, Moses and Aaron, are allowed for the first time to enter the house of the deity (Lev 9:23a), while the rest of the community is authorized to see the 'splendor' (*kavod*) of Yahweh (9:24a)."[22]

Some scholars assert that Leviticus 9 is P's version of the Sinai theophany. Exodus 24:15-18a introduces the first appearance of God's presence

21. Nihan, *From Priestly Torah to Pentateuch*, 90.
22. Ibid., 91.

at Sinai according to the priestly source, during which Moses ascends the mountain and YHVH's presence covers the mountain. The presence of YHVH settles on Mount Sinai, and the presence covers it for six days; on the seventh day, YHVH calls to Moses out of the cloud: "Now the appearance of the glory of the LORD was like a devouring fire on the top of the mountain in the sight of the people of Israel. Moses entered the cloud, and went up on the mountain" (Exod 24:17-18).

The next mention of God's כבוד occurs at the very end of Exodus where we read: "Then the cloud covered the tent of meeting, and the glory of the LORD filled the tabernacle. Moses was not able to enter the tent of meeting because the cloud settled upon it, and the glory of the LORD filled the tabernacle" (Exod 40:34-35). Leviticus 9 then picks up the narrative to describe the first time that YHVH's presence emerges from the holy of holies and consumes the first offering.

Baruch Schwartz suggests another way of understanding Leviticus 9 in light of the bigger picture of the priestly writings. If we read the P sections of Exodus–Leviticus apart from the other sources, we get the following story.[23] The Israelites arrive at Sinai in the third month after the exodus. The divine presence, enveloped by a fire cloud (that had been a pillar leading the people), settles on Mount Sinai; it is visible to the people. After six days, Moses ascends the mountain. God gives Moses instructions for the building of the tabernacle. Moses descends and proceeds to oversee the construction of the tabernacle, and, ten months later, at the first month of the next year, YHVH enters the tabernacle from the mountain and takes up residence in the holy of holies. Then YHVH's presence calls Moses in to set out the laws about sacrifices, which then enables the priests to be ordained and to begin their work. With these laws in hand and the consecration of priests and space, YHVH's fire bursts out of the holy of holies to consume the altar sacrifice, confirming before all witnesses that the system is essentially set up and ready to go. It is only then that the priestly laws concerning purity and impurity, along with a handful of other laws presented in the book of Numbers, mark the unfolding of the law to complete the process. In this reading, Sinai is not the holy mountain of God but rather the stopping place for the Israelites where they receive instructions for and then build the tabernacle. Schwartz emphasizes that Leviticus 9 is not the first time that

---

23. Baruch Schwartz identifies the following as P: Exod 19:1-2; 24:16-18a; 25:1–31:17; 31:18; 32:15; 34:29-35; 35:1-40; Lev 1–16.

the community witnesses God's presence; rather, it is the final stage in the divine presence settling into the tabernacle.[24]

Moses plays a key role in this chapter. He gives Aaron and his sons the instructions, and in verse 5 it is confirmed that they did as Moses has commanded. Then Moses confirms that this is what God had commanded (v. 6), although the Torah has no record of these words. Finally, in verse 21, the narrative of the offerings concludes with a statement that Aaron did everything as Moses had commanded it. Schwartz, in *The Jewish Study Bible*, states: "Rabbinic tradition acknowledges that Moses often commanded in the name of the LORD actions about which he had received no prior orders (e.g., Exod. 19:15; 32:27; elsewhere in P this occurs in Num. 30:2), implying that Moses' prophetic intuition was tantamount to explicit divine authority."[25] Again, as we saw in Leviticus 8, power and authority are conferred by YHVH via a sacred text and cannot be questioned. Moses's authority is unquestionable and absolute. The absolute authority of Moses is just one example of millennia of patriarchal institutions that confer power to one or the few over the many.

## Burning for God (10:1-7)

The culmination of the narrative block of materials in chapters 8–10 features a story radically at odds with all that has preceded it. Leviticus 1–9 presents a fantasy of a highly ordered and regulated world; chapter 10 introduces a moment of chaos that breaks through the order. The story of Nadav and Avihu offers a glimpse into the human impulse to break through a range of restrictions that societies place on individuals regarding gender-defined emotions and behavior.[26]

The chapter begins, "on the eighth day." For a full week, Nadav and Avihu have been sequestered with other new male initiates of the family of Aaron in the rather tight quarters of the tent of meeting in the midst of the desert. For seven days, they have been eating and drinking in

24. Baruch Schwartz, "The Priestly Account of the Theophany and Lawgiving at Sinai," in *Texts, Temples and Traditions: A Tribute to Menahem Haran*, ed. Michael V. Fox et al. (Winona Lake, IN: Eisenbrauns, 1996), 103–34.

25. Baruch Schwartz, "Leviticus," in *The Jewish Study Bible*, ed. Adele Berlin and Marc Zvi Brettler (Oxford: Oxford University Press 2004), 225.

26. Portions of this chapter are drawn from an earlier publication: Tamar Kamionkowski, "Nadav and Avihu and Dietary Laws: A Case of Action and Reaction," in *Torah Queeries: Weekly Commentaries on the Hebrew Bible*, ed. Gregg Drinkwater, Joshua Lesser, and David Schneer (New York: New York University Press, 2009), 135–39.

10:1Now Aaron's sons, Nadab and Abihu, each took his censer, put fire in it, and laid incense on it; and they offered unholy fire before the LORD, such as he had not commanded them. 2And fire came out from the presence of the LORD and consumed them, and they died before the LORD. 3Then Moses said to Aaron, "This is what the LORD meant when he said,

'Through those who are near me
   I will show myself holy,
and before all the people
   I will be glorified.'"

And Aaron was silent.

4Moses summoned Mishael and Elzaphan, sons of Uzziel the uncle of Aaron, and said to them, "Come forward, and carry your kinsmen away from the front of the sanctuary to a place outside the camp." 5They came forward and carried them by their tunics out of the camp, as Moses had ordered. 6And Moses said to Aaron and to his sons Eleazar and Ithamar, "Do not dishevel your hair, and do not tear your vestments, or you will die and wrath will strike all the congregation; but your kindred, the whole house of Israel may mourn the burning that the LORD has sent. 7You shall not go outside the entrance of the tent of meeting, or you will die; for the anointing oil of the LORD is on you." And they did as Moses had ordered.

the presence of God's fiery and smoky manifestations. Finally, on the eighth day, the same ritual day as a traditional circumcision, it is time for the new priests who have had a rare and almost unprecedented intimacy with God to take their place within the community. Nadav and Avihu, along with other initiates of the family, perform their priestly duties for the first time for the community of Israel. Likely inundated by the experiences of the past week (close proximity to other men, an abundance of food and drink, sleeping in a sacred space infused with divinely associated smells and sights), they must now perform a series of very carefully prescribed ritual actions. As in a drag show, the individual performer and the audience experience a transformation through the specific sights and sounds, the elaborate costumes, and every move of the performer. In the Torah narrative, the performance ends with an extraordinary climax: YHVH reveals himself to the entire community in a blaze of fire. According to the priestly perspective that is presented in this Torah portion, God reveals himself to the community only this one time—at the consecration of the sanctuary/tent of meeting and the ordination of the priests. As the community witnesses this extraordinary event, they shout out and fall to the ground.

It is against this backdrop that the famous story of Nadav and Avihu is set. On this eighth symbolic day a new beginning and a new level of inti-

macy with God is marked. As readers, we have only one verse in which
to understand what acts Nadav and Avihu perform. The verse gives us
no information about their state of mind or their intention. Instead, the
text specifies a series of actions. Each man takes his fire pan, puts coals
on the pan, places incense on the coals, and then offers God that which
he has just prepared (Lev 10:1). This may seem like rather innocuous
behavior; however, in a highly prescribed ritual world, they may have
broken a host of rules through these few actions. Did they use the right
coals? Did they use the appropriate incense? The only comment that we
have for guidance is the narrator's description of the final product that
they had created together as an אש זרה ("unholy fire," NRSV) or "strange
fire," which Moses had not commanded.

Immediately, a fire emerges "from before YHVH and consumes them
and they die before YHVH." Twice in this verse, the text says "before
YHVH," a rather uncommon occurrence. Some readers imagine that this
fire of God emerges from the heavens and descends on the two men. It
is more likely, however, that the fire emerged from the holy of holies, the
most holy inner sanctum of the tabernacle, just feet away from the outer
court by the entrance where they were most likely standing. Perhaps
the emphasis on the fact that they died in the presence of God stresses
what they were seeking in the first place. They were in fact taken into
the private divine sanctum and thus experienced what no other men had
experienced—a level of impassionate intimate connection with their God.

The history of interpretation on this passage has been complex and
voluminous. The most common reading is that Nadav and Avihu committed a willful sin, an offense against God, and that God punished them.
The dominant reading that they transgressed God's commandments,
God's wishes, and that God killed them reinforces the sin and punishment motif that is a central motif in biblical texts. Not every commentator, however, has agreed with this reading.[27] Philo reads the actions of
Nadav and Avihu and God's response as altogether positive. According
to Philo, Nadav and Avihu consciously chose to sacrifice or shed their
physical bodies in order to ascend to a more divine realm. In *De Som-
niis* 2.67,[28] Philo writes that they "consecrated their zeal, hot and fiery,

---

27. Opinions expressed in the Sifra, the Pesikta de-Rab Kahana, and Leviticus
Rabbah point to a line of interpretation arguing that Nadav and Avihu suffered the
death penalty through accidental transgressions and that God was saddened by the
death of the two men.

28. Translation taken from *Philo*, vol. 5, trans. F. H. Colson and G. H. Whitaker, LCL
275 (Cambridge, MA: Harvard University Press, 1934), 473.

flesh-consuming and swiftly moving, to piety, a zeal which was alien to creation, but akin to God. They did not mount by steps to the altar . . . but wafted by a favoring breeze and carried even to the revolving heavens were they like the complete and perfect burnt offerings resolved into ethereal rays of light."[29] Philo further argues that they had stripped themselves of all their garments and stood naked before God.[30]

We can expand Philo's reading through a queer reading lens. These men, having been in close proximity to other men for a week, and in the presence of the male figure that elicits trembling and passion and is seemingly unattainable, choose to risk all the cultural norms and legal prescriptions of their generation in order to merge with this ultimate male figure. In a world with highly prescribed rules regarding every aspect of their behavior, rules that are infused with strict boundaries regarding what it is to be male and female and what it means to be religious leaders, they break through all of the boundaries for the sake of love and the desire for an ultimate merging. The Indigo Girls express this idea more poetically in their song, "Strange Fire": "I come to you with strange fire / I make an offering of love / The incense of my soul is burned / By the fire in my blood."[31]

God accepts the men and takes them into his innermost sanctum, and he consumes them in an act of burning passion. There is no indication that God is angry with them; in fact, one could argue the opposite. God's verbal response is, "I am made holy through those that come close to me." Thus, God's holiness is supported and even enhanced by the acts of Nadav and Avihu. Therefore, Leviticus 10:1-2 can be read as an example of homoerotic attraction between human males and the male God of the Bible; each desires to come closer to the other. Nadav and Avihu strip themselves literally and figuratively—they strip themselves of their common clothing, of societal expectations, of confining rules, and they come forward. God meets them in a passion of fire, taking them in completely.

Nevertheless, the dominant postbiblical interpreters reconstruct a story of unbridled love into one of sin and punishment. The dominant narrative that emerges from rabbinic and medieval commentators is that Nadav and Avihu erred by making a decision on their own that had not

29. Although the early rabbis did not move in Philo's direction, the Kabbalists, centuries later, did consider the idea of Nadav and Avihu's merging with the divine both as worthy of honor and as dangerous.

30. *Legum Allegoriarum* 2.57-58, in *Philo*, vol. 1, trans. F. H. Colson and G. H. Whitaker, LCL 226 (Cambridge, MA: Harvard University Press, 1929), 259–61.

31. Indigo Girls, "Strange Fire," from their 1987 album *Strange Fire*, Epic/Sony Records.

been commanded by Moses (in other words, they acted with arrogance and challenged Moses's authority regarding matters of law), that they were not worthy to make such offerings because they were not married, or that they were drunk with wine and acted irresponsibly.[32] Within these rabbinic debates, a desire for intimacy with the divine and the merging of the human and divine male figures is completely erased.

While the "conservative" position has the last word in the interpretative life of Leviticus 10, the narrative of Nadav and Avihu remains front and center. For feminists who reject simple dualistic modes of thinking, Leviticus 10 can serve as an example of resistance or as a reminder that the tighter the controls, the stronger the impulse to break out of control.

## The Mission of the Priests (10:8-11)

The core of priestly responsibility is set out in Leviticus 10:8-11, immediately following the Nadav and Avihu narrative. The text begins with a command prohibiting priests from drinking wine or stronger alcoholic beverages while they are on duty. The seemingly odd placement of this prohibition following the narrative led the rabbinic imagination to posit that Nadav and Avihu had been drunk. In most cases the Hebrew Bible frowns on excessive drink (e.g., Isa 5:11; Prov 20:1), and it is explicitly prohibited for Nazirites (e.g., Num 6:3; Judg 13:4, 7, 14). The alcohol ban is followed by two instructions, each introduced with an infinitive construct: להבדיל ("to distinguish")[33] and להורות ("to instruct," NRSV). The text instructs the priests to distinguish between the holy and the common, and between the pure and impure, and to teach Israel the relevant laws. Leviticus 12–15 will set out the details of conditions that create impurities and mechanisms for the removal of impurities. Not surprisingly, with so much focus on the holy in Leviticus 1–16, Leviticus 10:10 is the only occurrence in the P writings of the word חל ("common"). This may be because the priest's primary concern is with maintaining holiness and the only force that is a threat to holiness is impurity. The pure state is

---

32. These interpretational lines can be found in sources such as Sifra, Pesikta de-Rab Kahana, and Leviticus Rabbah. For a solid presentation of postbiblical exegesis on this passage with a focus on Philo, see Robert Kirschner, "The Rabbinic and Philonic Exegesis of the Nadab and Abihu Incident (Lev. 10:1-6)," *JQR* 73 (1984): 375–93.

33. Watts, *Leviticus 1–10*, 539, suggests that the term להבדיל has the sense of "exercise judgment," based on the use of the same verb in Ezek 44:23: "They shall teach my people the difference between the holy and the common, and show them how to distinguish between the unclean and the clean."

⁸And the Lᴏʀᴅ spoke to Aaron: ⁹Drink no wine or strong drink, neither you nor your sons, when you enter the tent of meeting, that you may not die; it is a statute forever throughout your generations. ¹⁰You are to distinguish between the holy and the common, and between the unclean and the clean; ¹¹and you are to teach the people of Israel all the statutes that the Lᴏʀᴅ has spoken to them through Moses.

compatible with holiness. The goal of distinguishing between holy and common, between pure and impure, and of teaching Israel about these matters is to keep holiness and impurity from coming into contact.

### Food for the Priest's Family (10:12-15)

Moses then instructs Aaron to complete the rituals of the offerings set out in Leviticus 9 by having Aaron and his sons eat their due of the grain offering and having his entire family, sons and daughters, consume the thigh and breast of the well-being offering of the community. This instruction aligns with Leviticus 6:14-23 and 7:11-21, where the rules for eating consecrated foods are enumerated. The grain offering can be eaten only within the tabernacle and is restricted to the males, while the priestly portion of well-being offerings is to be consumed in a clean or pure place and is assigned to Aaron's sons and daughters. Watts notes that this is the first time that daughters from the Aaronide line are mentioned, while Aaron's sons have already been mentioned twenty-nine times.[34]

### Establishing the Chain of Command (10:16-20)

Leviticus 10:16-20 presents an inquiry regarding who has ultimate ritual authority: Moses or Aaron. The contest here is between two privileged men of power. In the contemporary period, we are witnessing women's claims for ritual authority in Jewish, Protestant, and Catholic circles. Significant forward progress continues for women wishing to serve as ministers and rabbis, while Catholic women face more severe obstacles. The verses at the end of Leviticus 10 illustrate the ongoing desire of religious leaders to serve as ritual performers.

---

34. Watts, *Leviticus 1–10*, 545.

*Lev 10:12-20*

¹²Moses spoke to Aaron and to his remaining sons, Eleazar and Ithamar: Take the grain offering that is left from the LORD's offerings by fire, and eat it unleavened beside the altar, for it is most holy; ¹³you shall eat it in a holy place, because it is your due and your sons' due, from the offerings by fire to the LORD; for so I am commanded. ¹⁴But the breast that is elevated and the thigh that is raised, you and your sons and daughters as well may eat in any clean place; for they have been assigned to you and your children from the sacrifices of the offerings of well-being of the people of Israel. ¹⁵The thigh that is raised and the breast that is elevated they shall bring, together with the offerings by fire of the fat, to raise for an elevation offering before the LORD; they are to be your due and that of your children forever, as the LORD has commanded.

¹⁶Then Moses made inquiry about the goat of the sin offering, and—it had already been burned! He was angry with Eleazar and Ithamar, Aaron's remaining sons, and said, ¹⁷"Why did you not eat the sin offering in the sacred area? For it is most holy, and God has given it to you that you may remove the guilt of the congregation, to make atonement on their behalf before the LORD. ¹⁸Its blood was not brought into the inner part of the sanctuary. You should certainly have eaten it in the sanctuary, as I commanded." ¹⁹And Aaron spoke to Moses, "See, today they offered their sin offering and their burnt offering before the LORD; and yet such things as these have befallen me! If I had eaten the sin offering today, would it have been agreeable to the LORD?" ²⁰And when Moses heard that, he agreed.

The final verses of Leviticus 10 describe an argument between Moses and Aaron. Although the text is somewhat elusive, it seems that Moses becomes angry because he notes that while the grain and well-being offerings were consumed by the priests, the meat of the purification offering had not been consumed as instructed in Leviticus 6:26. Moses rebukes Aaron's sons and claims that YHVH would not accept the purification offering on behalf of the people. The specific content of Aaron's response is difficult to understand, but it is clear that Aaron is claiming the authority to interpret the law and that Moses submits to Aaron's authority regarding ritual law.[35]

35. Nobuyoshi Kiuchi (*Leviticus*, ApOTC 3 [Nottingham: Inter-Varsity Press, 2007], 72–85) argues that Aaron did not eat the sacred meat because he felt responsibility and guilt for the deaths of Nadav and Avihu. Levine (*Leviticus*, 63) argues that Aaron did not complete the ritual because he was in mourning. For an exploration of the source of the disagreement, see Jacob Milgrom, *Leviticus 1–16*, AB 3 (New York: Doubleday, 1991), 635–40.

### A Brief History of the Roman Catholic Womenpriests Movement: 2002–2015

After the first 1996 European Women's Synod, Austrian Christine Mayr-Lumetzberger was moved to draft a preparation program for women and men priests in the Roman Catholic Church. Three groups of women, two Austrian and one German, began working the program as a group. Theologians participated as outside examiners.

In 2001, a group of Austrian and German women decided to go forward with ordination. In 2002, Mayr-Lumetzberger announced the plan to the media. However, the group had no bishop to ordain them. Mayr-Lumetzberger recalls thinking, "If Jesus wants women priests, God will get a bishop." Doors opened. Barriers came down. Bishops were found. On Palm Sunday 2002, a "Catacomb" Ordination took place in an Austrian home. Six women were ordained deacons by two bishops, Argentine Bishop Romulo Braschi[36] and a canonical bishop in good standing, whose identity is protected.

Plans began for an ordination to the priesthood. Mayr-Lumetzberger sent invitations to women of various countries who had theological and pastoral backgrounds. Women willing to risk excommunication to challenge Canon 1024 as an unjust law came forward.[37] June 29, 2002, the feast of Sts. Peter and Paul, was chosen, the same day on or near which priests throughout Europe were customarily ordained. The original plan was for twelve women to be ordained, but some declined or dropped out. Members of the Austrian and German group who did not seek ordination for themselves participated as advisors, planners, and organizers.[38] Diocesan bishops sent Mayr-Lumetzberger a warning not to proceed, threatening her with grave consequences. Despite resolve, there was fear of what would happen if they proceeded, fear that proceeding might even be dangerous. On June 29, 2002, seven women were ordained priests on the Danube River

---

36. Romulo Antonio Braschi was ordained a Roman Catholic bishop. Disillusioned by the church's identification with oppressive political forces in Argentina, he founded the Independent Catholic Church and married.

37. Canon 1024 states: "Only a baptized male can be validly ordained."

38. Lumetzberger's husband, Michael Mayr, and her sister, Elizabeth Grossegger, were heavily involved.

in international waters, where no bishop had jurisdiction.[39] Argentine Bishop Braschi and Bishop Rafael Regelsberger presided at the ordination.

News of the ordinations quickly reached the Vatican. On July 22, 2002, the feast of Mary Magdalene, the Vatican issued a *Monitum* threatening excommunication of the Danube Seven if they did not repudiate their ordinations. In January 2003, the women were excommunicated. Two filed appeals and were denied. Later in 2002, a Roman Catholic bishop in good standing, in a private ceremony, laid hands on the four women who became the leaders of the women's ordination movement to eliminate any question regarding the validity of their ordinations.[40]

In 2003, Mayr-Lumetzberger and Gisela Forster were ordained bishops privately by Roman Catholic bishops in good standing. In June 2003, the women bishops ordained Patricia Fresen to the priesthood in Barcelona, Spain.[41] A South African Dominican sister of forty-five years, Fresen was forced to leave her Dominican order, moved to Germany, and was eventually excommunicated.

By June 2004, women from other countries and continents emerged. Four women from Latvia, France, Switzerland, and Canada and two native-born US citizens were ordained deacons on the Danube River by Mayr-Lumetzberger and Forster.[42]

The movement rapidly burgeoned in the United States. In 2005, Victoria Rue and Phillip Faker, Via's husband, established the nonprofit Roman Catholic Womanpriests-U.S.A. (RCWP-USA) and its website. A European organization, Women's Ordination Worldwide, held a convention in Ottawa, Canada. Afterward, nine women were ordained priests or deacons on the St. Lawrence River near

---

39. These women were Christine Mayr-Lumetzberger, Pia Brunner, Gisela Forster, Iris Mueller, Ida Raming, Adelinde Therese Roitinger, and Angela White (Dagmar Braun Celeste, an Austrian-born naturalized US citizen and former first lady of Ohio).

40. These four were Gisela Forster, Christine Mayr-Lumetzberger, Iris Mueller, and Ida Raming.

41. Fresen participated in the antiapartheid movement, allowing black children to attend the Catholic school of which she was principal. For this she was arrested. Her South African experience sensitized her to apartheid against women in the Roman Catholic Church. As an English speaker, Fresen later led North American ordinations.

42. Astrid Indricane, Genevieve Beney, Monica Wyss, and Michele Birch-Connery were ordained with Victoria Rue and Jane Via (pseudonym Jillian Farley). The latter two were the first native-born US citizens to receive ordination in the movement.

Gannanaque,[43] one French, one Canadian, and seven US women.

Meanwhile, Fresen was consecrated a bishop in 2005 in a "Catacomb" ceremony in Austria by women bishops. In 2006, women bishops ordained four women on the Bodensee, one Swiss and three US citizens.[44] In the same year, Fresen presided at the first US ordination in the Pittsburgh area, where three rivers come together, ordaining eight women priests and several deacons; 2007 saw eleven US women ordained priests and thirteen ordained deacons.

By 2008, so many US women were seeking ordination that a bishop for the Americas was needed. Sibyl Dana Reynolds was elected and ordained the first woman bishop of the Americas.

In 2009, on the feast of Joan of Arc, the Vatican, no longer able to issue individual excommunications, issued a general excommunication order for any woman who "attempts" ordination and anyone who assists a woman in "attempting" ordination. By 2010, the US movement was so large that five regions emerged within the United States. Each region elected a bishop to ordain women within its region. In 2015, thirteen years after the Danube Seven, there are 145 women ordained worldwide and many in preparation for ordination.[45]

Womenpriests serve in virtually every capacity in which male priests serve. If the presence of women serving in priestly ministry is any indication, the Spirit is at work in this movement, despite the Vatican's continued refusal even to discuss women's ordination. "In truth, . . . God shows no partiality" (Acts 10:34).

*Jane Via*

43. Victoria Rue was ordained a priest, as was Sibyl Dana Reynolds, who would become the first woman bishop of the Americas, Canadian Michele Birch-Connery, Frenchwoman Genevieve Beney, and US women Jean Marie Marchant and Marie David. Kathleen Kunster, Roberta Meehan, Regina Nicolosi, and Kathy Vandenberg were ordained deacons.

44. Regina Nicolosi, Jane Via, and Monica Wyss were ordained priests. Andrea Johnson was ordained a deacon and later became the first bishop of the East Coast region of RCWP-USA.

45. In 2010, the Southern Region of RCWP-USA withdrew and formed the Association of Roman Catholic Womanpriests (ARCWP), with Bridget Mary Meehan as bishop. On September 24, 2015, Bishop Meehan and two other women bishops ordained three women bishops for ARCWP: Canadian Michele Birch-Connery, Columbian Olga Lucia Alvarez, and Mary Eileen Collingwood from the United States. In September 2015, ARCWP Bishop Mary Meehan estimates the number to be 215 women, a figure that would include Europe, RCWP, and ARCWP women. RCWP has also ordained a few men.

Watts argues that Leviticus 10 is about expanding priestly authority from sacrificial and temple matters to teaching law and making determinations regarding people's status.[46] Christophe Nihan sees verses 8-15 as "a hinge chapter" moving from sacrifices to matters of ritual impurity and ambiguity. He writes:

> By combining a story that illustrates the dangers posed by interpretive ambiguity with a story that illustrates the high priests' divinely ordained power to settle such ambiguities and forestall their dangers, the chapter enhances the mystique of the priestly office. To explain exactly why Nadav and Avihu's incense offering was wrong or exactly how Aaron reasoned regarding the eating of the sin offering would spoil the mystery of priestly service. The message from the priests to Israel is that "it is enough for you to know that our job is dangerous but God has given us the ability to handle it."[47]

Thus, Leviticus 10:16-20 brings the narratives of the dedication of the tabernacle and the ordination of the priests to a close by demonstrating Aaron's ultimate authority and Moses's acquiescence to matters of ritual law.

46. Watts, *Leviticus 1–10*, 537.
47. Nihan, *From Priestly Torah to Pentateuch*, 517.

# Leviticus 11:1-47

# *If You Must Eat Meat, Then . . .*

Probably food taboos (as unwritten social rules) exist in one form or another in every society on Earth, for it is a fact that perhaps nowhere in the world, a people, a tribe, or an ethnic group, makes use of the full potential of edible items in its surroundings. . . . One of many examples, although an especially well-studied one, involves the Ache people, i.e., hunters and gatherers of the Paraguayan jungle. According to Hill and Hurtado,[1] the tropical forests of the Ache habitat abound with several hundreds of edible mammalian, avian, reptilian, amphibian and piscine species, yet the Ache exploit only 50 of them. Turning to the plants, fruits, and insects the situation is no different, because only 40 of them are exploited. Ninety-eight percent of the calories in the diet of the Ache are supplied by only seventeen different food sources.[2]

Leviticus 11 has arguably had the most enduring influence on Jewish practice for over two millennia. Until just a few decades ago, keeping kosher was a central marker of Jewish identity for the majority of Jews around the world. The complex system of the laws of *kashrut* has its origins, in large part, in Leviticus 11 and its parallel in

1. Kim Hill and A. Magdalena Hurtado, "Hunter-Gatherers of the New World," *American Scientist* 77 (1989): 436–43.

2. Victor Benno Meyer-Rochow, "Food Taboos: Their Origins and Purposes," *Journal of Ethnobiology and Ethnomedicine* 5, no. 18 (2009), http://www.ethnobiomed.com/content/5/1/18.

Deuteronomy 14. Scholars have long debated the relationship between Leviticus 11 and Deuteronomy 14. Some scholars believe that the two texts have their origins in a common text, while others argue that one text is derived from the other. Howard Eilberg-Schwartz argues that Leviticus 11 reworks Deuteronomy 14 to bring the dietary laws into alignment with the creation story. He points out that Deuteronomy describes just one category of land animals while Leviticus addresses domesticated, wild, and swarming animals. Leviticus includes a category of swarming things in the waters; associates animals with the domains of land, water, and air; and presents the animals in an order that closely resembles that of Genesis 1.[3] Regardless of the relationship between the two texts, Leviticus certainly contains echoes of Genesis 1 and betrays an orientation toward classification and categorization. To some extent, Leviticus 11, with its detailed categorization of prohibited and permitted animals, serves as a counterbalance to the chaos of chapter 10.

## Hooves and Cud (11:1-8)

The dietary laws are presented in great detail and this degree of detail has led to significant scholarly attention on understanding the taxonomy of Leviticus 11.[4] John E. Hartley suggests that this chapter was a text of priestly instruction for the laity and is therefore presented didactically for the laity to understand.[5]

The chapter begins by designating which land animals are permissible for consumption. The text begins with a general principle: Israel may eat land animals that have divided hooves with a cleft in the hoof and that chew the cud (v. 3). The text then presents three animals—the camel, the rock badger, and the hare—that fulfill one condition, chewing the cud, but not the other, having divided hooves. The text also supplies an example of an animal that has divided hooves but that does not chew the

---

3. Howard Eilberg-Schwartz, "Creation and Classification in Judaism: From Priestly to Rabbinic Conceptions," *History of Religions* 26 (1987): 360–61.

4. Recent attempts at establishing the taxonomy or organizing principle of Leviticus 11 include Walter J. Houston, "Towards an Integrated Reading of the Dietary Laws of Leviticus," in *The Book of Leviticus: Composition and Reception*, ed. Rolf Rendtorff, Robert A. Kugler, and Sarah Smith Bartel (Leiden: Brill, 2003), 142–61; Naftali Meshel, "Food for Thought," *HTR* 101 (2008): 203–29; Lance Hawley, "The Agenda of Priestly Taxonomy: The Conceptualization of טמא and שקץ in Leviticus 11," *CBQ* 77 (2015): 231–49; and Jonathan Burnside, "At Wisdom's Table: How Narrative Shapes the Biblical Food Laws and Their Social Function," *JBL* 135 (2016): 223–45.

5. John E. Hartley, *Leviticus*, WBC 4 (Waco, TX: Word Books, 1992), 157.

11:1The LORD spoke to Moses and Aaron, saying to them: 2Speak to the people of Israel, saying:

From among all the land animals, these are the creatures that you may eat. 3Any animal that has divided hoofs and is cleft-footed and chews the cud—such you may eat. 4But among those that chew the cud or have divided hoofs, you shall not eat the following: the camel, for even though it chews the cud, it does not have divided hoofs; it is unclean for you. 5The rock badger, for even though it chews the cud, it does not have divided hoofs; it is unclean for you. 6The hare, for even though it chews the cud, it does not have divided hoofs; it is unclean for you. 7The pig, for even though it has divided hoofs and is cleft-footed, it does not chew the cud; it is unclean for you. 8Of their flesh you shall not eat, and their carcasses you shall not touch; they are unclean for you.

cud: the pig. Verse 8 provides the summary statement for the subunit, repeating the prohibition against eating these animals and adding a ban on touching the carcasses of these animals; a person becomes impure both by eating and by touching the carcasses of these animals. Quadrupeds forbidden for consumption could be touched and handled for other purposes, for example, using the camel for locomotion.

Of the four specific animals that the text provides as examples of prohibited quadrupeds, the pig has garnered the most attention by commentators perhaps because, of all the prohibited animals, pigs are common small farm animals and were routinely eaten in Canaan. Jacob Milgrom writes: "These criteria for edible quadrupeds were deliberately formulated in order to exclude the pig. Otherwise, Scripture could have stipulated one criterion—cloven hoofs—and it would have eliminated the other three quadrupeds."[6] He asserts, as many biblical interpreters have, that the pig was universally abhorred in the ancient Near East because it was regarded as dirty and repulsive and because it was associated with netherworld deities.[7]

Nicole Ruane has recently offered a fresh perspective on the pig ban. She suggests that pigs may have been forbidden because of their reproductive traits. While permitted land animals are uniparous (birthing one offspring or twins at a time), pigs are multiparous. So while pigs may have been a common staple on Canaanite farms and thus an obvious

6. Jacob Milgrom, *Leviticus 1–16*, AB 3 (New York: Doubleday, 1991), 649.
7. Ibid., 649–53.

food source, the fact that they birth litters may have conflicted with Israelite ideology. For example, Ruane notes that in multiparous births it is difficult to identify the firstborn and that this is at odds with the sanctity of the firstling. Pigs also bear offspring of multiple sires so paternity was impossible to identify, and this may have tapped into male paternity anxiety.[8] Finally, Ruane points out that the highly fertile nature of sows stands in tension with cultural norms of controlling female fertility. Pigs did not just produce many offspring; pigs actually symbolized fertility in ancient Near Eastern cultures. She cites a Hittite ritual discussed by Billie Jean Collins: "Just as a single pig gives birth to many piglets, let every single branch of this vineyard, like the pig, bear many grape clusters."[9] Ruane's astute observations consider modalities of reproduction in addition to other categories that have been considered, such as physical traits, means of locomotion, and eating practices. And Ruane's approach has the advantage of suggesting a link between Leviticus 11 and the impurity laws of Leviticus 12–15: "The laws of human impurity in Leviticus 12–15 and those of impure animals particularly in Leviticus 11 are less disjointed than they may initially appear. Reproductive concerns may be a matter for both forms of impurity."[10]

### Kashrut

Almost every religion arises in and is shaped by a place and teaches its adherents how to live in that place. In an ecosystem where humans depended on hunted game taken from large herds of wild animals, such as buffalo on the North American plains, the prohibition found in Leviticus against eating blood would be almost impossible to follow. But in the ecosystem of biblical Israel, where wild herds and habitats are less productive, a hunting culture is unsustainable. Instead, a culture where humans can carefully control the size of domesticated herds to fit both the limits of the ecosystem and the needs of the population is what's called

---

8. Nicole J. Ruane, "Pigs, Purity, and Patrilineality: The Multiparity of Swine and Its Problems for Biblical Ritual and Gender Construction," *JBL* 134 (2015): 489–504.

9. Ibid., 501, citing Billie Jean Collins, "Pigs at the Gate: Hittite Pig Sacrifice in Its Eastern Mediterranean Context," *JANER* 6 (2006): 162.

10. Ruane, "Pigs, Purity, and Patrilineality," 493. Ruane points to other indicators in Lev 11 for reproductive concerns and anxieties, like the association of the forbidden swarming animals with abundant reproduction of Israelites in Exod 1:7 and in Gen 9:7 (495–96).

for. That was the ecosystem that shaped the religion and rules of the Bible.

This brings us to those puzzling categorical rules that determine which animals are permitted for eating. Mammals that chew their cud and have split hooves are kosher; all other land animals are not (Lev 11 and Deut 14). What do these two characteristics of hoof and mouth mean? Anthropologically, historically, theologically, and personally, there may be many interpretations. Some of them can be found in Mary Douglas's celebrated work *Purity and Danger*.[11] But ecologically, there is a specific meaning, which goes far beyond any hygienic or moral or other rationalistic or symbolic interpretation. The depth of this meaning is not in generalities but in the details. That meaning, practically speaking, is straightforward: any animal that chews its cud can eat grasses and plants that are inedible to human beings. Any animal that has split hooves can walk, and therefore graze, on land that is too rocky to cultivate with a plow. In the extreme, mountain goats can be seen grazing small shrubs growing out of crevices on the sides of dams. These characteristics together mean one clear thing: the only land animals that can be eaten according to the laws of kashrut are animals that do not compete with human beings for food.

These rules, precisely tuned to the agriculture of hilly Canaan, would in their original context of the ancient Mideast have allowed a civilization to thrive without destroying the ecosystem it depended on. In that ecosystem, which was in some ways marginal—that is, which depended on intensive human input (agriculture and herding) as well as on intensive "divine" input (rain, as it was understood in biblical Israel)—there was no room for devoting good farming land to livestock.

Embedded in this wisdom about locale is another truth: any culture that allows domesticated herds to compete with humans for food also pits farmers against herders. More important, it pits the poor who have no land against owners who control both land and herds. We can easily see the dynamics of this problem in the modern world, where rising world food prices endanger the poor in many countries. Those prices are driven in part by the industrial practice of feeding grain to cattle instead of giving them their natural diet of diverse grasses and other pasture plants. They may also be driven more recently by the use of grain to make ethanol fuel. Instead of competition between

---

11. Mary Douglas, *Purity and Danger: An Analysis of Concepts of Pollution and Taboo* (London: Routledge, 2003).

herders and farmers, we have competition between feeding our SUVs and cattle and feeding other human beings.

In order to create a just society, which may be the most important value within Torah, there needs to be a way for farming and animal husbandry to produce enough for all people, poor and rich. The way to achieve this value in different ecosystems may differ, but any culture founded on justice will always find a way to bring this value into alignment with its ecosystem.[12]

*David Seidenberg*

## *Sacred Meat and Invisible Grains*

Interestingly, Leviticus 11:1-8 would have had very little impact on the daily lives of Israelites if these laws were ever put into practice in the biblical period. Livestock was used for heavy labor, milk, and wool. The average farm would have had neither the capacity nor the capital to raise livestock for human consumption. Studies of eating patterns in antiquity in the Palestinian region suggest that meat eating may have been limited to special holidays and feasts, so the dietary laws of Leviticus 11 would not have had much impact on the population. Roland Boer provides valuable data regarding subsistence farming in ancient Israel. He reports that in a small village, goats would have accounted for one-third of the domesticated animals and sheep for the other two-thirds. Bovines were rare because a cow requires twenty-five times as much water as a goat or sheep. Bovines also require much more pasturage. Male goats and sheep were culled at a young age to save on water and pasturage. They were used for meat and skins. Bovines would be culled at an older age, when they were no longer capable of traction work.[13]

12. David Seidenberg, "Kashroots: An Eco-History of the Kosher Laws," *The Jew and the Carrot: Jews, Food, and Contemporary Issues*, November 21, 2008, www.jcarrot.org/kashroots-an-eco-history-of-the-kosher-laws; revised for NeoHasid.org, September 2009, www.neohasid.org/torah/kashroots; Aloys Hüttermann, *The Ecological Message of the Torah: Knowledge, Concepts and Laws which Made Survival in a Land of Milk and Honey Possible* (Gainesville: University Press of Florida, 1999), 72.

13. Roland Boer, *The Sacred Economy of Ancient Israel*, LAI (Louisville: Westminster John Knox, 2015), 60–64.

By contrast, bread constituted 50 percent of caloric intake in Palestine; the diet of the average person consisted of dairy products, grains, and fruits; yet none of this is regulated in Leviticus 11. Evidence shows that women were the primary workers with grains. Carol Meyers estimates that it would have taken three hours of work each day to provide edible grain for six people.[14] Meyers argues that grain production by women would have entailed female control of complex technologies for transferring grain from its raw form into cooked breads and that, as women worked together to grind the grain and prepare food, a socio-political power base would have naturally occurred among women.[15] Early rabbinic evidence attests to women's sharing of ingredients, supplies, and workspaces. Cynthia Baker notes the likely sharing of small communal grinding mills.[16]

After the fall of the Second Temple, when first fruits could no longer be brought to the priests, it was women's responsibility to continue the practice in symbolic form. To this day, the preparation of challah always includes the separation of a portion of dough to be burnt in the oven as an offering to God. As b. Menachot 97a expresses: "When the Temple was standing, the altar atoned for sin. Now that the Temple no longer stands, a person's table atones for sin."

When we refer to Leviticus 11 as "the dietary laws," we privilege male priestly attention on meat while deflecting our attention from the "real" diets of grain, dairy, and fruit, of which women were the primary producers.

## Fish, Fowl, and Bugs (11:9-23)

Leviticus 11:9-12 moves from land animals to sea and water animals. Water animals are permitted for consumption as long as they have fins and scales (v. 9). This unit does not provide specific examples of water animals that may be difficult to classify. Instead, the text emphasizes the שֶׁקֶץ ("detestable" in vv. 10-12) nature of those animals that lack fins and scales. The summary statement (v. 12) repeats the prohibition against eating unfit animals and adds that touching the carcasses of these water animals is also detestable. Worthy of note is the fact that one cannot

---

14. Carol Meyers, "Having Their Space and Eating There Too: Bread Production and Female Power in Ancient Israelite Households," *Nashim* 5 (2002): 22.

15. Ibid., esp. 29–33.

16. Cynthia M. Baker, *Rebuilding the House of Israel: Architectures of Gender in Jewish Antiquity* (Stanford, CA: Stanford University Press, 2002), 39.

⁹These you may eat, of all that are in the waters. Everything in the waters that has fins and scales, whether in the seas or in the streams—such you may eat. ¹⁰But anything in the seas or the streams that does not have fins and scales, of the swarming creatures in the waters and among all the other living creatures that are in the waters—they are detestable to you ¹¹and detestable they shall remain. Of their flesh you shall not eat, and their carcasses you shall regard as detestable. ¹²Everything in the water that does not have fins and scales is detestable to you.

¹³These you shall regard as detestable among the birds. They shall not be eaten; they are an abomination: the eagle, the vulture, the osprey, ¹⁴the buzzard, the kite of any kind; ¹⁵every raven

become impure by eating or touching the forbidden water animals; instead, these animals are simply described as detestable.

Mary Douglas suggests that the prohibited water animals are those whose mode of locomotion defies proper movement in the water. For example, animals such as crabs and lobsters walk instead of swim.[17] Hartley argues that these water animals are called detestable rather than impure to emphasize that they were considered especially repulsive.[18] Milgrom argues more persuasively that "detestable" is here used in a more technical manner, indicating that the animal is forbidden for consumption but that it does not transmit impurity. He notes that the summary statement of this chapter in Leviticus 11:47 addresses two different issues that arise in the chapter: distinguishing between impure and pure and distinguishing between animals that may and may not be eaten. Milgrom asserts that the water animals, by virtue of existing in perpetually pure waters, cannot be impure. Additionally, the animals marked as detestable rather than impure all originate from the waters according to the creation story of Genesis 1. According to Genesis 1:20-21, both water animals and birds that fly came from the waters. Thus water animals, birds, and some reptiles are termed detestable and do not convey impurity.[19]

17. Douglas, *Purity and Danger*, 55.
18. Hartley, *Leviticus*, 158. So too, Nobuyoshi Kiuchi, *Leviticus*, ApOTC 3 (Nottingham: Inter-Varsity Press, 2007), 196.
19. Milgrom, *Leviticus 1–16*, 657–58.

of any kind; [16]the ostrich, the nighthawk, the sea gull, the hawk of any kind; [17]the little owl, the cormorant, the great owl, [18]the water hen, the desert owl, the carrion vulture, [19]the stork, the heron of any kind, the hoopoe, and the bat.

[20]All winged insects that walk upon all fours are detestable to you. [21]But among the winged insects that walk on all fours you may eat those that have jointed legs above their feet, with which to leap on the ground. [22]Of them you may eat: the locust according to its kind, the bald locust according to its kind, the cricket according to its kind, and the grasshopper according to its kind. [23]But all other winged insects that have four feet are detestable to you.

Naftali Meshel has engaged in an in-depth study of each animal that is mentioned in Leviticus 11 and has attempted to categorize the animals along several axis points, such as permitted or forbidden for consumption and pure or impure regarding contact. He notes, for example, that the consumption of a crow and of a camel are both prohibited, even though a crow is pure and a camel is impure. It is permissible to come into contact with a canary and a chameleon, even though the canary is pure and the chameleon is impure. Meshel concludes that this complex taxonomy, which almost seems to defy logic, indicates that the "legislator argued that permission and prohibition are divine decrees, which are imposed upon, not derived from, the natural order."[20]

Leviticus 11:13-19 focuses on the realm of the sky and forbidden birds. This subunit has a unique format. The text gives no specific qualities that would exclude specific birds; instead the text provides an extended list of twenty birds that are forbidden. Verses 20-23 deal with winged insects but reverse the format of the prior subunit. In this section, all winged insects are considered detestable, but certain exceptions are made: insects with jointed legs are permissible for ingestion. According to the text, these include locusts, crickets, and grasshoppers.[21]

---

20. Meshel, "Food for Thought," 222.

21. Milgrom posits that animals that move on all fours, such as locusts, were permitted as an exception because they were popularly enjoyed; see "Ethics and Ritual: The Foundations of the Biblical Dietary Laws," in *Religion and Law: Biblical-Judaic And Islamic Perspectives*, ed. Edwin Firmage, Bernard G. Weiss, and John W. Welch (Winona Lake, IN: Eisenbrauns, 1990), 189.

²⁴By these you shall become unclean; whoever touches the carcass of any of them shall be unclean until the evening, ²⁵and whoever carries any part of the carcass of any of them shall wash his clothes and be unclean until the evening. ²⁶Every animal that has divided hoofs but is not cleft-footed or does not chew the cud is unclean for you; everyone who touches one of them shall be unclean. ²⁷All that walk on their paws, among the animals that walk on all fours, are unclean for you; whoever touches the carcass of any of them shall be unclean until the evening, ²⁸and the one who carries the carcass shall wash his clothes and be unclean until the evening; they are unclean for you.

²⁹These are unclean for you among the creatures that swarm upon the earth: the weasel, the mouse, the great lizard according to its kind, ³⁰the gecko, the land crocodile, the lizard, the sand lizard, and the chameleon. ³¹These are unclean for you among all that swarm; whoever touches one of them when they are dead shall be unclean until the evening. ³²And anything upon which any of them falls when they are dead shall be unclean, whether an article of wood or cloth or skin or sacking, any article that is used for any purpose; it shall be dipped into water, and it shall be unclean until the evening, and then it shall be clean. ³³And if any of them falls into any earthen

## Contamination through Impure Animals (11:24-43)

Leviticus 11:24 constitutes the beginning of a new topic that shifts the focus from permissible and forbidden food for consumption to the consequences of touching impure animals. This block of material has no parallel in Deuteronomy 14 and is likely an addition to the dietary laws. These verses (esp. vv. 24-40) provide more detail on impurity contamination and purification processes caused by contact with forbidden animals. At some points, this block of material repeats information already provided in order to set the stage for purification instructions. Essentially, a person who incurs impurity through contact with the carcass of an animal is unclean until evening and must observe the usual practice for ridding oneself of minor impurities: bathing and laundering.

Verse 29 provides a list of swarming animals that cause impurity, augmenting the general statement that swarming animals are detestable in Leviticus 11:20-23. These swarming animals seem to fall under the category of rodents and amphibians. The text describes the variety of ways that contact impurities are transmitted. Carcasses transmit impurity not just to people who touch them but also to fabrics, skins, and vessel, all that is in it shall be unclean, and you shall break the vessel. [34]Any food that could be eaten shall be unclean if water from any such vessel comes upon it; and any liquid that could be drunk shall be unclean if it was in any such vessel. [35]Everything on which any part of the carcass falls shall be unclean; whether an oven or stove, it shall be broken in pieces; they are unclean, and shall remain unclean for you. [36]But a spring or a cistern holding water shall be clean, while whatever touches the carcass in it shall be unclean. [37]If any part of their carcass falls upon any seed set aside for sowing, it is clean; [38]but if water is put on the seed and any part of their carcass falls on it, it is unclean for you.

[39]If an animal of which you may eat died, anyone who touches its carcass shall be unclean until the evening. [40]Those who eat of its carcass shall wash their clothes and be unclean until the evening; and those who carry the carcass shall wash their clothes and be unclean until the evening.

[41]All creatures that swarm upon the earth are detestable; they shall not be eaten. [42]Whatever moves on its belly, and whatever moves on all fours, or whatever has many feet, all the creatures that swarm upon the earth, you shall not eat; for they are detestable. [43]You shall not make yourselves detestable with any creature that swarms; you shall not defile yourselves with them, and so become unclean.

other similar materials. Vessels are contaminated along with any food or liquid held by the vessel. Even a watered seed is contaminated if it comes into contact with the carcass. Exceptions to contagion are cisterns and dry seeds. Milgrom writes, "The basic principle is that the earth and everything that is embedded in it, such as cisterns (v. 36) and planted seeds (v. 37), are not susceptible to impurity. But objects unattached to the land such as vessels (vv. 32-33), solid food (v. 34a), potable drink (v. 34b), and loose seed (v. 38) are susceptible."[22]

## Eating as a Holy Practice (11:44-45)

Leviticus 11:44-45 provides a specific rationale for the dietary laws: since God is holy, Israel should strive toward holiness and one way to become more God-like is through eating habits. The language of verses 44-45 is so similar to the phraseology and theology of the Holiness

---

22. Milgrom, *Leviticus 1–16*, 680.

⁴⁴For I am the Lᴏʀᴅ your God; sanctify yourselves therefore, and be holy, for I am holy. You shall not defile yourselves with any swarming creature that moves on the earth. ⁴⁵For I am the Lᴏʀᴅ who brought you up from the land of Egypt, to be your God; you shall be holy, for I am holy.

Legislation, that many scholars believe that these verses are an insert from H into the P materials. Verses 44-45 focus on the theme of the Holiness Code—that YHVH is holy, so Israel too should be holy. In addition, the curtailing of seafood is odd insofar as ancient Israelites did not live in coastal lands and would not have consumed much by way of the sea. The forbidden quadrupeds would have been difficult to obtain because they lived in remote regions not easily accessible to average Israelite farmers. It may have been that only the priests would have had access to meat on a regular basis.

## Eating as a Boundary Marker (11:46-47)

The last two verses of chapter 11 reflect more normative priestly thinking, namely, that what we do with our bodies can determine whether we are impure or pure, and that mindfulness regarding permissible and forbidden animals helps to distinguish between the holy and the common.

Over the course of many centuries, readers of Leviticus 11 have attempted to explain the dietary laws in a variety of ways. One approach has been to explain the laws from a pragmatic perspective. One example is the claim that the dietary laws addressed public health issues and proper hygiene.[23] Another example of a pragmatic approach is that the dietary laws might have distinguished ancient Israelites from their neighbors.[24]

23. Maimonides argued that pork is forbidden because it is dirty and unhealthy; see *Guide for the Perplexed*, trans. M. Friedländer (London: Routledge, 1956), 370–80.

24. Baruch Levine, *Leviticus: A JPS Torah Commentary* (Philadelphia: Jewish Publication Society of America, 1989), 244. So too David P. Wright, "Observations on the Ethical Foundations of the Biblical Dietary Laws: A Response to Jacob Milgrom," in Firmage, Weiss, and Welch, *Religion and Law*, 193–98.

*Lev 11:46-47*

⁴⁶This is the law pertaining to land animal and bird and every living creature that moves through the waters and every creature that swarms upon the earth, ⁴⁷to make a distinction between the unclean and the clean, and between the living creature that may be eaten and the living creature that may not be eaten.

### Dietary Laws and Disease

In Leviticus 11 lists are provided of what is permissible for food among land animals, birds, insects, and fish. Apart from its original purpose of ritual cleanness, this regulation may also have relevance for food hygiene in view of the fact that the concept of clean and unclean animals can be understood within the context of food customs or dietary laws. Current dietary theory draws a link between cultural values and nutritive factors. This relationship is difficult to explain, but its possibility poses a probability with regard to dietary regulations in Leviticus. Hence it is not impossible that in ancient Israel the regulation that some animals could render persons ritually unfit might also reflect the people's dietary customs. The relevance of the regulation to environmental health is brought out clearly in the prohibition from touching the carcasses of unclean animals (v. 8), which in itself mandates that any person who had contact with these carcasses had to wash his or her clothes (v. 25). Even cooking utensils such as ovens or stoves were contaminated by contact with carcasses of unclean animals and should be destroyed (v. 35). This regulation incidentally anticipated certain modern scientific findings. Science has confirmed that contact with certain animals, dead or living, might cause diseases. L. J. Vorhaus[25] confirms this when he states that tularemia is an acute disease of a variety of animals that can be transmitted to humans by direct contact, as in skinning an infected rabbit. (Incidentally the rabbit is on the list of unclean animals in v. 6.) In April 2009 the whole world was threatened by swine influenza (or swine flu; H1N1 virus), an infectious disease believed to be transmissible from pigs to humans. Experts say that although the disease cannot be

25. L. J. Vorhaus, "Tularemia," Microsoft Student 2008 [DVD].

caught by eating pork, sporadic human infections with swine flu have occurred. Influenza viruses can be directly transmitted from pigs to people and from people to pigs. Human infection with flu viruses from pigs are most likely to occur when people are in close proximity to infected pigs, such as in pig barns and livestock exhibits housing pigs at fairs (see www.cdc.gov). Some countries are just recovering from Ebola, the deadly disease believed to be transmissible from bats to humans. Thus, the prohibition from touching putrefying animals anticipated ecological issues in modern times in the form of persons being rendered "unclean," not ritually, but in terms of being infected with certain diseases.

*Solomon Olusola Ademiluka*

The rabbis approached the dietary laws with the "just because God commanded it" approach. Rav[26] said: "The commandments were only given to purify people. For what difference does it make to the Holy One whether one slaughters from the throat or from the nape? Or what difference does it make to Him whether one eats unclean or clean substances?" In other words, the laws are arbitrary; what is important is that God commanded them, and it is for Israel to obey them.[27]

Perhaps the most common approach has been the symbolic or allegorical. The work of Mary Douglas has been most informative for biblical scholars in recent decades.[28] Generally stated, Douglas posited that the dietary laws serve to function as boundary markers. Animals that fall outside of what fits into the "natural" structure of the universe are forbidden. A common example might be animals like lobsters and crabs; as sea animals they belong in the water, yet they transgress their place in nature by walking on land as well.[29]

David C. Kraemer offers yet another attempt with the symbolic approach. Kraemer follows Eilberg-Schwartz, with some modifications, in

---

26. Abba Aricha, a third-century Talmudic scholar.

27. Tanhuma (a collection of Midrash), Parashat Shemini.

28. Douglas, *Purity and Danger* and later, "The Forbidden Animals in Leviticus," *JSOT* 59 (1993): 3–23.

29. For a detailed review of the scholarly literature on the rationale for the dietary laws, see Jiří Moskala, "Categorization and Evaluation of Different Kinds of Interpretation of the Laws of Clean and Unclean Animals in Leviticus 11," *BR* 46 (2001): 5–41.

arguing that "the dietary restrictions carve up the animal world along the same lines as Israelite thought."[30] Kraemer argues that metaphors in the Bible reveal that some animals were considered evil and other animals were associated with positive qualities. Evil or aggressive animals were not to be consumed because they stood for the opposite of the community's desired identity. Kraemer is pointing to the concept that "you are what you eat."

Finally, Jacob Milgrom posits an ethical rationale for Leviticus 11. He considers the dietary laws within the context of the blood prohibition, and he concludes that "its purpose is to teach the Israelite reverence for life by (1) reducing the choice of flesh to a few animals, (2) limiting the slaughter of even those few permitted animals to the most humane way, and (3) prohibiting the ingestion of blood and mandating its disposal upon the altar as acknowledgment that bringing death to living things is a concession of God's grace and not a prerogative of human whim."[31]

*Meat Eating and Gender*

Milgrom's opinion, that Leviticus 11 puts controls on meat eating in order to force the community to maintain its reverence for life, is appealing. When we add to this the claims made by the text itself, that Israel is to maintain these laws in order to strive for holiness and in order to maintain controls on what people consume, there is a great appeal to Leviticus 11. The ongoing impact of Leviticus 11 has led to thousands of years of mindfulness eating and has contributed to a powerful identity marker in Judaism. As Kraemer has written regarding special festive eating practices in ancient Israel: "On these occasions, Israel was celebrating her identity in multiple and various ways. What has not been before noticed is that one of the ways she was celebrating that identity was in what she ate. In fact . . . she was not only celebrating, *but also eating*, her national identity."[32] As true as this claim may be, it is crucial to remember that meat eating, especially sacralized meat eating, was actually limited to the wealthy (according to material and archaeological

30. Howard Eilberg-Schwartz, *The Savage in Judaism: An Anthropology of Israelite Religion and Ancient Judaism* (Bloomington: Indiana University Press, 1990), 195–216; and David C. Kraemer, *Jewish Eating and Identity Through the Ages* (London: Routledge, 2007), 21.

31. Milgrom, "Ethics and Ritual," 190.

32. Kraemer, *Jewish Eating*, 22.

records) and was governed by a male priesthood. If ancient Israel really was "what it ate," then Israel was primarily connected to the grains and fruits that the communities cultivated and to the dairy products that farm animals produced.

The trend of privileging meat eating with sacred practices (as in Lev 11) while giving no "textual space" to those parts of the diet that women produced and prepared effectively marginalizes what women bring to the table and the hard work behind it. Carol Adams's famous study, *The Sexual Politics of Meat*, argues that there is a direct correlation between meat eating and patriarchy. She quotes George Beard's assertion: "In proportion as man grows sensitive through civilization or through disease, he should diminish the quantity of cereals and fruits, which are far below him on the scale of evolution, and increase the quantity of animal food, which is nearly related to him in the scale of evolution, and therefore more easily assimilated."[33] Adams asserts that "the emphasis on the nutritional strengths of animal protein distorts the dietary history of most cultures in which complete protein dishes were made of vegetables and grains. Information about these dishes is overwhelmed by an ongoing cultural and political commitment to meat eating."[34]

The afterlife of Leviticus 11 perpetuated the association of meat with men in some Jewish literature. A famous Mishnah reveals that the rabbis claimed that only one who engaged in Torah study was allowed to eat meat.[35] Jonathan Brumberg-Kraus points out that the development of postbiblical dietary laws fostered distinctions between the rabbis (תלמדי חכמים) and the uneducated masses (עמי הארץ) insofar as the laws of meat eating were so complex that a commoner would be better off sticking with a vegetarian diet. Brumberg-Kraus suggests that "the 'acquired honor' of Torah learning has replaced the 'ascribed honor' of family lineage as the primary criteria [*sic*] for leadership and social status in the rabbinic system."[36]

---

33. Carol J. Adams, *The Sexual Politics of Meat: A Feminist-Vegetarian Critical Theory* (New York: Bloomsbury Academic, 2015), 8–9.

34. Ibid., 10.

35. b. Pes 49b: "This is the torah of beast and fowl (Lev 11:46) for all who engage in Torah, it is permitted to eat the flesh of beast and fowl. But for all who do not engage in Torah, it is not permitted to eat beast and fowl."

36. Jonathan D. Brumberg-Kraus, "Meat Eating and Jewish Identity: Ritualization of the Priestly 'Torah of Beast and Fowl' (Lev. 11:46) in Rabbinic Judaism and Medieval Kabbalah," *AJSR* 24 (1999): 249.

Within Jewish mystical circles of the medieval period, Kabbalists developed a notion that eating meat (symbolic sacrifices) was a way of approaching God that went hand in hand with Torah study; thus the gathering of learned men (as defined by the Kabbalists) to eat communally became a complex ritual event. Brumberg-Kraus suggests:

> This kabbalistic approach to meat-eating, especially with its extensive use of sacrificial language and images seems to support the late Nancy Jay's anthropological thesis that sacrifice is a "remedy for man having been born of women." That is to say, men use the blood and flesh of shared meat sacrifices to foster myths of communal origins and bonds that root group identity in institutions controlled by males, rather than in who one's mother is.[37]

Meanwhile women have served as the ritual experts in food preparation from the biblical period to contemporary times. Norma Baumel Joseph writes, "Is it coincidental or consequential that the food preparer—the neglected or invisible ritual expert and participant—is female? Food appears to play a profound part in Jewish communal identity and religious life, but the woman's responsibility for this domain has not been seen as critically influential."[38] As the women of Susan Sered's study note, the rabbi might study the law, but the women actually practice, enforce, and interpret the law! The sacred nature of meat eating may have been co-opted by Jewish literature produced by men, but women have been the actual preparers of food. "The fact that women prepare for holidays means that it is the women who are ritual experts, the guardians of law and tradition, the ones with the power to make and create, not simply participate."[39]

---

37. Ibid., 234.
38. Norma Baumel Joseph, "Introduction," *Nashim* 5 (2002): 7–13.
39. Susan Starr Sered, *Women as Ritual Experts: The Religious Lives of Elderly Jewish Women in Jerusalem* (Oxford: Oxford University Press, 1996), 135.

# Leviticus 12:1–15:33

# *Bodies and Access to the Holy*

## Impurity, Not Sin

As argued in the introduction, the English terms for "sin," "defilement," "purity," "impurity," and "atonement" are so bound up in hundreds of years of Christian theology that the use of these terms in biblical exegesis only obscures the meaning of the Hebrew text. A case in point comes from Gordon Wenham's commentary:

> After dealing with the uncleanness associated with animals, the law moves on to consider various bodily *defilements*. Ch. 12 deals with the *ritual defilement* that follows childbirth, chs. 13 and 14 with the *uncleanness* caused by skin diseases, and ch. 15 with the *uncleanness* associated with reproduction, including the woman's monthly cycle. . . . These chapters deal with internal *sources of pollution*; they arise from the constitution of man, not from his environment. Insofar as man can pollute himself through his own bodily functions as well as through his contact with animals, these uncleanness laws reflect the fact that Israel's status as a holy nation faces challenges inside and outside. *Sin is not merely a matter of environment but of individual failure.*[1]

---

1. Gordon J. Wenham, *The Book of Leviticus* (Grand Rapids: Eerdmans, 1979), 186 (italics mine).

The translations "defilement," "uncleanness," "sources of pollution," and "sin" (corresponding to the Hebrew word טמאה) all have negative connotations and have both informed and been informed by Christian theology; unfortunately, this negativity underlies the framework in which many readers encounter Leviticus. The overall mind-set created by a litany of deleterious words leads some interpreters to use these misleading translations to further build an inaccurate understanding of Leviticus. As Yvonne Sherwood has noted, often "commentators are, like henchmen, carrying out the threats in the text."[2] Note, for example, how Wenham connects "the constitution of man" to "individual failure," which all falls under the rubric of sin and how Wenham describes Leviticus 15 as concerned with reproduction and woman's monthly cycle without noting more accurately that the topic of the chapter is genital discharges.

If we focus instead on the meaning of the Hebrew words within the context of the text itself, several interesting observations arise. There are a host of terms for wickedness, evil, and sin in the Bible, such as פשע (e.g., Exod 23:21), עון (e.g., Exod 20:5), חטא (Deut 19:15), מעל (Num 5:6), רעה (Gen 6:5); however, an examination of the language in Leviticus 12–15 reveals that the word פשע ("transgression") does not appear in the impurity chapters until chapter 16! The term עון ("iniquity") never appears in Leviticus 12–15, nor does חטא as a *qal* verb ("to sin" or "miss the mark"). Even the term נסלח ("forgiven") never appears in these chapters. Thus טמאה (usually translated as "impurity," but which NRSV renders as "uncleanness"), a key term in Leviticus 12–15, has nothing to do with morality; nor is it even obvious that טמאה has any negative valence at all! In short, the primary concern in Leviticus 12–15 is determining the status of a woman or a man at any given time regarding their permissibility to enter YHVH's sanctuary or to partake of sanctified food. Leviticus 12–15 is about one's ontological status in relation to holiness. Absent the sanctuary these priestly categories would become utterly irrelevant. In fact, we might go so far as to say that these categories have nothing to do with God's will or moral imperative. In these chapters, God does not judge, warn, or praise the community in any way; טמאה simply drives away God's presence as two opposing magnets repel each other.

It is not surprising that the term טמאה has been widely misunderstood. The Bible does not define the word, and it is used in a variety of settings,

---

2. Yvonne Sherwood, *The Prostitute and the Prophet: Hosea's Marriage in Literary-Theoretical Perspective*, JSOTSup 212 (Sheffield: JSOT Press, 1996), 261.

which point to multiple translations. While Leviticus uses the term to indicate conditions that preclude an individual from coming in contact with the Holy, at times the word does seem to imply moral deficit. A productive avenue to better comprehend this complex terminology is to consider what is categorized as טמאה and what it is about those categories that repels the divine presence. David Wright distinguishes between forms of impurity that are "tolerated" (טמאה) and those that are "forbidden" (thus, connoting sin). He lists tolerated impurities as: (1) death related, (2) sexual, (3) disease related, and (4) cultic.[3] Forbidden impurities, which might reasonably be associated with "sin," fall into two categories: unintentional impurity, in which someone fails to abide by the purity regulations and does not address the impact of their tolerated purity on the sanctuary; and intentional impurities, which are willful refusals to engage in the proper purification rites.[4]

Leviticus 12–15 begins and ends by addressing certain types of blood loss from the human body. Blood is undoubtedly a central motif in Leviticus, but its conceptual associations are complex. On the one hand, the blood of animal sacrifice serves as a life-affirming substance that enhances the relationship between God and Israel. On the other hand, human female blood released through the vagina causes impurity. The shedding of human blood through violence or injury is not addressed at all. So what is going on here?

Howard Eilberg-Schwartz suggests that the factor of control plays a key role in determining the status of blood. Sacrificial slaughter is a highly controlled form of bloodshed, while genital discharges cannot be controlled.[5] Disorderly flows of genital blood are contaminating while sacrificial blood is the substance that cleanses impurity. Eilberg-Schwartz argues that the controlled bloodshed of sacrifice remedies the contamination resulting from disorderly discharge through its symbolic reversal. Instead of "deathly" blood flowing uncontrollably from the body and contaminating the tabernacle because of the impurity it generates, sacrificial blood is carefully collected and applied to specific parts of the tabernacle's structures in order to remove impurity. Blood is reordered

---

3. David P. Wright, "The Spectrum of Priestly Impurity," in *Priesthood and Cult in Ancient Israel*, ed. Gary A. Anderson and Saul M. Olyan, JSOTSup 125 (Sheffield: JSOT Press, 1991), 154.

4. Ibid., 159–64.

5. Howard Eilberg-Schwartz, *The Savage in Judaism: An Anthropology of Israelite Religion and Ancient Judaism* (Bloomington: Indiana University Press, 1990), 188.

in this process. What in one situation is "life" lost through leakage is, in sacrifice, life captured and given to God.[6]

In addition to uncontrolled genital blood, טמאה is also created through certain skin diseases, molds, and contact with corpses. Jacob Milgrom represents a common view in suggesting that all these things share one common denominator: death. For example, certain skin conditions may make a person look like she is rotting, and menstruation represents the loss of potential life. The death theory does not, however, explain every case of impurity. For example, sexual intercourse defiles, and yet, if anything, this act can result in life.

Another more recent approach to unpacking טמאה has been suggested by Yitzhaq Feder, who focuses on the concept of disgust. Feder has recently written:

> I wish to demonstrate that the ancient Israelite conception of pollution was grounded in concrete experience and should be analyzed from a phenomenological perspective that is philosophically non-dualistic, socio-culturally situated and appeals to the emotion-laden subjectivity of individual actors.[7]

Feder draws on concepts from embodiment theories and the emotional responses to apparent or real threats to the body. "In some cases, the assumption of a transfer of essence is corroborated by science (e.g., in germ-theory), but frequently it is based on an emotional bias that overwhelms cold reason. As a simple illustration, a person who picks up a piece of animal feces by means of a plastic bag is usually inclined to wash his hands afterwards, despite the absence of actual contact."[8] Feder asserts that in the prescientific era, there would not have been the same kinds of distinctions between contagion and defilement. For example, misfortune was considered contagious in many cultures; isolation of a cursed person would have been indistinguishable from isolation of a diseased individual. Feder's work serves as an important caution against trying to impose a logical and systematic structure onto the specific cases of impurity.

In short, despite the many theories that have been advanced regarding impurity and contagion, scholars have not come close to a consensus. The

---

6. Ibid.

7. Yitzhaq Feder, "Contagion and Cognition: Bodily Experience and the Conceptualization of Pollution (*ṭum'ah*) in the Hebrew Bible," *JNES* 72 (2013): 155.

8. Ibid., 156.

priestly notions of impurity and contagion continue to defy any single unifying theory. Mary Douglas does make one point, which I believe is important to emphasize in this commentary. Douglas notes that generally the phenomenon of contagion emerges from the general population of a society and serves to bolster the power of the dominant group. As an example, Douglas points to HIV hysteria, which led professional health-care workers and the general populace to take precautions that were not logically necessary. This fear of contagion enabled the dominant group to further marginalize gay men. In priestly texts, however, the regulations regarding contagion apply equally to all members of society, regardless of class, gender, or Israelite/non-Israelite. As Douglas puts it, "They maintain absolutely no social demarcation."[9] In my engagement with priestly biblical literature, I agree with Douglas' point and I believe that this point is important to keep in mind as we interpret the following chapters.

## The Mysteries of Blood in Childbirth (12:1-8)

Leviticus 12 may be the shortest chapter in Leviticus, but it is one of the most puzzling texts. The chapter addresses the issue of ritual impurity following childbirth. According to Leviticus 12, when a woman bears a son, she is impure for seven days and then she remains in a lesser state of impurity for another thirty-three days. During this period, she may not enter the sanctuary or come into contact with food that has been consecrated to YHVH. If she births a female, she enters a state of ritual impurity for fourteen days, followed by the lesser degree of impurity for sixty-six days. At the end of the two-stage period, whether she births a son or a daughter, she presents a lamb to the priest for a burnt offering and a pigeon or a dove for a purification offering. If she cannot afford a sheep, she may bring two birds, one for each offering. Again we observe the application of a sliding scale model.[10]

Leviticus 12:1-4 is replete with rare and unusual language, ambiguous terms, and mysterious logic. First, the phrase that is used to open the case of the parturient appears nowhere else: כי תזריע וילדה זכר (Lev 12:2).

9. Mary Douglas, "Atonement in Leviticus," *JSQ* 1 (1993/1994): 109–30, esp. 112–13.

10. For a review of the reception history of Leviticus 12, see Linda S. Schearing, "Double Time . . . Double Trouble? Gender, Sin, and Leviticus 12," in *The Book of Leviticus: Composition and Reception*, ed. Rolf Rendtorff, Robert A. Kugler, and Sarah Smith Bartel (Leiden: Brill, 2003), 429–50.

¹²:¹The Lord spoke to Moses, saying: ²Speak to the people of Israel, saying: If a woman conceives and bears a male child, she shall be ceremonially unclean seven days; as at the time of her menstruation, she shall be unclean. ³On the eighth day the flesh of his foreskin shall be circumcised. ⁴Her time of blood purification shall be thirty-three days; she shall not touch any holy thing, or come into the sanctuary, until the days of her purification are completed. ⁵If she bears a female child, she shall be unclean two weeks, as in her menstruation; her time of blood purification shall be sixty-six days.

⁶When the days of her purification are completed, whether for a son or for a daughter, she shall bring to the priest at the entrance of the tent of meeting a lamb in its first year for a burnt offering, and a pigeon or a turtledove for a sin offering. ⁷He shall offer it before the Lord, and make atonement on her behalf; then she shall be clean from her flow of blood. This is the law for her who bears a child, male or female. ⁸If she cannot afford a sheep, she shall take two turtledoves or two pigeons, one for a burnt offering and the other for a sin offering; and the priest shall make atonement on her behalf, and she shall be clean.

The *hiphil* of the verb זרע appears only here and in Genesis 1:11, which describes seed-bearing grass and fruit-bearing trees. In narrative texts we usually find הרה ("conceive") and ילד ("bear").[11] So why does the text employ תזריע instead of the more common הרה? Baruch Levine argues that תזריע means "when she is inseminated."[12] Levine's translation suggests that the woman is the passive recipient and that someone is doing something to her. If this were the case, the verb would be in a passive construction, but it is not. The verb is a *hiphil*, which indicates that she is the subject. It is worth noting that there is no male actor here who impregnates her. She is the sole subject! Dorothea Erbele-Küster notes that whatever the text really means, it does not refer to the role of the male in insemination.[13]

Milgrom suggests that since "seed" in Genesis 1:11 refers to fully developed fruit, תזריע here may indicate "produces offspring" or "comes

11. E.g., Gen 4:1; 16:11; 21:2; 29:32; 30:5; Exod 2:2; Num 11:12; Judg 13:3; 1 Sam 2:20; 2 Kgs 4:17; Isa 7:14; Hos 1:3.

12. Baruch Levine, *Leviticus: A JPS Torah Commentary* (Philadelphia: Jewish Publication Society of America, 1989), 72.

13. Dorothea Erbele-Küster, *Körper und Geschlecht: Studien zur Anthropologie von Leviticus 12 und 15*, WMAT 121 (Neukirchen-Vluyn: Neukirchener Verlag, 2008), 27.

to term."[14] The Samaritan addresses the problem by reading the verb as a *niphal*, which would translate as "is impregnated." Rashi argues that the verse means that even if the male is a stillborn, it renders the woman impure. Without knowing exactly what the biblical writers understood about conception and pregnancy, it is difficult to answer the question.[15]

Chapter 12 instructs that, immediately after childbirth, a woman is in a state of ritual impurity akin to that of menstruation. The terminology used to describe the woman's menstrual impurity in verse 2 is נדת דותה ("menstruation"). The root דוה refers to menstruation itself; it appears in Leviticus 15:33 and 20:18 in addition to our present text. The term נדה refers to a subcategory of טמאה, the impurity specifically created by menstrual blood. (See "Translation Matters" on page 143 for more on these two terms).

---

### The Churching of Women

Leviticus 12:1-8 was used as a basis for the Christian practice of excluding women who had just given birth from the eucharistic assembly throughout Christian history, but with some ambivalence regarding the validity of the Levitical practice for Christian women.

Origen (*Homilia* 8, early third century) poses the question of why a woman who provides a service for the world in giving birth to a child should be considered unclean and must make propitiatory sacrifice to God for her purification. He declares that all birth in the flesh results in impurity.

An interesting crossover took place in this argument. In Hebrew thought the need to maintain cultic purity resulted in laws, which enforced a temporary isolation of the new mother from the community, while sexual intercourse as such remained a holy act. Greek philosophical dualism and Christian ascetic tendencies, on the other hand, supported the fundamental baseness and defilement of human flesh in contrast to the spirit, particularly in the act of generation.

---

14. Jacob Milgrom, *Leviticus 1–16*, AB 3 (New York: Doubleday, 1991), 743.

15. There is some debate as to the purity status of the newborn. Leviticus 12 is silent on the matter, which leads many commentators to assume that the newborn does not share the mother's impurity status. This interpretation is supported by 4Q266 6.ii.10-11, which forbids a new mother to nurse her child and instead requires the use of a wet nurse to prevent impurity contagion. Luke 2:22 suggests that both the mother and child are impure.

The *Canons of Hippolytus* (mid-fourth-century Egypt; esp. Canon 18) include the attending midwife in the purity prescriptions:

> The midwives are not to partake of the mysteries, until they have been purified. Their purification shall be thus: if the child they delivered is male, twenty days; if it is female, forty days. . . . The woman who has given birth stays outside the holy place forty days if the child which she has borne is a male, and if it is female, eighty days. If she enters the church, she is to pray with the catechumens. The midwives are to be numerous so that they may not be outside all their life.

Almost all of the medieval penitential books stipulate that both a new mother and a menstruant are cultically unclean and may not enter a church or receive communion. To do so would incur a penance of forty days.

The twelfth-century Ritual of Wessobrunn cites Leviticus as the rationale for the rite and prays that the new mother be freed "from every stain of sin and every impurity of heart and body." This text is unusual in referring to Leviticus; usually the reference was to the purification of Mary in the temple, Luke 2:22-39.

The Roman Ritual of 1614 used source material, which eliminated overt reference to the motif of purification and penance as the rationale for the rite. The rite's verbal content emphasizes the mother's thankfulness for her survival and health. This rite would be used through the mid-twentieth century. Survey evidence of women in Europe who underwent the rite in the 1940s and 1950s before it fell out of use indicates that, although the rite remained in Latin, these women perceived that in fact the purpose of the rite was to "purify" them of the sin of concupiscence and childbearing. For that reason many decided on their own not to ask for the rite. Today a vestige of the rite remains in the Roman Catholic Rite of Baptism, in the priest's blessing on the new mother.

*Susan K. Roll*

For specific information about the nature of the first stage of impurity for the parturient, we must look to chapter 15 (see discussion below). Presumably, these laws regulate the conduct of a new mother as well. Leviticus 12:3 likely is a parenthetical insertion that mandates that the boy be circumcised on the eighth day. The wording of this verse acknowledges the eighth-day ritual but states it as a side note within the context of a discussion of the parturient and her responsibilities vis-à-vis the cult. The laws are addressed to the woman, and she bears the sole responsibility for keeping them.

The second stage of the woman's waiting period (i.e., thirty-three days after the birth of a son, sixty-six days after the birth of a daughter) has no parallel in the Bible. Leviticus 12:4-5 indicates that during this period, the woman cannot touch anything consecrated or enter the sanctuary. This prohibition implies that at any other time women did enter the sanctuary and did come in contact with consecrated foods. Many readers of Leviticus assume that the text supposes a cult system in which only men participate, but apart from the male priesthood, there is no difference between men and women as regards access to the sanctuary. It is only during the Second Temple period that the court of women was built to differentiate between male and female levels of access; no such court is mentioned in any of the biblical sources.[16]

## Menstrual Blood as a Purifying Agent

Procreation is arguably the most important role that the Bible assigns to women, and systems of women's reproductive cycles are also the sources of the longest periods of ritual impurity. Many modern commentators contend that postpartum ritual impurities are pervasive in ancient and modern cultures. Milgrom offers examples of childbirth impurities from a variety of cultures, and he concludes that the origin of childbirth impurity "cannot be traced to a creed or a ritual but must reside in some universal human condition that has evoked the same response all over the globe. In a word, we have to do with the human psyche."[17] Milgrom, like many other commentators, argues for the universality of menstrual and postpartum taboos as an apologetic response to a law that renders childbirth as impure.

The universality of taboos, however, has come into question. Thomas Buckley and Alma Gottlieb write in the introduction to their book *Blood Magic*:

> "The menstrual taboo" as such does not exist. Rather, what is found in close cross-cultural study is a wide range of distinct rules for conduct regarding menstruation that bespeak quite different, even opposite, purposes and meanings. Many menstrual taboos, rather than protecting

16. See Josephus, *Wars*, 5:198-99 and m. Mid 2:5-6 for descriptions of the Second Temple women's court.

17. Milgrom, *Leviticus 1–16*, 765.

society from a universally ascribed feminine evil, explicitly protect the
perceived creative spirituality of menstruous women from the influence of others in a more neutral space. . . . In other cultures menstrual
customs, rather than subordinating women to men fearful of them,
provide women with means of ensuring their own autonomy, influence
and social control. "The menstrual taboo," in short, is at once nearly
universal and has meanings that are ambiguous and multivalent.[18]

While childbirth restricts a woman's access to the sanctuary and to consecrated foods, Leviticus 12 says nothing about postpartum blood as taboo
or dangerous.[19] Perhaps Milgrom's apologetic is not even necessary.

The key to better comprehending Leviticus 12 may be found in the
phrase דמי טהרה, which is most intriguing. The name for this waiting
period after childbirth is called ימי טהרה ("days of purification" in v. 4) in
which the parturient is to remain in her דמי טהרה ("blood of purification"
in v. 5). The terms ימי טהרה and דמי טהרה appear nowhere else. Baruch
Schwartz is representative of most commentators when he writes that
"in a stage of blood purification, lit. 'In the blood of become pure,' that is,
she will continue to observe some discharge, and thus remain impure to
a lesser degree, before becoming fully purified."[20] The prohibition against
entering the sanctuary, coupled with our knowledge of lochia, makes
this reading of a lesser stage of impurity reasonable. Still, the explanation
fails to elucidate our understanding of this unusual terminology. Three
different translations of Leviticus 12:4a—"Her time of blood purification" (NRSV), "Then she will remain thirty-three days in blood purity"
(NET), and "She shall remain in a state of blood purification" (NJPS)—all
suggest the idea that a woman gradually moves from impurity to purity
as her blood discharge decreases. Erbele-Kürster suggests that Leviticus
12:4 refers to a conversion rite.[21] Thus purification, that is "blood purification," is intended as an act or process that moves one from impure to

18. Thomas Buckley and Alma Gottlieb, "A Critical Appraisal of Theories of Menstrual Symbolism," in *Blood Magic: The Anthropology of Menstruation* (Berkeley: University of California Press, 1988), 7.

19. Richard Whitekettle suggests that Levitical thought conceived of the womb
via a womb/well-spring homology (based, in part, on the Hebrew term מקור, which
is found in Lev 12:6-7 and in Lev 20:18). Menstruation and postpartum blood and
discharge were understood as the overflowing of the well-spring, which made the
womb/well-spring uninhabitable ("Levitical Thought and the Female Reproductive
Cycle: Wombs, Wellsprings, and the Primeval World," *VT* 46 [1996]: 376–91).

20. Baruch J. Schwartz, "Leviticus," in *The Jewish Study Bible*, ed. Adele Berlin and
Marc Zvi Brettler (Oxford: Oxford University Press, 2004), 222.

21. Erbele-Küster, *Körper und Geschlecht*, 32.

pure. If, however, we translate טהרה as "purity" (a condition) rather than "purification" (a process), then the woman is in a state of blood purity or, more literally, "blood of purity." The fact that the phrase for "blood purity" appears nowhere else in the Bible, not even to describe the blood used to purify the altar, is remarkable.

The discharge that women experience after childbirth generally goes through three stages: lochia rubra, lochia serosa, and lochia alba. The discharge gradually shifts from a deep red to brown to yellow and ultimately to white. It may have been that the appearance of blood that seems to clear itself from red blood to a white or clear discharge may have led to the term blood of purity—blood that transforms itself to another substance. No other blood changes its apparent composition.

Ulrike Steinert analyzes ancient Mesopotamian gynecological texts, and she cites several texts that address postpartum complications in which there is blockage of the flow of blood. One text reads: "You administer (it) to a woman who gives birth and subsequently her blood does not stop." Another text reads: "If a woman has given birth and subsequently she has intestinal fevers, vomits . . . the blood of that woman in childbed, which has been blocked/detained in her womb."[22] Reference to the "blood of purity" in Leviticus 12 may reflect the importance of postpartum discharges. Steinert also points to the work of Edward Shorter, who identifies the pervasiveness of peritonitis, which can develop within a few days after delivery due to a spreading postpartum bacterial infection at the site of the uterus, which articulates itself in a hard swollen belly, pain in "the lower part of the abdomen and stopping of the lochia. . . . In the past, the lifetime risk for women to get puerperal infection was high (estimated 25% risk), and few women passed through their childbearing without ever getting a puerperal infection."[23] Thus, the blockage of the discharge was a sign of illness and possible death, while the regular flow of blood, then lochia, was a sign of health and of life renewed.

Leviticus 12 does not require a woman to engage in ritual bathing prior to bringing her offering to the sanctuary. Her purification takes place internally as her lochia flows out of her body—she is engaged in a process of blood purity; her own bodily functions transform her internally from ritual impurity to ritual purity. Ritual bathing would be redundant.

---

22. Ulrike Steinert, "Fluids, Rivers and Vessels: Metaphors and Body Concepts in Mesopotamian Gynecological Texts," *Journal des Médecines Cunéiformes* 22 (2013): 5–6.

23. Ibid., 8 n. 18, cites Edward Shorter's *Women's Bodies: A Social History of Women's Encounter with Health, Ill-Health and Medicine* (New Brunswick: Transaction Publishers, 1997).

### The Rhetorical Reception of Childbirth Image of John 16:21 and Leviticus 12 and 15

Any inquiry into the influence of Leviticus 12 and 15 on the rhetorical reception of the childbirth image of John 16:21 in the late first century is tentative because the extent to which the *tame'* and *tahor* codes describe women's actual experience in religion of Israel, later rabbinic Judaism and Christianity, is unknown. Because these codes are found in sacred texts, however, they are prescriptive and shape later interpretation and practice. The woman-in-childbirth image invites a reading against the grain of the text. How might the text be heard and appropriated by women?

In Johannine interpretation, it is accepted that images function at two levels. First, they apply to Jesus and then to the disciples. The exception is the parable of the image of the woman in childbirth (16:21), which is interpreted as a waiting image for the disciples. I have argued extensively that this is an image for the death-resurrection of Jesus. Why has this level been obscured or ignored in the history of interpretation? How may late first-century people have heard this image? What influence was exerted by the holiness codes of Leviticus 12 and 15? Could a woman's body in childbirth serve as an image for the death-resurrection of Jesus?

Male creativity is enshrined predominately in the biblical traditions. At the divine level, the role of God as birth giver is presented as masculine and bloodless (Gen 2:7) or depicted in poetic metaphor (Deut 32:18). In the human beginnings myth, a presumably male character, *'adam*, gives birth to woman in the first human "birth"—a bloodless and painless event. Eve and her daughters cannot reproduce the original birth. Absent are the blood and birth pain so integral to women's experience of childbirth. All they are capable of is a messy, painful, and inexact imitation. Flowing blood and childbirth subjected women to the stipulations of pure and impure codes that function to protect male holiness and purity.

Birth, however, is an undeniably female activity, "a physically innovative act" in a Christian philosophy that privileges mind over body, idea over matter, "the word over the bloody, shitty mortal flesh."[24] Susan Stanford Friedman highlights how "women and men have encoded different concepts of creativity and procreativity" into the birth metaphor itself and that this "subversive inscription of women's (pro)creativity has

---

24. Sara Ruddick, *Maternal Thinking: Towards a Politics of Peace* (London: Women's Press, 1990), 48.

existed for centuries."[25]
    An example of "subversive inscription" and reading against the grain is found in a tension within the image of John 16:21. Its metaphorical power is inscribed in a parable. Theological layers mask the birth, for the word used for pain (*lupe*) is not pain of childbirth but that of the mental anguish and hardship experienced in the struggle for the necessities of life shared by both woman and man (LXX Gen 3:16-17).

*Kathleen Rushton*

## Boys 40, Girls 80

There are a number of explanations for the time differences in impurity when birthing male versus female infants. A fairly common explanation is that a female infant carries some of her mother's hormones and may have some vaginal spotting that would render the baby girl impure. Therefore, the eighty-day period serves to cover both the mother's and the daughter's impurities.[26] Levine suggests that simply the anxiety about a baby girl's potential for fertility extends the time.[27] David J. Macht, following the thinking of medieval commentators, suggests that women have different toxicity levels in their blood after the birth of male and female children. He concludes that the Jewish sages knew that there was a physiological difference.[28] Some of the earlier critical works suggest that women were more prone to attacks by demons; therefore, the birth of a girl attracted the demons more acutely and therefore it was more dangerous.[29]

Tarja Philip builds on Milgrom's note of seemingly parallel Hittite texts in which women are impure for a longer period when birthing females than when birthing males.[30] Based on Gary Beckman's collection and translation of Hittite birth-related texts, Philip notes that in both Hittite

---

25. Susan Stanford Friedman, "Creativity and the Childbirth Metaphor: Gender Difference in Literary Discourse," *Feminist Studies* 13 (1987): 50–51.

26. Jonathan Magonet, " 'But If It Is a Girl She Is Unclean for Twice Seven Days . . .': The Riddle of Leviticus 12.5," in *Reading Leviticus: A Conversation with Mary Douglas*, ed. John F. A. Sawyer, LHB/OTS 277 (Sheffield: Sheffield Academic, 1996), 144–52.

27. Levine, *Leviticus*, 250.

28. David I. Macht, "A Scientific Appreciation of Leviticus 12:1-5," *JBL* 52 (1933): 253–60.

29. Karl Elliger, *Leviticus*, HAT 1/4 (Tübingen: C. B. Mohr [Siebeck], 1966), 168.

30. Tarja S. Philip, *Menstruation and Childbirth in the Bible: Fertility and Impurity*, StBibLit 88 (New York: Lang, 2006), 118.

birth rituals and biblical priestly legislation, birth causes impurity; there are several stages of purification, and the period of impurity is longer for birthing females. Philip also notes that the Hittite birth rituals contain favorable pronouncements for the birth of both boys and girls. Finally, Philip points to the fact that the Hittite birth rituals do not generally mention blood, while the priestly legislation is entirely focused on blood.[31]

David Tabb Stewart argues that דמי טהרה has nothing to do with pollution. The boy's circumcision cleanses the son, while the girl is bonded to the mother in a consecutive forty-day separation from the tabernacle public space.[32] Elizabeth W. Goldstein writes: "Ultimately Leviticus 12 states the obvious, that female bodies have a higher potential for *tumah* than do the bodies of men. . . . Female reproductive blood has a higher polluting factor than male reproductive fluid."[33]

Philip believes that the insertion of circumcision "evokes the role of the father in the process of generation." She reads circumcision here against the backdrop of Genesis 17, concluding that "only in Leviticus 12 is circumcision mentioned in the context of impurity, but not the impurity of semen, rather of the parturient's bleeding, thus contrasting in this context impure female blood and fertile male seed."[34]

The rabbis also found the difference between the birth of boys and girls odd. B. Niddah 31b captures some of their confusion:

> R. Simeon b. Yohai was asked by his disciples: Why did the Torah ordain that a woman after childbirth should bring a sacrifice? He replied: When she kneels in bearing she swears impetuously that she will have no intercourse with her husband. The Torah, therefore, ordained that she should bring a sacrifice. (R. Joseph demurred: Does she not act presumptuously in which case the absolution of the oath depends on her regretting it? Furthermore, she should have brought a sacrifice prescribed for an oath!) And why did the Torah ordain that in the case of a male [the woman is clean] after seven days and in that of a female after fourteen days? [On the birth of a] male with whom all rejoice she

---

31. Ibid., 118–19.

32. David Tabb Stewart, "Parturient's Ritual for a Girl: The Puzzle of Double Pollution," in *Hermeneutics, Gender and Biblical Law*, ed. Athalya Brenner and F. Rachel Magdalene (Sheffield: Sheffield Phoenix, forthcoming), 65–73.

33. Elizabeth W. Goldstein, *Impurity and Gender in the Hebrew Bible* (Lanham, MD: Rowman & Littlefield, 2015), 38.

34. Tarja Philip, "Gender Matters: Priestly Writing on Impurity," in *Embroidered Garments: Priests and Gender in Biblical Israel*, ed. Deborah W. Rooke (Sheffield: Sheffield Phoenix, 2009), 47–48.

regrets her oath after seven days, [but on the birth of a female] about whom everybody is upset she regrets her oath after fourteen days.

The rabbis sought to explain the difference with an anachronistic projection. The claim that she regrets her oath sooner for a boy ignores the objection by R. Joseph that the sacrifice prescribed is not for overturning an oath!

Many modern Christian commentaries connect Leviticus 12 to Genesis 2–3. For example, John E. Hartley presents a theological explanation for the woman's impurity. "In giving birth the woman challenges the penalty of death on mankind for sinning against God in the Garden of Eden (Gen 2:16-17), for each birth insures the continuation of the race. Symbolically each birth strikes a blow on the head of the paradisiacal serpent, the champion of death (Gen 3:15)."[35] Unfortunately, this kind of theological commentary deflects our attention from the fascinating questions that emerge from within Leviticus 12 and redirects our attention to negative portrayals of women and procreation.

### Ambiguity of Blood: On Threshold of Life and Death

The parable of the woman in childbirth in John 16:21 taps into the symbolism of John's gospel significantly because birth evokes the archetypical symbols of blood and water, which are Johannine symbols. Scholarship has not alluded to the possibility that in the polyvalence of this gospel's symbolism, blood and water, as the archetypical symbols for life, could evoke the female arena of birth. My understanding is that the image of birth as evoked by John 16:21 was employed to make theological meaning of the death-glory of Jesus throughout a strand of the gospel (see John 1:12-13; 3:3-8; 7:37-38; 16:21-22; 19:25-27, 30, 34).

The language and imagery of human generation, which is used to express the relationship between God and human, contains the potential for ambiguity. Those who believe are given power to "become children of God . . . born . . . of God" (1:12). This potential relationship is conveyed by the verb γεννάω. For the reader, ambiguity is evoked because this may be predicated to a woman or a man to describe generativity from the female or male

---

35. John E. Hartley, *Leviticus*, WBC 4 (Waco, TX: Word Books, 1992), 169.

principle. Female participation in human generation is found overtly in the first negation of John 1:13 when the reader allows the understanding of contemporaneous Greek physiology to inform the meaning of the phrase οὐκ ἐξ αἱμάτων, literally meaning "not of bloods." This phrase refers possibly to the drops of blood required for the human embryo formed from the seed of the father and the blood of the mother.

Biblical symbolism constantly disrupts perception. The symbolism of blood is deep within the texts and tradition of Christianity and has the potential to be deeply subversive. In the prescription of male-written and male-centered texts that are not necessarily descriptive of woman's experience, woman's role as birth-giver exudes power and mystery. Male perceptions of woman as the source of life and death in her capacity to give birth, as well as the cyclical menstruation in which she bleeds without dying are found cross-culturally. Like her voice, woman's blood stirs ambivalence.[36] Flowing female blood and the female birth-giver are perceived to defile. In contrast, the flowing blood of the male Jesus saves.

The image of John 16:21, which spans cultural and religious ambiguities and prescriptions, has the potential to cross those boundaries not only in its world of origin but in the many layers of the Christian tradition. It has the potential to redefine Jesus' and God's activity, asserting that the female person in her body may, does, and must image God. Any feminist reading must be underpinned by a theory of parables that regards the activity of the woman in the parable as participative action in the sphere of God's action. By aligning Jesus with God, by implication birth, a uniquely female activity, is associated with the divine in the patriarchal and androcentric Johannine universe. That activity, in the case of the parable of John 16:21, is childbirth in which a woman hovers on the threshold of life and death. Childbirth, an undeniable activity of "symbolic, emotional and ultimately political significance"[37] evoking female presence and power, as in this parable, may make theological meaning of the death-resurrection of Jesus.

*Kathleen Rushton*

36. Roslyn Lacks, *Woman and Judaism: Myth, History, and Struggle* (Garden City, NY: Doubleday, 1980), 150–51.

37. Ruddick, *Maternal Thinking*, 48.

### Psalm 24 in the Churching of Women

The rite of the "churching of women after childbirth" in the Roman Ritual used from 1614 until 1964, introduced the use of Psalm 24 to shift the theme from purification from evil and contamination to a theme of joyous entry into the church. The woman would wait at the church door holding a lighted candle in her hand while the priest sprinkled her with holy water and recited Psalm 24. Then the priest would extend the left end of his stole for the woman to hold and lead her into the church with these words, "Enter the temple of God, adore the Son of the Blessed Virgin Mary, Who has given thee fruitfulness of offspring."

The use of Psalm 24 can be interpreted several ways: those who emphasize the abolition of the purification motif cite the use of this psalm elsewhere as a psalm of joyful entrance, as if welcoming a king or a conqueror, and in fact some evidence for this analogy can be found in African texts concerning a new mother emerging from her home. Verses 3-5—"Who shall ascend the hill of the Lord? And who shall stand in his holy place? Those who have clean hands and pure hearts, who do not lift up their souls to what is false, and do not swear deceitfully"—point, however, to a motif of renunciation of evil and of purification as prerequisites for "standing in the holy place."

Right up to the mid-twentieth century, to the extent that the rites were in Latin, the woman was unlikely to comprehend what was being said or why. The choice of one psalm or another, or the content of the blessing text, would have said nothing at all to the mother.

The few women still alive who remember the rite are likely to report discomfort, confusion, a feeling that they were being insulted, and, more important, a sense that the act of giving birth was regarded by their church as shameful. A woman might report she was churched after the first baby and then refused to do it again. Women themselves made the connection between the churching rite and purification and often reacted strongly: "It was as if I had committed murder!"

The shape of the rite itself communicated clearly to the women the ambivalence, at best, and the fear and repulsion, at worst, of churchmen toward women's sexuality and childbearing. In effect, the rite represented a reverse symbolic birth: the woman is brought into church as if on a leash, a symbolic umbilical cord in an act of (re-)birth by the priest into her rightful place as a baptized Christian within the church. The use of Psalm 24, if the woman understood the text, would say nothing about childbirth but makes a passing reference to clean hands and pure heart as a prerequisite to entering the sanctuary, which women could not do in any case except as sacristans. In the end, women themselves boycotted the rite by individual choice, and thus in the mid-twentieth century the rite fell into disuse.

*Susan K. Roll*

## Introduction to Pus, Sores, Rashes, and Scabs

Many readers of the Bible quickly skim over Leviticus 13–14, with its detailed description of dermatologic disorders. Most of us prefer narratives, poetry, and lofty commandments when we engage with the Bible. But then we come across details regarding skin sores, pus, discoloration, rashes, and burns. The text continues on and on with painstaking detail, asking us to read material that we would not otherwise encounter. So why is this material in the Bible? In order to understand Leviticus 13–14, we must first dispel a number of myths and misunderstandings about these two chapters.

### Skin Ailments, not Leprosy

The LXX translation for צרעת is *lepra*, which was a general term in Greek for a wide variety of skin ailments. Thus, the LXX translators understood the skin ailments in Leviticus 13 to include a variety of ailments. According to E. V. Hulse, it was not until medieval times that *lepra* was associated with the disease that would come to be known as Hansen's disease.[38] The trajectory from צרעת as "skin afflictions" (my translation), to Greek *lepra* (also indicating "skin afflictions"), to *lepra* as "leprosy" (the medieval connotation, which is now associated with Hansen's disease) has led to a complete distortion of the early meanings of Leviticus 13–14. This unfortunate association has meant that, for centuries, when readers encountered Leviticus 13–14 they would conjure up frightening images of mutilated bodies. In Hansen's disease particular bacteria target the skin, nasal membranes, and lymph nodes. As the bacteria attack nerve fibers, parts of the victim's body are gradually mutilated. These symptoms

---

38. E. V. Hulse, "The Nature of Biblical 'Leprosy' and the Use of Alternative Medical Terms in Modern Translations of the Bible," *PEQ* 107 (1975): 88–89. See also more recently Samson O. Olanisebe, "Laws of *Tzara'at* in Leviticus 13–14 and Medical Leprosy Compared," *JBQ* 42 (2014): 121–27.

are completely absent in the biblical text. There was no natural reason to equate צרעת with leprosy, since the conditions described in Leviticus 13–14 are radically different from leprosy. Unfortunately, once these chapters were translated and interpreted as pertaining to "leprosy," discourse about them was dominated by that lens instead of understanding צרעת more appropriately as "skin conditions."

## Skin Ailments, not Sin

Biblical narratives and postbiblical interpretation associate the skin conditions described in Leviticus 13 with (or as) punishments by God for grave sins. Indeed, there are non-P texts that describe צרעת as a punishment from God.[39] Traditional Jewish thinkers have understood צרעת in a variety of ways. The Talmud lists seven reasons one might be afflicted with the disease, including murder, perjury, forbidden sexual relationships, arrogance, theft, and envy (b. Ar 16a). Many Jewish textual traditions associate this text with Numbers 12, where Miriam is afflicted with צרעת and is sent out of the camp until she is healed. The association of these two texts gave rise to midrashic interpretations connecting this ailment to gossip and to women's behavior. Part of this interpretive tradition connects the word מצרע (*metzora'*), a person afflicted with the condition, to מוציא שם רע, a person guilty of slander or libel, via associative wordplay, which is central to Midrash.

While not the first to make a counterclaim, Joel S. Baden and Candida R. Moss set out a compelling series of arguments to prove that in the priestly material צרעת is not at all connected with sin. "Of all the eccentricities and diversities of human embodment, no physical abnormality seems to have captured the imagination of biblical authors so much as צרעת ('skin disease') which is accorded detailed treatment in both Priestly legislation and non-Priestly narratives."[40] They argue that the association of צרעת with sin arises by reading non-P צרעת texts and carrying over their assumptions and claims. Baden and Moss point out that Leviticus 13–14 are devoid of words for sin or the language of נסלח לו ("he is forgiven").

> In relation to the priestly regulations concerning sin in Leviticus 4–5, the section on צרעת in Leviticus 13–14 lacks any introductory statement identifying the specific sin committed, as in Lev 5:1-4, 20-22, or even a statement noting that there has been any sin at all, such as we find in

---

39. See, e.g., 2 Kgs 5; Num 12:10; 2 Chr 26:16-21.
40. Joel S. Baden and Candida R. Moss, "The Origin and Interpretation of Sara'at in Leviticus 13–14," *JBL* 130 (2011): 643.

4:2, 13, 22, 27; 5:15, 17. There is no moment at which the sufferer realizes his sin, as in the cases of 4:13-14, 22-23, 27-28; 5:17, 23, or confesses
his guilt, as in the case of 5:5. Most notably, even after the offering of
sacrifices, the מצרע is not said to be forgiven (נסלח לו), as in 4:20, 26, 31,
35; 5:10, 13, 16, 18, 26; rather, precisely in the place where we find the
statement of forgiveness in Leviticus 4–5, we find in 14:20b the proclamation "he is clean" (וטהר).[41]

Additionally, fabrics and homes can acquire the same growths and
certainly these things are not capable of sinning. Samuel E. Balentine
writes: "The lack of sin language in Leviticus 13–14 may be more than a
curious omission. It is plausible to suggest that the priests were aware of
the popular connection between affliction and sin and sought to reframe
the issue in a ritual context that permitted a different assessment."[42]
Hartley, for whom צרעת is not "leprosy" but rather a variety of skin ailments including psoriasis, eczema, and fungal infections, describes the
condition that causes impurity to be loathsome and repulsive, even as he
notes that the text never associates the condition with sin in Leviticus.[43]
צרעת has wrongly been associated with sin for hundreds of years.

### Rashes, Scabs, Boils, and Burns (13:1-28)

The first 28 verses of Leviticus 13 address four categories of skin conditions: eruptions of the skin, such as swellings and scabs (vv. 1-8), raw flesh
and skin whiteness (vv. 9-17), boils (vv. 18-23), and burns (vv. 24-28). The
instruction begins by stating that someone with a potential skin condition is brought to Aaron or one of his sons (v. 2). Wilda C. Gafney writes:

> The text is clear that women and men experience the same disease,
> diagnostic rituals, and treatment program. However, it strikes me as
> unreasonable that, given Israel's modesty codes, men would examine
> women's bodies for any reason, including disease or contagion. It is
> possible to read *kohen* as "person from the priest-clan," which would
> include women.[44]

Gafney posits that the terminology usually translated as "or to one of his
sons, the priests," can also be read more broadly. She suggests:

41. Ibid., 646–47.
42. Samuel E. Balentine, *Leviticus* (Louisville: Westminster John Knox, 2002), 105.
43. Hartley, *Leviticus*, 200.
44. Wilda C. Gafney, *Womanist Midrash: A Reintroduction to the Women of the Torah
and the Throne* (Louisville: Westminster John Knox, 2017), 114.

Lev 13:1-28

13:1The LORD spoke to Moses and Aaron, saying:

2When a person has on the skin of his body a swelling or an eruption or a spot, and it turns into a leprous disease on the skin of his body, he shall be brought to Aaron the priest or to one of his sons the priests. 3The priest shall examine the disease on the skin of his body, and if the hair in the diseased area has turned white and the disease appears to be deeper than the skin of his body, it is a leprous disease; after the priest has examined him he shall pronounce him ceremonially unclean. 4But if the spot is white in the skin of his body, and appears no deeper than the skin, and the hair in it has not turned white, the priest shall confine the diseased person for seven days. 5The priest shall examine him on the seventh day, and if he sees that the disease is checked and the disease has not spread in the skin, then the priest shall confine him seven days more. 6The priest shall examine him again

Israel does not have a female priesthood, even though women do serve in other capacities, including at the wilderness sanctuary and temple. However, *banayv* (plural possessive), means more than "his sons"; it can mean "his children," "his descendants," or even "his disciples/ apprentices." I believe it likely that the daughter of a priest, a *bat kohen*, examined the suspicious areas on women's bodies and consulted with her father, brother, or husband, perhaps concealed behind a curtain, who made the final determination.[45]

The first case (vv. 2-8) is typical of most of the other cases. If a person has a swelling or a scab on the skin, the priest looks at the skin; if the hair on the swelling is white or if the swelling runs below the surface of the skin, the priest confirms that it is נגע צרעת ("leprous disease," NRSV; better, "skin disease"), and the priest declares the person impure (v. 3). If the priest cannot determine the status of the individual, the person is quarantined for seven days and then reexamined; if the situation is still unclear, there is one more round of quarantine before reexamination (vv. 4-5). If there is no spread of symptoms and the condition is clearing up, the priest declares him pure, noting that it is just a scab, and the person's clothing is to be laundered (v. 6). If the scab or swelling spreads, then the priest declares him impure (vv. 7-8).

45. Ibid.

on the seventh day, and if the disease has abated and the disease has not spread in the skin, the priest shall pronounce him clean; it is only an eruption; and he shall wash his clothes, and be clean. ⁷But if the eruption spreads in the skin after he has shown himself to the priest for his cleansing, he shall appear again before the priest. ⁸The priest shall make an examination, and if the eruption has spread in the skin, the priest shall pronounce him unclean; it is a leprous disease.

⁹When a person contracts a leprous disease, he shall be brought to the priest. ¹⁰The priest shall make an examination, and if there is a white swelling in the skin that has turned the hair white, and there is quick raw flesh in the swelling, ¹¹it is a chronic leprous disease in the skin of his body. The priest shall pronounce him unclean; he shall not confine him, for he is unclean. ¹²But if the disease breaks out in the skin, so that it covers all the skin of the diseased person from head to foot, so far as the priest can see, ¹³then the priest shall make an examination, and if the disease has covered all his body, he shall pronounce him clean of the disease; since it has all turned white, he is clean. ¹⁴But if raw flesh ever appears on him, he shall be unclean; ¹⁵the priest shall examine the raw flesh and pronounce him unclean. Raw flesh is unclean, for it is a leprous disease. ¹⁶But if the raw flesh again turns white, he shall come to the priest; ¹⁷the priest shall examine him, and if the disease has turned white, the priest shall pronounce the diseased person clean. He is clean.

In the next case (vv. 9-17), if a person has a mark of צרעת, that person is brought to a priest and if there is swelling with white discoloration, with some white hair and with some raw flesh in the swelling, it is צרעת נושנת ("a chronic leprous disease" in v. 11). The priest declares the person impure. The text makes a point of saying that this person is not to be quarantined because he has already been declared impure. This seems to conflict with Leviticus 13:46, which requires an impure person to remain outside the camp for the duration of the impurity. In the first case, an individual who may have a skin ailment may be set apart for seven days because her status vis-à-vis her ritual purity is uncertain.

Verses 12-17 have puzzled interpreters. As verse 10 notes, the skin condition causes impurity if the skin turns white, the hair on the skin turns white, and there is raw flesh within it. Leviticus 13:12-17 addresses cases in which the same condition spreads throughout the entire body. When the condition spreads throughout the entire body, from head to toe, the priest declares the individual ritually pure because she is all

¹⁸When there is on the skin of one's body a boil that has healed, ¹⁹and in the place of the boil there appears a white swelling or a reddish-white spot, it shall be shown to the priest. ²⁰The priest shall make an examination, and if it appears deeper than the skin and its hair has turned white, the priest shall pronounce him unclean; this is a leprous disease, broken out in the boil. ²¹But if the priest examines it and the hair on it is not white, nor is it deeper than the skin but has abated, the priest shall confine him seven days. ²²If it spreads in the skin, the priest shall pronounce him unclean; it is diseased. ²³But if the spot remains in one place and does not spread, it is the scar of the boil; the priest shall pronounce him clean.

²⁴Or, when the body has a burn on the skin and the raw flesh of the burn becomes a spot, reddish-white or white, ²⁵the priest shall examine it. If the hair in the spot has turned white and it appears deeper than the skin, it is a leprous disease; it has broken out in the burn, and the priest shall pronounce him unclean. This is a leprous disease. ²⁶But if the priest examines it and the hair in the spot is not white, and it is no deeper than the skin but has abated, the priest shall confine him seven days. ²⁷The priest shall examine him the seventh day; if it is spreading in the skin, the priest shall pronounce him unclean. This is a leprous disease. ²⁸But if the spot remains in one place and does not spread in the skin but has abated, it is a swelling from the burn, and the priest shall pronounce him clean; for it is the scar of the burn.

white (vv. 12-13)! And then again, if raw skin appears at a later time, she is declared impure (vv. 14-15); yet, if raw skin turns white again, she is declared pure (vv. 16-17).

One question with which interpreters have contended is why the spread of white skin throughout the entire body would render someone ritually pure. Nobuyoshi Kiuchi argues that being all white does not represent healing, but it does represent cleanness (which may sometimes precede healing!). When a person is all white, there is no possibility of hiding a sin, so the person is clean (i.e., not hiding from God).⁴⁶ Kiuchi's argument is based on troubling assumptions about the symbolism of whiteness. Milgrom argues that complete whiteness is a sign that the condition has healed;⁴⁷ so too Schwartz: "The spreading of the scales to

46. Nobuyoshi Kiuchi, *Leviticus*, ApOTC 3 (Nottingham: Inter-Varsity Press, 2007), 232.

47. Milgrom, *Leviticus 1–16*, 785.

the entire body rather than deepening and causing erosion in specific spots indicates that healing is under way and the person is pronounced pure."[48] Hartley argues that the person is clean because there are no open sores nor is there evidence of illness under the skin's surface.[49] Erhard S. Gerstenberger tentatively raises the possibility of social "consideration for the person already marked by death," or perhaps "a positive estimation regarding the rare instance when total infection appears."[50] Kiuchi similarly proposes that the complete whiteness is an indication that he is in fact approaching death.

A different interpretation is given by Hanna Liss,[51] who distinguishes between the "dynamic" state of צרעת, in which the skin is patchy and the disease spreading, and the "static" state described in Leviticus 13:12-13. She argues that in the static state, impurity does not transfer and that therefore the המצרע, the afflicted one ("leprous"), may be declared clean, since he represents no danger to the community or the sancta.

The next two cases, of boils (vv. 18-23) and burns (vv. 24-28), follow the same pattern as the prior discussion of skin conditions in Leviticus 13. The priest examines boils and burns to determine whether the conditions extend below the surface of the skin, whether there is discoloration, and whether the condition has spread. These indicators generally lead the priest to declare the person to be ritually impure.

## Scales and Spots around Hair (13:29-44)

The next case (Lev 13:29-37) addresses skin ailments on the head. The new key element in this case regards the color of the hair as an indicator of the condition. Yellow hair is a sign of impurity while black hair is a marker of ritual purity. Gafney writes:

> As an Afro-diasporic reader in a Euro-centric world that frequently embodies white-supremacist norms, I was delighted as a young reader to discover a text that demonstrated blond was not normative hair color for the people of Israel. Blond hair can be only a potential indicator for disease in a community in which blondness is uncommon or

48. Schwartz, "Leviticus," in *The Jewish Study Bible*, 224.

49. Hartley, *Leviticus*, 191.

50. Erhard S. Gerstenberger, *Leviticus*, OTL (Louisville: Westminster John Knox, 1996), 163.

51. Hanna Liss, "Ritual Purity and the Construction of Identity: The Literary Function of the Laws of Purity in the Book of Leviticus," in *The Books of Leviticus and Numbers*, ed. Thomas Romer, BETL 215 (Leuven: Peeters, 2008), 329–54.

[29]When a man or woman has a disease on the head or in the beard, [30]the priest shall examine the disease. If it appears deeper than the skin and the hair in it is yellow and thin, the priest shall pronounce him unclean; it is an itch, a leprous disease of the head or the beard. [31]If the priest examines the itching disease, and it appears no deeper than the skin and there is no black hair in it, the priest shall confine the person with the itching disease for seven days. [32]On the seventh day the priest shall examine the itch; if the itch has not spread, and there is no yellow hair in it, and the itch appears to be no deeper than the skin, [33]he shall shave, but the itch he shall not shave. The priest shall confine the person with the itch for seven days more. [34]On the seventh day the priest shall examine the itch; if the itch has not spread in the skin and it appears to be no deeper than the skin, the priest shall pronounce him clean. He shall wash his clothes and be clean. [35]But if the itch spreads in the skin after he was pronounced clean, [36]the priest shall examine him. If the

perhaps unnatural. This was long before I understood the implications of geography; Sinai, Canaan, and subsequently Israel form the land bridge between Africa and Asia; neither continent is known for indigenous blonds. In modernity, blonds signify a particular construction of whiteness as a category that excludes so-called people of color and leads to the intentional exclusion of black and brown girls from dominant-culture beauty standards, even though blond hair naturally occurs in persons of African descent. However, yellow hair bears a different significance in the text. According to Leviticus, the presence of yellow hair is a call for closer inspection to determine whether quarantine and other subsequent procedures are in order, to protect the community.[52]

Leviticus 13 addresses issues pertaining to both men and women, although verse 29 is the only verse that explicitly refers to "a man or woman." Hartley believes that both men and women are mentioned in 13:29 to ensure that readers know that, even in a condition in which facial hair is mentioned, both men and women are still being addressed.[53] (Hartley seems to be implying that readers may associate facial hair with men only.) As the case unfolds, the text defaults to third-person masculine singular, but the introduction in verse 29 makes it clear that the laws regarding skin ailments may apply equally among men and women.

52. Gafney, *Womanist Midrash*, 112–13.
53. Hartley, *Leviticus*, 192.

*Lev 13:29-44 (cont.)*

itch has spread in the skin, the priest need not seek for the yellow hair; he is unclean. ³⁷But if in his eyes the itch is checked, and black hair has grown in it, the itch is healed, he is clean; and the priest shall pronounce him clean.

³⁸When a man or a woman has spots on the skin of the body, white spots, ³⁹the priest shall make an examination, and if the spots on the skin of the body are of a dull white, it is a rash that has broken out on the skin; he is clean.

⁴⁰If anyone loses the hair from his head, he is bald but he is clean. ⁴¹If he loses the hair from his forehead and temples, he has baldness of the forehead but he is clean. ⁴²But if there is on the bald head or the bald forehead a reddish-white diseased spot, it is a leprous disease breaking out on his bald head or his bald forehead. ⁴³The priest shall examine him; if the diseased swelling is reddish-white on his bald head or on his bald forehead, which resembles a leprous disease in the skin of the body, ⁴⁴he is leprous, he is unclean. The priest shall pronounce him unclean; the disease is on his head.

One of the outstanding features of Leviticus 13–14 is the role of the priest. The priest's role is not medical—he does not provide a diagnosis or prognosis; he takes no action toward healing. Rather, the priest's job is to look and declare: "pure!" or "impure!" The declaration of "impure!" is conveyed in the *piel* conjugation. Remarkably, it is not the person's condition but rather the priest's pronouncement that renders him impure; until the priest declares him impure he is not impure! Thus, the priest's declaration in fact is what changes the person's status at that moment. Jonathan Sacks expounds: "Words are remarkable in another way as well. We can use language not just to describe or assert. We can use it to create new moral facts. The Oxford philosopher J. L. Austin called this special use of language 'performative utterance.'"⁵⁴

The culmination of this priestly role comes at the end of this unit (v. 44) where the root טמא is used three times in one verse: the person is described by the narrative voice as impure, the priest declares that the person is impure, and the force of the declaration is emphasized with an infinitive absolute of the same Hebrew root.

54. Jonathan Sacks, *Covenant and Conversation: A Weekly Reading of the Jewish Bible; Leviticus: The Book of Holiness* (Jerusalem: Koren Publishers, 2015), 204. Sacks refers to J. L. Austin's *How to Do Things with Words* (Cambridge, MA: Harvard University Press, 1962).

## "Impure, Impure!" (13:45-46)

Leviticus 13:45-46 may be read as the conclusion of the last case specifically, or more generally as the conclusion of all of the cases enumerated in Leviticus 13. Regardless, once the priest has pronounced an individual impure, the person tears his clothes, messes up his hair, covers the upper lip, and cries out, "Impure, impure!" The person is impure for the duration of the skin condition. She is to live alone outside of the camp. Kiuchi interprets, "The sense of the rule is that the leprous person, without his lips seen by others, must cry 'Unclean, unclean!' This gesture as a whole, then, conveys an ambivalent message: while he must indicate that he is unworthy to speak, he must also make it public that he is in the sphere of death."[55] Contrast this interpretation with that of Baruch Schwartz: "This is not in order to arrest the spread of the disease but rather to check the spread of the potent impurity that it is believed to produce, lest this have an irreversible effect on the sanctuary."[56] The question that lies behind the two interpretations is this: does the person with a skin ailment need to be separated from the community in order to prevent the spread of the disease or in order to prevent the spread of impurity? Since Leviticus does not discuss the dangers of any other diseases, it appears that for the priest, the primary concern is impurity contagion, not disease contagion.

### Misreading Leprosy and Social Control

The afterlife of Leviticus 13 has influenced not only the textual and theological spheres; the associations of skin afflictions with leprosy and with sin have been used to subjugate peoples. Ron Amundson and Akira Oakoakalani Ruddle-Miyamoto provide a study of a recent example of such subjugation: European colonialists have exploited the erroneous equation of צרעת with leprosy to denigrate native populations. In the following example, a somewhat benign disease is recast as "biblical leprosy," which then enables colonialists to quarantine and stigmatize natives of the land. In a study of the social history of Hawaiian forced exiles, Amundson and Ruddle-Miyamoto argue persuasively that prior to colonialism, Hawaiian natives with leprosy were not stigmatized and

---

55. Kiuchi, *Leviticus*, 237.
56. Baruch J. Schwartz, "Leviticus," in *The New Interpreter's Bible*, ed. Beverly Roberts Gaventa and David Petersen (Nashville: Abingdon, 2010), 68.

*Lev 13:45-46*

⁴⁵The person who has the leprous disease shall wear torn clothes and let the hair of his head be disheveled; and he shall cover his upper lip and cry out, "Unclean, unclean." ⁴⁶He shall remain unclean as long as he has the disease; he is unclean. He shall live alone; his dwelling shall be outside the camp.

lived with their families and communities.[57] The bodily disfigurements were understood as within the range of what bodies could look like. When Europeans colonized Hawaii, they used the language of leprosy, with its biblical connotations, to define the entirety of the indigenous people and to legitimize separating out non-European populations. Colonialists used leprosy to define race and to distinguish between indigenous peoples and European newcomers.[58] Amundson and Ruddle-Miyamoto describe the phenomenon powerfully:

> The stigmatized traits of the body—the loosened skin, softened nose bridge, blistered and misshapen hands and feet—explain why it was leprosy rather than tuberculosis, smallpox, syphilis, measles, or influenza that was chosen to be criminalized in Hawaii. The functional impairments that leprosy caused—the loss of vision and hearing, and functional impairments of the extremities—were well known, and surely contributed to the public fear. But the public discourse of the period indicates that the functional impairments were secondary to sheer "loathsomeness" as triggers of disgust. In today's world (roughly the post–World War II world) it is hard to comprehend the 19th and

57. Ron Amundson and Akira Ruddle-Miyamoto, "A Wholesome Horror: The Stigmas of Leprosy in 19th Century Hawaii," *Disability Studies Quarterly* 30 (2010): http://dx.doi.org/10.18061/dsq.v30i3/4.1270.

58. Douglas C. Baynton, "Disability and the Justification of Inequality in American History," in *New Disability History: American Perspectives*, ed. Paul K. Longmore and Lauri Umansky (New York: New York University Press, 2001), 33–57. This view is consistent with the work of Douglas Baynton, who has shown that "concepts of race and sex that were prevalent in the early 20th century presupposed that the stigmatized groups (women, ethnic or 'racial' minorities) were literally disabled, in the sense that they were functionally impaired when compared to white men." Bayton concludes that "the concept of race was conflated with certain kinds of disability; the concept of a nonwhite race as distinct from disability did not exist for most nineteenth century thinkers."

early 20th century attitudes towards aesthetic judgments of human ugliness or "loathsomeness." Social Darwinism combined with eugenics to give a certain privilege to the judgments of ugliness that one human group passed on another, especially when a member of a "higher" group judged a "lower." These judgments were regarded as legitimate and objectively valid. The ugliness that eugenic authors attributed to "lower" races reflected their status in the racial hierarchy.[59]

### Skin Afflictions and Human Bodies

Leviticus 13 actually undermines popular contemporary attitudes toward diseases and bodily differences. Instead of encouraging the common tendency to look away with disgust, thus feeding fears about illness and disease, Leviticus 13 pushes individuals to pay attention to bodies, not to avert the gaze, but rather to require the gaze. The task of the priest is to do just that—to look, to examine in great detail. (The root ראה indicating "to see" appears thirty-nine times in this chapter!) As Joel S. Baden and Candida R. Moss show, the texts do not attach any stigma to these conditions; to the contrary, they provide a calm, thoughtful, and systematic exploration of each condition in detail.[60]

In Leviticus 13, there is no focus on healing whatsoever. The priest does not offer a prognosis and does not offer medicinal treatments. Leviticus 13 focuses on the myriad ways that the exterior of a human body can present itself. Some of these manifestations release impurities that can affect God's holy objects and some of these manifestations have no impact on holiness. Because of the potent impurity that skin ailments create, the person is separated from the community to avoid impurity contagion. It is crucial to remember that P is concerned with purity/impurity issues. There were likely community healers who may have attended to the symptoms and may have offered comfort, but the priestly concern was specifically with impurity. The gospels tell stories about how Jesus miraculously heals lepers; in contrast to Leviticus 13, the focus in the gospels is on the miraculous power of the healer to do what others cannot.

59. Amundson and Ruddle-Miyamoto, "A Wholesome Horror."
60. Baden and Moss, "The Origin and Interpretation of Sara'at."

### Jesus and the Lepers

In the Christian gospels, Jesus heals "lepers," always depicted as male although he heals women afflicted with other conditions of impurity (Matt 8:2-3; Mark 1:40-42; Luke 5:12, 13). He visits a "leper's" home (Matt 26:6; Mark 14:3), sends the disciples to cleanse "lepers" (Matt 10:8), refers to healing "lepers" in his mission statement (echoing Isa 29:18-19; 35:5-6; 42:18; 61:1), and refers to Naaman, the Syrian, whose leprosy was healed. The Greek words used are ὁ λεπρὸς and its cognates or ἡ λέπρα. Jesus' actions show he understands that "lepers" are ritually, not medically, impure. He touches "lepers" (Luke 5:13; Mark 1:41; Matt 8:3), rendering himself ritually unclean, and tells lepers to present themselves to the priest upon healing (see Lev 13:6, 28, 37). There is no evidence that Jesus visits priests for personal ritual purification.

*Jane Via*

Leviticus 13–14 may be interpreted as putting controls on potential sources of fear. Ayala Sha'ashoua Miron writes:

> The cohen, the priest, representing society, is the one who defines the Nega, the affliction. He offers the necessary steps to redeem the infection and invites the infected back into society, through his touch of grace. The priest is called to visit the infected, to examine their conditions, to measure the marks on their skin and pay careful attention to the differences that they show over time. The priest is called to frame and reframe the Nega, the "touched" area. His willingness to look and get in touch with the infected body, his closeness, and his repeated attention are all part of a gesture that turns the site of "infection" into one of "purity."[61]

The person with skin conditions is not automatically טמא or טהור. Only when someone takes the time to look very closely at a bodily expression, can that condition be named. The priest does not heal, does not provide a prognosis; this is not about medicine or sickness. It is about noticing the details that most of us prefer to avoid. Leviticus 13 publicly acknowledges that boils, rashes, scabs, and pus are all possible expressions of the human body. The priests categorize some physical expressions as טמא or טהור based on criteria that are long lost to us. As readers of these texts,

---

61. Ayala Miron, "Nagu'a: Touched by the Divine," in *Torah Queeries: Weekly Commentaries on the Hebrew Bible*, ed. Gregg Drinkwater, Joshua Lesser, and David Shneer (New York: New York University Press, 2009), 142.

we are momentarily asked to pay attention, as the priests were required to do. Instead of reading these chapters with disgust or boredom, we might approach them with curiosity and with awe for all the ways that the body can express itself in the course of living and healing. Rashes occur as a bodily defense against toxins. Scabs mean that the body is regenerating itself. This is the stuff of life.

---

### Quarantine and Sanitation

From the foregoing description, it is clear that the main purpose of the diagnostic guidelines for צרעת was to prevent the spread of the disease and the consequent danger to the health of the community. This ecological value of the diagnostic process is set out particularly in the use of quarantine for suspected patients. Quarantine is now an internationally employed device. Travelers across countries are inspected, and if one is found with a contagious disease he or she is isolated for a period of time. Thus, quarantine as used in ancient Israel anticipated its employment in modern times. The treatments prescribed for houses suspected to have been infected with צרעת have relevance for environmental sanitation. They anticipated modern methods of solid waste disposal, which involve the disposal of solid or semisolid materials that are useless, unwanted, or hazardous. Sometimes they involve the demolition of houses, too.[62]

*Solomon Olusola Ademiluka*

---

## "Skin Afflictions" on Fabrics and Hides (13:47-59)

Leviticus 13:47 introduces a new topic altogether: that of צרעת on fabrics and on hides and skins. The fact that the same term is used for a condition both on human skin and on fabrics bolsters the argument that this condition has nothing to do with sin (unless fabrics have a moral compass!). A priest declares fabrics, hides, and yarn or threads impure if the object has a greenish or reddish growth on it. As is the case with persons, the fabric should be set aside for seven days to determine whether or not the growth is spreading. If the growth has spread, the object is considered impure and is burned in fire. If the growth has not spread, but fails to be cleansed away completely when washed, it is also considered impure

---

62. J.Y.C. Huang, "Solid Waste Disposal," *Microsoft Student 2008* (DVD).

⁴⁷Concerning clothing: when a leprous disease appears in it, in woolen or linen cloth, ⁴⁸in warp or woof of linen or wool, or in a skin or in anything made of skin, ⁴⁹if the disease shows greenish or reddish in the garment, whether in warp or woof or in skin or in anything made of skin, it is a leprous disease and shall be shown to the priest. ⁵⁰The priest shall examine the disease, and put the diseased article aside for seven days. ⁵¹He shall examine the disease on the seventh day. If the disease has spread in the cloth, in warp or woof, or in the skin, whatever be the use of the skin, this is a spreading leprous disease; it is unclean. ⁵²He shall burn the clothing, whether diseased in warp or woof, woolen or linen, or anything of skin, for it is a spreading leprous disease; it shall be burned in fire.

⁵³If the priest makes an examination, and the disease has not spread in the clothing, in warp or woof or in

and burned in fire. If the priest determines that the fabric no longer carries the growth, then it is ceremonially washed and rendered pure.

This section of text (vv. 47-59) uses a couple of words that appear only here in the Bible and that offer a glimpse into women's work. The text does not simply mention fabrics; it specifies the warp, the threads that run lengthwise in a loom, and the woof, the horizontal threads that are woven into the loom. Since textile production in the homes fell under the domain of women's work (2 Chr 2:7; Judg 16:14; 2 Kgs 23:7),⁶³ it must have been the responsibility of women to notice potential cases of צרעת and to work with priests to remedy the impurities. David Tabb Stewart notes that the section on moldy fabric refers to the priest in the third-person masculine singular but that the owner of the fabric is addressed in the second-person masculine singular: "You shall burn it" (vv. 55, 57). Stewart suggests that the common reading is incorrect and that the grammatical form should be read as the third-person feminine singular, "She shall burn it."⁶⁴ Since this section on moldy fabrics was likely addressed to women, Stewart's reading is quite compelling.

---

63. Elizabeth Wayland Barber, *Women's Work: The First 20,000 Years; Women, Cloth and Society in Early Times* (New York: Norton, 1996); for more recently discovered evidence, see Jennie Ebeling, "Women's Daily Life in Bronze Age Canaan," in *Women in Antiquity: Real Women Across the Ancient World*, ed. Stephanie Lynn Budin and Jean Macintosh Turfa (London: Routledge, 2016), 465–76.

64. David Tabb Stewart, "Does the Priestly Purity Code Domesticate Women?," in *Perspectives on Purity and Purification in the Bible*, ed. Pamela Barmash, Shachar Pinsker, and Rick Painter, *HS* 50 (2009): 70.

anything of skin, [54]the priest shall command them to wash the article in which the disease appears, and he shall put it aside seven days more. [55]The priest shall examine the diseased article after it has been washed. If the diseased spot has not changed color, though the disease has not spread, it is unclean; you shall burn it in fire, whether the leprous spot is on the inside or on the outside.

[56]If the priest makes an examination, and the disease has abated after it is washed, he shall tear the spot out of the cloth, in warp or woof, or out of skin. [57]If it appears again in the garment, in warp or woof, or in anything of skin, it is spreading; you shall burn with fire that in which the disease appears. [58]But the cloth, warp or woof, or anything of skin from which the disease disappears when you have washed it, shall then be washed a second time, and it shall be clean.

[59]This is the ritual for a leprous disease in a cloth of wool or linen, either in warp or woof, or in anything of skin, to decide whether it is clean or unclean.

Milgrom believes that the text mentions the warp and the woof to ensure that the reader understands that צרעת may appear on fabrics and on yarns and threads on a loom.[65] That is, P acknowledges that a ball of yarn could suffer mold or other fungi.

## An Unusual Purification Ritual (14:1-9)

In Leviticus 14 the focus shifts from diagnosis to performance of a purification ceremony. The priest leads the individual (male or female) through a three-stage ritual ceremony that includes novel ritual substances. The first stage of the ritual takes place outside the camp, after the priest has ascertained that the afflicted individual is healed. The following materials are brought on behalf of the person to be declared pure: two pure living birds, cedar wood, crimson yarn, and hyssop (v. 4). While cedar wood was a relatively common substance in ancient Near Eastern rituals, the use of this material is attested only in this ritual and in the ritual of the red heifer (Num 19). In both cases, it is likely that the red color of the wood made it attractive for use. The next substance, שני תולעת ("crimson yarn"), means literally "scarlet of a worm," which KJV translates simply as "scarlet." The phrase may derive from an insect

65. Milgrom, *Leviticus 1–16*, 809–10.

¹⁴:¹The Lord spoke to Moses, saying:

²This shall be the ritual for the leprous person at the time of his cleansing:

He shall be brought to the priest; ³the priest shall go out of the camp, and the priest shall make an examination. If the disease is healed in the leprous person, ⁴the priest shall command that two living clean birds and cedarwood and crimson yarn and hyssop be brought for the one who is to be cleansed. ⁵The priest shall command that one of the birds be slaughtered over fresh water in an earthen vessel. ⁶He shall take the living bird with the cedarwood and the crimson yarn and the hyssop, and dip them and the living bird in the blood of the bird that was slaughtered over the fresh water. ⁷He shall sprinkle it seven times upon the one who is to be cleansed of the leprous disease; then he shall pronounce him clean, and he shall let the living bird go into the open field. ⁸The one who is to be cleansed shall wash his clothes, and shave off all his hair, and bathe himself in water, and he shall be clean. After that he shall come into the camp, but shall live outside his tent seven days. ⁹On the seventh day he shall shave all his hair: of head, beard, eyebrows; he shall shave all his hair. Then he shall wash his clothes, and bathe his body in water, and he shall be clean.

that was used as a color extract. Again, like the cedar wood, the red color of the material is key.

The priest kills one of the birds and collects its blood into a vessel that is filled with fresh water (v. 5). The priest dips the living bird along with the cedar wood, scarlet, and hyssop into the vessel with watered-down blood (v. 6); then he sprinkles the healed individual seven times and makes a declaration: "pure!" (v. 7).[66] The living bird is released alive into an open field and the individual in the process of purification washes her clothes, shaves all of her body hair, and bathes in water (v. 8). This completes the first stage of purification. The second stage allows for the person to enter the camp as long as she does not enter her tent. After a seven-day waiting period, she shaves again, washes her clothes, and bathes. At that point, she has completed the second stage of purification (v. 9).

66. In Num 19:6, a priest makes use of cedar wood, scarlet, and hyssop for a ritual of burning. Thus, in two cases, materials are used to enhance the red coloring either in a water mixture (Lev 14) or in an ash mixture (Num 19).

This unique ritual has elicited many questions but few conclusive answers. The slaughter of a bird outside the sanctuary is unusual, as is the sprinkling of blood on a layperson. The birds are not described as pigeons or turtledoves (birds used for the altar), so these were likely wild birds and were not intended to function as sin offerings. Many interpreters assume that this ritual reflects early pagan rites of elimination, whereby the impurity was transferred to the live bird that carried away the contaminating elements. It is unclear, however, how the priestly writers understood the purpose of this ritual. Milgrom goes so far as to suggest that the "bird rite plays no role whatsoever in the actual purification of the healed."[67] The priests may have adapted an earlier pagan ritual, but it must have had some significance for them that is lost to us.

## Purification at the Sanctuary (14:10-32)

The final stage of purification addresses both the purification of the sanctuary and of the healed individual. Leviticus 14:10-20 describes an altar ritual that most closely mirrors that of the priestly ordination (see Lev 8). The healed person brings two male lambs, one female ewe, a cereal offering mixed with oil, and additional oil (vv. 10-11). The first sacrifice is a guilt offering, and the blood of that sacrifice is placed on the right ear, right thumb, and right big toe of the person who is being cleansed (vv. 12-14). This parallels the placement of blood on the priests when they are ordained with the offering of ordination (see Lev 8:22-24)! Perhaps the transition that a healed individual makes from standing outside of the camp to being incorporated back into the community parallels the transition that new priests undergo from laity to priesthood. The ritual continues with the priest presenting the oil to God and sprinkling it on the altar (v. 15). What remains goes on the priest's left palm, and, with his right hand, he places oil on the person as he did with the blood (vv. 17-18). The rest of the oil is poured on the person's head and the priest makes atonement (כפר) or mitigates on behalf of the person (v. 19). The ritual concludes with a purification offering, a burnt offering, and a grain offering (v. 20).[68]

---

67. Milgrom, *Leviticus 1–16*, 838.

68. On the ritual of Lev 14:1-20 as divinatory and exorcistic, see most recently Adriana Destro and Mauro Pesce, "The Ritual for the Leper in Leviticus 14," in *Ancient Israel: The Old Testament in Its Social Context*, ed. Philip F. Esler (Minneapolis: Fortress, 2006), 66–77.

[10]On the eighth day he shall take two male lambs without blemish, and one ewe lamb in its first year without blemish, and a grain offering of three-tenths of an ephah of choice flour mixed with oil, and one log of oil. [11]The priest who cleanses shall set the person to be cleansed, along with these things, before the LORD, at the entrance of the tent of meeting. [12]The priest shall take one of the lambs, and offer it as a guilt offering, along with the log of oil, and raise them as an elevation offering before the LORD. [13]He shall slaughter the lamb in the place where the sin offering and the burnt offering are slaughtered in the holy place; for the guilt offering, like the sin offering, belongs to the priest: it is most holy. [14]The priest shall take some of the blood of the guilt offering and put it on the lobe of the right ear of the one to be cleansed, and on the thumb of the right hand, and on the big toe of the right foot. [15]The priest shall take some of the log of oil and pour it into the palm of his own left hand, [16]and dip his right finger in the oil that is in his left hand and sprinkle some oil with his finger seven times before the LORD. [17]Some of the oil that remains in his hand the priest shall put on the lobe of the right ear of the one to be cleansed, and on the thumb of the right hand, and on the big toe of the right foot, on top of the blood of the guilt offering. [18]The rest of the oil that is in the priest's hand he shall put on the head of the one to be cleansed. Then the priest shall make atonement on his behalf before the LORD: [19]the priest shall offer the sin offering, to make atonement for the one to be cleansed from his uncleanness. Afterward he shall slaughter the burnt offering; [20]and the priest shall offer the burnt offering and the grain offering on the altar. Thus the priest shall make atonement on his behalf and he shall be clean.

Leviticus 14:21-32 offers an alternative ritual for those who cannot afford two lambs and one ewe. The same ritual may take place with one lamb for the guilt offering and two birds, one as a purification offering and one as a burnt offering. As we have seen time and time again, the priestly writers offer alternative donations for those who do not have the means to provide the necessary cattle or flock.

This ritual is never attested in narrative texts, although Numbers 12 tells the story of Miriam who, when she challenges the authority of Moses, is punished by God with a skin affliction. That narrative tells us that Miriam remains outside of the camp for the duration of her condition, but there is no mention of ritual practices. Meanwhile, the entire camp of Israelites remains encamped until Miriam is ready to travel again.

²¹But if he is poor and cannot afford so much, he shall take one male lamb for a guilt offering to be elevated, to make atonement on his behalf, and one-tenth of an ephah of choice flour mixed with oil for a grain offering and a log of oil; ²²also two turtledoves or two pigeons, such as he can afford, one for a sin offering and the other for a burnt offering. ²³On the eighth day he shall bring them for his cleansing to the priest, to the entrance of the tent of meeting, before the LORD; ²⁴and the priest shall take the lamb of the guilt offering and the log of oil, and the priest shall raise them as an elevation offering before the LORD. ²⁵The priest shall slaughter the lamb of the guilt offering and shall take some of the blood of the guilt offering, and put it on the lobe of the right ear of the one to be cleansed, and on the thumb of the right hand, and on the big toe of the right foot. ²⁶The priest shall pour some of the oil into the palm of his own left hand, ²⁷and shall sprinkle with his right finger some of the oil that is in his left hand seven times before the LORD. ²⁸The priest shall put some of the oil that is in his hand on the lobe of the right ear of the one to be cleansed, and on the thumb of the right hand, and the big toe of the right foot, where the blood of the guilt offering was placed. ²⁹The rest of the oil that is in the priest's hand he shall put on the head of the one to be cleansed, to make atonement on his behalf before the LORD. ³⁰And he shall offer, of the turtledoves or pigeons such as he can afford, ³¹one for a sin offering and the other for a burnt offering, along with a grain offering; and the priest shall make atonement before the Lord on behalf of the one being cleansed. ³²This is the ritual for the one who has a leprous disease, who cannot afford the offerings for his cleansing.

## Impurity Contamination in Houses (14:33-53)

In the second half of Leviticus 14, the focus shifts to cases in which צרעת is found in homes. Verse 33 indicates that these laws are to be applied once the people are settled in the land of Canaan (and thus have homes!). The pattern is similar to the process of inspection, identification, and purification of impurity in individuals. Verses 35-36 state that it is the responsibility of the homeowner to call a priest if he suspects that there is a growth somewhere in the house. The accountability for ensuring that the community combats impurities lies with homeowners of the community. Before the priest arrives to make an examination, the homeowner is to remove everything from the house because, if the objects are removed before the priestly declaration, then they are not

³³The LORD spoke to Moses and Aaron, saying:

³⁴When you come into the land of Canaan, which I give you for a possession, and I put a leprous disease in a house in the land of your possession, ³⁵the owner of the house shall come and tell the priest, saying, "There seems to me to be some sort of disease in my house." ³⁶The priest shall command that they empty the house before the priest goes to examine the disease, or all that is in the house will become unclean; and afterward the priest shall go in to inspect the house. ³⁷He shall examine the disease; if the disease is in the walls of the house with greenish or reddish spots, and if it appears to be deeper than the surface, ³⁸the priest shall go outside to the door of the house and shut up the house seven days. ³⁹The priest shall come again on the seventh day and make an inspection; if the disease has spread in the walls of the house, ⁴⁰the priest shall command that the stones in which the disease appears be taken out and thrown into an unclean place outside the city. ⁴¹He shall have the inside of the house scraped thoroughly, and the plaster that is scraped off shall be dumped in an unclean place outside the city. ⁴²They shall take other stones and put them in the place of those stones, and take other plaster and plaster the house.

⁴³If the disease breaks out again in the house, after he has taken out

considered contaminated, but if they are in the home when the priest pronounces impurity, then everything in the home is considered contaminated and must be destroyed.

Again, the objects in the home are not rendered impure by virtue of their potential contact with the growth; the objects are made impure through the priest's declaration. This demonstrates that there is nothing physically or scientifically contagious in the house; it is the priest's declaration that makes it so. When Adam names each animal in Genesis 2:20, he is, in effect, defining the animal and placing it within a larger constellation of animals. When Hagar names God "El Roi" (Gen 16:13), she is placing her own personal stamp on God's identity. Likewise, one of the priest's most significant powers is his ability to make declarations that influence reality.

Leviticus 14:37-53 describes the process by which the priest makes his examination. If the status of the mold or fungus is unclear, the house is shut for seven days. At the end of that period, if the growth has spread, the priest has the plaster and stones of the affected area removed and replaced (vv. 37-42). The house is inspected one more time at the end of another seven-day period, and if the growth has returned, the house the stones and scraped the house and plastered it, ⁴⁴the priest shall go and make inspection; if the disease has spread in the house, it is a spreading leprous disease in the house; it is unclean. ⁴⁵He shall have the house torn down, its stones and timber and all the plaster of the house, and taken outside the city to an unclean place. ⁴⁶All who enter the house while it is shut up shall be unclean until the evening; ⁴⁷and all who sleep in the house shall wash their clothes; and all who eat in the house shall wash their clothes.

⁴⁸If the priest comes and makes an inspection, and the disease has not spread in the house after the house was plastered, the priest shall pronounce the house clean; the disease is healed. ⁴⁹For the cleansing of the house he shall take two birds, with cedarwood and crimson yarn and hyssop, ⁵⁰and shall slaughter one of the birds over fresh water in an earthen vessel, ⁵¹and shall take the cedarwood and the hyssop and the crimson yarn, along with the living bird, and dip them in the blood of the slaughtered bird and the fresh water, and sprinkle the house seven times. ⁵²Thus he shall cleanse the house with the blood of the bird, and with the fresh water, and with the living bird, and with the cedarwood and hyssop and crimson yarn; ⁵³and he shall let the living bird go out of the city into the open field; so he shall make atonement for the house, and it shall be clean.

and all its contents are destroyed (vv. 43-45), but if the growth has not returned, then the priest leads the ritual of the two birds, cedar wood, crimson, and hyssop (vv. 49-51). In this case, the house itself is sprinkled with blood. Verse 43 indicates that the purification ritual is to לחטא (*piel* of חטא), which may best be understood as "to purge" (or, as v. 53 indicates, "make atonement for") the house. Baruch Schwartz notes this oddity: "Make expiation for, Heb 'kiper' is used anomalously here . . . to refer to the decontamination of a person. No purification of the sacred sphere is prescribed, since if the 'zaraʿat' is deemed severe the house is destroyed before the impurity spreads to the sanctuary."[69]

### Epilogue (14:54-57)

Verses 54-57 summarize the materials presented in Leviticus 13 and 14, indicating that these are laws that address צרעת, whether on people, fabrics, or houses. The fact that houses are included in these chapters

---

69. Schwartz, "Leviticus," in *The Jewish Study Bible*, 240.

⁵⁴This is the ritual for any leprous disease: for an itch, ⁵⁵for leprous diseases in clothing and houses, ⁵⁶and for a swelling or an eruption or a spot, ⁵⁷to determine when it is unclean and when it is clean. This is the ritual for leprous diseases.

calls attention to the fact that, even today, our homes can be toxic and we must deal with those poisons systematically and with proper leadership. Lead paint that still lines the walls, windows, and doors in older housing stock, where people (sometimes single mothers or immigrants and refugees) with low incomes are trying to raise families, is literally toxic. Often low-income families live in mold-infected homes in rural communities hit by floods or other severe weather events. Only those families with the means to purchase home insurance and with the power to influence insurance companies receive the attention to remove the toxins. Leviticus 14 ends with the statement "to determine when it is clean or when it is unclean" (v. 57), emphasizing the priests' role in making distinctions through examination and proclamation, regardless of the family's economic class.

## Leviticus 15: An Introduction to Genital Emissions

The content of Leviticus 15 and its afterlife or reception history provide an excellent example of the ways in which patriarchal culture and misogyny rework ancient texts, each generation building on the prior, until the original text is almost completely obscured. For example, the Rastafarian role of women calls to mind a profound misreading of Leviticus 15: "The Adam and Eve myth tells the tale of what lies in store for man if woman is allowed to control him. . . . Man is vulnerable during woman's menstrual flow, and to avoid all possibilities of contamination male and female underwear are strictly segregated. Indeed, only a woman herself may wash her own underwear. Pregnant and menstruating women are thought to have a malignant effect on certain crops."[70] This kind of rhetoric may be found in abundance in early and

70. Barry Chevannes, "Rastafari: Toward a New Approach," *New West Indian Guide* 64 (1990), 132; as quoted by N. Samuel Murrell, "Woman as Source of Evil and Contaminant in Rastafarianism: Championing Hebrew Patriarchy and Oppression with Lev 12," *Proceedings: Eastern Great Lakes and Midwest Biblical Societies* 13 (1993): 195.

medieval Christian and Jewish works such as that of Nahmanides, who writes: "For the ancients in their wisdom knew that their [women's] breath is harmful, their gaze detrimental and makes a bad impression, as the philosophers have explained."[71] In fact, Leviticus 15, a source text for these attitudes, does not contain a hint of this misogyny!

## Genital Emissions from a Penis (15:1-18)

Leviticus 15 begins with instruction about abnormal genital discharges from a penis (בשר, "member"), whether the discharge is runny or thick and congealed (Lev 15:2-15). This condition renders a man impure until the condition ends,[72] at which point he must wait seven days, bathe in the evening, and bring two birds to the priest on the following day.[73] While in his impurity, he transmits his impurity through direct contact in a variety of ways, including to his bedding, to anything he sits on (including a saddle), and to any earthen or wooden vessels (vv. 4, 9, and 12). If anyone touches any of these things, that person develops a secondary level of impurity and must bathe and wait until evening (vv. 5-6). Additionally, the man with the discharge can transmit his impurity to others via his spittle (v. 8). Verse 11 indicates that the impure man can touch another person only if he has washed his hands.

Interestingly, in the midst of the list of items that can transmit the impurity, verse 7 indicates that anyone who touches the man's בשר ("body," NRSV) becomes impure until evening. Since בשר indicates genitalia ("member," NRSV) throughout this chapter, the most likely translation for בשר here must also refer to genitalia; thus whoever touches the man's penis is impure until evening. Most commentators argue, however, that בשר here means any part of his body, probably reflecting embarrassment or anxiety regarding the notion of men touching each other's penises.

71. Ramban, *Commentary on the Torah*, trans. Charles B. Chavel (New York: Shiloh, 1974), 255.

72. Note that the NRSV uses the term "ceremonially unclean" to describe impurity of abnormal male discharge, while it uses "impurity" in reference to women's discharge.

73. Judith Romney Wegner has noted that Lev 15:14 instructs the male to come "before YHVH" at the entrance to the tent of meeting to bring his offering but that the parallel instruction for a female to bring her offering in Lev 15:29 omits the phrase "before YHVH." Wegner uses this discrepancy to argue that women were excluded from the priestly cult (" 'Coming Before the Lord': The Exclusion of Women from the Public Domain of the Israelite Priestly Cult," in *The Book of Leviticus: Composition and Reception*, ed. Rolf Rendtorff, Robert A. Kugler, and Sarah Smith Bartel [Leiden: Brill, 2003], 451–65).

¹⁵:¹The Lᴏʀᴅ spoke to Moses and Aaron, saying: ²Speak to the people of Israel and say to them:

When any man has a discharge from his member, his discharge makes him ceremonially unclean. ³The uncleanness of his discharge is this: whether his member flows with his discharge, or his member is stopped from discharging, it is uncleanness for him. ⁴Every bed on which the one with the discharge lies shall be unclean; and everything on which he sits shall be unclean. ⁵Anyone who touches his bed shall wash his clothes, and bathe in water, and be unclean until the evening. ⁶All who sit on anything on which the one with the discharge has sat shall wash their clothes, and bathe in water, and be unclean until the evening. ⁷All who touch the body of the one with the discharge shall wash their clothes, and bathe in water, and be unclean until the evening. ⁸If the one with the discharge spits on persons who are clean, then they shall wash their clothes, and bathe in water, and be unclean until the evening. ⁹Any saddle on which the one with the discharge rides shall be unclean. ¹⁰All who touch anything that was under him shall be unclean until the evening, and all who carry such a thing shall wash their clothes, and bathe in water, and be unclean until the evening. ¹¹All

A fact that has not received sufficient attention in commentaries is that a man with an abnormal genital discharge has the most communicable form of impurity among all the impurities. Nine verses are devoted to the communicability of abnormal male discharge (vv. 4-12). To avoid communicating the impurity, the man must sleep alone, eat separately with his own utensils, avoid direct contact with others, and speak to others at a distance lest he get his spittle on them!

While the irregular genital discharges flank the outer part of the unit (vv. 2-15 and vv. 25-31) the interior sections address regular emissions of semen and menstruation. When a man has a discharge of semen, his body is impure until evening, as is his clothing with which the semen has come into contact. A man's semen similarly renders a woman impure when he ejaculates into her during sexual intercourse. The man, his clothing, and his sexual partner are required to bathe and remain impure until evening (vv. 16-18).⁷⁴

---

74. Note that Deut 23:10 (in NRSV, Heb 23:11) uses specific terminology for nocturnal emissions: מקרה־לילה (literally, "incident of the night").

those whom the one with the discharge touches without his having rinsed his hands in water shall wash their clothes, and bathe in water, and be unclean until the evening. ¹²Any earthen vessel that the one with the discharge touches shall be broken; and every vessel of wood shall be rinsed in water.

¹³When the one with a discharge is cleansed of his discharge, he shall count seven days for his cleansing; he shall wash his clothes and bathe his body in fresh water, and he shall be clean. ¹⁴On the eighth day he shall take two turtledoves or two pigeons and come before the Lord to the entrance of the tent of meeting and give them to the priest. ¹⁵The priest shall offer them, one for a sin offering and the other for a burnt offering; and the priest shall make atonement on his behalf before the Lord for his discharge.

¹⁶If a man has an emission of semen, he shall bathe his whole body in water, and be unclean until the evening. ¹⁷Everything made of cloth or of skin on which the semen falls shall be washed with water, and be unclean until the evening. ¹⁸If a man lies with a woman and has an emission of semen, both of them shall bathe in water, and be unclean until the evening.

## Genital Emissions from a Vagina (15:19-33)

When a woman menstruates,[75] she is in a state of ritual impurity for seven days (presumably the count begins at the onset of menstruation).[76] Anyone who touches a menstruating woman is impure until evening (15:19), and anyone who touches any of her bedding or seating is impure until evening and must launder and bathe (vv. 21-22) or simply remain impure until evening (v. 23). There seems to be an internal debate within the text regarding the communicability of menstrual discharge. Jonathan Magonet convincingly argues that verses 21-22, which describe the requirement for bathing after second-degree impurity, were added later to align the laws for women to the laws for men, which do require bathing (see Lev 15:5-13). Magonet argues that verse 23 represents the original text and that no bathing was required.[77] The final statement on menstrual discharge is that if a man lies with a woman during her menstrual period,

75. See Gen 31:35; 1 Sam 21:5; and 2 Sam 11:4 for narrative references to menstruation.

76. In traditional Jewish law, the counting of seven days begins after bleeding stops. The law assumes a five-day period plus seven days as mandated by the Bible. Thus, there is a twelve-day period of separation between husband and wife in traditional Jewish practice.

77. Magonet, " 'But If It Is a Girl,' " 144–52.

*Lev 15:19-33*

¹⁹When a woman has discharge of blood that is her regular discharge from her body, she shall be in her impurity for seven days, and whoever touches her shall be unclean until the evening. ²⁰Everything upon which she lies during her impurity shall be unclean; everything also upon which she sits shall be unclean. ²¹Whoever touches her bed shall wash his clothes, and bathe in water, and be unclean until the evening. ²²Whoever touches anything upon which she sits shall wash his clothes, and bathe in water, and be unclean until the evening; ²³whether it is the bed or anything upon which she sits, when he touches it he shall be unclean until the evening. ²⁴If any man lies with her, and her impurity falls on him, he shall be unclean seven days; and every bed on which he lies shall be unclean.

²⁵If a woman has a discharge of blood for many days, not at the time of her impurity, or if she has a discharge beyond the time of her impurity, all the days of the discharge she shall continue in uncleanness; as in the days of her impurity, she shall be unclean. ²⁶Every bed on which she lies during all the days of her discharge shall be treated as the bed of her impurity; and everything on which she sits shall be unclean, as in the uncleanness of her impurity. ²⁷Whoever touches these things shall be unclean, and shall wash his clothes, and bathe in water, and be unclean until the evening. ²⁸If she is cleansed of her discharge, she shall count seven days, and after that she shall be clean. ²⁹On the eighth day she shall take two turtledoves or two pigeons and bring them to the priest at the entrance of the tent of meeting.

he takes on the same seven-day impurity that she carries (15:24). Thus, her state of impurity is transmissible only to her bedding, her seating, and her sexual partner (Lev 15:19-20). If we assume that Magonet is correct, then contact with menstrual blood did not necessitate bathing—not for those who came in contact with the blood or for the menstruating woman herself!

Neither male nor female healthy and natural discharges require offerings. Semen renders one ritually impure until the man bathes and evening comes. Women are not required to bathe at the end of their seven-day ritual impurity.[78]

78. Nicole J. Ruane notes that the only time a woman is required to bathe is when she comes in contact with sperm during sexual intercourse (v. 18). Ruane argues that bathing is gendered insofar as men are required to bathe in a variety of instances while women do not bathe. In fact, men are not required to bathe after sexual intercourse with a menstruant because the impurity is gendered as female! ("Bathing, Status and Gender in Priestly Ritual," in *A Question of Sex? Gender and Difference in the Hebrew Bible and Beyond*, ed. Deborah W. Rooke, HBM 14 [Sheffield: Sheffield Phoenix, 2009], 66–81, esp. 78–79.)

³⁰The priest shall offer one for a sin offering and the other for a burnt offering; and the priest shall make atonement on her behalf before the Lord for her unclean discharge.

³¹Thus you shall keep the people of Israel separate from their uncleanness, so that they do not die in their uncleanness by defiling my tabernacle that is in their midst.

³²This is the ritual for those who have a discharge: for him who has an emission of semen, becoming unclean thereby, ³³for her who is in the infirmity of her period, for anyone, male or female, who has a discharge, and for the man who lies with a woman who is unclean.

## TRANSLATION MATTERS

As we noted earlier, the terminology used to describe the woman's menstrual impurity in Leviticus 12:2 is נדת דותה ("menstruation"). At the end of Leviticus 15:33, the phrase הדוה בנדתה ("for her who is in the infirmity of her period") is used to refer to a menstruating woman. The NRSV, like other translations, does not consistently translate the two Hebrew words that appear in Leviticus 12:2 and 15:33 to describe a menstruating woman. The adjective דוה literally means "menstruous" in Leviticus 12:2; 15:33; and 20:18. The root appears only a few times in the Bible. Outside of Leviticus, it is used figuratively to describe one who is faint, dispirited, or unwell (as an adjective in Isa 1:5; and Lam 1:13; 5:17; and as a noun in Ps 41:4). The term is never used in a derogatory sense; it connotes suffering. Our closest analogous terms might include cramping and bloating!

The term נדה refers to a subcategory of טמאה, the impurity specifically created by menstrual blood.[79] Ezekiel takes this innocuous term and extends its use figuratively to describe moral impurity (Ezek 7:19-20; see also Lam 1:17; 2 Chr 29:5; Ezra 9:11).[80] In Zechariah 13:1, נדה is used as a parallel to טמאה. These later renderings of נדה as "sinfulness" or "depravity," coupled with the term's association with women's physiology, have fed into a long and painful history of misogyny within Judeo-Christian traditions. If we can strip those later meanings from the earliest use of נדה in Leviticus, we can reclaim נדה simply as a technical subcategory of ritual impurity. Thus, the most literal translations of Leviticus 12:2 and 15:33 are, respectively, "the impurity of her menstruating" and "the menstruous one in her impurity."

---

79. BDB, 622 does not list a single occurrence of this word as meaning "menstruation."

80. See Moshe Greenberg, "The Etymology of *niddah* (Menstrual) Impurity," in *Solving Riddles and Untying Knots: Biblical, Epigraphic and Semitic Studies in Honor of Jonas C. Greenfield*, ed. Ziony Zevit et al. (Winona Lake, IN: Eisenbrauns, 1995), 69–77. See also Erbele-Küster, *Körper und Geschlecht*, 115–34.

### Irregular Menstrual Flow: A Gospels Prespective

Leviticus 15:26 describes transmission of this vaginal discharge impurity to people and things. Under Priestly law, as opposed to other primitive societies, neither menstruation nor chronic bleeding result in isolation from community or restriction to home, but only impurity transmission by touch of things *under her* (bedding, seat)[81] and others touching her. Women were not banished from the home during bleeding, but continued to clean, cook, and serve food, to the benefit of men.[82] The text is unclear whether her touch of others transmits impurity.[83] The male with abnormal discharge transmits uncleanness if he touches another with unrinsed hands (v. 11). Logically, women with abnormal flow would also transmit impurity since blood impurity is greater.

Were biblical women "rarely excluded from the cult" because of constant pregnancy or nursing, implicitly suffering no greater cultic alienation than men in the Priestly era?[84] Arguably, women were more often excluded from the cult *because* they bled *regularly* when not pregnant or nursing. In the Middle Ages, Christian men excluded women deacons from service at the altar because they might be menstruating.[85]

A woman who has suffered a flow of blood for twelve years touches Jesus (Mark 5:25-34; Matt 9:20-22; Luke 8:43-48)[86] and is healed by "power" (Mark 5:30; Luke 8:46) that passes through Jesus to her. Afterward, Jesus affirms her action and healing. He does not instruct her to submit to purification rituals, nor is there evidence he sought them if her touch transmitted her uncleanness. Jesus' willingness to minister to women and girls is evident throughout the gospels.

*Jane Via*

---

81. This is in contrast to the scale-diseased person who is banished because he will contaminate all persons and objects with him under the same roof ("overhang"); see Jacob Milgrom, *Leviticus: A Book of Ritual and Ethics; A Continental Commentary* (Minneapolis: Fortress, 2004), 154–55, 159–60.

82. Milgrom, *Leviticus 1–16*, 953.

83. Milgrom, *Leviticus: A Book of Ritual and Ethics*, 141, 156.

84. Milgrom, *Leviticus 1–16*, 953.

85. Gary Macy, William T. Ditewig, and Phyllis Zagano, *Women Deacons: Past, Present, Future* (Mahwah, NJ: Paulist, 2011), 30–32.

86. In all three gospels, this story is inserted into a passage in which Jesus raises the only girl child of a synagogue official from the dead, consistent with the theory that blood flow (normal or abnormal) is connected to death impurity.

Leviticus 15:24 concludes the section on healthy menstrual flows, indicating that a man enters into a seven-day period of ritual impurity when he has intercourse with a menstruating woman. Gordon Wenham believes that verse 24 applies only in the following case: "Should a woman's period commence while she is having intercourse with her husband, he becomes unclean like her."[87] Wenham, like many others, reads verse 24 through the context of passages like Leviticus 18:19; 20:18 and even Ezekiel 18:6 and 22:10, all of which ban sexual intercourse with a menstruating woman. These texts are not P texts, however, and therefore cannot inform the text before us. Leviticus 15 does not ban heterosexual intercourse while the female partner is menstruating.

Women with an irregular vaginal discharge communicate their impurity only by direct contact or contact with their bedding or seat (Lev 15:25-30). On completion of the discharge, the woman must wait seven days and bring two birds to the priest on the next day, just as males do in cases of abnormal genital discharge. Again, the text itself does not require the woman to bathe. (See below, "Discharge, Gender, and Realia," pp. 149–51.) Almost all commentators assume that the requirement to bathe is implied because explicit mention of so obvious a ritual would have been considered unnecessary by the biblical writers. In fact, the impurities that require bathing in מים חיים ("fresh water") are only mandated for corpse contamination (Lev 17:15), skin afflictions (Lev 14:5, 50), and abnormal male genital discharge (Lev 15:13).

## Gender Ideology and Chapter Structure

The structure of Leviticus 15 appears to be quite straightforward: the first half of the chapter addresses abnormal and then normal male discharges, while the second half of the chapter addresses normal and then abnormal female discharges. The chapter begins and ends with the abnormal conditions while placing regular healthy discharge in the interior of the chapter. Close readings suggest, however, that the chapter is more complicated and that one's understanding of the structure impacts one's interpretation of the chapter and, in particular, that of gender ideology.

The two most common organizational principles are chiasm and parallel structure. Wenham divides Leviticus 15 into two sections in which verses 2-18 address male discharges and verses 19-30 address female

---

87. Wenham, *Leviticus*, 220; also Hartley, *Leviticus*, 212.

discharges. Within each of these units, Wenham discerns a further division between long-term and transient discharges.[88] Milgrom offers an idea from a student, James Randolph, who suggests that verse 18 is an inverted hinge, "a transitional unit of text, independent to some degree from the larger units on either side, which has affinities with each of them and does not add significant information to that of its neighbors. . . . The inserted hinge offers the pattern A/ba/B and reverses the order of the joining elements of the longer block of text."[89] The fact that verse 18 begins with the word אשה ("woman"), although the man is still the subject, suggests the A/ba/B pattern.

Richard Whitekettle argues that verse 18 stands on its own,[90] as its own case within the chapter as a whole. He identifies a chiastic structure of ABCB'A': abnormal male genital discharges; typical male genital discharges; normal sexual intercourse; typical female genital discharges; and abnormal female genital discharges. Abnormal discharges are pathological; typical discharges are regular but not ideal; and normal heterosexual intercourse, which is addressed in verse 18, is an ideal condition. Whitekettle argues that the chapter as a whole points to the centrality of sexual intercourse as the most desirable state.

> Section C, as the fulcrum of the chapter, portrays sexual physiology in its fully functional setting. The reproductive system of neither individual is showing signs of a life-threatening or degenerating condition. But also, each evidences physiology which is appropriate for the ideal sexual physiological setting of intercourse: ejaculation in the male and the absence of menstrual discharge in the female.[91]

According to Whitekettle, abnormal discharges (addressed in sections A and A' of the chapter) disallow the possibility of procreation, normal discharges (sections B and B') mark lost opportunities, and sexual intercourse (section C) is the ideal state.

So why does sexual intercourse, if it is the ideal, still create impurity? According to Samuel Balentine, the fact "that Israel's priests viewed the sexual sphere as a matter of ritual concern indicates neither a unique

---

88. Milgrom, *Leviticus 1–16*, 904, names the subdivision as "long term" and "short term."

89. Ibid., 930–31, quoted from H. Van Dyke Parunak, "Transitional Techniques in the Bible," *JBL* 102 (1983): 541.

90. So too Balentine, *Leviticus*, 121.

91. Richard Whitekettle, "Leviticus 15:18 Reconsidered: Chiasm, Spatial Structure and the Body," *JSOT* 49 (1991): 38; also see Erbele-Küster, *Körper und Geschlecht*, 69.

nor repressive attitude toward the importance, worth and enjoyment of sex."[92] Whitekettle suggests that the ambiguous functioning of the penis as both seed giver and pollutant discharger (urine) accounts for this impurity. Hartley believes that sexual intercourse causes impurity in order to ensure that no sex acts take place within the environs of the tabernacle.[93]

Dorothea Erbele-Küster questions whether verse 18 should be understood as the central point of the chapter. She notes that while portions of Leviticus 15 have terminological similarities, the symmetry of the chapter breaks down in several places. For example, the term זב ("discharge") is absent from the unit on ejaculation, and this topic does not seem to belong to the chapter. The consistent term throughout the chapter is בשר ("genitalia"). Erbele-Küster offers an alternative structure: a/b/a'/a", male discharge (זב), ejaculation, female discharge (זב), and extended female discharge (זב). Additionally, she dismisses any categorization of the chapter by normal versus abnormal discharges because that language is not in the text itself.[94] She also notes that the summary of the chapter in verses 32-33 tells the reader that the chapter is about emissions, not sexual intercourse, and this leads Erbele-Küster to see verse 18 as somewhat redundant, given that verse 16 addresses cultic impurity by means of direct contact with the semen. Perhaps her description of verse 18 as "Der Vers bildet das imaginäre Zentrum des Kapitels" ("The verse comprises the imaginative center of the chapter"),[95] with its complex syntax, suggests that the emission of semen in the context of sexual intercourse *also* defiles.

Deborah Ellens notes yet another structure within Leviticus 15. Ellens analyzes Leviticus 15 by noting two contrasting conceptualizations embedded within the text. Ellens notes that there are signs within the text that point to a view of woman as marginalized, objectified, and periodically unhealthy: at the end of the chapter, the woman is referred to as a דוה ("menstruant" in v. 33; see "Translation Matters" above); in reference to sexual intercourse, she is an object (v. 18); and the primary audience of the chapter is the male community. Ellens then shifts her focus to the structure of the chapter itself, and in this she finds a very different attitude toward women. Ellens asserts that the writer has inherited the view

92. Balentine, *Leviticus*, 119.
93. Hartley, *Leviticus*, 211.
94. Erbele-Küster, *Körper und Geschlecht*, 54–59.
95. Ibid., 67; my translation.

of woman as marginalized and objectified but that, in the construction of the chapter, the writer communicates a conceptual framework that does view women as marginalized.

Ellens argues,[96] against Milgrom, that the syntax of verse 18 does not follow the expected pattern of "hinge" verses because, by separating verse 18 from what precedes it, the balance between the sections on male discharges and female discharges is disrupted; further, separating verse 18 from what follows it makes it difficult to account for the function of verse 24. In other words, Ellens argues that verse 18 is integrally connected to verses 16-17, as is verse 24 in relation to verses 19-23. Verses 18 and 24 both address sexual intercourse. Most commentators read verse 18 as the climax and most important verse of the chapter, while reading verse 24 as a subsection of the unit of women's discharges. Ellens argues convincingly that verses 18 and 24 are, in fact, talking about the same thing: what happens when semen or menstrual blood is present during sexual intercourse. Both types of discharges cause impurity equally. Verse 18 addresses the case of a male discharge, while verse 24 addresses the case of a female discharge. The text does not idealize sexual intercourse at all; it is concerned with how discharges impact ritual purity.

Thus, genital discharge—not the woman, not the man, not intercourse per se, and not the functional ambiguity of the penis—is the source of the impurity addressed in Leviticus 15:18. The construction of verse 18 is a result of the writer's concern to emphasize the fact that during the "desirable" act of intercourse, which every married couple was expected to perform, both individuals are defiled by impurity. Thus, inasmuch as Second Temple literature and texts from later periods are known for their misogynistic characterizations of menstruating women, such allusions are nowhere to be found in P literature!

In a similar vein, Tarja Philip points out that gender is not at the center of Leviticus 15. In alignment with Ellens's view, Philip notes the structure of the chapter and argues that the structure underlines equality between the sexes. She notes that while the methods for the disposal of impurity from normal menstrual blood and from semen are different, they are not related to gender. For example, both the male and female are impure until evening after they have been exposed to semen; similarly, both the male

---

96. See Deborah L. Ellens, "Leviticus 15: Contrasting Conceptual Associations regarding Women," in *Reading the Hebrew Bible for a New Millennium*, ed. W. Kim et al. (Harrisburg, PA: Trinity Press International, 2000), 2:131–36, 138–41. Goldstein, *Impurity and Gender in the Hebrew Bible*, generally agrees with Ellens's arguments.

and female are impure for seven days after they have been exposed to menstrual blood.[97]

## Discharge, Gender, and Realia

Saul Olyan emphasizes the gender-based impact of the genital emissions regulations. He argues that we might not think that exclusion from the cult matters that much, but, because cultic sites were the primary places for the slaughter, processing, and distribution of meat, exclusion from those activities was significant. "To lose access—even for a relatively short period of time—to cultic and quasi-cultic contexts would surely have been viewed as a hardship, given the value and attractiveness attributed to meat, the desirability of participation in sacrificial rites, and the fact that such participation is enjoined in a variety of contexts."[98]

An important contribution that Olyan brings to the conversation is consideration of age and stage of life as additional indicators of status vis-à-vis the cult. He draws a contrast between "simple impurity" (until sunset) for male ejaculation and "grave impurities" for the menstruant, parturient, and people with skin diseases and corpse contamination. Olyan asserts that, given the impurities laws for the parturient and the weeklong exclusion during menstruation, women must have been excluded significantly more than men. Olyan further speculates that prepubescent girls and postmenopausal women would have had the fewest obstacles to access to the cult, but he also states, "I do not imagine that older women and young girls could escape completely from the cultural stigma of a distinctly feminine impurity such as menstruation."[99]

Nicole J. Ruane approaches the text from a different perspective. Ruane asserts that the sexual impurity texts function: "1) to put controls on sexuality and reproduction to limit their potentially damaging effect on lineage and social order and 2) to create gender distinctions for the purpose of defining social roles."[100] Ruane raises several points in response to the work of Ellens. She argues that the seven-day impurity period for

---

97. Philip, *Menstruation and Childbirth in the Bible*. See also Gordon Wenham, "Why Does Sexual Intercourse Defile (Lev 15,18)?," *ZAW* 95 (1983): 432–34.

98. Saul M. Olyan, *Rites and Rank: Hierarchy in Biblical Representations of Cult* (Princeton: Princeton University Press, 2000), 55.

99. Ibid., 56.

100. Nicole J. Ruane, *Sacrifice and Gender in Biblical Law* (Cambridge: Cambridge University Press, 2013), 175.

abnormal discharges "causes menstruation to resemble illness as well as death in a way that ejaculation does not."[101] In addition, a woman's normal discharge and abnormal discharge are both blood; there is no differentiation in the substance of the material. For men, the normal substance is semen and the abnormal substance is a different type of discharge. Ruane asserts that there is a closer association of women's blood than male secretions with pathology.

While Ellens argues that the source of impurity is only the discharge, Ruane asks why a woman is always rendered impure for seven days even if the blood flow stops before that time. Additionally, why would someone become impure through contact with the individual but not necessarily with the substance? Blood from a penis does not defile, and nonblood discharges from a vagina do not defile; therefore, "P constructs somewhat arbitrary sex-specific substances to correlate to these sex-specific events. The fluid is not really the problematic element, rather the distinction between male and female is the true importance; the labeling of certain substances is merely the means of making the distinction."[102] Finally, Ruane suggests that, for P, sexual intercourse is a moment in which the boundaries between male and female can become blurred. Females can take on what is generally a male impurity, and males can take on what is generally a female impurity, "so that gender itself can become contagious, if you will."[103] The rituals that P prescribes put gender lines back into place. In the end, female impurities are more severe, more pathological, and last longer than male impurities.

I appreciate the corrective that Ruane adds to Ellens's work; the discharges cannot be completely divorced from the body that emits them. P is not exhaustive in listing the full range of genital discharges that both male and female bodies experience; blood discharge is the sole concern regarding females, and diseased and/or seminal fluids are associated with males. I am not convinced, however, that the seven-day period of impurity for blood means that women's sexual discharges render women lower on a ladder of holiness. The P texts never assign value to the length of an impurity, and if there is no moral implication in impurity, then the length of an impurity is less relevant than whether or not an offering is required for the tabernacle. Arguments can be made that if a woman does not have access to the tabernacle for seven days, then she is excluded

101. Ibid., 177.
102. Ibid., 181.
103. Ibid., 182.

from society. If, however, we were to add up the number of times each week that an average young man has sexual intercourse, masturbates, or has nocturnal emissions, then men could be out of commission more frequently than women![104] In addition, women would be able to anticipate the times when they would not have access to the sanctuary, while men's impurities would be much more unpredictable. We simply do not know how these rules, if ever practiced in ancient Israel, would have played out in the arena of gender identity.

In addition, there is no evidence that gender boundaries can be blurred during sexual intercourse or that the sharing of genital fluids, and thus taking on impurities related to blood or semen, is a corrective to that potential blurring. Does a man blur his boundaries with a woman during sexual intercourse only when the woman is menstruating? As Ellens contends, it is all about the discharge even if those discharges are defined differently for men and women. Charlotte Elisheva Fonrobert asserts,

> In rabbinic literature, we can observe a sliding of the two conceptual frameworks into each other, primarily on a linguistic level. On the one hand, the rabbinic texts continue to distinguish halachically conceptually between the two in traditional Jewish law. . . . That is, the system of impurity follows certain rules of the production and transference of a status of impurity. In and by themselves, these are completely independent from the issue of sexual prohibition. On the other hand, the rabbis employ the language of impurity as an expression describing the woman's condition in which she is prohibited from having sexual relations.[105]

## Menstruation and Mikveh

Interestingly, but not surprisingly, the most important family impurity law that was retained in early Judaism and to the present in some

---

104. Charlotte Elisheva Fonrobert cites a text from the *Didascalia* in which the *Didascalia* is trying to get Jewish converts to Christianity to refrain from believing that they are impure while menstruating: "For if, when a man shall have intercourse, or flux come out from him, he must be bathed, let him also wash his mattress—and he will have this travail and unceasing vexation: he will be bathing and he will be washing his clothes and his mattress, and he will not be able to do anything else" (*Menstrual Purity: Rabbinic and Christian Reconstructions of Biblical Gender* [Stanford, CA: Stanford University Press, 2002], 184).

105. Ibid., 27. See also Michael Rosenberg, "The Conflation of Purity and Prohibition: An Interpretation of Leviticus 18:19," *HTR* 107 (2014): 447–69.

communities is that concerning the menstruating woman. The legal system is quite complex, and there is a full tractate of the Talmud that is titled *niddah*. As we have already noted, Leviticus requires only men to bathe after genital discharges; however, in the course of interpretation this requirement was shifted to women after menstruation. Traditional Jewish law requires a woman to immerse in a *mikveh*, which is a pool of water, a certain percentage of which must be derived from a natural source, such as rain or a body of water. Immersion takes place after sunset in the *mikveh*, with accompanying rituals that ensure that the woman's entire body comes into contact with the water at the same moment. Leviticus 15:18 is used as the primary biblical proof text for this practice. It is only after the ritual water immersion that a husband and wife can touch one another again.

With the advent of the Jewish feminist movement of the 1970s and 1980s, Jewish women began to reject this practice, though it continues to be practiced regularly in Orthodox circles and among Jewish feminists who seek to reclaim the practice. For some, the practice of *mikveh* is interpreted as yet another example of women's oppression; for others, the practice has been reaffirmed and reconstructed as a sacred space for women. Some couples have found that the abstinence period helps them to strengthen their sexual desires for one another.

# Leviticus 16:1-34

# *Purifying the Sancta: "It Takes a Village"*

## Overview

Leviticus 16 has been key in the history of Jewish practice and Christian theology. For well over two thousand years, Yom Kippur, the Jewish Day of Atonement, has been considered the Sabbath of Sabbaths:

> Although it is ambiguous when exactly Yom Kippur had been considered the holiest day of Judaism, in the post-exilic time—definitely in the late Second Temple period—the day was considered as such, and has been so ever since. Yom Kippur was considered so by the Qumranites; the Sadducees, the Pharisees and their followers, the Rabbinites (who dedicated a special Talmudic tractate to Yom Kippur); by the Karaites (ca. 750 C.E. and on), and by all modern Jewish religious denominational groups—Yoma [= "The Day"]—in Mishnah, in the Tosefta, and in both Talmudim. This was and is the approach towards Yom Kippur in all the Jewish communities—Sephardi, Oriental, Ashkenazi, Italian, and Yemeni—in the Land of Israel as well as all over the diaspora, although there were and are some differences in how to maintain Yom Kippur's rituals.[1]

1. Isaac Kalimi, "The Day of Atonement in the Late Second Temple Period: Sadducees' High Priests, Pharisees' Norms, and Qumranites' Calendar(s)," *Review of Rabbinic Judaism* 14 (2011): 72 n. 4.

Leviticus 16 brings together all that has preceded it: consecrated priests, dedicated sanctuary, regulations for sacrificial offerings, and information about impurities. This chapter serves as the culmination and conclusion of the priestly manual of instructions. Thus far, Leviticus has provided details regarding the mechanics of the sacrificial system, an account of the investment of Aaron and his sons, the dedication of the sanctuary, and the impurity laws. Leviticus 16:1 states that YHVH spoke to Moses, following the deaths of the sons of Aaron when they approached YHVH and died. Aaron was to be told that he should not enter into the most holy sanctum, beyond the veil at just anytime lest he die, because God appears in a cloud over the כפרת ("mercy seat," NRSV; others, e.g., NJPS, translate "covering"). This term refers to the gold slab that rested on the ark in the holy of holies, and the Hebrew word itself derives from the root כפר. Thus, the term for the covering over the ark (כפרת), the verb (כפר) that is associated with atonement and expiation, and the name of the Jewish holiday that derives from Leviticus 16 (יום כפור) all share the same Hebrew root.

### Atonement

Women theologians from different perspectives, arising from their countries of origin, culture, race, class, and churches, have posited a range of solutions, which either reject, or restore, or reclaim, or reconfigure the problematic character of the central Christian belief in redemption and atonement. The perimeters of this debate may not be described or addressed adequately here. In the main, these discussions and critiques are conducted at the level of Anselmian theology or later reinterpretations. Elisabeth Schüssler Fiorenza points to the necessity of engagement with the Christian Scriptures themselves and the advantages of learning from these earliest attempts to make meaning of the death of Jesus. She identifies four similarities between these and feminist "naming" processes. First, both discourses arise out of situations and experiences of violence and oppression. Second, both discourses use the language world of their own times. Third, a multiplicity of images are evoked that articulate diverse, and even contradictory, insights into the process of meaning making. Fourth, the resurrection is interpreted as transformative of the world as it is known.[2]

2. Elisabeth Schüssler Fiorenza, *Jesus: Miriam's Child, Sophia's Prophet; Critical Issues in Feminist Christology* (New York: Continuum, 1995), 120–21.

The greatest obstacle to change is the narrowness of categories within which people can operate.[3] There have to be other voices. Among these is the image of John 16:21 and the strand of birth imagery in John that, as I have argued, functions to explain the death-resurrection of Jesus.[4] Arguably, in this gospel, on questions concerning the atoning of sin, the forgiveness of sin "plays out in a different mode."[5] The death of Jesus is presented not as an atoning sacrifice but as the Passover lamb, a sign of liberation. Jesus as "the Lamb of God who takes away the sin of the world" (John 1:29) dies at the hour the Passover lambs are being killed in the temple (19:33). His legs are not broken (19:33; see Exod 12:46). The forgiveness of sin is spoken of in the context of giving power to the disciples to continue the mission of Jesus (John 20:22-23).

To expand this brief overview, five criteria, which emerge from positions representative of the multiplicity of women's voices on this central Christian mystery, are helpful.[6] First, theological meaning making must not obscure that the death of Jesus happened because his actions, life, and ministry in some way threatened the interests of religious and political authorities. The consequence was a violent public execution carried out under the auspices of imperial authorities. Second, interpretations of the death-glory of Jesus must take into account his life, ministry, and resurrection. Third, the images and metaphors employed for theological meaning making are influenced by the culture and historical period in which the interpreter is immersed. Fourth, theological interpretations of the death-glory of Jesus have rhetorical effects that have consequences for the intrapersonal, interpersonal, and interstructural relationships of humankind and social systems and the relationship with the Divine and creation. Fifth, theological interpretations of the death-resurrection of Jesus must not gloss over the reality of suffering and death in his life and that of all human persons, yet it must address life and transformation.

*Kathleen Rushton*

3. Mary Grey, *Redeeming the Dream: Feminism, Redemption and Christian Tradition* (London: SPCK, 1989), 154.

4. Kathleen P. Rushton, *The Parable of the Woman in Childbirth of John 16:21: A Metaphor for the Death and Glorification of Jesus* (Lewiston: Mellen, 2011).

5. Barbara E. Reid, *Taking up the Cross: New Testament Interpretations through Latina and Feminist Eyes* (Minneapolis: Fortress, 2007), 17.

6. Rushton, *Parable of the Woman in Childbirth*, 6–14.

Without getting into the history of the composition of Leviticus, it is worth noting that Leviticus 16 most likely would have followed chapter 10, the narrative about Nadav and Avihu. In that location, Aaron would have received the details about a special ritual ceremony that was to be conducted once a year. This would fit nicely with the consecration of the priests, the dedication of the sanctuary, the mistake of Nadav and Avihu, admonitions for the newly minted priests, and then instructions for the core ritual ceremony of the year. As the text now stands, we have been immersed in laws regarding impurities connected to childbirth, skin conditions and mold, and genital discharges. The instructions given in Leviticus 16 are delayed because the Day of Purification ceremony would have made no sense without information about what and how the sanctuary would have needed to be purified.

Leviticus 16 describes a two-part annual ceremony of cultic decontamination and community reset. This chapter has been the focus of so much attention because the priestly agenda is slightly expanded during the course of this ritual and terminology appears here that is absent from the first part of the book. The primary components of the ritual are easily understood in the context of the priestly material that is presented in Leviticus 1–15; for example, the use of offerings and blood manipulation in the sanctuary. In addition, there are new elements that we have not encountered in Leviticus or that have been under the radar, elements that tend to focus outside of the sanctuary and within the camp. The addition of new elements combined with the dominant motifs and practices lead to challenges in understanding key terminology, which is now expanded beyond its prior technical uses. For example, while the term כפר occurs with great frequency throughout the priestly section of Leviticus, most scholars base their study of this term on its particular use in Leviticus 16. In part, this is because, frankly, the use of כפר in this chapter is messy and confusing.

In most cases, when a person comes into a state of ritual impurity two things need to happen. First, the individual waits the prescribed period of time and then launders clothing and bathes in water; often the text indicates that the person is no longer impure. (See discussion of Lev 13–14 above.) In most cases, however, that individual still needs to bring an offering to the sanctuary on the following day. Milgrom's explanation for this is that impurity impacts directly on the sanctuary, so once the person is no longer impure, she or he still needs to attend to the impact of her or his condition on the sanctuary.[7] Milgrom emphasizes that these states of impurity that impact negatively on the sanctuary are strictly ritual impurities, not sins.

Interestingly, while the Second Temple period attests to the importance of the Day of Purification for Jewish practice and for early Christian theology, the Hebrew Bible itself does not acknowledge this special day. Most commentators begin with the question of the origins of the Day of Purification, but, as I will argue, this is the wrong question to ask.

Leviticus 16 does not provide a name for this day, and it is only in the epilogue (vv. 21-34) that a particular day of the year is designated. The holiday calendar of the Holiness Code (Lev 23:26-32) refers to this day as "the Day of Purification" and describes it similarly to how it is discussed in the epilogue to Leviticus 16. In describing the calculations for the Jubilee Year, Leviticus 25:9 says that the Jubilee begins on the sacred day, the tenth day of the seventh month. Numbers 29:7-11, another holiday calendar, also mentions this date along with a series of offerings that do not correspond to Leviticus 16. The Hebrew Bible does not refer or even allude to this day in any other place. The epilogue and calendars describe the day as one of fasting and self-denial, but they do not mention any of the rites of the high priest or of the treatment of the goat. Thus, more fruitful questions might be: what kind of vision of the community does the text describe? What ideology drives this text?

While the overwhelming concern of the priests is the wellbeing of the sanctuary, they also recognize that even ritual impurity, which has no social stigma (except in the case of skin afflictions), may have a negative emotional impact on individuals. We find recognition of this in the regulations for the חטאת and אשם. While the first three offerings are described consistently and in an orderly fashion, the chapters on purification and guilt offerings are somewhat inconsistent. The language of "feeling guilty," "recognizing guilt," and "being forgiven" does not have the same precision that is expected of priestly texts. The material loses precision because the dynamics of guilt and forgiveness in the human

---

7. Jacob Milgrom first espoused this idea in his article "Israel's Sanctuary: The Priestly 'Picture of Dorian Gray,'" *RB* 83 (1976): 390–99, in which he compared the impact of Dorian Gray's immorality on his portrait. Although the character does not seem to be impacted, his portrait is.

psyche are neither precise nor logical. As the Psalms attest, guilt is a complicated feeling (e.g., Pss 7; 22; 25; 31; 38; 41).

Leviticus 16 provides a complex series of rituals that attend both to the precise mechanics of a well-run cultic system, in which the natural flows of the human body are regulated vis-à-vis God's need for static conditions of holiness and purity, and to the irrational emotions of guilt and fear that the humans experience within highly subjective conditions. The first part of the ritual thus focuses on blood purification in the holy arena, while the second part focuses on the needs of the community to express guilt, release emotions, and witness them symbolically leaving the camp. The first part of the ritual takes the high priest in to the very presence of God, while the second part extends the ritual beyond the camp. This ritual goes into the deepest core and outermost fringes of the physical space of the camp. The ritual is the ultimate reset button for restoring the community to a state of purity.

We have no evidence that the ritual as described in Leviticus 16 was ever enacted in the First Temple period. By the Second Temple period, we have evidence that there was an annual practice at the Second Temple that was based on Leviticus 16, but even during that period there was substantial disagreement among Jewish sects as to how the rite was to be observed. The disagreement was based on textual interpretation; in other words, the Second Temple practices were based on a variety of interpretations of Leviticus 16 and were influenced by other rituals of the Second Temple period, but actions described in the text could not be followed exactly because there was no ark or כפרת in the Second Temple. Nevertheless, Leviticus 16 did provide a rough blueprint for an elaborate ritual, which took place in the temple along with observances by laypeople. Following the destruction of the temple, Jews solemnized this day through prayer, fasting, and atonement. Among Christians, Leviticus 16 was read as the necessary forerunner to Jesus who, in suffering like the goat and giving his life, made atonement for all believers in Christ.[8]

## The Ritual Preparations (16:1-10)

The atonement ritual is described in such detail that it merits a careful examination. Verse 3 indicates that Aaron should approach the most holy

---

8. For example, see Rom 5:6-11 and Heb 9:11-14.

<sup>16:1</sup>The Lord spoke to Moses after the death of the two sons of Aaron, when they drew near before the Lord and died. <sup>2</sup>The Lord said to Moses:

Tell your brother Aaron not to come just at any time into the sanctuary inside the curtain before the mercy seat that is upon the ark, or he will die; for I appear in the cloud upon the mercy seat. <sup>3</sup>Thus shall Aaron come into the holy place: with a young bull for a sin offering and a ram for a burnt offering. <sup>4</sup>He shall put on the holy linen tunic, and shall have the linen undergarments next to his body, fasten the linen sash, and wear the linen turban; these are the holy vestments. He shall bathe his body in water, and then put them on. <sup>5</sup>He shall take from the congregation of the people of Israel two male goats for a sin offering, and one ram for a burnt offering.

<sup>6</sup>Aaron shall offer the bull as a sin offering for himself and for his house. <sup>7</sup>He shall take the two goats and set them before the Lord at the entrance of the tent of meeting; <sup>8</sup>and Aaron shall cast lots on the two goats, one lot for the Lord and the other lot for Azazel. <sup>9</sup>Aaron shall present the goat on which the lot fell for the Lord, and offer it as a sin offering; <sup>10</sup>but the goat on which the lot fell for Azazel shall be presented alive before the Lord to make atonement over it, that it may be sent away into the wilderness to Azazel.

קדשׁ ("sanctuary" in NRSV refers to the inner shrine, sometimes called קדשׁ קדשׁים, "holy of holies") with a bull for a purification offering and a ram for a burnt offering. He should wear special vestments: a linen tunic, linen breeches upon his genitalia, a linen sash, and a linen turban. These garments are designated as "holy clothing" (v. 4). It is interesting to note that this clothing varies sharply from the usual ostentatious priestly vestments. Traditional Jewish interpretation suggests that the high priest wears this clothing to appear humble before God and to represent the regular individual. Before he dresses, he washes his flesh. Then Aaron should take two male goats from the congregation of Israel to serve as purification offerings and a ram to function as a burnt offering, and he should get ready to offer his bull as a purification offering to make expiation for himself and his household (vv. 5-6). Aaron also readies the male goats by bringing them to the entrance of the tent of meeting and placing lots upon them, one that says "for YHVH" and one that says "for Azazel." The goat designated for Azazel is put before YHVH to make expiation upon it, to send him into the wilderness to Azazel. (See below for a discussion of Azazel.)

## The Ritual Actions, Scene 1 (16:11-19)

Description of the ritual begins in Leviticus 16:11, with Aaron's slaughter of the bull for expiation on his own behalf and on behalf of his household. He then takes a censer full of coals from the incense altar that is located in the inner sanctum along with two handfuls of fine spicy incense. He brings the censer through the veil burning the incense so that an incense cloud covers a clear view of the כפרת within which the testimony is contained; Aaron creates the incense cloud so that he will not die (vv. 12-13). He takes the bull's blood and with a finger sprinkles some of the blood toward the כפרת; he does this seven times (v. 14). Aaron repeats the process with the community's goat offering in the same manner (v. 15). Verse 16 provides the reason for these ritual activities: this is done to expiate upon the most holy from the impurities of the Israelites and from their wrongs and all their sins.

From the point when Aaron enters until he exits the most holy, nobody else is allowed in; Aaron must present himself before YHVH alone (v. 17). Aaron then moves to the outer altar and repeats the sevenfold sprinkling of the blood of the bull and the goat, in addition to placing blood on the horns of the altar (vv. 18-19). Thus, Aaron purifies and sanctifies the altar from the impurities of the Israelites.[9]

There is a rigorous and ongoing debate among scholars about the meaning of כפר in this chapter. Much of the debate centers on the specific meaning of "atone" with different prepositions in relation to the חטאת offering. Milgrom asserts that the חטאת never purifies the offerer, but that the חטאת blood purges the sancta. He argues that the translation "make expiation on behalf of" is indicated when כפר is followed by the prepositions בעד and על and that these two prepositions are interchangeable when a person is the object. Milgrom continues, however, if the object is inanimate then the prepositions על, ב, and את signify "make expiation upon." In verse 16, purging takes place upon (על) the כפרת, and in verse 20 purging happens in (ב) the most holy. "Thus for both Israel and her neighbors impurity was a physical substance, an aerial miasma that possessed magnetic attraction for the realm of the sacred. . . . Impurity is the implacable foe of holiness where it exists; it assaults the sacred realm

---

9. See Naphtali Meshel, *The "Grammar" of Sacrifice: A Generativist Study of the Israelite Sacrificial System in the Priestly Writings* (Oxford: Oxford University Press, 2014), 147–53, for a discussion of the six verbs that P uses to describe blood manipulation.

[11]Aaron shall present the bull as a sin offering for himself, and shall make atonement for himself and for his house; he shall slaughter the bull as a sin offering for himself. [12]He shall take a censer full of coals of fire from the altar before the LORD, and two handfuls of crushed sweet incense, and he shall bring it inside the curtain [13]and put the incense on the fire before the LORD, that the cloud of the incense may cover the mercy seat that is upon the covenant, or he will die. [14]He shall take some of the blood of the bull, and sprinkle it with his finger on the front of the mercy seat, and before the mercy seat he shall sprinkle the blood with his finger seven times.

[15]He shall slaughter the goat of the sin offering that is for the people and bring its blood inside the curtain, and do with its blood as he did with the blood of the bull, sprinkling it upon the mercy seat and before the mercy seat. [16]Thus he shall make atonement for the sanctuary, because of the uncleannesses of the people of Israel, and because of their transgressions, all their sins; and so he shall do for the tent of meeting, which remains with them in the midst of their uncleannesses.[17]No one shall be in the tent of meeting from the time he enters to make atonement in the sanctuary until he comes out and has made atonement for himself and for his house and for all the assembly of Israel. [18]Then he shall go out to the altar that is before the LORD and make atonement on its behalf, and shall take some of the blood of the bull and of the blood of the goat, and put it on each of the horns of the altar. [19]He shall sprinkle some of the blood on it with his finger seven times, and cleanse it and hallow it from the uncleannesses of the people of Israel.

even from afar."[10] Milgrom further argues that biblical impurity occurs in graded power. A person's severe physical impurity impacts the altar, an inadvertent transgression affects the inner altar, and an intentional transgression pierces through the veil to the most holy. The Day of Purification remedies the impact of impurities on all three levels.[11]

## The Ritual Actions, Scene 2 (16:20-22)

When Aaron has finished purging the most holy, the inner sanctum, and the altar, he brings forth the remaining living goat designated for Azazel (Lev 16:20). There are different theories regarding the name

10. Jacob Milgrom, *Leviticus 1–16*, AB 3 (New York: Doubleday, 1991), 257.
11. See ibid., 254–58 for a concise explanation of his proposal.

*Lev 16:20-22*

²⁰When he has finished atoning for the holy place and the tent of meeting and the altar, he shall present the live goat. ²¹Then Aaron shall lay both his hands on the head of the live goat, and confess over it all the iniquities of the people of Israel, and all their transgressions, all their sins, putting them on the head of the goat, and sending it away into the wilderness by means of someone designated for the task. ²²The goat shall bear on itself all their iniquities to a barren region; and the goat shall be set free in the wilderness.

Azazel; most commentators conclude that this was the name of a demon, perhaps originally a designation for the Canaanite god of death, Mot. While Azazel may have been a demon, the text never describes the demon and never makes any other reference to it. Baruch Levine notes Ibn Ezra's comment on Leviticus 16:8: "If you are able to understand the mystery of the word 'Azazel' you will comprehend both its mystery and the mystery of its name, for it has analogies in Scripture. And I will disclose to you a bit of the mystery: When you understand thirty-three, you will know it." Levine then explains that counting thirty-three verses beyond 16:8, the reader arrives at 17:7, which refers to the cult of the goat demon.[12] According to Levine, the ritual of the goat betrays ancient Israel's ongoing beliefs in magic and otherworldly creatures (even in P), while Milgrom believes that the reference to Azazel is completely demythologized. According to Milgrom, Azazel may have been known in popular Israelite folklore and was co-opted by P.

While the writers designate this goat as a חטאת (v. 21), this goat's blood is never used in the ritual; nor is the animal even sacrificed! The ritual of the goat addresses transgressions, sins, and iniquities while the blood ritual, which immediately precedes it, addresses transgressions, sins, and impurities.

The high priest places both of his hands on the head of the living goat and confesses on it all of the iniquities of the Israelites, their transgressions, and all their sins; he places all of this on the head of the goat (v. 21). David Wright has convincingly demonstrated that the two-handed

---

12. Baruch Levine, *Leviticus: A JPS Torah Commentary* (Philadelphia: Jewish Publication Society of America, 1989), 252. For a more comprehensive presentation of Azazel interpretations, see Bernd Janowski, "Azazel עזאזל," in *Dictionary of Deities and Demons in the Bible*, ed. Karel van der Toorn, Bob Becking, and Pieter W. van der Horst, 2nd rev. ed. (Leiden: Brill and Grand Rapids: Eerdmans, 1999), 128–31.

ritual focuses attention on the goat as the recipient of the community's sins.[13] Then a designated man sends the goat out into the wilderness. There is no agreement as to the identity of the person who accompanies the goat; suggestions include a priest, a criminal, or a layperson.[14] Baruch Levine first argued in 1974 in *In the Presence of the Lord*, as well as in his JPS commentary, that the Hebrew word התודה (NRSV, "confess") in verse 21 has a particular valence because it comes from the root ידה, which means "to reveal oneself." Thus, as the high priest confesses the sins of the people he is basically exposing the sins (which may have been supposed to have had some demonic power) and then trapping them in the goat. "Ancient peoples believed that sinfulness, like impurity, was an external force that had clung to them; it was necessary, therefore, to 'drive out,' or detach sins."[15] Milgrom, by contrast, argues that the function of the Azazel goat was to carry off the people's impurities and that, at a later stage, the people believed that the goat carried off all of their sins.[16]

One more observation warrants attention regarding the second part of the Day of Purification ritual. It is unique in the Hebrew Bible, the only case of a two-handed ritual with confession and a send-off. While the first component of the ritual builds on known P rituals, the goat is extraordinary. There are two stages in the goat ritual. First the priest transfers the sins and impurities from the people to the goat, and then the contaminated goat is sent away, effectively disposing of the sins and impurities. Instead of transfer, some scholars believe that this is a ritual of substitution. "In substitution, the evil is not just transferred for the purpose of disposal, it is transferred so that the consequences of the evil will fall on the bearer of impurity instead of the patient."[17] The issue of substitution

---

13. David P. Wright, "The Gesture of Hand Placement in the Hebrew Bible and in Hittite Literature," *JAOS* 106 (1986): 436.

14. Meir Malul, "עתי אִישׁ (Leviticus 16:21): A Marginal Person," *JBL* 128 [2009]: 437–42) argues convincingly that the phrase אישׁ עתי designates any person who is marginal to society, like a woman, a leper, or a criminal. Raymond Westbrook argues that the person is specifically a criminal who is given a chance to atone by performing this task (Raymond Westbrook and Theodore J. Lewis, "Who Led the Scapegoat in Leviticus 16:21?," *JBL* 127 [2008]: 417–22).

15. Baruch Levine, *In The Presence of the Lord: A Study of Cult and Some Cultic Terms in Ancient Israel*, SJLA 5 (Leiden: Brill, 1974), 82; and later in *Leviticus*, 106.

16. Milgrom, *Leviticus 1–16*, 1041–45, 1064.

17. David P. Wright, *Disposal of Impurity: Elimination Rites in the Bible and in Hittite and Mesopotamian Literature* (Atlanta: Scholars Press, 1987), 37.

raises two important questions: Did the writers believe that God would punish the people for their sins? If so, was the ritual of transferring their sins to the goat intended to deflect the punishment off of them?

The substitution concept plays an important role in some Christian formulations, as Jesus is understood to have taken on the sins of others and to have died on their behalf. As Eric Gilchrest notes, "It is my opinion that part, if not much, of the reason atonement in the Hebrew Bible is read through the lens of substitutionary death is because of the tendency among some scholars to speak about biblical theology with a Pauline accent, in particular Paul's statement that 'the wages of sin is death' (Rom. 6:23)."[18] Gilchrest offers a modified substitution theory, wherein the people expect to be banished by God, not put to death, so the goat is banished in place of the people. Banishment is necessary because God needs boundaries to be maintained between the holy and the unholy.[19] As Howard Cooper has written,

> Suffice it to say here that whether we think of the impulses that the scapegoat symbolically carries in terms of Jung's shadow or Freud's id, it would seem that the original ritual was a highly organised attempt to ensure that potentially destructive impulses (ones that could lead to so-called "sin") were not repressed from consciousness, were not split off and disowned, but were transferred consciously to the so-called "scapegoat," who would then take them into a space of their own. In addition, the knowledge that this was happening would help generate in the people a sense of hopefulness, a sense that instinctual life was complex and demanding yet potentially liberating. The community would not be enslaved to elemental passions as long as they accepted these passions as a natural part of the human condition, rather than impulses that had to be condemned and eradicated.[20]

## The Concluding Actions (16:23-28)

Aaron then takes off the special garments of linen and leaves them in the most holy; he washes his flesh with water in a holy place and dresses in his usual priestly garb. Then he goes out to officiate over the burnt

18. Eric Gilchrest, "For the Wages of Sin Is . . . Banishment: An Unexplored Substitutionary Motif in Leviticus 16 and the Ritual of the Scapegoat," *EvQ* 85 (2003): 44 n. 30.

19. Ibid., esp. 44–46.

20. Howard Cooper, "Some Thoughts on 'Scapegoating' and Its Origins in Leviticus 16," *European Judaism* 41 (2008): 118.

²³Then Aaron shall enter the tent of meeting, and shall take off the linen vestments that he put on when he went into the holy place, and shall leave them there. ²⁴He shall bathe his body in water in a holy place, and put on his vestments; then he shall come out and offer his burnt offering and the burnt offering of the people, making atonement for himself and for the people. ²⁵The fat of the sin offering he shall turn into smoke on the altar. ²⁶The one who sets the goat free for Azazel shall wash his clothes and bathe his body in water, and afterward may come into the camp. ²⁷The bull of the sin offering and the goat of the sin offering, whose blood was brought in to make atonement in the holy place, shall be taken outside the camp; their skin and their flesh and their dung shall be consumed in fire. ²⁸The one who burns them shall wash his clothes and bathe his body in water, and afterward may come into the camp.

offerings, and he makes expiation on his behalf and on behalf of the community (vv. 23-25). Meanwhile, the person who accompanied the goat out to the wilderness launders his clothing, bathes in water, and then returns to the camp (v. 26). The bull and goat that were slaughtered for their blood are taken outside the camp, where they are burnt up completely (v. 27). The person who takes care of this then launders and bathes in water and reenters the camp (v. 28). This concludes the ritual.

## The Epilogue (16:29-34)

The final six verses of Leviticus 16 seem to be a composite of explanations for the atonement ritual itself that reveals some level of disagreement regarding the actual purpose of the ritual. First, the epilogue provides a fixed date for the annual ritual so that a one-time event described in Leviticus becomes an annual holiday (v. 29). The epilogue adds the dimensions of the human state of mind and intention for the day, including self-humbling and refraining from work (vv. 30-31). The final words mark the Day of Atonement as the Sabbath of Sabbaths, in which the anointed priest purges the inner sanctum and the sacrificial altar each year (vv. 32-34). The epilogue contains inserts from the H source, which add the popular practice of self-affliction and fasting to the ritual laws.

In Judaism, the Day of Atonement, Yom Kippur, incorporates the text of Leviticus 16 into its liturgy for the day. Yom Kippur has become a day of fasting and prayer, a day of חשבון נפש, taking account of one's soul. The

²⁹This shall be a statute to you forever: In the seventh month, on the tenth day of the month, you shall deny yourselves, and shall do no work, neither the citizen nor the alien who resides among you. ³⁰For on this day atonement shall be made for you, to cleanse you; from all your sins you shall be clean before the Lord. ³¹It is a sabbath of complete rest to you, and you shall deny yourselves, it is a statute forever. ³²The priest who is anointed and consecrated as priest in his father's place shall make atonement, wearing the linen vestments, the holy vestments. ³³He shall make atonement for the sanctuary, and he shall make atonement for the tent of meeting and for the altar, and he shall make atonement for the priests and for all the people of the assembly. ³⁴This shall be an everlasting statute for you, to make atonement for the people of Israel once in the year for all their sins. And Moses did as the Lord had commanded him.

Day of Atonement is preceded by weeks of introspection and by trying to make amends for wrongs committed against others. Making things right with God can come only after doing the best we can to make things right with others. We must seek to right the wrongs בין אדם לחברו ("between human beings") before righting wrongs בין אדם למקום ("between the individual and God"). In a sense, then, the heart of the ritual of Leviticus 16 requires us to pay attention both inwardly, to the relationship between God and ourselves, and outwardly, to our relationships with others. The responsibility for taking account of one's wrongs on Yom Kippur transcends gender. Both women and men are required to rectify wrongs, whether in relationship to God or to other members of the community. The high priest confesses the sins of the community as a whole.

# Leviticus 17:1-16

## A Bloody Mess

### Entering the Holiness Legislation

Just as the Covenant Code (Exod 20:22–23:33) and the Deuteronomic Law Code (Deut 12:2–26:15) begin by addressing the practice of sacrifices, so too the Holiness Legislation (Lev 17:1–26:46) begins with statements regarding the proper site for sacred offerings. Scholars have long agreed that the Covenant Code assumes that people can make offerings anywhere, as long as an altar is set up for this purpose. Deuteronomy, by contrast, insists that all sacred offerings be made at only one centralized location (later interpreted as Jerusalem). The claims in Leviticus 17 are more ambiguous, and there is no scholarly consensus regarding the specific assertions about sites of worship. Leviticus 17 insists that the slaughter of sacrificial animals must take place at the entrance to the tent of meeting, but it is not clear if this is *the* tent of meeting or *any* tent of meeting. In other words, was the author of this work assuming a system of centralized worship at only one legitimate cultic site or a system of multiple places of worship?

Under the initial influence of Julius Wellhausen, who believed that the priestly writings (P) and holiness legislation (H) material were the latest layer of the Pentateuch, many scholars believe that P/H must have assumed a system of centralized worship as set up by the Deuteronomist (D). Because P/H inherited this system, there would have been no need for the priestly writers to assert what was already the practice. This position is based, however, on a number of assumptions—all of which have been questioned in recent years. I am persuaded by the arguments in favor of multiple sites of worship in H's worldview because H also advocates that all meat must first be presented at an altar as a well-being offering. Therefore, the consumption of meat must go hand in hand with accessible altar sites. It may be that P/H was not written after D, regardless of the absolute (specific) dating of the documents. It may be that P/H is not familiar with D. It may be that P/H is simply not interested in the D agenda. The application of D's program of centralization was short-lived in any case, so its longstanding influence may have been quite minimal.

As I have done elsewhere in this volume, I will take the position that D and P/H have different interests and different agendas and do not necessarily polemicize against one another. If we refrain from making assumptions about what P/H knew or did not know about other schools of thought, then we are brought back to the text itself to reflect on what this particular text is addressing.

## No Slaughtering Outside the Tent of Meeting (17:1-7)

Leviticus 17 sets out five distinct yet related cases. Verses 3-4 state that if a person slaughters an ox, a lamb, or a goat within the camp or outside of the camp and does not bring the animal to the tent of meeting to offer it as a sacrifice to YHVH, that person's crime is the symbolic equivalent to murder, and that person shall be cut off from the people. Verses 5-7 provide the reasoning for this legislation. Instead of slaughtering animals out in the open fields, people should bring the animals to the tent of meeting and to the priest, so that the slaughter functions as a well-being offering for YHVH instead of an offering to the goat demons in the field. This legislation ensures that offerings are made within the priestly cultic system, but what constitutes an offering in this text? Is the legislation about animals that have been set aside specifically for a sacred offering, or does the legislation address the slaughter of any animal that is to be consumed? There is a longstanding debate over this question among ancient and modern interpreters of the text, going back to the Talmud (b. Hul 16a-17a). Rabbi Akiva says that since שחט means "slit the throat," the law applies only to sacrificial animals intended for the altar. Therefore, other means of killing animals would have been permitted. Rabbi Ishmael argues that the law applies to all animals that are killed as

17:1The LORD spoke to Moses:

2Speak to Aaron and his sons and to all the people of Israel and say to them: This is what the LORD has commanded. 3If anyone of the house of Israel slaughters an ox or a lamb or a goat in the camp, or slaughters it outside the camp, 4and does not bring it to the entrance of the tent of meeting, to present it as an offering to the LORD before the tabernacle of the LORD, he shall be held guilty of bloodshed; he has shed blood, and he shall be cut off from the people. 5This is in order that the people of Israel may bring their sacrifices that they offer in the open field, that they may bring them to the LORD, to the priest at the entrance of the tent of meeting, and offer them as sacrifices of well-being to the LORD. 6The priest shall dash the blood against the altar of the LORD at the entrance of the tent of meeting, and turn the fat into smoke as a pleasing odor to the LORD, 7so that they may no longer offer their sacrifices for goat-demons, to whom they prostitute themselves. This shall be a statute forever to them throughout their generations.

food sources in addition to those that are intended for the altar.[1] Baruch Schwartz argues that the law prohibits all profane slaughter and that, in the theologies of both P and H, the only way to consume meat is via a well-being offering.[2]

We can only wonder which members of a farming household would have had the primary responsibility for bringing domesticated farm animals to the priest for ritual slaughter. We must also keep in mind that the consumption of meat from cattle and flock correlated with economic class and only the wealthiest families would have had the luxury of slaughtering animals for their meat.

## Offer Sacrifices Only at the Tent of Meeting (17:8-9)

The second piece of legislation in this chapter may help to clarify the first. Leviticus 17:8-9 states that if an Israelite or a resident alien who dwells among Israelites wishes to offer a burnt offering or a well-being offering, but does not bring that offering to the tent of meeting to offer

1. Jacob Milgrom, *Leviticus 17–22*, AB 3A (New York: Doubleday, 2000) seems to agree with R. Ishmael's point, noting that שחט is used in the Bible for nonsacrificial slaughter as well (1453–54).

2. Baruch Schwartz, "'Profane' Slaughter and the Integrity of the Priestly Code," *HUCA* 67 (1996): 15–42.

[8]And say to them further: Anyone of the house of Israel or of the aliens who reside among them who offers a burnt offering or sacrifice, [9]and does not bring it to the entrance of the tent of meeting, to sacrifice it to the LORD, shall be cut off from the people.

it before YHVH, that person will be cut off from the people. This law essentially insists that if someone plans to make a sacred offering, it must be brought to YHVH at the tent of meeting. If the first law refers only to the slaughter of animals intended as a sacred offering, then the laws are redundant and we must ask why the resident alien is included in one but not the other.

Milgrom argues that the גר ("alien") is absent from the first law because the גר is only required to follow prohibitive laws in order to avoid the release of impurity in the community; the גר is not required to follow performative or positive commandments since refraining from positive commandments is an act of inaction—and in this case, inaction does not lead to impurity.

## Do not Consume Blood! (17:10-12)

Leviticus 17:10-12 introduces the third unit of legislation, which bans the ingestion of blood. Any Israelite or resident alien who lives among Israelites and who eats blood will suffer two consequences: God will set God's face against the person and God will cut that person off from the community.

The reasoning for the prohibition is presented in verse 11: (1) the life force of all flesh (i.e., living beings) is in the blood; (2) I (YHVH) have given (the blood) for you upon the altar to effect expiation (NRSV, "making atonement") by means of life force. The punishment for eating blood is quite severe and stands out among only a handful of severe punishments. The first two laws indicate the punishment with the כרת ("cut off") formula in its most common iteration—with a *niphal* (passive) verb form. For the blood prohibition (vv. 10-12), however, punishment begins with the statement that YHVH will turn YHVH's attention to the offender with hostile intent. Then the text uses the כרת formula with a *hiphil*, indicating that YHVH will actively and directly execute the punishment.[3] Given the

---

3. The *hiphil* of this verbal root indicates a more violent demise than does the *niphal*. The *hiphil* is used by H only for the blood prohibition and for Molech worship (see Lev 20:3, 5, 6).

*Lev 17:10-12*

[10]If anyone of the house of Israel or of the aliens who reside among them eats any blood, I will set my face against that person who eats blood, and will cut that person off from the people. [11]For the life of the flesh is in the blood; and I have given it to you for making atonement for your lives on the altar; for, as life, it is the blood that makes atonement. [12]Therefore I have said to the people of Israel: No person among you shall eat blood, nor shall any alien who resides among you eat blood.

harsh language here and the fact that the blood prohibition appears in a variety of biblical sources (see Gen 9:4; Lev 3:17; 7:26-27; and Deut 12:16, 23-25), it is safe to assume that the consumption of blood was a central taboo. The reason for this taboo is not entirely clear. Some interpreters argue that clauses 1 and 2 (v. 11a and b) were originally independent and competing rationales; that is, for some ancients blood as life force was the source of the taboo, while for others blood was to be used for the altar site.

One interesting observation about this legislation is the statement in verse 11b that YHVH has provided blood in order to make expiation on the altar, a view that is contrary to P materials, which never indicate that the well-being has any expiatory function but rather is an expression of joy and thanksgiving. Why would H connect the layperson's eating of meat with an expiatory function?[4] Baruch Schwartz offers a compelling reading: clause 1 (v. 11a) asserts that blood is the seat of life. Clause 2 (v. 11b) asserts that blood is to be used for expiation. And clause 3 (v. 11c) combines the two prior statements to provide the ultimate reason against eating blood: blood serves as ransom for human life, which kills in order to eat meat.

> This is the only place in which the action כפר attributed to blood has the sense of ransom rather than purification. The verse takes a word, or rather a cultic concept—that blood is מכפר—a concept which generally has one meaning, and gives it an entirely new one. This new meaning, contained in the third clause's synthesis of the first two, is that blood, by virtue of the life of which it is the seat, has been assigned by God

---

4. Rolf Rendtorff brought this question to the fore in "Another Prolegomenon to Leviticus 17:11," in *Pomegranates and Golden Bells: Studies in Biblical Jewish and Near Eastern Ritual, Law and Literature in Honor of Jacob Milgrom*, ed. David P. Wright, David Noel Freedman, and Avi Hurvitz (Winona Lake, IN: Eisenbrauns, 1995), 23–28.

to the altar, i.e., commanded to be offered to God, in order to serve as ransom for human life.[5]

Schwartz argues that H is engaging with P's view of the function of blood. While P believes that blood purifies the sancta from contamination, H argues that blood also serves as a ransom to redeem oneself from extreme culpability. Thus, if the role of blood is to ransom lives, then it cannot be ingested. If Schwartz is correct, the text provides an example of what we will see throughout the Holiness Legislation: a shift in focus from the sanctuary, with its limited access, to the responsibilities of each individual in the community.

### Honoring All Life

It is very clear in the Torah that the animals we use have some kind of status as ethical ends, and many of the laws appear to have consideration for the subjectivity and intrinsic needs of the creatures we care for. That animals have standing is reflected at an even more fundamental level in the Torah's use of the same vocabulary for human and animal bodies. Both an animal and a human are called נפש, which most accurately means body imbued with breath; and the substance of both is called בשר, without the distinction we have in English of meat versus flesh. Though the Torah makes no firm distinction between soul and body, to the extent that one can speak of נפש as representative of the concept of soul or subjectivity in Torah, animals were also imbued with this נפש.[6]

Yet the Torah did permit the eating of certain animals, so it was essential to make some kind of substantive distinction between a human נפש and an animal נפש, between human and animal bodies and souls. Instead of doing this by denying the subjecthood and subjectivity of animals, as late Western thought did, ancient Hebrew culture used rituals to physically and symbolically inscribe different meanings onto

5. Baruch Schwartz, "The Prohibitions Concerning the 'Eating' of Blood in Leviticus 17," in *Priesthood and Cult in Ancient Israel*, ed. Gary A. Anderson and Saul M. Olyan, JSOTSup 125 (Sheffield: JSOT Press, 1991), 56. See Jay Sklar, "Sin and Impurity: Atoned or Purified? Yes!," in *Perspectives on Purity and Purification in the Bible*, ed. Baruch J. Schwartz, David P. Wright, Jeffrey Stackert, and Naphtali S. Meshel, LHB/OTS 474 (New York: T&T Clark, 2008), 30–31 for a refutation of Schwartz's argument.

6. See David Seidenberg, *Kabbalah and Ecology: God's Image in the More-Than-Human World* (Cambridge: Cambridge University Press, 2016), chaps. 4–5.

animal and human bodies. The sacrificial system of the קרבנות ("animal offerings") inscribed holiness onto an animal's body by dividing up the body into parts that were sacred and parts that could be used, whereas the purification system of טמאה and טהרה ("cultic impurity" and "cultic purity," respectively) inscribed holiness in the human body by valorizing its wholeness and reconstituting the body's unity through immersion in "living waters" and related purification rituals. The importance of inscribing these differences is reflected in the many chapters of Leviticus (esp. 1, 3, 4, and 7) devoted to detailing how the body of an animal sacrifice is to be dissected, which parts go on the altar, and how to treat the blood of a slaughtered animal, as well as in the many chapters devoted to the problem of צרעת (leprosy) and issues or changes in the human body and the rituals needed to restore the body's wholeness (12–15).

The temple was the ground and center where these two symbolic systems and ritual regimes overlapped and interacted. Sacrifices in the temple overcame the tension between the intrinsic value of an animal's life and its use-value for us by harvesting, as it were, the intrinsic value of the animal for an end greater than human needs or desires, something we might term its "holiness-value." Fundamentally, this holiness-value was located in the blood of the animal, "for the נפש of all flesh is its blood," כי נפש כל בשר דמו היא (Lev 17:14; see also Gen 9:4; Lev 17:10-12; Deut 12:23-25). Here נפש is rightly interpreted as soul in an animistic sense. In essence, the נפש was localized to the blood so that the בשר or flesh could become permissible for eating. Because of this sanctity, the only valid use for blood was on the altar.[7] Leviticus 17:11 explains the exchange value that mediates between the systems of embodied meaning: "For the נפש of flesh is in the blood, and I have given it to you for the altar to atone for your נפשות, for the blood is that in the נפש that will atone."[8]

The secret of both the red heifer ritual for cleansing after contact with a dead body (Num 19) and the ritual of cleansing from צרעת (Lev 14) may be hidden in the need to tie together these two systems. The red heifer or פרה אדומה must be wholly red, אדומה (i.e., the color of earth/אדמה)—reminiscent of both Adam/אדם, and blood/דם. In the red heifer ritual, which incorporated other red items—cedar wood, hyssop, and crimson—the redness of blood/דם was externalized and the body of the animal was burned whole, thereby combining elements of

---

7. See David Seidenberg, "Brit Taharah: Reconstructing the Covenantal Body of the Jew," in *Sh'ma* 25/486 (January 20, 1995).

8. Author's translation.

the טהרה system and the קרבנות.
The resulting ashes were used
to restore the wholeness of the
human body in the case of its
most extreme breach, contact with
a human corpse, which is also
called נפש (Num 5:2). In Leviticus
14, the ritual for purification
from צרעת (leprosy), which was
a disease that damaged the
wholeness of the human body,
also involved cedar wood,
hyssop, and crimson, and like the
red heifer it combined elements
of wholeness and sacrifice, taking
a live whole bird, and dipping
it in the blood of a slaughtered
bird. Both these rituals happened

outside the temple and the camp,
thus forming the second pole of a
circuit whose opposite pole was
the *mishkan* or temple altar, where
perfect whole humans offered
the blood and parts of perfect
animals.

What we may find amid all
these details is a core ethical ideal
supported by a vast network
of ritual. That ideal is simply
that if humans are to use the
lives of other animals to sustain
ourselves, we can and must do it
in a manner that honors the full
ethical and spiritual value, the
נפש, of the lives we take.

*David Seidenberg*

## Game Meat and Blood Disposal (17:13-14)

The fourth piece of legislation (Lev 17:13-14) addresses the treatment
of the blood of animals that are hunted, game. Game is not suited for
sacrifice at the altar for both ideological and pragmatic reasons. It is not
practical to gather the seeping blood of the animal and transport it to
an altar, so the blood is to be poured on the ground and covered with
dust. There is no agreement among commentators as to the purpose of
covering the blood. Some argue that the blood should be covered so that
another living being does not eat it. Others argue that the blood must
be covered so that the blood does not cry out for vengeance or so that
the blood can be properly returned to God. The outstanding feature in
this legislation is the number of times that blood is identified with life.
The text says: "life is in the blood," "blood is in the life," and "blood is
life." The equation of blood and life also occurs in Deuteronomy 12:20-
24, which also deals with animal slaughter. In that text, game is placed
in the same category as non-sacrificial animal slaughter.

## Congealed Blood and Carcasses (17:15-16)

The final legislation (Lev 17:15-16) contains no prohibition. The legislation states that if anyone consumes an animal that has died of natural

¹³And anyone of the people of Israel, or of the aliens who reside among them, who hunts down an animal or bird that may be eaten shall pour out its blood and cover it with earth.

¹⁴For the life of every creature—its blood is its life; therefore I have said to the people of Israel: You shall not eat the blood of any creature, for the life of every creature is its blood; whoever eats it shall be cut off.

¹⁵All persons, citizens or aliens, who eat what dies of itself or what has been torn by wild animals, shall wash their clothes, and bathe themselves in water, and be unclean until the evening; then they shall be clean. ¹⁶But if they do not wash themselves or bathe their body, they shall bear their guilt.

causes (נבלה) or an animal that has been killed as prey by another animal (טרפה), that person needs to wash and launder in order to remove the impurity. This law must assume that congealed blood does not fall under the same category as fresh blood. In the postbiblical period, the dietary laws of rabbinic Judaism strictly forbid even the consumption of נבלה and טרפה.

## Who Are the Savages?

Leviticus 17 is not often cited in contemporary food discourse, but it should be. This chapter reflects a profound reverence for life even as it accepts the carnivorous nature of most human beings. In modern slaughterhouses, whether they are small and oriented toward humane treatment of animals or enormous industrial factories, regulations and best practices for slaughter are as follows. Once the animal enters the stunning box, a stunner is used to shoot a metal rod into the brain to render the animal insensible.[9] The animal is then lifted up by one of its back hooves and a worker uses a knife to sever all the arteries from the heart. The ideal time period between stunning and bleeding is fifteen seconds to ensure that the animal does not come out of the stun. When the arteries are severed, blood gushes out in gallons very quickly. It is the bleeding out that kills the animal in seconds. In small facilities, the blood may be caught with a large tub and in larger facilities the blood flows into huge vats. An entire subfield of waste management is now focused

---

9. Kosher and Halal slaughtering practices sever the throat and do not use stunners before the slaughter.

on blood and fat disposal. Generally, trucks come to the slaughterhouse facilities to pick up vats of blood for disposal or recycling. Blood is most commonly repurposed as an ingredient in animal feed, or it becomes an ingredient for fertilizer or compost. If companies dispose of the blood in sewers or landfills, regulations mandate that the companies must decontaminate the blood before disposal.

In the context of today's practices, the mandates in Leviticus take on a new meaning. Leviticus 17 claims that the slaughter of an animal is akin to murder and that the only way to make things right with God is to return the blood of the animal back to God. The "recycling" of blood takes on a sacred dimension and demands that each person recognize that slaughter is the taking of a life. God does not forbid the eating of meat, but H requires that every time someone wants to eat meat, they must engage in a ritual that honors the life and acknowledges the problematic act of killing. The Deuteronomic school privileges the value of centralization of worship over the sanctity of the animal; H maintains the sanctity of life as most important. Put in more contemporary language, if you want to have a barbeque with friends, you cannot just slaughter the animal and move on to the grilling; you must step aside from the mundane and slaughter the animal at a sacred site in which a trained professional transforms the disposal of blood into a ritual act.

The sentiments of these writers are so extremely removed from the way in which we eat meat today. Ironically, readers have consistently expressed disgust with the focus on blood in Leviticus. Interpreters have described the material as primitive and cruel and blood-obsessed. Yet, when we endorse the taking of lives on a mass scale without any ongoing and institutionalized mechanism to remind us of what we are doing, it's fair to ask where the cruelty really lies. Perhaps our disgust with so much of Leviticus stems from an underlying guilt; Leviticus does not allow us to forget that while we eat meat purchased at the market, a spilling of blood lies behind the packaging. How many of us are willing to face this head on as the priestly writers do?

# Leviticus 18:1–20:27

# From Ritual Impurity
# to Ethical Transgressions

Leviticus 18–20 addresses the lay community, setting out laws that focus on behavior in the home and within the community. Leviticus 18 and 20 both deal with the same issues, namely, forbidden sexual encounters and Molech worship. Leviticus 19 stands between these two parallel chapters. Leviticus 18 and 20 give the impression of an envelope in which the heart of the Holiness Legislation (Lev 19) rests.

## Introduction to Incest Laws

Leviticus 18 deals, in large part, with laws prohibiting certain incestuous relationships.[1] Before looking at the text itself, we should note that incest was not generally condemned in biblical texts. As a matter of fact, there are several narratives in which incest occurs, and not a single one of those narratives expresses a condemnation of the act of incest. In

---

1. Johanna Stiebert questions whether these prohibitions should be read as laws at all, given the unusual formulaic language and inconsistencies. Johanna Stiebert, *First-Degree Incest and the Hebrew Bible: Sex in the City*, LHB/OTS 596 (London: Bloomsbury T&T Clark, 2016), 62.

2 Samuel 13:13, when Tamar realizes that her brother Amnon is going to rape her, she entreats her brother to get the permission of their father David, who would certainly not object. The issue at stake in this text is rape, not incest! Abraham and Sarah share a common parent. Jacob marries two sisters. Judah has sexual intercourse with his daughter-in-law Tamar, and while he is ignorant of the fact at the time of the sex act, by the end of the story Tamar receives praise for her actions. One of the most distasteful stories, from our modern perspective, is the seduction of Lot by two of his daughters in Genesis 19:30-38. Not only does the text fail to condemn this father-daughter sexual union, but the Bible also lays out a direct lineage from this incestuous act to the Messiah. According to Genesis 19:37-38, the Ammonite and Moabite peoples descended from the children of Lot's daughters. Ruth, the Moabite, marries Boaz and from their lineage comes King David from whom the Messiah was destined to come (Ruth 4:17-20; see also Isa 11:1-9 and Matt 1:5-6).

Within the context of the narrative material, the incest prohibitions in Leviticus 18 are radical and at odds with general practice, if the narratives reflect social norms.[2] Baruch Levine notes the discrepancies between narrative and legislation and suggests that "the rules governing incest underwent considerable development."[3] By this he means that laws governing marriage to half-sisters or to two sisters while they are both alive became stricter over time and are reflected in Leviticus 18, but Levine also asserts that "the prohibition of incest reflects the almost universal, natural feelings of a person toward those with whom he has been reared and toward those with whom his closest relatives have had sexual relations."[4]

Social scientists have long been engaged in a debate regarding the factors behind the almost universal incest taboos for nuclear families. The English anthropologist Edward Tylor presented his alliance theory in the 1870s, arguing that marrying outside the family was necessary for alliance-building and growing families for survival. A couple of decades later, Edvard Westermarck promoted his aversion theory, that people raised closely together are less likely to be attracted to one another based

---

2. See, most recently, ibid. for a comprehensive study of both narrative and nonnarrative texts regarding incest in the Hebrew Bible. See also Athalya Brenner, "On Incest," in *A Feminist Companion to Exodus to Deuteronomy*, FCB 6 (Sheffield: Sheffield Academic, 1994; repr. 2001), 113–38 for a discussion on incest in biblical narrative and juridical material.

3. Baruch Levine, *Leviticus: A JPS Torah Commentary* (Philadelphia: Jewish Publication Society of America, 1989), 253.

4. Ibid., 254.

on a natural human instinct.[5] Westermarck referred to this phenomenon as reverse sexual imprinting. In more recent years, socio-biologists have focused on genetics and the human instinct to birth healthy children. These theories offer plausible explanations for sexual prohibitions between the closest blood relations, but they do not address the much more complex series of incest laws in Leviticus 18 and Leviticus 20.

## Don't Be Like the Canaanites (18:1-5)

Chapter 18 reminds the reader that all of Leviticus is set in the wilderness, so it makes sense that the text reminds the people that while in Egypt they were not to act like the Egyptians and admonishes them not to follow the ways of the Canaanites upon settling in the land.[6]

### What Is at Stake in Leviticus 18:3?

What is at stake in walking in the ways of the oppressor or of those the Israelites conquer?

In an early rabbinic commentary on this verse,[7] the rabbis initially suggest "their ways" refers to planting plants or building buildings like these foreign nations do. The focus of this prohibition is not a critique of the moral nature of the behaviors themselves (there is nothing inherently wrong with their plants or buildings) per se, but rather, it promotes an ethic of distinctiveness—maintaining the uniqueness of a people. The text goes on to reject this possibility, though, and asserts that "neither shall you walk in their ways" refers to the practice that, "A man would marry a man, a woman would marry a woman, a man would marry a woman and her daughter, and a woman would marry two men."[8] Prohibiting these relationships replaces plants and buildings as the path to Israelite distinctiveness. This shift in prohibition begs the question: does this shift raise moral questions about the behaviors themselves (i.e., there is something essentially undesirable about these sexual behaviors) or are they as value-neutral as plants and buildings?

As Leviticus introduces sexual prohibitions in just a few verses,

---

5. Gregory C. Leavitt, "Tylor vs. Westermarck: Explaining the Incest Taboo," *Sociology Mind* 3 (2013): 45–51.

6. For a more comprehensive commentary on the function of "othering" the Canaanites, see discussion below of Leviticus 20.

7. Sifra (a work of halachic Midrash on Leviticus) Parashat Acharei Mot 9.

8. Ibid.

<sup>18:1</sup>The LORD spoke to Moses, saying: <sup>2</sup>Speak to the people of Israel and say to them: I am the LORD your God. <sup>3</sup>You shall not do as they do in the land of Egypt, where you lived, and you shall not do as they do in the land of Canaan, to which I am bringing you. You shall not follow their statutes. <sup>4</sup>My ordinances you shall observe and my statutes you shall keep, following them: I am the LORD your God. <sup>5</sup>You shall keep my statutes and my ordinances; by doing so one shall live: I am the LORD.

are these laws laced with a moral critique of the behaviors themselves or is their prohibition primarily rooted in the ethic of distinctiveness? Leviticus 18 concludes by reminding us that these practices were previously done in the land and therefore the Israelites should not do them. There may be a moral valence in these prohibitions, but the emphasis remains primarily on maintaining Israelite distinctiveness. Sexual morality, if present at all, is simply a means to an ethic of distinctiveness.

One might argue that the presence of the word תועבה (often translated as "abomination") signals that this should be read as a moral transgression and not as a matter of assimilation. In Genesis 43:32, the word תועבה is used to say that Egyptians are not to eat meals with Israelites—it is a תועבה for Egyptians. This is not a moral transgression. It is a boundary concerned with cultural mixing that may lead to undesired assimilation. If this is the case, then we can read Leviticus 18 as a chapter on anti-assimilationist sexual practices, encouraging us to identify the problematic norms of the dominant, erotic culture and reject them. Today, these may include rape culture, slut-shaming, and compulsory heterosexuality.

*Alex Weissman*

## Incest Laws, Version 1 (18:6-18)

By addressing incest and other prohibited sexual unions, Leviticus 18 defines what constitutes a family both through consanguineous (blood) relations and by affinity (marriage). Verse 6 sets out some key terminology for the rest of the chapter. שאר like בשר has both the literal meaning of "flesh" (i.e., "food") and a more figurative meaning of "kin." The phrase שאר בשרו indicates "flesh of his flesh," that is, his own flesh. Regarding

[6]None of you shall approach anyone near of kin to uncover nakedness: I am the LORD. [7]You shall not uncover the nakedness of your father, which is the nakedness of your mother; she is your mother, you shall not uncover her nakedness. [8]You shall not uncover the nakedness of your father's wife; it is the nakedness of your father. [9]You shall not uncover the nakedness of your sister, your father's daughter or your mother's daughter, whether born at home or born abroad. [10]You shall not uncover the nakedness of your son's daughter or of your daughter's daughter, for their nakedness is your own nakedness. [11]You shall not uncover the nakedness of your father's wife's daughter, begotten by your father, since she is your sister. [12]You shall not uncover the nakedness of your father's sister; she is your father's flesh. [13]You shall not uncover the nakedness of your mother's sister, for she is your mother's flesh. [14]You shall not uncover the nakedness of your father's brother, that is, you shall not approach his wife; she is your aunt. [15]You shall not uncover the nakedness of your daughter-in-law: she is your son's wife; you shall not uncover her nakedness. [16]You shall not uncover the nakedness of your brother's wife; it is your brother's nakedness. [17]You shall not uncover the nakedness of a woman and her daughter, and you shall not take her son's daughter or her daughter's daughter to uncover her nakedness; they are your flesh; it is depravity. [18]And you shall not take a woman as a rival to her sister, uncovering her nakedness while her sister is still alive.

his own flesh, he may not approach to uncover nakedness (have sexual relations). These flesh relations are identified in Leviticus 21:2-3 as one's mother, father, daughter, son, sister, and brother. As regards affinity, when a man marries a woman, the wife's sisters and children by another marriage are forbidden to the man. The situation is complicated by the fact that a man could marry more than one woman, thus extending potential prohibited relations. Deborah W. Rooke suggests that the term שאר points to a gender that is neither male nor female. Bodies that are שאר undermine the idealized dimorphic gender concept. Rooke suggests that שאר bodies are intersex bodies from the male perspective. "Physically female, they are nevertheless of the same flesh . . . as the male; these bodies therefore destabilize the normal male/female divide, threatening the binary categorization of human bodies, because they participate in both genders."[9]

9. Deborah W. Rooke, "The Bare Facts: Gender and Nakedness in Leviticus 18," in *A Question of Sex? Gender and Difference in the Hebrew Bible and Beyond*, ed. Deborah W. Rooke, HBM 14 (Sheffield: Sheffield Phoenix, 2009), 31.

Rooke's observations are just one among many issues that emerge when reading this text from a feminist perspective: (1) What is the relationship between verse 6 and what follows? (2) Where is the daughter? (3) Does heterosexual normativity govern the incest laws? (4) To what extent is women's sexuality the property of men? (5) Why do incest laws serve as book endings for Leviticus 19, the center point of the Holiness Legislation?

The first issue that we encounter as we read the introductory verse to the incest regulations concerns the specific meaning of שאר. Leviticus 21:2-3 defines שאר as a man's mother, father, daughter, son, sister, and brother. The context in Leviticus 21 concerns the family members for whom a priest may mourn. If we assume that the שאר in Leviticus 18 and 21 are the same, we encounter some difficulties. First of all, does verse 6 imply that a man is forbidden to engage sexually with his father, son, and brother? If so, Leviticus 18:6 is addressing heterosexual and same-sex relationships side by side. Second, if שאר implicitly includes the mother and sister, why do the incest laws repeat these prohibited relations?

One of the most disturbing omissions from the incest laws is the absence of a prohibition regarding sexual relations between a father and daughter.[10] There are several explanations for this absence. Levine asserts that "the law does mention granddaughters, however (v. 10), and it is to be assumed that since a daughter is more closely related than a granddaughter, she would be forbidden, a fortiori."[11] In other words, some assert that the absence of the father-daughter prohibition indicates that this kind of sexual relationship was unthinkable. Johanna Stiebert asserts that the missing law does not mean that father-daughter incest was permitted. Rather, she argues that the necessary formulation would have been "her nakedness is your nakedness," and this would have sounded awkward to ancient readers.[12] Henry Sun suggests that father-daughter incest is missing from the list because the daughter was considered to be

10. It is interesting to note that the *Code of Hammurabi* forbids father-daughter incest (par. 154) and the Hittite laws prohibit a man from approaching his blood daughter (par. 189).

11. Levine, *Leviticus*, 120.

12. Johanna Stiebert, *Fathers and Daughters in the Hebrew Bible* (Oxford: Oxford University Press, 2013), 109–15. Stiebert is following Jan Joosten, "La non-mention de la fille en Lévitique 18: exercise sur la rhétorique du Code de Sainteté," *ETR* 75 (2000): 415–20, who argues that the writer left out father-daughter sexual relations because it would have been distasteful to the audience.

the father's property, and the biblical text would not legislate what one could do with one's own property.[13] Scholars who accept the absence of the daughter from this list generally say that it would have been unlikely that a father would have sexually abused his daughter because then her value as a virgin bride would be lost. Tirzah Meacham observes that in the biblical narratives, there are no cases of father-daughter incest among the patriarchs or heads of Israelite tribes. "It is thus possible to understand the incest code as a reaction to the actions of the patriarchs, the head of tribes and leaders, and an attempt to discourage emulation of such deeds."[14]

Another line of argumentation seeks to find the missing daughter within the text. Susan Rattray argues that in Leviticus 21:2-3, we can find a full definition for the term שאר, which also appears in our passage. There, the list includes mother, father, sister, brother, daughter, and son. Thus, she notes that the daughter is included with the first prohibition against sexual relations with one's שאר. If this is the case, then one should not expect one's mother, father, sister, brother, daughter, or son to be mentioned in the rest of the list because they too are already covered under שאר. That leads to the question of why the prohibition against sexual relations with one's mother is listed separately in verse 7; Rattray argues that the writers of the text highlight the mother-son prohibition because it is the most abhorrent case and best illustrates the principle of forbidden relationships.[15]

Eve Levavi Feinstein argues that Leviticus 18 is an expansion of Leviticus 20 and that the latter never provides a comprehensive list of prohibited sexual relationships. Leviticus 18 expands the list by explicating the implications of Leviticus 20, even to the point where there are some redundancies. Feinstein argues that the daughter was originally added to a highly repetitive text (Lev 18) but was subsequently inadvertently dropped by a copyist. "You shall not uncover

---

13. Henry T. C. Sun, *An Investigation of the Compositional History of the So-Called Holiness School: Leviticus 17–26* (PhD diss., Claremont Graduate School, Claremont, CA, 1990), 151.

14. Tirzah Meacham, "The Missing Daughter: Leviticus 18 and 20," *ZAW* 109 (1997): 258.

15. Susan Rattray, "Marriage Rules, Kinship Terms and Family Structure in the Bible," in *Society of Biblical Literature 1987 Seminar Papers* (Atlanta: Scholars Press, 1987), 537–44. Ellens generally follows Rattray's position (Deborah L. Ellens, *Women in the Sex Texts of Leviticus and Deuteronomy: A Conceptual Analysis*, LHB/OTS 458 [London: T&T Clark, 2008], 87–91).

the nakedness of your daughter. You shall not uncover the nakedness of your son's daughter or your daughter's daughter, for they are your nakedness." The copyist may have skipped over the first "nakedness of your daughter" to the second occurrence of this word pair in the same verse (*homoioarcton*).[16]

It is interesting to note that most of the incest prohibitions in Leviticus are not considered incest in the United States; yet, Leviticus is silent with regard to one of the greatest ills that we confront in contemporary culture, namely, father-daughter incest. Judith Herman and Linda Hirschman argue that incest taboos are created and enforced by men; often these taboos have to do with agreements made among men regarding the exchange of women. They argue that in patriarchal societies, a boy is less likely to approach his mother because she belongs to his father who may respond with rage; in time, presumably, the boy will have a woman of his own. By contrast, with father-daughter incest, there is no threat of a punishing father. And while she will not marry her father, she may well marry a man like her father. Thus patriarchal cultures have supports in place to make room for father-daughter incest.[17]

Most readers assume that the incest laws ban only cases of heterosexual sex. There are some indicators, however, that point to a different reading. Leviticus 18:7 reads: "Your father's nakedness, that is, the nakedness of your mother you shall not uncover; she is your mother, you shall not uncover her nakedness." The lack of symmetry in this verse has confounded traditional and critical scholars for centuries. Is the individual prohibited from sexual relations with his father and his mother? If so, what is the function of the second part of the verse? Similarly, verse 14 reads: "The nakedness of your father's brother you shall not reveal; you shall not approach his wife, she is your aunt" (NRSV). The most common translation of this verse is: "The nakedness of your father's brother you shall not reveal; that is, you shall not approach his wife . . ." This translation suggests that the prohibition is between the individual and his aunt because his aunt equals his uncle's nakedness. Feinstein argues that:

---

16. Eve Levavi Feinstein, *Sexual Pollution in the Hebrew Bible* (Oxford: Oxford University Press, 2014), 170–73.

17. Judith Herman and Linda Hirschman, "Father-Daughter Incest," *Signs* 2 (1977): 735–56.

In my view, the expression "it is YHVH's nakedness" in Leviticus 18
and 20 is best understood as an anatomical metaphor, similar to the
metaphor expressed by the word "flesh." While consanguineous kin
share the same flesh, according to this view sexual partners share the
same "nakedness," having been joined at the genitals. As a result, when
ego uncovers the nakedness of his father's wife, he also uncovers the
nakedness of his father, who is ego's own "flesh."[18]

But Feinstein's translation reads words into the Hebrew that are not
there and this reading is driven by heterosexist assumptions. There are
only three cases in Leviticus 18 in which a prohibition is connected to
someone else's nakedness:

verse 8 forbids going to one's father's wife because she is the nakedness of the father

verse 10 forbids going to one's granddaughter because she is one's
own nakedness

verse 16 bans approaching a brother's wife because she is the brother's
nakedness

Only two other prohibitions give an explicit reason for the ban. Leviticus 18:12-13 bans going to one's father's sister or mother's sister
because the sisters are the שאר of the parent. The other incest laws do not
explicitly connect a family member with another family member. Earlier
generations of Jewish exegetes read this text more directly. b. Sanhedrin
54a offers the opinion that verses 7 and 14 prohibit sexual relations with
the individual's father and the individual's uncle. It is only in verses 7
and 14 that the phrase "do not uncover the nakedness of X" refers to
a male X. Further interpretation suggests that these two male relatives
should be accorded a high degree of respect and that such sexual relations would negatively impact their due respect. Since the ban on male-
male sex later in the chapter seems to render these verses redundant, the
rabbis suggest that if the homosexual act takes place between a father
and son without their knowing it, then they have to atone for two sins:
a homosexual act and incest.[19]

---

18. Feinstein, *Sexual Pollution*, 111.
19. Feinstein assumes that ego will mate only with females (ibid., 104).

### Gendering Nakedness (ערוה) and Sexual Policing

Leviticus 18 and 20 contain the most comprehensive lists of sexual prohibitions. These prohibitions are exclusively addressed to men (with the possible exception of bestiality involving a woman and an animal [18:23; 20:16]), setting the social taboos that limit their sexual privileges, particularly over women. The repeated expression "do not expose the nakedness of [a certain woman]" presupposes male agency and authority over female sexuality, albeit circumscribed, and female sexual passivity. The fact that these prohibitions are addressed only to men suggests that women are not sexually autonomous. Underlying these sexual prohibitions is a power dynamic that serves to privilege male control over female sexuality by assigning gendered nakedness and sexual policing to male jurisdictions.

"Nakedness" (ערוה) is a major concept in Leviticus, which contains thirty of the fifty-four occurrences of the term in the Hebrew Bible. In Leviticus, as in ancient Southwest Asian culture, female nakedness is generally used to represent men's object of desire, a symbol of sexual allure, to be exposed by a male subject for his jouissance. The sight of naked female genitals is titillating and seductive. Naked exposure is often portrayed as a foreplay to coitus. As a part of maintenance of social order, however, sexuality was regulated in ancient Mesopotamia, insofar as it is regarded as a pleasurable and celebrated experience.

In ancient Southwest Asia, male nakedness carries a different set of cultural meanings than does female nakedness. In Assyrian war reliefs, only the defeated or dead enemies are represented as nude. In some artistic depictions of royal-court entertainment, female musicians and dancers perform in the nude, while their male counterparts rarely appear undressed.[20] The gendered differentials of nakedness are also common in ancient Mesopotamian literature. In *Enki and Ninhursag* and *Enlil and Ninlil*, female nudity is portrayed as seductive, irresistible, and sensuous, presented for male voyeuristic enjoyment.[21] In the *Epic of Gilgamesh*, when Shamhat, the harlot, saw Enkidu, the savage man who lived among the beasts in a primitive style, she stripped

---

20. Zainab Bahrani, *Women of Babylon: Gender and Representation in Mesopotamia* (London and New York: Routledge, 2001), 59-65.

21. Ibid., 55; Gwendolyn Leick, *Sex and Eroticism in Mesopotamian Literature* (London: Routledge, 1994), 49.

herself naked, exposed her breasts and overpowered the yet sexually innocent Enkidu with her voluptuousness. Satiated after a week of sexual activity, Enkidu became aware of his primitive state of being. Shamhat then adorned Enkidu with clothes and brought him to the city. Being clothed signifies the initiation to civilization. Male nakedness, when it is isolated from the sexual act, typically occupies a literary topos of shame, humiliation, deprivation, and savagery. The deprecating meanings of "male nakedness" are also employed in the Hebrew Bible (e.g., Isa 20:4; Ezek 22:10).

The gendered differentials in the cultural meanings of nakedness reflect the perceived ideal of femininity and masculinity from a male-normative perspective. In light of these gendered differentials, the illicit act of exposing a forbidden woman's nakedness in Leviticus 18 and 20 constitutes not only a transgression of sexual boundaries set in the community but also an equivalent act of exposing the nakedness of the man who was regarded as the rightful owner of her sexuality, namely, of shaming and humiliating him (18:7, 8, 10, 16; 20:11, 20, 21). If the offender is the paterfamilias (18:10), he brings disgrace upon himself.

The transgression of sexual boundaries is considered not only a breach of public mores but also a cultic offense against YHVH. The members of the community (male by default) are responsible for sexual policing, carrying out death sentences and social exclusion against the sex offenders along with their victims (Lev 20). Should there be a breach, the sexual boundaries are to be strictly enforced, even at the expense of the lives of victims. If men are the subjects of action (who strip, sleep with, and "take" a woman, as Lev 18 and 20 portray) and women are the passive sexual objects to be acted upon, why then are women held unquestionably to be accomplices in illicit sexual relations and penalized by the same capital punishment or social exclusion as their sexual predators? Women become the double victims under these Levitical laws of sexual prohibitions. Not only is their sexual agency denied and their sexuality reduced to passivity, in the case of a breach they are deprived of the victim status, prosecuted along with the male offenders, and scapegoated in order to maintain the ideal social boundaries of sexuality imposed by the patriarchal authority. These laws reinforce the patriarchal ideal of chaste women and defend the circumscribed male sexual privileges at the expense of women's subjectivity and lives.

*Sonia K. Wong*

*What Is the Function of the Incest Laws?*

Adrian Schenker suggests that these laws existed to ensure the well-being of the entire household. "The sexual potential which in virtue of erotic attraction is capable of creating new promising relations for the future is consciously and intentionally kept away from existing family relations in order to preserve from confusion the clear social order, which is an absolute necessity for the family."[22] Schenker further argues that the prohibitions that extend beyond incest, like bestiality or sacrificing children to Molech, also disrupt the social fabric of a household.

Madeline Gay McClenney-Sadler suggests that the incest laws must be understood in relation to Israelite kinship terms. After studying over three thousand kinship terms in the Bible, she concludes that Israelite kinship most closely approximates what has been termed the Hawaiian kinship pattern,[23] in which there is no differentiation between siblings and cousins and in which terminology for aunts and uncles is bifurcate-collateral; that is, Hebrew kin distinguishes between a mother's sister and a father's sister (unlike English which uses "aunt" whether the woman is related to the father or mother). While her conclusions are far ranging, for our purposes we are interested in how she analyzes the organization of incest prohibitions in Leviticus 18. She argues that the שאר rights belong to YHVH and are explicated in verse 6. In other words, sexual engagement with any שאר is an affront to YHVH.

McClenney-Sadler notes that the phrase "uncovering the nakedness of y" refers to a sex act with person y and the phrase "it is the nakedness of x" refers to the party whose rights have been violated.[24] Thus, Leviticus 18:7a, which forbids the uncovering of nakedness of one's father because it is the nakedness of one's mother, must mean that EGO is forbidden from sexual relations with his father, because that act violates the rights

22. Adrian Schenker, "What Connects the Incest Prohibitions with the Other Prohibitions Listed in Leviticus 18 and 20?," in *The Book of Leviticus: Composition and Reception*, ed. Rolf Rendtorff, Robert A. Kugler, and Sarah Smith Bartel, vol. 3 (Leiden: Brill, 2003), 167.

23. Madeline Gay McClenney-Sadler (*Recovering Daughter's Nakedness: A Formal Analysis of Israelite Kinship Terminology and the Internal Logic of Leviticus 18*, LHM/OTS 476 [New York: T&T Clark, 2007], 26) is here referring to one of the six kinship systems that social scientists have identified in all cultures. English kinship terminology falls under the Eskimo system. The six are Iroquois, Hawaiian, Eskimo, Crow, Omaha, and Sudanese.

24. Ibid., 80.

of the mother!²⁵ The second part of the verse protects the father's rights by forbidding sexual access to the mother. McClenney-Sadler interprets verse 9 as addressing three kin relations: full sister, a father's daughter, and a mother's daughter. Regarding verse 11, she explains that "You shall not uncover the nakedness of your father's wife's daughter, begotten by your father, since she is your sister," means that "a man must abstain from sexual relations with a half-sister, that is, a father's daughter or a mother's daughter (v. 9) and he must abstain from sexual relations with a half-sister born of a woman other than his mother who is 'legally' neither a 'father's daughter' nor a 'mother's daughter' but a 'father's wife's daughter' (v. 11)."²⁶

For McClenney-Sadler, the incest laws are about protecting the rights of certain members of the family. Thus, she asserts that verse 7a protects the mother's right by forbidding a son or daughter to go to their father (her husband). Verses 7b-11 protect a father's rights, verse 12 protects a father's father's rights, verse 13 protects a mother's father's rights, verse 14 addresses the rights of the father's brother, followed by the rights of the son (v. 15), the rights of the brother (v. 16), and finally the wife's rights (vv. 17-18). McClenney-Sadler concludes by noting that the "jural-literary movement from 'mother's rights' to 'wife's rights' forms an inclusio that makes the first last and the last first. Consequently, the importance of wives and mothers in ancient Israelite culture is emphasized literarily, thus balancing gender asymmetry in these laws."²⁷

Deborah Ellens is less concerned with the sociology of incest laws and more interested in what the incest laws teach us about Leviticus. Ellens claims that if one studies the sex-related texts in Leviticus and in Deuteronomy, one finds two very different, although sometimes overlapping, concerns. Leviticus is primarily concerned with ontology, category establishment, and maintenance, while Deuteronomy's sex laws are primarily concerned with property issues. Ellens distinguishes:

---

25. A different approach is taken by Bruce Rosenstock ("Incest, Nakedness, and Holiness: Biblical Israel at the Limits of Culture," *JSQ* 16 [2009]: 333–62). He argues that these incest laws must be understood in light of the P text in Gen 2:23-24, about a husband and wife becoming one flesh. The conjugal unit is therefore one flesh. Rosenstock asserts that the phrase *legalot ervah*, which is used almost exclusively for incest, not other sexual transgressions, means that the ideal one flesh is revealed and thus goes against God's desire that to be in the image of God is to be a heterosexual conjugal unit.

26. McClenney-Sadler, *Recovering Daughter's Nakedness*, 84.

27. Ibid., 91.

(1) point-of-view, which she argues is always gender-asymmetrical; (2) "language-depicting-the-sex-act" or women's objectification; and (3) women's focalization, which "is the expectation the text harbors for the man and the woman with respect to the ideal which it 'prescribes' for the community through the laws it articulates."[28] Put differently and somewhat simplified, the texts are patriarchal and androcentric, but that is not all they are. Within the patriarchy, there are other driving concerns that might present women as agents or property, as valued or forgotten, to use Ellens's terminology.

Ellens argues persuasively that the incest laws in Leviticus 18 are not about women as property belonging to fathers or husbands but mainly about purity. Ellens notes that Leviticus 18:19-23 (possibly excluding v. 20) does not deal with property rights at all but rather with purity or "genital boundaries." Regarding Molech worship, Ellens cites John Day's claim that verse 21 stands in its present "sexual context because the Molech cult is thought of metaphorically as an adulterous one vis-à-vis Yahweh."[29] Having set purity and "genital boundaries" as the theme of the chapter, Ellens concludes: "This text of sexual affairs illustrates the woman's overall dependence and subordination in Leviticus 18, but not her lack of responsibility. . . . Thus woman is marginalized and objectified. But she is also focalized as agent. And she is not focalized as property."[30]

Eve Levavi Feinstein comes to similar conclusions via a different line of argument. Feinstein explores the idea of sexual pollution in the Bible through the lens of the work of Thomas Kazen, who argues that pollution language emerges from a sense of disgust. The problem with the tendency to set ritual pollution and moral pollution as separate categories is reflective of modernity's assumptions that the moral emerges from the rational and that the ritual emerges from the embodied and the emotional side of life. Pollution as rooted in disgust breaks down the barriers between how we think about moral pollution and ritual pollution.

Feinstein begins her study of sexual pollution with an examination of the Suspected Adulteress (Num 5:11-31), the pollution of Woman Israel

28. Ellens, *Women in the Sex Texts of Leviticus and Deuteronomy*, 6–7.

29. John Day, *Molech: A God of Human Sacrifice in the Old Testament*, University of Cambridge Oriental Publications 41 (New York: Cambridge University Press, 1989), 23. Ellens also cites Moshe Weinfeld's argument that, in this case, זרע can be understood here not only as offspring but as "semen" (Moshe Weinfeld, *The Worship of Molech and of the Queen of Heaven and Its Background* [Butzon & Bercker, 1972], 144.)

30. Ellens, *Women in the Sex Texts of Leviticus and Deuteronomy*, 99.

as expounded by a number of prophetic texts, the restoration of marriage legislation (Deut 24:1-4), and the narrative of Dinah and Shechem (Gen 34). Comparing Leviticus 18 to these other works, she concludes that "whereas the conception of sexual pollution that we saw in the preceding chapters rests on a view of women as sexual property, in Leviticus 18 the pollution concept is completely divorced from this idea. Not only is pollution language applied to transgressions that have nothing to do with sexual property, but it is applied to men, and the text in fact seems far more concerned with the sexual pollution of men than that of women." She explains this difference as a result of Holiness theology, which requires the community to maintain a state of holiness and purity.[31]

## Keep Your "Seed" Out of the Following (18:19-23)

Leviticus 18:19-23 presents five additional prohibitions that are loosely connected by the topic of male "seed"; in other words, these prohibitions are about where men should not release their sperm. Verse 19 prohibits a man from having sexual intercourse with a woman while she is menstruating. Leviticus 20:18 contains a parallel law: "If a man lies with a woman having her sickness and uncovers her nakedness, he has laid bare her flow and she has laid bare her flow of blood; both of them shall be cut off from their people." Leviticus 18:19 and 20:18 illustrate how the Holiness Legislation takes P material that is nonjudgmental of menstruation and shifts the concern from ritual impurity to moral judgment. (See discussion of Lev 15, above.) It is possible that the primary concern behind the prohibition in 20:18 is not sexual intercourse with a menstruant but sexual intercourse with a woman who is not well. This may include a woman's discomfort during menstruation and other conditions in which there is a genital flow due to illness.

Leviticus 15:24 establishes a period of seven days of impurity for a man who lies with a menstruant, but the act itself is not prohibited. In contrast, Leviticus 20:18 prescribes כרת for both sex partners, a cutting off from the community, either as an untimely death or some other form of exclusion. Since Leviticus 20:18 punishes both the man and the woman, it is unlikely that the prohibition is about protecting a woman during her time of discomfort. Leviticus 15 is concerned with impurities and their contagion, while Leviticus 18:19 and 20:18 attempt to curtail sexual intercourse during menstruation. In other words, the same act is viewed

---

31. Feinstein, *Sexual Pollution*, 129.

## Lev 18:19-23

¹⁹You shall not approach woman to uncover her nakedness while she is in her menstrual uncleanness. ²⁰You shall not have sexual relations with your kinsman's wife, and defile yourself with her. ²¹You shall not give any of your offspring to sacrifice them to Molech, and so profane the name of your God: I am the LORD. ²²You shall not lie with a male as with a woman; it is an abomination. ²³You shall not have sexual relations with any animal and defile yourself with it, nor shall any woman give herself to an animal to have sexual relations with it: it is perversion.

differently through two different social and theological lenses. Herein we have another example of H's democratization of holiness beyond the priest and the sanctuary to the entire community, but in the process of democratization, women's natural body functions are assigned a moral significance that stigmatizes women's bodies but not men's.

The reference to Molech worship in Leviticus 18:21 seems, at first glance, out of place, since the prohibition addresses offspring and not sperm. A connection becomes apparent, however, in view of the range of meanings of the Hebrew word זֶרַע ("seed"), which can refer to plant seed, sperm, or offspring/progeny. Debate continues regarding the practices involved in Molech worship and the Bible's polemical descriptions of such practices; the most common understanding of Molech worship is that it involved child sacrifice. The ban against engaging in Molech worship appears in Leviticus 20:2-5 and in Deuteronomy 20:1-5. The book of Kings also mentions a practice wherein individuals (including kings) would sacrifice their children by putting them to fire for the worship of Molech, the god of the Ammonites, who were Israel's neighbors to the east (1 Kgs 11:7; 2 Kgs 23:10).[32] The inclusion of Molech worship in a list of forbidden sexual unions (Lev 18:19-23) makes sense because each prohibition involves wasted seed: sexual intercourse during menstruation is less likely to result in pregnancy (v. 19); if a man impregnates his neighbor's wife (v. 20), the husband claims the children; and sacrificing one's own children results in an obvious loss of progeny (v. 21).

---

32. Molech has traditionally been associated with the deity of the Ammonites, Milkom, but it is also possible that Molech was Malik, a Mesopotamian underworld deity. For research into the identification of Molech and ritual practices associated with him, see George C. Heider, *The Cult of Molek: A Reassessment*, JSOTSup 43 (Sheffield: JSOT Press, 1985); John Day, *Molech*; and Jacob Milgrom, *Leviticus 17–22*, AB 3A (New York: Doubleday, 2000), 1551–65.

*Male-Male Sexual Penetration*

Leviticus 18:22 (see also Lev 20:13) is arguably the most notorious verse in Leviticus. Broadly speaking, there tend to be two approaches to interpreting this verse: a broad reading and a strict one. A broad reading interprets the verse as a ban on homosexual sex acts. A strict reading interprets the verse as a prohibition against a specific sexual encounter that was meant to distinguish the Israelites from the surrounding nations. In rabbinic literature, there is a famous case referred to as *ben sorer u'moreh*, which is a response to the law in Deuteronomy 21:18-21 concerning the fate of a rebellious son. When the rabbis encountered the commandment to stone a rebellious son to death, they began to read limitations into the text. They created so many limitations regarding the child's age—the agreement of the parents' assessment, the sameness of the parents' own heights and appearances, the specific rebellious action and a particular history of prior misconducts and warnings by a court—that a rebellious son vanished.[33] To a lesser extent, progressive interpretations of Leviticus 18:22 move in this same direction to eradicate the perceived ban on same-sex relations between men.

A caveat is needed here. The prohibition concerns an act, not an identity or even a desire. LGBTQ[34] identity, as with any other identity marker, is a complex construction of which sex acts are just a part. The fundamentalist lens for which Leviticus 18:22 is often cited (but surrounding laws are ignored) was effectively parodied in an anonymous letter to Dr. Laura Schlessinger, a socially conservative radio show host.[35] This letter has now floated around the internet for over a decade and is worthy of citation in a Leviticus commentary given the rising transphobia and threats to LGBTQ rights. The letter writer raises ten questions for Dr. Laura; I include the first three here:

> Dear Dr. Laura:
> Thank you for doing so much to educate people regarding God's Law. I have learned a great deal from your show, and try to share that knowledge with as many people as I can. When someone tries to defend the homosexual lifestyle, for example, I simply remind them that Leviticus 18:22 clearly states it to be an abomination. . . . End of debate.
> I do need some advice from you, however, regarding some other elements of God's Laws and how to follow them.

33. b. Sanh 71a.
34. An acronym for lesbian, gay, bisexual, transgender, queer.
35. Dr. Laura Schlessinger is a conservative social commentator who was especially renowned in the late 1990s for her syndicated talk radio show called the *Dr. Laura Program*.

1. Leviticus 25:44 states that I may possess slaves, both male and female, provided they are purchased from neighboring nations. A friend of mine claims that this applies to Mexicans, but not Canadians. Can you clarify? Why can't I own Canadians?

2. I would like to sell my daughter into slavery, as sanctioned in Exodus 21:7. In this day and age, what do you think would be a fair price for her?

3. I know that I am allowed no contact with a woman while she is in her period of menstrual uncleanliness—Lev. 15:19-24. The problem is how do I tell? I have tried asking, but most women take offense.[36]

Whether the prohibition appears in Leviticus 18:22 as part of incest taboos or as part of an attempt to self-differentiate from the Canaanites, the concept of a penetrator and penetrated one comes down to power relationships. The penetrator is the person with power, and the receptive partner is of a lesser status. In Greco-Roman culture, an adult man could sexually penetrate a woman, a male slave, or a boy without any censure, because he was abiding by the power dynamics of those relationships. An adult male who allowed himself to be penetrated, however, was condemned (as was a woman who played the role of a penetrator) because this act was contrary to sanctioned power relationships. As Michael Satlow and others have argued, in early Judaism under Hellenistic influence, the Jewish sources often describe the deviation from the normative penetrating role as going against the laws of nature.[37]

Against the backdrop of the Holiness Legislation, we see that the maintenance of power structures and hierarchical relationships is legitimized by placing laws such as Leviticus 18:22 within legislation about holy community. Thus, the so-called homosexuality ban in Leviticus 18:22 is really a prohibition against deviation from the prescribed norms of masculinity.

## The Debate over Leviticus 18:22

In the following section I will explain the difficulties in the Hebrew text that give rise to a variety of interpretations, and then I will present some of the most compelling interpretations of this verse. It is not my

36. The origin of this letter is a matter of debate. According to Snopes.com, the letter was written by Kent Ashcraft in May 2000 and quickly went viral. The letter was reproduced in a variety of contexts online. See https://www.snopes.com/politics/religion/drlaura.asp for a copy of the letter in its entirety.

37. Michael L. Satlow, "'They Abused Him Like a Woman': Homoeroticism, Gender Blurring, and the Rabbis in Late Antiquity," *Journal of the History of Sexuality* 4 (1994): 1–25.

intention to argue that any one of these is correct or most persuasive. By revealing the varieties of readings of this verse I hope to demonstrate that we simply do not know what the verse means! Any religious-moral arguments that are based primarily on this verse stand on shaky ground.

The difficulties in the text are revealed by comparing a few English translations of Leviticus 18:22:

> You shall not lie with a man as with a woman. (NRSV)
> Do not lie with a male as one lies with a woman. (NJPS)
> With a male you are not to lie (after the manner of) lying with a woman.[38]

Notice that each translation provides a word that is absent in the Hebrew: "as" or "after the manner of." They also omit a word that is present in the Hebrew and that forms a construct with the word "woman." The construct translates literally as "lying down of a woman." Thus the most literal translation of the verse is: "You shall not lie the lying down of a woman with a man." And regarding its rough parallel legislation in 20:13: "As for the man who lies the lying down of a woman with a male, they, both of them, have committed an outrage; they shall certainly be put to death, their blood is upon them."

The first scholar to revisit this verse in light of modern historical-critical and linguistic tools is Saul Olyan, who argues that an analogous phrase to משכבי אשה ("lyings of a woman") occurs in Numbers 31 and Judges 21, in which the difference between a virgin and nonvirgin are described. In these texts, a virgin is one who has not experienced משכב זכר ("lying of a man"). Olyan argues that since the issue at stake in these texts is virginity, משכב זכר must indicate vaginal penetration. Olyan then reasons that משכבי אשה must indicate the corollary: vaginal receptivity. Thus, anal penetration was seen as analogous to vaginal penetration.[39] Olyan also argues that the law is directed against the penetrator and that the inclusion of both participants in Leviticus 20 is the result of editorial changes.[40]

---

38. Everett Fox, *The Five Books of Moses: Genesis, Exodus, Leviticus, Numbers, Deuteronomy; A New Translation with Introductions, Commentary, and Notes* (New York: Schocken Books, 1997).

39. Saul Olyan, "'And with a Male You Shall Not Lie the Lying Down of a Woman': On the Meaning and Significance of Leviticus 18:22 and 20:1," *Journal of the History of Sexuality* 5 (1994): 179–206, esp. 183–86.

40. Jerome T. Walsh ("Leviticus 18:22 and 20:13: Who Is Doing What to Whom?," *JBL* 120 [2001]: 208) modifies Olyan's theory to suggest that the case in Lev 18:22 is specifically "about anal sex between two men, one of whom is a free adult Israelite and takes the passive sexual role of being penetrated by the other."

Olyan points out that the receptive role in the sex act became gendered ("the bounding of receptivity exclusively to women") and became associated with the role of the woman, who was also seen as passive.

> Each penetrator was seen as an agent acting on the body of his receptive partner (the woman in the case of adultery; the penetrated male in a male coupling); the receptive partner was in turn viewed as a passive recipient of that action rather than an active participant in his or her own right. Receptivity, if viewed as passivity, would perhaps have rendered them guiltless.[41]

More recently, David Tabb Stewart suggests that this ban is connected to the incest laws of the chapter. He notes that "the lying of a male" indicates deflowering a virgin but that the phrase "the lyings (pl.) of your father" means "incest with the (step)mother" (Gen 49:40). Stewart suggests that the plural of lyings in these constructs has the technical sense of incest. He thus concludes:

> The lyings-of-a-woman still presumes the agency of a male but refers to an act with another male by a kind of literary gender play. Just as the "lyings-of-your-father" refers to a usurpation of the father's bed by the son, the "lyings-of-a-woman" metonymically refer to a male as incestuous object—a metonym because elaboration of the incest category has been (primarily) in terms of female objects (Lev. 18.7-16).[42]

In other words, the verse is an expansion on the incest laws regarding male relatives of the same degree as the laws regarding women relatives that are enumerated in verses 6-18. For Stewart, there is no ban against unrelated male-male sex.

---

41. Olyan, "And with a Male," 189. Also in 1994, Daniel Boyarin published an article entitled, "Are There Any Jews in 'The History of Sexuality'?" in which he came to essentially the same conclusion as Olyan, that is, that the text is addressing male anal penetration only. His argument is based on rabbinic literature and Roman texts. Boyarin says, "The Torah's language is very explicit; it is the use of a male as a female that is *toevah*, the crossing of a boundary from one God-given category to another. . . . Moving a male body across the border into female metaphysical space transgresses the categories in the same way as putting on a female garment" (Daniel Boyarin, "Are There Any Jews in 'The History of Sexuality'?," *Journal of the History of Sexuality* 5 [1994]: 343–44). Both Olyan and Boyarin argue that the writers of this material associated maleness with penetration and femaleness with receptivity.

42. David Tabb Stewart, "Leviticus," in *The Queer Bible Commentary*, ed. Deryn Guest, Robert Goss, and Mona West (London: SCM Press, 2015), 97.

K. Renato Lings presents a meticulous study of the grammatical and syntactical problems of verse 22, and his conclusions are similar to Stewart's:

> Sexual intercourse with a close male relative should be just as abominable to you as incestuous relationships with female relatives. If the whole of ch. 18 is read in this light, by the time we reach 18.22 virtually all possible combinations of incest are clearly forbidden. Then, the purpose of the added phrase of *miškevē 'iššâ* is to make sure that the general prohibition against incest applies in all directions. Thus, the Leviticus legislator is warning Israelite men that incestuous acts with members of either sex are punishable.[43]

Lings understands the phrase משכבי אשה as a reference to all the prohibited incestuous relationships listed in regard to female relatives. One suggestive and compelling rephrasing that he offers is: "With a male relative you shall not engage in sexual relationships prohibited with female relatives."[44] This verse therefore takes its natural place with the incest laws.

### Bestiality

Leviticus 18:23 and 20:16 ban bestiality for both men and women. In 18:23, bestiality is called a perversion; 20:15-16 repeats the ban in slightly different language and proscribes death for both the person and the animal. Leviticus 20:16 makes the woman the subject and the agent of the sexual act: "If a woman approaches any animal and has sexual relations with it." Similarly, Leviticus 18:23 reads, "nor shall any woman give herself to an animal to have sexual relations with it." Given how rare it is for biblical texts to ascribe agency to women in sexual acts, it is disappointing to find some commentators rephrasing the text in ways that mask this agency. For example, John E. Hartley comments: "A man is not to lie with an animal, and a woman is not to flaunt herself seeking to seduce a beast."[45] Ellens argues that in this bestiality law (Lev 20:15-16), the male יתן שכבתו ("has sexual relations" in v. 15), while the woman תקרב . . . לרבעה אתה ("approaches . . . and has sexual relations" in v. 16). She notes that the phrase for depositing seed in Leviticus 18 and 20

---

43. K. Renato Lings, "The 'Lyings' of a Woman: Male-Male Incest in Leviticus 18.22?," *Theology & Sexuality* 15 (2009): 245.

44. Ibid., 246.

45. John E. Hartley, *Leviticus*, WBC 4 (Waco, TX: Word Books, 1992), 297.

occurs only with regard to non-affinal/non-consanguine relationships; thus יתן (literally, "to give") with seed refers to depositing seed outside the spheres of species, cult, or marriage. She also argues that שכבתו ("to lie down," perhaps "to copulate") has the sense of breeding. Thus, men deposit seed through orgasm and women breed and produce offspring.[46]

In order to understand why bestiality is included in the prohibitions, we must examine another text in which animals and humans come into close contact. In the case of a goring ox (Exod 21:28), if an ox kills a man or a woman, the ox is stoned to death. According to Jacob Finkelstein, the animal is put to death because it has crossed boundaries and has essentially inverted the order of humankind having dominion over the animals. Similarly, Finkelstein remarks that "bestiality offends against divine creation in two respects. First, it violates the hierarchical order of the universe, in which man occupies an exclusive superior position vis-à-vis all other terrestrial life. Secondly, it aims directly at the very principle of Creation: the separation of species and even of such phenomena as day and night."[47] Thus, when it comes to women and animals, women are the agents and therefore, *contra* Hartley and Ellens, subject to penalties similar to those against men who violate H's sexual boundaries.

## The Land Vomits (18:24-30)

Leviticus 18:24-30 and Leviticus 20:22-26 warn the people of Israel that if they do not follow God's laws, they will be cast out of the land like its prior inhabitants, the Canaanites and other native nations. The specific wording of Leviticus 18:24-30 (and 20:22-26) reveals a unique theological premise of the Holiness Legislation: the land as a living agent with a body. Leviticus 18:24-25 is key in understanding this H theology. There were other people living on the land, but they defiled themselves and the land with their sexual transgressions. As a result, YHVH punished the land for its iniquity, and the land vomited out its inhabitants. Several points are important here: the actions of the inhabitants had an impact on the land and not just on the people. YHVH punished the land, which presumes that YHVH held the land accountable in some way, and then the land itself vomited out the inhabitants of the land. For the writers of the Holiness Legislation, the entire Land of Israel was God's holy

46. Ellens, *Women in the Sex Texts of Leviticus and Deuteronomy*, 130.
47. Jacob J. Finkelstein, "The Ox That Gored," *Transactions of the American Philosophical Society* 71 (1981): 71.

²⁴Do not defile yourselves in any of these ways, for by all these practices the nations I am casting out before you have defiled themselves. ²⁵Thus the land became defiled; and I punished it for its iniquity, and the land vomited out its inhabitants. ²⁶But you shall keep my statutes and my ordinances and commit none of these abominations, either the citizen or the alien who resides among you ²⁷(for the inhabitants of the land, who were before you, committed all of these abominations, and the land became defiled); ²⁸otherwise the land will vomit you out for defiling it, as it vomited out the nation that was before you. ²⁹For whoever commits any of these abominations shall be cut off from their people. ³⁰So keep my charge not to commit any of these abominations that were done before you, and not to defile yourselves by them: I am the LORD your God.

sanctuary. Just as the priests bear responsibility for keeping the sanctuary pure and holy, the inhabitants of the land bear responsibility for the state of the land. Just as cultic impurities could threaten the sanctuary, so moral impurities could threaten the land. As such, all of the people throughout the land must maintain holiness and purity, to allow for the holy community and the land to coexist.[48]

The H writers took one further step in their understanding of the land: they described the land as analogous to a human body with the agency and vulnerabilities of human bodies. Leviticus 25:18 and 23 state that the land does not belong to the people; rather, the land belongs to God, just as the people belong to God. The people are simply tenants upon the land. Both the land and the people have their own covenantal relationships with God. The land is mentioned ten times in Leviticus 18–27.[49] The land rests, observes, and enjoys its Sabbath, devours, vomits, and fornicates, just as human bodies do. When a human body is defiled, however, it can undergo rituals of purification while the land has no parallel mechanisms. As Nobuyoshi Kiuchi points out, the land has no Day of Atonement for an annual cleaning of the sanctuary, so its only avenue for cleansing is vomiting.[50]

---

48. For an excellent treatment of land issues in the Holiness Legislation, see Jan Joosten, *People and Land in the Holiness Code: An Exegetical Study of the Ideational Framework of the Law in Leviticus 17–26*, VTSup 67 (Leiden: Brill, 1996).

49. Lev 18:25, 28; 19:29; 20:22; 25:2, 4, 5; 26:34, 38, 43.

50. Nobuyoshi Kiuchi, *Leviticus*, ApOTC 3 (Nottingham: Inter-Varsity Press, 2007), 339.

## Echoes of the Decalogue (19:1-4)

Leviticus 19, which contains some of the most well-known laws of the Bible, weaves ritual, civil, criminal, and ethical law into a tapestry. Unlike many other tapestries, however, there is no readily apparent order or pattern in this one. With our limited knowledge about the composition of this text, it seems that H did not order the material by category or topic. The refrain "I am YHVH" appears seventeen times within this chapter, yet it does not seem to mark the beginning or the end of any particular unit. Most of the laws here either appear elsewhere in the Bible in a slightly different form or seem to refer to laws found elsewhere in the Bible. Within this chapter we find, for example, references to the Decalogue, laws governing the well-being sacrifices, legislation addressing economic justice, prescriptions for right intention, case law regarding a betrothed female slave, legislation to promote land sustainability, prohibitions against divination and magic, and protections for the stranger.

A few other biblical passages present a tightly packed smorgasbord of material and have been compared to Leviticus 19. For example, Ezekiel 22:6-12 reads:

> The princes of Israel in you, everyone according to his power, have been bent on shedding blood. Father and mother are treated with contempt in you; the alien residing within you suffers extortion; the orphan and the widow are wronged in you. You have despised my holy things, and profaned my sabbaths. In you are those who slander to shed blood, those in you who eat upon the mountains, who commit lewdness in your midst. In you they uncover their fathers' nakedness; in you they violate women in their menstrual periods. One commits abomination with his neighbor's wife; another lewdly defiles his daughter-in-law; another in you defiles his sister, his father's daughter. In you, they take bribes to shed blood; you take both advance interest and accrued interest, and make gain of your neighbors by extortion; and you have forgotten me, says the Lord GOD.

In this passage, Ezekiel covers the mistreatment of parents, exploitation of the stranger, profanation of the Sabbath, slander, violation of family purity laws, usury, and exploitation of one's neighbor. Some of the vocabulary in Ezekiel 22 and Leviticus 19 is strikingly similar. It is certainly possible that Ezekiel drew on the Holiness Legislation in composing this condemnation of Israelite practices, but it is not likely that H derived its material from Ezekiel. In fact, Ezekiel is not presenting casuistic and apodictic laws; he assumes these laws already exist in order to make his case that Israel has failed to obey the law. Deuter-

*Lev 19:1-4*

¹⁹:¹The Lᴏʀᴅ spoke to Moses, saying: ²Speak to all the congregation of the people of Israel and say to them: You shall be holy, for I the Lᴏʀᴅ your God am holy. ³You shall each revere your mother and father, and you shall keep my sabbaths: I am the Lᴏʀᴅ your God. ⁴Do not turn to idols or make cast images for yourselves: I am the Lᴏʀᴅ your God.

onomy 27 offers another possible parallel in that the series of curses that the people shout from the mountains condemn worshiping other gods, mistreatment of parents, exploiting the blind and the stranger, violating family impurity laws, and committing murder and bribery. There are, however, as many differences between the content of Deuteronomy 27 and Leviticus 19 as there are similarities. Thus, Leviticus 19 occupies a truly unique place in the Bible.

Within Leviticus 19, subunits have their own structure and content, shifting from apodictic to casuistic law. That each unit has its own structure suggests that this chapter may be a compilation of varied material rather than a coherent composition.[51] It is possible that H, in appropriating bits from various law codes and other sources, is affirming each body of work from which the material comes, while also modifying some of that material. David Tabb Stewart suggests that the writers of Leviticus 19 used literary conventions that may be difficult for modern readers to recognize. He posits that the allusion to other biblical laws is not to harmonize them or to raise up their importance but to act as "an aid to recollection that 'simultaneously activates' two or more texts and holds them in dialectical tension."[52] In any case, all of these laws are subsumed

51. There continues to be much debate about the structure and compositional history of Lev 19. During the mid-twentieth century German scholars sought to find a priestly decalogue or dodecalogue in this chapter, and a majority of more recent scholars cite some kind of relationship between Lev 19 and the Sinaitic Decalogue. See David Tabb Stewart, "Leviticus 19 as Mini-Torah," in *Current Issues in Priestly and Related Literature: The Legacy of Jacob Milgrom and Beyond*, ed. Roy E. Gane and Ada Taggar-Cohen (Atlanta: SBL Press, 2015), 300–301 for a summary of such views. See also Jonathan Magonet, "The Structure and Meaning of Leviticus 19," *HAR* 7 (1983): 151–67.

52. Stewart, "Leviticus 19 as Mini-Torah," 323. See also the work of Mary Douglas, *Thinking in Circles: An Essay on Ring Composition* (New Haven: Yale University Press, 2007); and Moshe Kline, "'The Editor Was Nodding': A Reading of Leviticus 19 in Memory of Mary Douglas," *JHebS* 8 (2008): 1–59 for new literary analyses of the structure of Leviticus.

under the primary directive of the chapter: whether one is engaged in sacrifice or agricultural work or relationships with one's neighbor, each moment is about *imitatio dei*, acting in ways that emulate YHVH and that thereby bring holiness into the community.

Leviticus 19 begins with a refrain that occurs several times throughout the chapter: "You shall be holy, for I, YHVH, am holy." It is this phrase that gave rise to the title for the Holiness Legislation. The use of the imperfect תהיו ("You shall be") indicates an ongoing, habitual activity, a call to aspiration, to behave in ways that emulate God's holiness. The verb is not an imperative, a command, but a call to a particular orientation in life. God is "holy," and engaging in *imitatio dei* is a lifelong striving toward holiness.

Verses 2-3 echo the Decalogue.[53] The commands—respecting one's parents, observing the Sabbath, and the prohibition against observing other gods—mark the central motifs in the Decalogue (Exod 20; Deut 5). In Leviticus 19, respect for one's parents, that is, attention to relationships within the family, appears before the prohibition against worshiping other gods. This different order signifies an orientation toward relationship among people and not only relationship with God. Whereas most biblical passages that mention parents list the father first and then the mother (see Exod 20:12; 21:15, 17; Deut 5:16; 21:8; Prov 1:8; 20:20), the inverted order in Leviticus 19 accords honor first to the mother. This order may simply reflect a literary technique in the Bible whereby the order of elements is reversed when a writer wishes to recall another text.

## Democratizing Worship (19:5-8)

Leviticus 19:5-8 makes a seemingly sudden shift from moral instruction to particular ritual instruction. The center of the discussion is the well-being offering. In contrast to its treatment in P, this H text concerns itself only with the role of the layperson. While Leviticus 7:11-21 breaks down this offering into three subcategories (i.e., thanksgiving, votive, and freewill offering), the H writers address the offering in its broader scope. Among all the types of sacrifices, it is only the well-being that affords the lay offerer the opportunity to partake of the meat. With other offerings, the lay role ends with the slaughter and cutting up of the

---

53. In Midrash Vayikra Rabbah 24:5, Rabbi Levi finds ten statements in Lev 19 that correspond to the Ten Commandments.

⁵When you offer a sacrifice of well-being to the Lᴏʀᴅ, offer it in such a way that it is acceptable in your behalf. ⁶It shall be eaten on the same day you offer it, or on the next day; and anything left over until the third day shall be consumed in fire.

⁷If it is eaten at all on the third day, it is an abomination; it will not be acceptable. ⁸All who eat it shall be subject to punishment, because they have profaned what is holy to the Lord; and any such person shall be cut off from the people.

animal. Furthermore, the H writers reinforce the importance of the lay role in consuming the meat properly. The exposition begins: "If you offer a well-being sacrifice to YHVH, sacrifice it לרצנכם." That term, which is an infinitive construct with a second masculine plural pronominal suffix, creates semantic ambiguity. The text can express both "be sure that the offering is acceptable [to YHVH]" and "be sure that the sacrifice is offered by you willingly." H adds the dimension of intentionality to the sacrificial system. The well-being may be consumed on the day of the sacrifice or the next day, but if it is eaten on the third day, לא ירצה ("it will not be accepted"). This instruction suggests that ritual efficacy is dependent not solely on the priest's manipulation of blood but on the manner in which the laypeople consume the meat. The ritual space extends from the sanctuary to the family's dining space and, in fact, even to the layperson's body itself! This move by H is paradigmatic of its revisions of the P system. Holiness in this H model is expanded beyond the scope of priestly control and beyond the sacred space of the sanctuary. Ultimately, one who eats the meat after the proscribed time period profanes the holiness or sacred space of YHVH.

## Economic and Social Justice (19:9-16)

The next section (Lev 19:9-16) shifts from the ritual sphere to the domain of economic justice. The H writers acknowledge the realities of the uneven distribution of wealth, and they design measures to ensure that those inequalities are addressed, even if only in some small measure. Deuteronomy 24:19-20 addresses a similar practice, emphasizing that whatever falls to the ground during the reaping season cannot be picked up during a second pass. Specifically, the edges of a field are to be left untouched and that which is missed during the gleaning from the rest of the field must also be left for the poor and the stranger. Regarding the

⁹When you reap the harvest of your land, you shall not reap to the very edges of your field, or gather the gleanings of your harvest. ¹⁰You shall not strip your vineyard bare, or gather the fallen grapes of your vineyard; you shall leave them for the poor and the alien: I am the Lord your God.

¹¹You shall not steal; you shall not deal falsely; and you shall not lie to one another. ¹²And you shall not swear falsely by my name, profaning the name of your God: I am the Lord.

¹³You shall not defraud your neighbor; you shall not steal; and you shall not keep for yourself the wages of a laborer until morning. ¹⁴You shall not revile the deaf or put a stumbling block before the blind; you shall fear your God: I am the Lord.

¹⁵You shall not render an unjust judgment; you shall not be partial to the poor or defer to the great: with justice you shall judge your neighbor. ¹⁶You shall not go around as a slanderer among your people, and you shall not profit by the blood of your neighbor: I am the Lord.

¹⁷You shall not hate in your heart anyone of your kin; you shall reprove your neighbor, or you will incur guilt yourself. ¹⁸You shall not take vengeance or bear a grudge against any of your people, but you shall love your neighbor as yourself: I am the Lord.

vineyard, עללות are the fruit clusters that have not yet ripened enough to be picked. When they mature, they can only be picked by the needy; similarly, the פרט ("fallen grapes") refers to the grapes that fell but were not collected during the picking. Maurice Harris notes that "this isn't an urging of private landowners to give charity—no, it's a legally required redistribution of wealth from haves to have-nots; a tax, if you will, on the profits of each year's agricultural yield designated for the needs of the poor."[54]

The inclusion of the poor and the stranger here together is interesting. The book of Ruth offers a rare example of a narrative that correlates with this legal material. In Ruth, Naomi instructs her daughter-in-law to glean from Boaz's fields. The text implies that such gleaning by women could be dangerous. Boaz says to Ruth, "Keep your eyes on the field that is being reaped, and follow behind them. I have ordered the young men not to bother you" (Ruth 2:9). So while the needy could glean from the fields of the prosperous, they were not guaranteed safety. Women, in particular, were at risk of being molested or raped.

---

54. Maurice D. Harris, *Leviticus: You Have No Idea* (Eugene, OR: Cascade Books, 2013), 79.

### Leviticus 19:9-10 as a Basis for Poverty Alleviation Today

Leviticus 19 deals with miscellaneous matters. In verses 9-10, the farmer is forbidden to reap his field right to the edge of the farm; he shall not gather the gleanings after his harvest; he shall not gather the fallen grapes of his vineyard; all shall be left for the poor and the sojourner (see 23:22; Deut 24:19-22).

The welfare provision in Leviticus 19:9-10 is for the poor and the sojourner (עני and גר, respectively). The term עני is frequently used synonymously with אביון and דל to express the difficulty accompanying a lack of material possessions.[55] Financially, the עני lives from day to day. God instructs the Israelites to grant loans to the עני even when he has only his outer garment as collateral or pledge (Exod 22:25-26). The term גר, which also means "alien" or "stranger," refers to someone who does not enjoy the rights usually possessed by the resident, although the גר did enjoy some of those rights and was not to be oppressed (Exod 22:21 [Heb 20]; Lev 19:3; Jer 7:6; 22:3). The clearest sense of the word is used of Israel in their sojourn in Egypt (see Exod 23:9; Gen 15:13).[56]

Abraham, Isaac, and Jacob lived as strangers in Canaan (Exod 6:4), meaning that they had no property rights there. As clearly implied in our text and others (see Deut 14:29; 16:11, 14; 24:17; 26:13; 27:19), the גר is effectively (or practically speaking) of the same social status as the poor, orphans, and widows.

From Leviticus 19:9-10 it is clear that gleaning was part of Israel's system of welfare provision for the poor and aliens.[57] In addition to this annual help, they had the benefit of the triennial tithe on produce that was stored as a food reserve for distribution to the needy (Deut 14:28-29) and the free use of the produce of the land in the sabbatical year (Exod 23:10-11). Thus, the relief of poverty in Israel was built into economic and legal structures. The landowner had to make sure there was something left to be gleaned. This law thus sets possession of resources in a framework of duty to God and others and rejects the idea that private property is an absolute right.

Regarding the pattern of distribution of wealth between the rich and the poor, Leviticus 19:9-10 is relevant

55. Leonard J. Coppes, "עני" in *TWOT*, ed. R. Laird Harris et al. (Chicago: Moody Press, 1980), 683–84.

56. Harold G. Stigers, "גר" in *TWOT*, 155–56.

57. Christopher J. H. Wright, "Leviticus," in *New Bible Commentary*, ed. G. J. Wenham et al. (Nottingham: Inter-Varsity Press, 1994), 147.

for contemporary times, particularly in developing countries in Africa and elsewhere, where the leaders often expropriate the common resources, thereby relegating a large portion of the population to poverty.[58] Hence, the first step toward alleviating poverty in these countries, in light of Leviticus, is to curb corruption in order to make the resources accessible to all. The next step is to identify the rich, represented by the farmers in Leviticus. In contemporary times, these are all taxable income earners, business tycoons, companies, etc., who should be made to pay proportionate tax to the government. With corruption curbed and taxes adequately harnessed, the government is in the position to give employment to many and also to empower the private sector to do same. With these steps, the population living in poverty is drastically reduced, making it possible for the government to pay some allowances.

*Solomon Olusola Ademiluka*

H's idea of economic justice extends to prohibitions against stealing, defrauding, robbery, deception by lies, and holding back wages from a hired hand (Lev 19:11-13). There are only two cases in the Bible of women stealing: the matriarch Rachel steals her father's תרפים when she leaves his household (Gen 31:19), and the princess Jehoshabeath steals the prince-child Joash to protect him from a military coup (2 Chr 22:11, see also 2 Kgs 11:2). In both cases, the act of theft is motivated by a desire to protect the continuity of the family line.

In the midst of these brief prohibitions that address economic justice, we find the following in verse 12: "you shall not swear falsely by my name, profaning the name of your God; I am YHVH." The grammatical structure of this verse is significant: an imperfect followed by a converted perfect. This sequence indicates that the consequence of using the divine name improperly results in the profanation of the divine name. (See chapter 24 for a full discussion of "profaning the divine name.")

58. Solomon Olusola Ademiluka, "Prophetic Intervention in Eighth-Century Israel: A Recipe for Socio-Economic Recovery in Africa," *Uma: Journal of Philosophy and Religious Studies* 2 (2007): 37; Biodun Ogunyemi, "Beyond the Security Threats," *The National Scholar: A Publication of the Academic Staff Union of Universities* (ASUU) 9 (2012): 36–37; E. Oju, "Nigerians Have Stolen N7.9 Trillion," *Daily Times, Nigeria* (2013): 6; A. A. Olaniyi, "The Dal in Exodus 30:15 and Poverty Alleviation in Nigeria," *ASUU Journal of Humanities: A Journal of Research and Development* 2 (2012): 130.

The placement of verses 14-15 within the section on economic justice reveals a sophisticated understanding of the dynamics of power, privilege, and class. Cursing a deaf person and putting a stumbling block before a blind person both involve the intentional exploitation of a person's weakness. A deaf person cannot defend herself from a curse because she is not even aware that she has been cursed; the case is similar for a blind person who cannot see what trap lies ahead.

These verses also use the phrase "you shall fear your God" as the culminating statement. This phrase appears a handful of times in the Holiness Legislation, and in each case the law concerns the arena of behavior that transcends reward or punishment. For example, Leviticus 25:39-43 deals with the release of Hebrew slaves at the Jubilee. This law can be enforced among a community of people; however, H extends the legislation to indicate that the master should not oppress the slave and that the master should fear God. A student of mine described the call for the fear of God in these contexts as a call to be a Mensch. The cases in which the fear of God is invoked are laws that cannot necessarily be enforced and that have to do with just being a good person.

It is important to highlight that H sees the deaf and the blind in their full humanity and therefore worthy of protection. In other cases, H determines that certain classes of people—like daughters or men who have anal sex with other men—are not worthy of protection. H seems to have a hierarchy of humanity, which, like US law, relegates certain classes of people as unworthy of full protection or civil rights (e.g., Dreamers and transsexual individuals).[59] These people are treated with indifference, humiliation, and even cruelty. Unfortunately this kind of exploitation continues to be pandemic in our own age.

## The Power of Speech

The Hebrew root of the NRSV's "slanderer" (רכיל in v. 16) can also refer to trading or being a trader. Merchants were not permanent residents of a community and were therefore held in suspicion. Traders would have dealt not only in goods and commodities but also in information. Someone who acts like a merchant is someone who benefits by collecting

59. The term "Dreamers" refers to non-American-born individuals who were brought to the United States illegally at a very young age, usually by a parent from Mexico or another Latin American country. Political debate continues to challenge the legal protection of Dreamers in the United States under the 2012 legislation, "Deferred Action for Childhood Arrivals."

and sharing information about other people. This may be how the same root came to be associated with gossip. The power and potential misuse of speech is an important motif in biblical literature.

Unfortunately, by the rabbinic period, לשון הרע ("harmful speech") was associated primarily with women by the rabbis. According to them, one of the characteristics of women is that they gossip; in fact, a strand of rabbinic interpretation reinterprets Miriam's challenge to Moses's authority in Numbers 12 from a question of leadership to women's gossip. According to this thread of interpretation, Miriam is punished with a skin affliction because she was gossiping behind Moses's back.[60] More recent scholarship on Numbers 12 and Miriam suggests that Miriam was performing her role as a leader of the community to ensure that ancient customs were honored.[61]

Throughout verses 15-16, the writers define who is included in these commandments. The words all indicate members of one's own community. Whether or not the writers would have agreed that everyone is to be treated according to these ethical standards, the world of the writers is the world of the specific community.

"You shall not profit by the blood of your neighbor" (Lev 19:16) is more literally translated as "you shall not stand on the blood of your neighbor." The phrase עמד על can be taken in different ways. Baruch Levine summarizes the three main possibilities: The first "has the sense that one ought not to stand by inactively when one's neighbor's life is in danger." The second interpretation is based on Targum Onkelos, which reads, "Do not rise up against the life of your comrade," understood literally as murder. The third common reading is based on Ezekiel 33:26, which Levine summarizes as follows: "One ought not pursue one's own livelihood in a manner that endangers another or at the expense of another's

60. The Ramban writes the following in *Sefer Devarim*, in the context of the commandment to remember Amalek, that Israel "is also commanded to remember what God did to Miriam: we are commanded to inform our children of her actions, and to speak of them from generation to generation. We must do this, even though it would have been appropriate to hide her behavior, since it is generally proscribed to speak negatively and embarrassingly about righteous individuals. The Torah, however, commanded us to proclaim her actions and to reveal them, in order to set a warning against evil speech . . . since evil speech is such a great sin that causes overwhelming amounts of evil in the world and people constantly stumble" (*Sefer Devarim* 25:17).

61. See Tamar Kamionkowski, "Will the Real Miriam Please Stand Up," http://thetorah.com/will-the-real-miriam-please-stand-up/.

well-being."[62] One can only wonder how H would have responded to the historic exploitation of workers in sweatshops or to rampant human trafficking around the globe.

Verse 17 gave rise to a substantial body of literature in Jewish post-biblical sources regarding תוכחה, that is, how, when, and why a person should reprove another. Proverbs 26:24-25 teaches that hating someone in one's heart can lead to acts of deceit; Proverbs 10:18 argues that concealing one's feelings can lead to slander; and Proverbs 25:9-10 advises a person to confront the other directly and to avoid talking to third parties about a concern.[63]

Leviticus 19:18 contains the source text for the Golden Rule. The first part of the verse bans both taking revenge and bearing a grudge. The rabbis describe the difference between these two actions or attitudes via example:

> "You shall not take revenge." What is the scope of vengeance? If x says to y "Lend me your sickle," and y refuses to lend it; and the next day y says to x "Lend me your ax," and x replies "I will not lend you an ax because you refused to lend me a sickle," that is what is forbidden by the law, "You shall not take revenge."
>
> What is the scope of bearing a grudge? If x says to y "Lend me your ax," and y refuses to lend it; and the next day y says to x "Lend me your sickle," and x replies "Take it! I'm not like you who would not lend me an ax," that is what is forbidden by the law, "You shall not bear a grudge."[64]

Verse 18 begins with a warning about behaviors and feelings, a trope which permeates much of Leviticus 19. Action and intention are interwoven. The Bible stands alone among ancient Near Eastern legal traditions in dictating feeling and intention. "You shall love your neighbor as yourself" has been the source of much interpretation within both Jewish and Christian traditions.

In fact, almost every word in this verse has been the object of interpretation. For example, there have been a variety of suggestions regarding the meaning of the word "neighbor." Earlier rabbinic interpretation tended to interpret the word "neighbor" as a member of one's own

---

62. Levine, *Leviticus*, 129.

63. For a presentation of postbiblical Jewish interpretations of Lev 19:17, see James L. Kugel, "On Hidden Hatred and Open Reproach: Early Exegesis of Leviticus 19:17," *HTR* 80 (1987): 43–61.

64. Sifra, Parashat Kedoshim, 2:4.

community. In a debate with Akiba, we find the following: "'You shall love your neighbor as yourself.' Rabbi Akiba says, 'This is a great principle in the Torah.' Ben Azzai says 'This is the book of the generations of Adam' is a greater principle than that one.'" Shimon ben Azzai (Sifra Parashat Kedoshim 4:12) argued that it is impossible for a person to fully love oneself and thus, if one despises oneself, should one despise the other? By placing the teaching that humans are created in the image of God (Gen 1:27) as more important than Leviticus 19:18, a base standard is set for everyone.[65] Luke 10:25-37, building on the statements in Mark 12:28-34 and Matthew 22:34-40, defines a neighbor as "the one who showed mercy" (v. 37) through the parable of the Good Samaritan.

Franz Rosenzweig interpreted the כמוך as an adjective modifying the neighbor, thus, one like you. "'Like you,' and thus not 'you.' You remain You and remain just that. But he is not to remain a He for you, and thus a mere It for your You. Rather he is like You, like your You, a You like You, an I—a soul."[66] The word כמוך can also be rendered an adverb, modifying the verb "love." In this case, the text would read: "Love your neighbor to the same degree that you love yourself."

Finally, the preposition ל that follows the verb "to love" can be interpreted as either an accusative (the direct object) or as a dative (the indirect object). Paul Mendes-Flohr distinguishes between the two eloquently: "As the direct object of love, *re'a* would be the addressee of love's emotional embrace; as the indirect object of love, *re'a* would be the intended recipient of love's deeds."[67] The medieval commentators read the preposition as a dative marker and as an accusative, so that loving one's neighbor as oneself means wishing for one's neighbor what one would wish for oneself. In addition, Mendes-Flohr reports on a booklet that was written by the great Jewish philosopher Hermann Cohen, about Jewish neighborly love, arguing that "neighbor" refers to all human beings. The booklet was published as an act of defiance at the rise of the Third Reich.[68]

The seemingly simple statement "you shall love your neighbor as yourself" is anything but simple in its Hebrew original. Indeed, the

65. See Reinhard Neudecker, "'You Shall Love Your Neighbor as Yourself—I Am the Lord' (Lev 19, 18) in Jewish Interpretation," *Bib* 73 (1992): 496–517 for an in-depth study of the history of interpretation within Jewish tradition.

66. Franz Rosenzweig, *The Star of Redemption*, trans. William Hallo (New York: Holt, Rinehart and Winston, 1973), 239–40.

67. Paul Mendes-Flohr, *Love, Accusative and Dative: Reflections on Leviticus 19:18*, The B.G. Rudolph Lectures in Judaic Studies (New York: Syracuse University Press, 2007), 11.

68. Ibid., 7.

multiple ambiguities in the Hebrew have allowed for a rich and varied history of interpretation.

## Maintaining Separation and Categorization (19:19-22)

Leviticus 19:19 encapsulates the priestly notion that categories should not be mixed: cattle should mate with cattle, one kind of seed is to be sown only with its own kind, and different kinds of fabrics should not be mixed in the same garment. The Hebrew term שעטנז ("different materials") appears in the Bible only here and in Deuteronomy 22:11. There is no clear cognate in related languages, although Deuteronomy 22:11 suggests that this enigmatic term refers to a combination of wool and linen. The rationale behind the prohibitions in verse 19 is the same as the one for prohibiting sexual acts between men,[69] namely, the maintenance of clear boundaries and hierarchies. While the H writers expand P's notions of holiness from static to more dynamic, the H writers still root their thinking in the concept of separation, of binaries, of distinct categories. This is in line with the story of creation in Genesis 1, where the world is created through the process of separation and categorization.

---

*On Leviticus 19:19, כלאים*

Broadly speaking, the Torah seems very concerned with preserving the boundaries between categories of natural beings, as one finds in the creation story of Genesis 1; in the laws about which animals can be eaten (Lev 11 and Deut 14); and in the prohibitions on כלאים or mixtures (Lev 19:19 and Deut 22:9-11), including mixing agricultural species in a single plot of land and cross- breeding animal species, and, at least according to rabbinic interpretation, grafting one species of tree onto another. In rabbinic terminology, the ordering of creation, סדרי בראשית, has an inherent sanctity. Accordingly, Ellen Davis believes that the כלאים prohibition could be applied today to genetic engineering.[70] Indeed, in rabbinic law, these prohibitions have a universal dimension, in that they apply both in the land of Israel

---

69. Lesbianism is not forbidden because the biblical understanding of sex was defined by the act of penile penetration. The assumption was that there was no penetrator in lesbian sex acts.

70. Ellen Davis, *Scripture, Culture, and Agriculture: An Agrarian Reading of the Bible* (Cambridge: Cambridge University Press, 2009), 86–88.

[19]You shall keep my statutes. You shall not let your animals breed with a different kind; you shall not sow your field with two kinds of seed; nor shall you put on a garment made of two different materials.

[20]If a man has sexual relations with a woman who is a slave, designated for another man but not ransomed or given her freedom, an inquiry shall be held. They shall not be put to death, since she has not been freed; [21]but he shall bring a guilt offering for himself to the LORD, at the entrance of the tent of meeting, a ram as guilt offering. [22]And the priest shall make atonement for him with the ram of guilt offering before the LORD for his sin that he committed; and the sin he committed shall be forgiven him.

and outside the land (m. Qidd 1:9). But the rules of כלאים, which also prohibit weaving together wool and linen in clothing, may also be thought of as purely cultic rules rather than ecological rules. Moreover, in the eyes of Jewish law, because they are part of the Holiness Code, they apply only to Jews, which limits their moral impact.

I think therefore that the answer is more complicated. We know that during the course of Earth's history, the orders of creation, of life, have changed many times over. If we take a long view of evolution, there is no essential "truth" to the array of species that define life at this moment, even though they are the species with whom we create our home. Evan Eisenberg, in *The Ecology of Eden*,[71] even argues that genetic engineering should be seen as being modeled on Nature to the same extent as any other human techne. In fact, recent research suggests that evolution itself is as much or more directed by mechanisms that cells have to manipulate their own genes, as it is by random mutation.[72] Moreover, though it may be bizarre to environmentalists, creating GMOs (genetically modified organisms) in some abstract sense also adds to life, and, in fact, genetic engineering may become a necessary if frightening tool for stewarding species so that they don't become extinct.

The relevant question may not be whether something is

71. Evan Eisenberg, *The Ecology of Eden: An Inquiry into the Dream of Paradise and a New Vision of Our Role in Nature* (New York: Vintage Press, 1999), 321–25.

72. James Shapiro, *Evolution: A View from the 21st Century* (Upper Saddle River, NJ: FT Press, 2011).

"natural" but whether and when we should exercise the capacity, ability, or right to control nature to this degree. The deeper lessons of Leviticus and the whole Torah—of shabbat, rest, and the demand that we relinquish the idea that we can own the Earth—suggest at least that we should hesitate. Given the possible ecological (and spiritual) impact of these technologies, and the impossibility of knowing and limiting the consequences of GMOs released into the wild, where they can spread and displace non-GMOs or crossbreed with them, the precautionary principle would also urge us not to take such risks. But even if we do take a more conservative view and affirm that the sacredness of the order of creation should apply to genetic engineering, this still would not mean that all genetic engineering should be prohibited.

Perhaps two distinctions should be made. The first is whether something will be released into the field or only used in a laboratory setting, which would apply in all cases. This can be related to כלאים because כלאים is specifically concerned with how one plants one's field. The second is whether genetic engineering takes genes from one species and implants them in another or simply edits the existing genome within a single species. This distinction can only be applied to creatures that reproduce sexually or, in biblical terms, "according to their species" (למינה or למינהו) (Gen 1:12, 21, 25)—in other words, plants, fungi, and animals. Because bacteria and many protista do not reproduce sexually, and bacteria can share genetic material through conjugation across species lines, the concept of species itself can only apply approximately to them, so כלאים could not really be applied. GMOs that can both be completely isolated and are used to save lives, such as bacteria modified so as to produce a certain drug in a laboratory reactor, or lab mice manipulated by the CRISPR process to test how a particular gene affects a certain illness, are ethically different from GMOs whose goal is merely (and questionably) to "enhance" lives, like Bt (genetically modified) corn.

*David Seidenberg*

The connecting feature in Leviticus 19:19 and 19:20-22 is the mixing of categories. Leviticus 19:20-22 presents instructions on how to deal with "mixing" that involves sexual relations when the status of one participant is unclear. An unidentified man has sexual intercourse with a slave woman who also has another status: she is נחרפת ("designated" in v. 20). Most scholars assume that she is promised to another man for marriage but that no formal betrothal arrangements have been set yet. The text gives us no information about the fate of the woman or the man to whom she is promised. The guilty party is the man who has initiated sexual activity, having offended both the current owner of the slave and God, to whom the offender must make amends through a guilt offering. The fate of the woman is not the concern of the writers of this unit.

Assuming that H was familiar with legal material from the Covenant Code, the writer might be addressing a perceived gap in the law regarding young girls who are sold into slavery. According to Exodus 21:7-11, if a man purchased a girl as a slave, he had three options upon her coming of age: he could marry her, he could give her to one of his sons as a wife, or he could sell her to another man to be a wife. Leviticus 19:20-22 addresses what happens if the owner has made an arrangement with another man but then another man has sexual relations with the slave woman. Assuming that the writers of the Holiness Legislation were familiar with other legal traditions, if the woman had not been a slave, the law in Deuteronomy 22:23-27 would have applied, proscribing the death penalty for the man and the woman involved in the sexual act, but the woman in Leviticus 19:20-22 is in an ambiguous state, for she is both a slave and a betrothed woman.

Moshe Kline has argued that Leviticus 19:20-22 is the central point of the book,[73] a view that I will return to after taking a closer look at some of the ambiguous terminology that renders verses 20-22 difficult to interpret. For example, what does it mean for a slave woman to be "assigned"? What is the בקרת ("inquiry," v. 20)? Why is an אשם ("guilt offering," v. 21) required? Who is the perpetrator and what is the nature of the crime?

Interestingly, this legal case is the only one in the Bible in which an "inquiry" is required. The P material (e.g., Lev 13:36; 27:33) uses the verbal form ("to inquire") to indicate when a skin disease requires deeper examination; Leviticus 19:20 may be addressing a similar situation. According to verse 20, however, the woman's status as both slave and as betrothed is complex but clear, the status of the owner is irrelevant to the case, and the perpetrator's guilt is implied. Levine, following Ephraim Speiser, connects the Hebrew בקר to the Akkadian *baqaru*, "to make good on a claim," and concludes that this refers to the payment imposed on the party responsible for the violation.[74]

Baruch Schwartz's interpretation of בקרת may be most compelling. The sole concern of Leviticus 19:20-22 is that the perpetrator bring a well-

---

73. Kline, "The Editor Was Nodding," 58.
74. Levine, *Leviticus*, 130.

being offering to the priest so that he may be forgiven by God for his sin. In this case, sexual intercourse takes place in a condition in which the status of the woman is unclear. As a slave, she is a man's property. As an assignee, she is in transition out of slavery and into the hands of another man. There is disagreement whether the perpetrator is the slave owner or a third party. Regardless, the case ultimately focuses on the perpetrator's requirement to offer a well-being sacrifice.[75]

Diane Kriger suggests that נחרפת means "to be trifled with." She argues that sexual intercourse with the first male partner should have constituted a marital-like bond between him and the שפחה. "Due, however, to the dubious nature of the intercourse—engaged in by the man with no intention of creating a permanent relationship, given the woman's unfree status and therefore her inability to protect herself—no such bond is created." Thus נחרפת ("assigned") is similar to בעלת בית ("mistress of the house"; see 1 Kgs 17:17), though this term cannot be used here because the woman is not to be considered a potential wife.[76] In this scenario, the first man has a claim on the slave woman and the second man brings a well-being because he has committed a trespass against God.

Kriger argues that נחרפת does not mean "betrothed" but rather sexually humbled[77] and that בקרת "refers to a claim, in the general sense of a contestation of a relationship. It need not imply a return of the item claimed, but it may include a right to be compensated or a right to dispute a status."[78] She concludes, "In what seems to be a conflict between sex rights and some idea of property rights, the case was resolved according to property rights. . . . The שפחה נחרפת may be understood as an upset of the dependence continuum. For the slave it is a crime of trespass and for the wife a crime of adultery."[79]

So is there significance to Kline's observation that this legal case is at the center of Leviticus? This is the only case in Leviticus in which the issue is not about respecting or transgressing categories. This case is about acting in a void. The status of the woman is complicated; she defies categorization. For this she is not regarded as guilty or culpable. The man who sexually engages with someone who defies classification, however, has

---

75. Baruch J. Schwartz, "A Literary Study of the Slave-Girl Pericope: Leviticus 19:20-22," *Scripta Hierosolymitana* 31 (1986): 241–55.

76. Diane Kriger, *Sex Rewarded, Sex Punished: A Study of the Status 'Female Slave' in Early Jewish Law* (Boston: Academic Studies Press, 2011), 153.

77. Ibid., 168–71.

78. Ibid., 217.

79. Ibid., 350.

*not* transgressed the law of the community. His sin is more severe; he has stepped outside the system altogether. In doing so, he has insulted God's system, God's ideological property. Thus a well-being offering is required.

### First Fruits (19:23-25)

Leviticus 19:23-25 teaches that the community of Israel maintains holiness not only in the way it treats its members and the *sancta* (sacred things) but also in the way it cares for the fruit of the land (vv. 23-37). The first instruction is that one should not pick new fruit-bearing trees for three years after planting them; then, in the fourth year, Israelites should dedicate the first fruits to God (vv. 23-24).

Literally, verse 23 reads: "you shall treat as foreskin its foreskin with its fruit." The term ערל ("uncircumcised") here has both a literal meaning (referring to the bud) and a metaphoric meaning (referring to its forbidden nature). Jacob Milgrom has argued that the foreskin refers to the fruit while it is still in its bud; therefore, the text commands the removal of the buds with the incipient fruit inside during the first few years after the tree is planted. The fruit of the nascent tree is not to be eaten until the fifth year.

### Unsanctioned Ritual Practices (19:26-31)

The following cluster of laws bans a variety of practices that, while popular with the populace, may have been incompatible or even a threat to official state-sanctioned practices. Verse 26 appears to be yet another ban on consuming blood, but Milgrom convincingly suggests that the wording may point to a different practice. The text does not say, "Do not eat the blood"; rather, it reads literally, "Do not eat over the blood" (*contra* NRSV, "You shall not eat anything with its blood"). The issue is that the verse uses the preposition על (literally, "on, over"). Milgrom argues that the prohibited practice here may be chthonic worship involving the consultation of ghosts. Milgrom refers to practices in which blood would be poured into a pit to get the attention of demons or ancestors. People would eat over the pit to inquire of the ancestors; thus a form of divination.[80] NRSV translates the second half of verse 26 as "You shall not

---

80. Milgrom, *Leviticus 17–22*, 1685–86, who is influenced by Ramban; also Hartley, *Leviticus*, 319–20.

²³When you come into the land and plant all kinds of trees for food, then you shall regard their fruit as forbidden; three years it shall be forbidden to you, it must not be eaten. ²⁴In the fourth year all their fruit shall be set apart for rejoicing in the LORD. ²⁵But in the fifth year you may eat of their fruit, that their yield may be increased for you: I am the LORD your God.

²⁶You shall not eat anything with its blood. You shall not practice augury or witchcraft. ²⁷You shall not round off the hair on your temples or mar the edges of your beard. ²⁸You shall not make any gashes in your flesh for the dead or tattoo any marks upon you: I am the LORD.

²⁹Do not profane your daughter by making her a prostitute, that the land not become prostituted and full of profanity. ³⁰You shall keep my sabbaths and reverence my sanctuary: I am the LORD.

³¹Do not turn to mediums or wizards; do not seek them out, to be defiled by them: I am the LORD your God.

practice augury or witchcraft." The term "witchcraft" may be misleading here since the two Hebrew terms seem to refer to forms of divination, that is, the practice of divining the future rather than attempting to alter events. Perhaps "You shall not practice augury or divination" is more accurate and better fits into the first part of the verse.

Verses 27-28 prohibit making changes to one's body associated in other cultures with mourning practices. The second part of verse 28 contains the Hebrew phrase כתבת קעקע, translated by NRSV as "tattoo any marks" while NJPS reads "incise any marks." The Hebrew phrase is a *hapax legomenon*; it appears only here in the Bible and thus we cannot know with precision what the biblical writers intended. It was common practice in the ancient Near East to brand people and animals to mark ownership;[81] however, traditional Jewish commentary has tended to interpret the phrase as tattooing rather than branding.[82]

On the surface, verse 29 simply seems to prohibit the use of daughters as prostitutes. There is some debate as to why a father would use his daughter as a prostitute. Some believe that the father might be dedicating his daughter to some sex cult[83] (although there is no evidence for

---

81. *Code of Hammurabi*, 146, 226–27.

82. For a more detailed discussion, see Gilad J. Gevaryahu, "Ketovet Ka'aka (Leviticus 19:28): Tattooing or Branding?," *JBQ* 38 (2010): 13–20.

83. Gordon J. Wenham, *The Book of Leviticus* (Grand Rapdis: Eerdmans, 1979), 272; Erhard Gerstenberger, *Leviticus*, OTL (Louisville: Westminster John Knox, 1996), 275–76.

this), while others argue that prostitution was necessitated by economic hardship.[84] The key word in this verse is חלל ("profane," NRSV), which should be rendered more accurately as "desecrate." The verb חלל is a technical term in the Holiness Legislation indicating a decrease in the level of holiness. If a father puts his daughter in a position that diminishes her holiness, that action affects the entire land negatively. This point is made even more strongly by coupling this teaching with a reminder in verse 30, to observe Shabbat and to keep watch over God's holy space. To some degree, the holiness of a daughter is akin to the holiness of the sanctuary. Deborah Ellens understands this text a bit differently: "Thus a daughter in Israel is holy. That is, she is consecrated or set aside. One component of her holiness is most certainly the fact that she is set aside for sexual access by one man, evidently in the context of marriage. Just as Israel is consecrated to Yhwh, so also the woman is consecrated to one man."[85]

The prohibition against turning to mediums or wizards in Leviticus 19:31 brings us back to the prohibitions in verse 26. The four terms that are used in verses 26 and 31 to describe illicit divination are equally associated with men and women when we look to narratives that ban such persons. The fact that the bans in Leviticus 19 do not target only women does not mean, however, that these texts are not oppressive for women. The priesthood naturally prohibits all access to the divine world that stands independent of its own monopoly on sanctuary-based practices. While this impacts both nonpriestly men and women, it completely erases any legitimate form of access to the divine for all women in Israel. In fact, the only named biblical character who is identified as a necromancer is the woman of Endor (1 Sam 28). When Saul is eager to receive counsel regarding an impending war with the Philistines, he begins by seeking God through dreams, Urim, and prophets. When he gets no response via these state-sanctioned mechanisms, Saul surreptitiously seeks help from "a woman who is a medium" (1 Sam 28:7). Thomas Overholt translates verse 7 more literally as "a woman who is a mistress of a ghost."[86] Saul himself had banned all necromancers and

---

84. Hartley, *Leviticus*, 321; Kiuchi, *Leviticus*, 359.

85. Ellens, *Women in the Sex Texts of Leviticus and Deuteronomy*, 116.

86. Thomas Overholt, "1 Sam 28:7-25 Medium of Endor," in *Women in Scripture: A Dictionary of Named and Unnamed Women in the Hebrew Bible, The Apocryphal/ Deuterocanonical Books and the New Testament*, ed. Carol Meyers, Toni Craven, and Ross S. Kraemer (Boston: Houghton Mifflin, 2000), 244–45.

mediums (v. 3), but his willingness to approach this woman and his trust in her abilities suggests that Saul's ban had nothing to do with the efficacy of the practice but rather with politics.

Esther Hamori points out that "work on ancient Near Eastern divination tends to focus on technical or academic methods, such as extispicy and omen compendia—logically enough, since these are by definition the types for which we have the most textual evidence. Because academic divination was overwhelmingly a male profession, such research is naturally focused on men. The next step is more problematic: divination is then circularly defined to be male."[87] Hamori's project is to highlight women's divination practices as witnessed through biblical narratives. In many of these cases, women's practices are functionally equivalent to other divinatory practices, but they are identified by the biblical writers as not having any official role.

In Mesopotamia, Tzvi Abusch explains that the *kassaptu*, a witch, is usually depicted as a woman who performs malevolent magic. She harms her victims through indirect contact, manipulating objects with which her victim has been in contact, creating figurines to represent the victim, and then manipulating the figurine to cause pain and malady. In contrast, the *asipu* is a legitimate practitioner of magic, who uses magic to protect clients. Abusch says: "Although witch and asipu are opponents, they nonetheless are almost mirror-images of each other insofar as they use many of the same techniques, though presumably in the service of conflicting social goals and norms."[88] Abusch also notes that the *asipu* and his clientele generally come from the upper classes. The male exorcist appropriates the practices of the witch, refines incantations to make them more "scholarly" and establishes a dichotomy between the witch and the exorcist. In Babylonia, the use of magic is in itself not condemned, yet female witches are unknown, mysterious, acting from afar and with malevolent intention, while male practitioners are known, legitimized as trained scholars, and act to protect members of society.

---

87. Esther Hamori, *Women's Divination in Biblical Literature: Prophecy, Necromancy and Other Arts of Knowledge*, ABRL (New Haven: Yale University Press, 2015), 10. See also Madeline McClenney-Sadler, "Cry Witch! The Embers Still Burn," in *Pregnant Passion: Gender, Sex, and Violence in the Bible*, ed. Cheryl A. Kirk-Duggan (Atlanta: SBL Press, 2003), 117–41.

88. Tzvi Abusch, *Mesopotamian Witchcraft: Toward a History and Understanding of Babylonian Witchcraft Beliefs and Literature*, Ancient Magic and Divination 5 (Leiden: Brill, 2002), 7.

Abusch furthermore argues that the image of the witch is transformed over time by the exorcists in two ways: "The witch is transformed into a supernatural demonic force" and "The witch is transformed into a powerful human figure who introduces chaos into the social order and even intrudes on the divine world."[89] This extension of the witch's powers correlates to the increasing power of the exorcist.

### Caring for the Vulnerable (19:32-37)

Leviticus 19:32 commands respect for the elderly within the community. The verb הדר ("defer," NRSV, or "show deference") is also used in Leviticus 19:15, which states that one should not show deference to the rich in courts of justice. Verse 32 is especially relevant in the twenty-first century as people live longer lives. As women are outliving men in most countries of the world, there are increasing needs for supports for elderly women. Globally, among people over the age of eighty, older women outlive men 100-to-61, yet women are less likely to receive old-age pensions than men in most countries of the world.[90]

Every law collection in the Bible advocates care for the גר ("foreigner" or "alien") who resides in the land of Israel (Lev 19:33-34; see also Exod 22:20; 23:9; Deut 14:29; 24:14, 17). A גר was a non-Israelite who lived either temporarily or for a longer period in the land of Israel but did not belong to the ethnic (later political) body of Israel. Elsewhere in the Bible, the stranger is mentioned alongside the widow and orphan, suggesting that men who were strangers were considered vulnerable and worthy of care. These admonitions frequently remind the reader that the Israelites were once strangers in the land of Egypt and that they should remember the vulnerability of the outsider, a particularly challenging instruction in light of today's worldwide migration crisis.

The formula אני יהוה ("I יהוה" or "I am יהוה") appears fifteen times in Leviticus 19, and in verse 36 it appears in its fullest form. This phrase encourages the reader to remember that one must emulate God and seek to become holy because God saved Israel in the past. What God has done—saved Israel—is the basis for one's commitment to the process of seeking to become holy.

---

89. Ibid., 14.

90. http://www.unwomen.org/en/digital-library/multimedia/2015/10/infographic-progress-ageing-has-a-female-face.

³²You shall rise before the aged, and defer to the old; and you shall fear your God: I am the Lord.

³³When an alien resides with you in your land, you shall not oppress the alien. ³⁴The alien who resides with you shall be to you as the citizen among you; you shall love the alien as yourself, for you were aliens in the land of Egypt: I am the Lord your God.

³⁵You shall not cheat in measuring length, weight, or quantity. ³⁶You shall have honest balances, honest weights, an honest ephah, and an honest hin: I am the Lord your God, who brought you out of the land of Egypt. ³⁷You shall keep all my ordinances, and observe them: I am the Lord.

## Honoring the Divine Name (20:1-5)

Leviticus 20 mirrors Leviticus 18 in its content, but the material in the two chapters is organized differently. In chapter 20, transgressions are ordered by level of severity and degree of punishment. Leviticus 18 frames the sexual prohibitions with anti-Canaanite rhetoric; that is, the overarching theme is that the Israelites should not act like the Canaanites. Leviticus 20 sets similar material within a slightly different framework: the people of Israel should not engage in illicit sexual encounters because Israel must separate itself from all other peoples (Lev 20:24-26).

The prohibitions begin with the topic of Molech worship (see Lev 18). The language of verse 3 reveals a key theological motif for the observance of laws: "I myself will set my face against them, and will cut them off from the people, because they have given of their offspring to Molech, *defiling my sanctuary and profaning my holy name*" (emphasis mine). According to this verse, Molech worship affects God in two ways: first, it defiles God's sanctuary; second, it desecrates God's name.[91] Are these two parallel statements two sequential results of Molech worship,[92] or

---

91. Lev 18:21 forbids the dedication of children to Molech as well and teaches that the result of this act is the desecration of the Name. See Lev 20:2-5; 1 Kgs 11:7; 2 Kgs 23:10; Isa 57:9; Jer 32:33. See Baruch J. Schwartz, *The Holiness Legislation: Studies in the Priestly Code* (Jerusalem: Magnes Press, 1999), 187–203.

92. Tannaitic literature seems to take these two phrases sequentially; see Sifra Parashat Kedoshim, 10:8: "'And so defiled My sanctuary and profaned My holy name': this teaches that [Molech worship] defiles the sanctuary, profanes the Name, causes the Divine Presence to depart, brings the sword upon Israel, and exiles them from their land." For a thorough analysis of this text and related tannaitic sources, see Jonathan Klawans, *Impurity and Sin in Ancient Judaism* (Oxford: Oxford University Press, 2000), 118–34.

*Lev 20:1-5*

²⁰:¹The LORD spoke to Moses, saying: ²Say further to the people of Israel:

Any of the people of Israel, or of the aliens who reside in Israel, who give any of their offspring to Molech shall be put to death; the people of the land shall stone them to death. ³I myself will set my face against them, and will cut them off from the people, because they have given of their offspring to Molech, defiling my sanctuary and profaning my holy name. ⁴And if the people of the land should ever close their eyes to them, when they give of their offspring to Molech, and do not put them to death, ⁵I myself will set my face against them and against their family, and will cut them off from among their people, them and all who follow them in prostituting themselves to Molech.

do they signify two different effects of sin? Certain wrongdoings (cultic/ ritual for P and more expansive for H) can have a direct negative impact on the sanctity of God's sanctuary. טמא ("defiling," in v. 3) is created by human actions and attaches itself not to God but to God's objects, that is, the sanctuary and its contents.[93] P offers a priestly prescription for cleansing the טמאה from the individual(s) and from the sanctuary through blood sacrifice (see Lev 4:5-7, 16-18, 24-25, 29-30, 33-34; 5:8-9; 16:14-15, 18-19). In contrast, H raises an additional concern regarding "desecration of my holy name." While P is exclusively concerned with the maintenance of the sanctity of the cultic site in order to ensure God's כבוד ("presence," usually rendered "glory" in NRSV) in the midst of the people, H's inclusion of the term שם ("name") adds a new theological dimension to the former nonanthropomorphic, static theology of P. It is no longer sufficient to ensure the presence of the כבוד, argues H, but Israel must also work to maintain the holiness of God's שם.

If H democratizes P, as has been argued by several scholars, then God's שם is that aspect of God that is accessible to all of Israel and not just to the priests. Milgrom argues that "God's name is the only sanctum other than the meat of the well-being offering that can be utilized by the laity."[94] The P writers argued that impurities have an impact on the sanctuary and may ultimately drive God's כבוד away, but H counters that while impurities and ethical wrongdoings have an impact on the sanctuary, they also directly impact an aspect of the divine being. The

93. Jacob Milgrom, *Leviticus 1–16*, AB 3 (New York: Doubleday, 1991), 258–61.
94. Milgrom, *Leviticus 17–22*, 1634–36.

untouchable כבוד is replaced, or rather supplemented, by the relational שם. The inaccessible, force-like God of the P writers is here changed into the more accessible, intimate God of H.

Traditional Jewish commentators have interpreted this phrase, חלול השם ("desecration of the Name"), to mean that one can damage God's reputation among the nations of the world through wrong actions. The phrase חלול השם is still used today to describe public acts that can bring shame on the people Israel and their God. In the context of the Holiness Legislation, however, this teaching is much more profound, for the message is that wrong human actions can actually have an impact on that aspect of God known as שם, "name."

## Avoid Mediums and Sanctify YHVH (20:6-8)

The ban on practicing necromancy and certain types of divination appears three times in Leviticus, with the punishment designated for such practices becoming more severe in each successive case: declaration of impurity (19:31), being cut off from one's people (20:6), and the death penalty (20:27). In contrast to the Covenant Collection in Exodus, the Holiness Code rarely refers to women explicitly. Therefore, to mention them in Leviticus 20:27 (see 19:31 and 20:6) suggests that one of the priestly writers' concerns was with women's accessing the divine realm. First Samuel 28 tells the story of King Saul's consultation with the woman of Endor, who provides him with access to the ghost of the prophet Samuel. The woman fears for her life because she knows that necromancy is banned, yet Saul has recognized that some Israelites must nevertheless be practicing it and that he needs the woman's assistance. In a world in which only men could enter into the priesthood and in which men dominated the prophetic guilds, it is likely that women used other forms of divination to access the divine realm.

Interestingly, H never bans sorcery (כשף) as Exodus 22:18 (Hebrew v. 17) and Deuteronomy 18:10 do. In fact, the Exodus text specifically targets female sorcerers.[95] The H writers are consistently concerned with practices that seem to be focused on divination and cults of the dead.

Leviticus 20:7-8 expresses the heart of the Holiness Legislation: "Sanctify yourselves and strive to be holy because I am YHVH your God. Keep

---

95. In Isa 57:3, female sorcerers and adulterers are grouped together, presumably because both roles represented infidelity to God and to husbands.

⁶If any turn to mediums and wizards, prostituting themselves to them, I will set my face against them, and will cut them off from the people. ⁷Consecrate yourselves therefore, and be holy; for I am the LORD your God. ⁸Keep my statutes, and observe them; I am the LORD; I sanctify you.

my statutes, and observe them; I am YHVH; I sanctify you" (translation mine). This exhortation begins with the Hebrew root קדשׁ in *hitpael* form, marking the community's responsibility to sanctify itself, and it ends with the same root in the *piel*, marking God's role in sanctifying the people. The ultimate goal is for the community to sanctify itself by observing the precepts outlined in the Legislation and to strive for holiness at all times. The reason behind this goal is that God is holy, and the proper "medium" for making a connection between God and Israel is holy action. Through proper action (and not divination, for example) the people come closer to God, and God reaches out toward the community.

## Incest Laws, Version 2 (20:9-21)

Leviticus 20:9-21 closely parallels the material found in Leviticus 18:6-23. Both units list incest taboos, laws against male anal penetration, and prohibitions against adultery, bestiality, and Molech worship. Leviticus 20:9 adds a prohibition against cursing one's parents. While Leviticus 18 organizes the bans according to familial relationships, Leviticus 20 organizes these laws by the severity of the punishment. The wording of some of the specific laws differs, but the basic sense of the prohibitions is similar in the two units.

As I argued regarding Leviticus 18, the sex act was understood as involving one who penetrates and one who is penetrated, so it is not surprising that there is no prohibition against sex acts between women. What we today might define as sexual or erotic activity between two women was not a category of concern in the biblical mindset. Apparently, the "problem" with sex acts between men was that it put one man in the receptive position, thus emasculating him and confusing sex roles. (See discussion of Lev 18 and 19:19.) Saul Olyan argues that while Leviticus 18 addresses only the penetrator, in Leviticus 20:13 both parties involved in a prohibited sexual act are addressed.[96]

96. Olyan, "'And with a Male,'" 187.

*Lev 20:9-21*

[9]All who curse father or mother shall be put to death; having cursed father or mother, their blood is upon them.

[10]If a man commits adultery with the wife of his neighbor, both the adulterer and the adulteress shall be put to death. [11]The man who lies with his father's wife has uncovered his father's nakedness; both of them shall be put to death; their blood is upon them. [12]If a man lies with his daughter-in-law, both of them shall be put to death; they have committed perversion, their blood is upon them.

[13]If a man lies with a male as with a woman, both of them have committed an abomination; they shall be put to death; their blood is upon them. [14]If a man takes a wife and her mother also, it is depravity; they shall be burned to death, both he and they, that there may be no depravity among you. [15]If a man has sexual relations with an animal, he shall be put to death; and you shall kill the animal. [16]If a woman approaches any animal and has sexual relations with it, you shall kill the woman and the

### Naked Exposure as a Shaming Device: A Cross-Cultural Perspective

According to Leviticus 20, when a transgression of sexual boundaries arises, the (male) members of the community are to act collectively as the dispensers of justice and penalize all parties involved. The violators, along with their victims, are to be put to death or cast out by the community. In order to achieve the effect of deterrence, however, the casuistic laws may be harsher in theory than in practice. In some ancient southwest Asian cultures, proven adultery was punishable by death and mutilation (such as cutting off the nose, laceration of the face, and castration of the paramour). The punishment could be mitigated, however, by having the female offender paraded naked in public, giving the cuckolded husband the right of filing a divorce without compensational payment to the wife, demanding that the paramour pay a ransom to the husband, or simply granting a pardon.[97]

Similar mitigating measures are found in the sexualized metaphor of Israel's reliance on foreign imperial powers (Ezek 16:36-41; 23:9-35; Isa 47:1-3; Lam 1:8). Instead of executing the adulterous Israel and her paramours (the mega-powers with which Israel consorted), YHVH, the cuckolded husband,

97. Hennie J. Marsman, *Women in Ugarit and Israel: Their Social and Religious Position in the Context of the Ancient Near East* (Leiden: Brill, 2003), 170.

*Lev 20:9-21 (cont.)*

animal; they shall be put to death; their blood is upon them.

[17]If a man takes his sister, a daughter of his father or a daughter of his mother, and sees her nakedness, and she sees his nakedness, it is a disgrace, and they shall be cut off in the sight of their people; he has uncovered his sister's nakedness, he shall be subject to punishment. [18]If a man lies with a woman having her sickness and uncovers her nakedness, he has laid bare her flow and she has laid bare her flow of blood; both of them shall be cut off from their people. [19]You shall not uncover the nakedness of your mother's sister or of your father's sister, for that is to lay bare one's own flesh; they shall be subject to punishment. [20]If a man lies with his uncle's wife, he has uncovered his uncle's nakedness; they shall be subject to punishment; they shall die childless. [21]If a man takes his brother's wife, it is impurity; he has uncovered his brother's nakedness; they shall be childless.

punished his adulterous wife by beating her and exposing her "nakedness" to her paramours, even though adultery was, in theory, a capital offense.

While female nakedness in general is regarded as a symbol of sexual attraction in ancient Southwest Asia, the naked exposure of an adulterous wife in public stands out as an act of shaming and humiliation.[98] As a punishment, it is only meted out to adulteresses. The shaming device serves multiple functions of social control: the punitive humiliation of the adulterous wife, a deterring effect on the female spectators (see Ezek 16:41; 23:10), and reinforcement of the sexual norms among the general public by triggering the psychogenesis of conscience. Of course, these functions could only be fulfilled given the voyeuristic desire of the spectators.

Naked exposure as a means of shaming adulterers is not strictly an ancient phenomenon,[99] as it is attested even in our times. For instance, in recent decades, there have been numerous newspaper reports on incidents of an alleged mistress being violently stripped naked or half-naked

---

98. See Sonia Wong, "Gendering Nakedness (ערוה) and Sexual Policing: A Cross-Cultural Perspective," a session paper presented at the annual meeting of the Society of Biblical Literature, San Antonio, TX (November 2016).

99. Mario Jacoby, *Shame and the Origins of Self-Esteem: A Jungian Approach*, trans. Douglas Whitcher (London: Routledge, 1994; repr., 2003), 11.

(with top or bottom attire torn) in public and brutally assaulted, usually by a gang of women led by the alleged paramour's wife in various major cities of mainland China.[100] The media have attributed the cause of this rising trend of public shaming to the booming Chinese mistress culture that has accompanied the economic growth of the country. The physical battering in these incidents is often deliberately targeted at the face, breasts, and groin of the victim, presumably with the intent to sabotage the sexual appeal of these body parts. Some assailants even video the entire process of the assault and upload the clip on social media with the intent of propagating and perpetuating the shaming. The practice has become normalized and tacitly accepted by the Chinese public, to the extent that it has been dubbed "vigilante justice." Of the fifteen incidents that I found online, in no single incident did the passersby attempt to rescue the defenseless victim, presumably because of the morally higher ground enjoyed by the assailant-wife, who is usually regarded as the true victim of the extramarital affair. The victim of the assault is, on the other hand, considered the true culprit who deserves to be shamed. To the general

public, this kind of dispute is "an affair of the heart," and public intervention is considered an infringement of domestic matters.

It is not difficult to see that female assailants in these incidents follow the longstanding patriarchal proclivity to hold the female party more accountable for extramarital affairs, while exonerating or even exculpating the male party involved. Only the "mistress" bears the guilt of the affair and hence deserves to be brutalized and shamed publicly. Under the patriarchal assumptions, women involved in illicit sexual affairs are always scapegoated. Violent acts against them become justifiable on the basis of their sexual culpability.

In feudal China, it was the responsibility of the local patriarchal authority to condemn a married woman who was involved in extramarital affairs. A common punishment was to drown the woman in a bamboo container used for pig transport, similar to the Babylonian chastity test called the "river ordeal" (*Code of Hammurabi* 132). While the "vigilante justice" of our times is meted out by women, gender-biased values and male-privileged positions are adopted wholesale. The assailant-wife and her

---

100. For instance, read a report of such an incident by Matthew Blake published on October 13, 2014, in the *Daily Mail* of the United Kingdom (http://www.dailymail.co .uk/news/article-2791108/mob-rule-chinese-adulteress-stripped-naked-beaten -senseless-latest-attack-kind.html#ixzz3wVBf9Hv1).

gang act as sexual police, a role previously taken by the patriarchal authority. They too only took revenge on the "mistress" and exonerated the husband. In contrast, while the Levitical sexual prohibitions are concerned with the maintenance of proper sexual boundaries and uphold gender-biased values and male-privileged positions, the casuistic laws make no distinction between the aggressors and possible female victims, for the death penalty or social exclusion is prescribed to both. In both the Levitical and Chinese cases, gender justice is at stake. The former is at risk of incriminating female victims of rape. In the case of Chinese "vigilante justice," it would not be wrong to call this kind of public shaming "rape," if "rape" is by definition a violation of the genitals of another person by physical force or power maneuvering. The assailant-wives in these incidents behave as sexual violators inasmuch as they violate other women to quench their thirst for scapegoating vengeance.

*Sonia K. Wong*

### The Things That Stay With Us

Just an hour ago, before sitting to write this, I received an apology for a wound I have carried for over twenty years. I had signed up for a two-day class with a teacher who was visiting from out of state. The teacher's name was familiar, but I thought it unlikely it would be the same person who first taught me Leviticus 20:13 when I was ten years old, a person I had not seen since then but have thought of often as I have considered my relationship to God and Torah. Through God's mysterious grace, the teacher of this short class had indeed been my fifth-grade religious teacher.

I was unsure if and how to broach the subject with him. At the end of the two days, I lingered as others left. Graciously, he was open to a conversation and I shared the pain and disappointment I experienced in how he had taught the verse to me as a ten-year-old. I appreciated that he taught it to me and did not shy away from such a challenging text, and I expressed the pain that I felt with how he taught it. His intentions were progressive, attempting to undermine the homophobia often interpreted out of the verse, but his execution fell short. I had needed more resources to engage this verse. Without them, I remained unconvinced of his progressive reading. As a pre-teen with only a hint of awareness of my own queerness, I had nowhere to go with my questions or my pain.

After sharing, he put his hand on his heart and closed his eyes. When he opened them, his eyes were watery as he apologized for not putting enough thought or care into his teaching. My eyes watered as well. I thanked him and we hugged.

I think we were both reminded of the deep power of these sacred words—to hurt, to heal, to inspire, and to soothe. As teachers, we wield this sacred and intimate power. I pray that in my own teaching, I will do my best to teach the risky texts with the necessary care and attention and, when I fall short, that I will find the grace and humility my teacher showed me.

*Alex Weissman*

## Holy Land and Holy People (20:22-27)

The concluding verses of chapter 20 find a rough parallel in Leviticus 18:24-25, which indicates that the Canaanites are to be dispossessed because of their sexual transgressions and not because they were generally disloyal to YHVH, the god of the land. Leviticus 18:24-30 and 20:22-26 regard the Canaanites as inherently impure and thus not deserving of the land. While evidence from a variety of ancient Near Eastern sources points to a rather similar discourse about incest taboos and normative sexual activity, the Bible portrays sexual purity as unique to Israel. Paul Stevens, responding to the works of Regina Schwartz and Michael Walzer[101] who advocate for the liberating impulse of "Exodus thinking," argues that "Leviticus thinking" represents a drive for order and uses sexual transgression as a mythic tool to separate Israel from other peoples. Leviticus 18 and 20 in particular "reveal . . . a classic process of othering, that is, naturalizing the differences, imagined or otherwise, between ourselves and other communities in such a way as to justify our possession of what belongs to them."[102] Stevens demonstrates how early American colonialists used these Leviticus passages to justify their possession of the land and the destruction of the native communities. Stevens quotes Purchas, who comments on the Algonquian uprising of

101. Regina Schwartz, "Joseph's Bones and the Resurrection of the Text: Remembering in the Bible," *PMLA* 103 (1988): 114–24; and Michael Walzer, *Exodus and Revolution* (New York: Basic Books, 1985).

102. Paul Stevens, " 'Leviticus Thinking' and the Rhetoric of Early Modern Colonialism," *Culture* 35 (1993): 451.

²²You shall keep all my statutes and all my ordinances, and observe them, so that the land to which I bring you to settle in may not vomit you out. ²³You shall not follow the practices of the nation that I am driving out before you. Because they did all these things, I abhorred them. ²⁴But I have said to you: You shall inherit their land, and I will give it to you to possess, a land flowing with milk and honey. I am the LORD your God; I have separated you from the peoples. ²⁵You shall therefore make a distinction between the clean animal and the unclean, and between the unclean bird and the clean; you shall not bring abomination on yourselves by animal or by bird or by anything with which the ground teems, which I have set apart for you to hold unclean. ²⁶You shall be holy to me; for I the LORD am holy, and I have separated you from the other people to be mine.

²⁷A man or a woman who is a medium or a wizard shall be put to death; they shall be stoned to death, their blood is upon them.

1622 through the "mediating glass of Leviticus 18, and the Indian rebellion is represented as sexual transgression: 'When Virginia was violently ravished by her owne ruder Natives, yea her virgin cheekes dyed with the bloud of three colonies. . . . Temperance could not temper her selfe, yea the stupid Earth seems distempered with such bloudy potions and cries that shee is ready to spue out her inhabitants.'" In other words, this rhetoric argues, the natives lost their land because they were unclean, not because of English aggression.[103]

Leviticus 18–20 establishes a set of norms and provides legislation for the community of Israel. The focus of Leviticus has shifted outward from the inner workings of the tabernacle to the whole of the community, from ritual law to ethical precepts. As Israel Knohl writes in the final pages of his work, *The Sanctuary of Silence*,

> HS abandoned Priestly separatism and addressed the people, adopting elements of faith and worship popular among the nation at large. The religious language of HS is imbued with the spirit of popular faith: God is described in anthropomorphic language, and the commandments are presented in the framework of a covenant of mutual obligation.[104]

103. Ibid., 455.
104. Israel Knohl, *The Sanctuary of Silence: The Priestly Torah and the Holiness School* (Winona Lake, IN: Eisenbrauns, 2007), 223–24.

In fact, in some ways, Leviticus 19 has set the bedrock for key teachings in both Judaism and Christianity.

We must also keep in mind, however, that—in the midst of gems like loving one's neighbor as oneself, not bearing grudges, leaving the edges of the field for the poor, and being aware of the power of speech—we must also contend with problematic teachings including deprecating attitudes toward menstruation, some measure of xenophobia, and prohibitions against divinatory practices that were often in the domain of women.

# Leviticus 21:1–22:33

# *Protecting Priestly Privilege*

## Mourning, Marrying, and Piercing Boundaries (21:1-15)

Leviticus 21 is devoted to three areas of the law that apply specifically to priests. These laws govern burial and mourning practices for priests and the high priest, marriage restrictions for the priest and high priest, and a list of physical conditions that disqualify priests from service at the sanctuary.

The chapter begins with the restriction of a priest's permissibility to mourn the death of kin (vv. 1-5). He may defile himself for his mother, father, son, daughter, or brother and for his sister who is not and who has never been married. Although verse 4 is not altogether clear, the sense is that the priest is specifically forbidden from mourning his wife,[1] which suggests that blood ties supersede marriage even in the case of a wife.[2]

---

1. An explicit example of this practice appears in Ezek 24:15-18.

2. Many interpreters believe that this verse bans mourning for kin related by marriage and not the wife. John E. Hartley (*Leviticus*, WBC 4 [Waco, TX: Word Books, 1992], 348) argues that the ban is on the wife's relatives and that the wife is considered part of the שאר and would of course be mourned by her priest-husband. Gordon J. Wenham (*The Book of Leviticus* [Grand Rapids: Eerdmans, 1979], 290) interprets v. 4 as anticipating v. 7: that a priest should not marry an unfit woman.

*Lev 21:1-15*

²¹:¹The LORD said to Moses: Speak to the priests, the sons of Aaron, and say to them:

No one shall defile himself for a dead person among his relatives, ²except for his nearest kin: his mother, his father, his son, his daughter, his brother; ³likewise, for a virgin sister, close to him because she has had no husband, he may defile himself for her. ⁴But he shall not defile himself as a husband among his people and so profane himself. ⁵They shall not make bald spots upon their heads, or shave off the edges of their beards, or make any gashes in their flesh. ⁶They shall be holy to their God, and not profane the name of the God; for they offer the LORD's offerings by fire, the food of their God; therefore they shall be holy. ⁷They shall not marry a prostitute or a woman who has been defiled; neither shall they marry a woman divorced from her husband. For they are holy to their God, ⁸and you shall treat them as holy, since they offer the food of

The hereditary nature of the priesthood is deeply embedded in shared holy blood—he shares the blood of his father. When the priest mourns his father, mother, son, daughter, brother, or sister, he is honoring the shared holy blood. In the case of marriage, his wife has no blood ties with him; she functions as a vessel to transmit his own seed/blood. If a priest mourns his wife, he makes himself impure, with the result that he desecrates (note: חלל is reflexive; "profane") himself. Verse 5 further limits actions priests can take when mourning close blood relatives: they are not to engage in cutting or in shaving their hair because these actions are associated with non-Israelite practices.[3]

Apart from what the priest may do to render himself impure (e.g., coming in contact with impurities and failing to undergo purification rites), according to H there are two situations in which he may be desecrated (חלל). The two potential sources of desecration emerge from females in his family: his wife and his daughter. As we noted above, if a priest chooses to mourn for his wife, he is not only placing himself into a temporary state of impurity (טמא), he is also desecrating himself (חלל, v. 4). There is only one other case in Leviticus that deals with desecrating oneself; namely, if a priest's daughter engages in prostitution, she desecrates both herself and her father (חלל, v. 9). Thus, the greatest threats to a priest's

3. See 1 Kgs 18:28; Jer 9:26 (v. 25 Hebrew).

your God; they shall be holy to you, for I the LORD, I who sanctify you, am holy. ⁹When the daughter of a priest profanes herself through prostitution, she profanes her father; she shall be burned to death.

¹⁰The priest who is exalted above his fellows, on whose head the anointing oil has been poured and who has been consecrated to wear the vestments, shall not dishevel his hair, nor tear his vestments. ¹¹He shall not go where there is a dead body; he shall not defile himself even for his father or mother. ¹²He shall not go outside the sanctuary and thus profane the sanctuary of his God; for the consecration of the anointing oil of his God is upon him: I am the LORD. ¹³He shall marry only a woman who is a virgin. ¹⁴A widow, or a divorced woman, or a woman who has been defiled, a prostitute, these he shall not marry. He shall marry a virgin of his own kin, ¹⁵that he may not profane his offspring among his kin; for I am the LORD; I sanctify him.

status emerge from his own temptation to mourn his wife and from the actions of his daughter, whom he may or may not be able to control. As Erhard Gerstenberger puts it, "The male cult is threatened above all by females and their behavior."[4]

As we will see in Leviticus 22, the women in priestly families had access to consecrated foods that were forbidden to the rest of Israel. The women of these families thus had access to more food and, by extension, to more wealth. We know nothing, however, about the roles they might have played in their households and in the community. It is probable that they had privileges that other women did not have, but it is equally probable that they experienced greater restrictions on their autonomy, especially if a priest's daughter's sexual engagements could impact the reputation and status of her father. Exodus 38:8 and 1 Samuel 2:22 refer to women serving at the entrance to the tent of meeting, but we do not know what kind of service this entailed and we have no information to suggest that these women were members of priestly families.

---

4. Erhard S. Gerstenberger, *Leviticus*, OTL (Louisville: Westminster John Knox, 1996), 314.

## TRANSLATION MATTERS

*Desecration (חלל) in H's Theology*

Two key terms are used in Leviticus to indicate a reduced state of holiness. The term טמא ("to be impure"; "defile" in 21:1) occurs many times in P to designate a person who is ritually impure restricted from eating sacred food and from entering God's holy space (e.g., Lev 12:2-4; 15:2). H uses טמא in a similar way to indicate ritual impurity (e.g., Lev 21:3 identifies a priest as ritually impure when he engages in mourning practices). H also supplements P's system, however, by recognizing an additional status change: under certain conditions, a priest is not only rendered ritually impure but also חלל ("desecrated"; "profane" in 20:3). The term חלל appears ten times in Leviticus 20–21 and a total of fourteen times in the Holiness Legislation; however, the term for desecrate never occurs in P![5] This raises a question about the difference between "defile" and "desecrate" and what the presence of "desecrate" in H but not in P suggests about the divergent theologies of Leviticus's priestly writers.

The most frequently mentioned object of desecration is God's holy name (appearing six times).[6] God's holy place is also mentioned several times as the object of desecration. For example, Leviticus 21:12 commands the priest not to leave the sanctuary, presumably in order to mourn a family member while he is on duty.[7] The result of this transgression is desecration (חלל) of the sanctuary. Jacob Milgrom describes the use of חלל here as imprecise because, according to Numbers 6:6-7, corpse contamination results in impurity (טמא), not desecration.[8] Jan Joosten argues that חלל is just a first step in profanation, which may later lead to impurity. For him, the more dangerous state is טמא because that is the state that drives the divine out of the sanctuary.[9] The one other text in which H describes the desecration of the sanctuary states that a priest with a blemish may not approach the veil or the altar (Lev 21:23);[10] doing so results in desecration (חלל) of the sanctuary, but not in impurity (טמא). Besides the sanctuary, objects that have been consecrated to God can also be desecrated. Thus, Leviticus 19:8 teaches that improper consumption of a well-being offering desecrates (חלל) the offering.

According to H, in addition to God's name, God's holy place, and Israel's offering, people—a priest, his offspring (who specifically include his daughter), and his potential wives—can also be objects of desecration. For example, a priest who comes in contact with a corpse both defiles himself (טמא) and desecrates himself

---

5. NRSV routinely uses the English word "profane" as a translation for חלל; however, I prefer the term "desecrate," which more pointedly denotes the opposite of "sanctify" or "make holy."

6. E.g., Lev 18:21; 19:12; 20:3; 21:6; and 22:2, 32.

7. See discussion in Jacob Milgrom, *Leviticus 17–22*, AB 3A (New York: Doubleday, 2000), 1818. 1QM 9:8 makes reference to priestly oil of anointment and desecration.

8. Milgrom, *Leviticus 17–22*, 1818.

9. Jan Joosten, *People and Land in the Holiness Code: An Exegetical Study of the Ideational Framework of the Law in Leviticus 17–26*, VTSup 67 (Leiden: Brill, 1996), 126–27.

10. Milgrom argues that this law applies only to the high priest (*Leviticus 17–22*, 1832).

(חלל), according to Leviticus 21:4.[11] A priest can also be desecrated by the sexually illicit behavior of his daughter (Lev 21:9). b. Sanhedrin 52a interprets this verse to mean that others in the community will no longer treat the priest with respect due to the behavior of his daughter. John E. Hartley suggests that, because "the family was a solid unit, the activity or character of each member reflected on the other members."[12] Milgrom, influenced by postbiblical understandings of חלול שם ("desecration of the Name") believes that Leviticus 21:9 must be metaphorical. The priest is not literally stripped of his status, but he is shamed by his daughter's actions and therefore his reputation is diminished. Milgrom writes, "It is as though he were disqualified [from being a priest]."[13] Milgrom adduces no evidence, however, to support his argument, though he does write elsewhere that in H, the priests are enjoined to observe the commandments in order to retain their holy status.[14] This implies that priests can lose their status as well as retain it, and the evidence in H shows that the priest has in fact been diminished in status.[15]

A woman of a priestly family can also be desecrated, although it is not altogether clear under what circumstances this desanctification occurs.[16] Leviticus 19:29 and 21:9 address situations in which the daughter of a priest has engaged in some sort of illicit sexual activity (see discussion of "Pierced Women" below). In the latter case, she is held responsible for her shift in status, and in the former, the father bears the responsibility.

In summary, we have seen that people (especially those of the priestly family), the sanctuary, and sanctified objects can all become desecrated, and Milgrom argues that we should read this language metaphorically in most instances. If, however, H's view is that holiness is dynamic, such that people and things can move toward greater (or lesser) degrees of holiness, then it stands to reason that people or things can also experience a reduction in holiness. A sacrificial food can lose its sacred quality and become a source of impurity. The sanctuary can experience the withdrawal of the holy presence, and a priest can lose his status for himself and/or his descendants. The sacrifice becomes just a piece of meat, the sanctuary just a building, and the priest just a man. In each of these cases, the H writers use the language of חלל in addition to P's טמא terminology. In other words, H overlays standard P material with the concept of חלל. In H, חלל signifies a real (ontological), not just metaphorical, reduction in holiness status. The condition of impurity may be remedied through specific purification rites; desecration is more permanent.

---

11. The verbal form is a reflexive *niphal*.

12. Hartley, *Leviticus*, 349.

13. Milgrom, *Leviticus 17–22*, 1810. Baruch Levine, *Leviticus: A JPS Torah Commentary* (Philadelphia: Jewish Publication Society of America, 1989), 144 implies the same reading of the text.

14. Jacob Milgrom, "The Changing Concept of Holiness in the Pentateuchal Codes with Emphasis on Leviticus 19," in *Reading Leviticus: A Conversation with Mary Douglas*, ed. John F. A. Sawyer (Sheffield: Sheffield Academic, 1996), esp. 70.

15. See 4Q213a 3–4 3: "She will profane her name and her father's name."

16. For a discussion of this case, see Milgrom, *Leviticus 17–22*, 1696–97.

### "Pierced" Women

Leviticus 21:7 states that a priest may not marry a prostitute, a חללה ("woman who has been defiled"), or a divorcee. In other words, a priest must marry a widow or a virgin. Verses 13-15 indicate that the high priest must marry a virgin of his own kin and that he is prohibited from marrying a widow, a divorcee, a חללה, or a prostitute. Thus all priests are forbidden from marrying prostitutes, חללה, and divorcees. The meaning of חללה is uncertain because the root חלל can mean "to be desecrated" or "to be pierced." Some commentators believe that this category refers to women who have been raped,[17] while others believe that it is a term for any nonvirgin (pierced).[18] Another possibility, which has been reaffirmed as recently as Hartley's 1992 commentary, suggests that a חללה was a cultic prostitute or a hierodule.[19] This interpretation derives from the root חול ("dancer"). The Bible never uses חלל or חול, however, to describe cultic prostitution or even pagan rites; in fact, the only term that may refer to a woman involved in a sacred cult is קדשה. The idea of cultic prostitution in Israel has no basis in any evidence from the Bible and the extrabiblical evidence is highly suspect.[20]

Let us, for a moment, accept the possibility of the חללה as a hierodule. If this were the case, the ban would suggest that an Israelite priest might choose to marry a priestess from a different cultic system. Hartley remarks that, "Whenever Israel came under strong pagan influence, it would be conceivable that the ideal woman for a priest, who was holy, should be such a holy woman."[21] This certainly makes sense. As we know, prohibitions tend to be put in place to counter the very practices that they ban. Is it possible that an Israelite priest would marry into the cultic competition? It is difficult to imagine an independent working priestess giving up her own religion, position, and rank to become an

---

17. Ibid., 1807. Levine, *Leviticus*, 143 takes *zonah v'halalah* as a hendiadys, "degraded harlot."

18. Nobuyoshi Kiuchi, *Leviticus*, ApOTC 3 (Nottingham: Inter-Varsity Press, 2007), 394.

19. Hartley, *Leviticus*, 348. Mordechai Zvi Levin, "Hallalah (Profaned) / חללה," *Beit Mikra: Journal for the Study of the Bible and Its World* 29 (1984): 180–81 (Hebrew). Levin focuses on traditional postbiblical interpretations that associate this term with cultic dancers.

20. See, most recently, Stephanie Lynn Budin, *The Myth of Sacred Prostitution in Antiquity* (Cambridge: Cambridge University Press, 2008); also, Joan Goodnick Westenholz's earlier study, "Tamar, *Qedesa, Qadistu*, and Sacred Prostitution in Mesopotamia," *HTR* 82 (1989): 245–65.

21. Hartley, *Leviticus*, 348.

Israelite priest's wife, unless these wives had privileges, which are nowhere suggested in the Bible. I bring up this scenario because scholars who continue to perpetuate the fantasy of cultic prostitutes/hierodules must play out their positions to their logical conclusions. If Israelite priests could consider marrying priestesses, a host of radical implications must be associated with this idea.[22]

Eve Levavi Feinstein convincingly concludes that a חללה probably refers to any woman who has sex out of wedlock. This is to be differentiated from a professional prostitute who has sex habitually. Feinstein, influenced by Milgrom, posits a hierarchy of "problematic" potential wives from most problematic to least: prostitute, חללה, divorcee, widow, virgin. Feinstein argues that a woman who has had sex out of wedlock is contaminated, while "a woman who has had sex within marriage is not inherently polluted, but from the perspective of a man other than her husband who might have sex with her, she is in some sense contaminated, 'marked' by the essence of another man." Finally, the distinction between the divorcee and the widow is that the divorcee might seem defective in some way because a man has rejected her.[23] Thus the laws governing eligible wives for priests have to do with both purity and social status. Feinstein also notes that genealogical purity is an issue only for the high priests, although it did become a more central concern applied to laypeople as well as priests during the Second Temple period.[24]

## Priestly Bodies (21:16-24)

The final portion of Leviticus 21 lays out disqualifications of priests from presiding over sacrificial and cereal offerings. Verses 17, 21, and 23 state that a disqualified priest may not "approach to offer the food of his God,"[25] or "come near to offer the LORD's offerings by fire (NRSV; better:

---

22. Savina Teubal (*Sarah the Priestess: The First Matriarch of Genesis* [Athens, OH: Swallow Press, 1984]) presents the possibility that much of the family drama presented in the Genesis narratives reflects remnants of the clash between Abraham's patriarchal YHVH-centered religion and Sarah's priestess traditions with their roots in Ur.

23. Eve Levavi Feinstein, *Sexual Pollution in the Hebrew Bible* (Oxford: Oxford University Press, 2014), 92–95. Hilary Lipka understands *halah* as "sexual acts that result in religious defilement" (*Sexual Transgressions in the Hebrew Bible*, HBM 7 [Sheffield: Sheffield Phoenix, 2006], 140 n. 58).

24. Feinstein, *Sexual Pollution*, 95.

25. The P writers avoid anthropomorphisms and thus never use the term לחם ("food") to indicate what is being offered to God. The H writers use the term "food" nine times in Lev 21–22 (Lev 21:6, 8, 17, 21-22; 22:7, 11, 13, 25).

*Lev 21:16-24*

¹⁶The LORD spoke to Moses, saying: ¹⁷Speak to Aaron and say: No one of your offspring throughout their generations who has a blemish may approach to offer the food of his God. ¹⁸For no one who has a blemish shall draw near, one who is blind or lame, or one who has a mutilated face or a limb too long, ¹⁹or one who has a broken foot or a broken hand, ²⁰or a hunchback, or a dwarf, or a man with a blemish in his eyes or an itching disease or scabs or crushed testicles. ²¹No descendant of Aaron the priest who has a blemish shall come near to offer the LORD's offerings by fire; since he has a blemish, he shall not come near to offer the food of his God. ²²He may eat the food of his God, of the most holy as well as of the holy. ²³But he shall not come near the curtain or approach the altar, because he has a blemish, that he may not profane my sanctuaries; for I am the LORD; I sanctify them. ²⁴Thus Moses spoke to Aaron and to his sons and to all the people of Israel.

"come near to offer YHVH's food gifts"), or "come near the curtain or approach the altar." Verse 22, however, indicates that a disqualified priest may still partake of the sacred meals, including the most holy foods, which may be eaten only in the sacred court (Lev 6:9; 7:6). In other words, Leviticus 21:17-23 only concerns disqualifying priests from officiating over offerings (ritual leadership), not from entering the sacred space or partaking of the most holy foods.

Leviticus 21:18-20 describes conditions that ban a priest from ritual leadership; these conditions are grouped under the term "blemish" (מום). The first two conditions are "blind" and "lame." These two words tend to function as a pair in a number of biblical texts (e.g., 2 Sam 5:6, 8; Jer 31:8; Mal 1:8, 13; Job 29:15). The next two terms, translated by NRSV as "mutilated face" and "limb too long," are uncertain. The Hebrew word חרם is a *hapax legomenon*; that is, the word appears only here. Some interpreters translate the term as "short-limbed" so that it works with the next term, "limb too long." Even the second word is uncertain, however, because it appears as a *qal* verb only here and in the list of blemishes on animals in Leviticus 22:23. NJPS translates the two terms as "limb too short" and "limb too long"; KJV reads "flat nose" and "anything superfluous."

The next pairing of blemishes in verse 19 refers to broken legs and broken hands. The question is whether these broken bones were understood as permanent defects (that is, unhealed broken bones) or temporary conditions. Given its context in the list of blemishes, verse 19 probably intends permanent damage. Verse 20 lists an additional six blemishes. The first pairing is generally translated as "hunchbacked" and "dwarf" but again it is important to note that these translations are merely educated guesses. The idea of "hunchback" comes from a phrase in Psalm 68:17 that describes "jagged mountains." The term for "jagged" may derive from the same Hebrew root as the first term in verse 20 (גבן). The literal translation of דק ("dwarf," NRSV) is "thin" or "withered." The next blemish refers to some discoloration or defect of the eye. This is followed by two terms that are associated with skin ailments (although neither of the Hebrew words appears in the myriad skin conditions discussed in Lev 13–14). The final blemish is a "crushed testicle." The Hebrew term for testicles, אשׁך, is another *hapax legomenon*, as is the word for "crushed" (מרוח). Again, these Hebrew terms are obscure and the translations are highly speculative.

The only conditions whose meanings are certain are the first two: blindness and lameness. Apart from the first two conditions, the others in this list never appear in any of the many narratives that describe diseases and impairments. So, without certainty about the meaning of the terms in this list of blemishes, we can only speculate about what all of these conditions have in common or why these specific conditions were included in the list. It is commonly speculated that these blemishes share one feature in common: they are visible, noticeable on the exterior of the body. Saul Olyan effectively complicates our understanding of blemishes when he points out that the skin diseases described in Leviticus 13 and 14, which are clearly visible, are not described as blemishes, and neither are tattoos or gashes on the skin, while crushed testicles, covered with breeches and other priestly vestments, would not be visible.[26] Jeremy Schipper and Jeffrey Stackert argue that the concern is not what the human eye sees but what YHVH perceives.[27]

The list of defects says nothing about diseases that do not manifest externally. This suggests that the concern is with the idealized perfect body and not with good health. The ideal body is male, without any

---

26. Saul Olyan, *Disability in the Hebrew Bible: Interpreting Mental and Physical Differences* (Cambridge: Cambridge University Press, 2008), 28–30. Milgrom, following Elliger, argues that crushed testicles were added to the list of priestly defects in order to match more closely the list of defects in sacrificial animals (*Leviticus 17–22*, 1838–39).

27. Jeremy Schipper and Jeffrey Stackert, "Blemishes, Camouflage and Sanctuary Service: The Priestly Deity and His Attendants," in *Hebrew Bible and Ancient Israel: Bodies and Religion* 4 (2013): 463.

visible divergence from the norm. Limbs must be in proper proportion to one another and fully functional, the back must be erect, the face must contain properly functioning eyes, and facial features must fall within "normal" parameters. It is unclear whether the female body is, by definition, blemished, because it does not have the idealized male anatomy.[28]

Sarah Melcher builds on Rebecca Raphael's language, that "the Bible is disabled, and much biblical interpretation is a prosthetic performance,"[29] as she asserts:

> In the Priestly system, the blemished body represents what God is not and the blemished body is depicted as something that threatens holy status. The blemished body is disruptive to the system. If the blemished body approaches the altar, then the holy place where God is worshiped is profaned (Lev 21:23). The blemished body can alter the status of the sanctuary, according to the Priestly literature. It must be brought under the restriction and control of the priests.
>
> The blemished body also serves as a prosthesis that qualifies the priesthood. The priesthood is defined as those sons of Aaron who are unblemished.[30]

Schipper and Stackert point out that a blemished priest is still holy because he partakes of the holy foods. Thus, a blemished priest represents what they call a paradox in that "that which is cultically holy can profane the holy."[31]

---

28. Sarah Melcher notes that Aaronide women and Aaronide men with blemishes occupy the same rung on the hierarchical ladder in "Blemish and Perfection of the Body in the Priestly Literature and Deuteronomy," *Journal of Religion, Disability & Health* 16 (2012): 5.

29. Rebecca Raphael, *Biblical Corpora: Representations of Disability in Hebrew Biblical Literature*, LHB/OTS 445 (London: T&T Clark, 2008), 142.

30. Melcher, "Blemish and Perfection," 13.

31. Jeremy Schipper and Jeffrey Stackert ("Blemishes, Camouflage and Sanctuary Service," 468) argue that the blemished priests must be interpreted within the larger framework of YHVH as divine king. If blemished priests were to offer sacrifices or come to the curtain, their imperfections would irritate YHVH and remind YHVH that his creation is not perfect. Similarly, they argue, the elaborate priestly vestments help to "camouflage" priests so that they do not bother the divine king in his repose. While divine kingship is certainly a common metaphor in the Hebrew Bible, I find little evidence that P or H conceptualized God in this way.

### What Are Embodied Qualifications?

For those of us who meet the embodied qualifications to step behind the veil, we might imagine our bodies are more holy than the bodies of those that do not qualify. We may cling to the idea of an unblemished body, feeling a sense of superiority over those who do not qualify.

The rabbis of the Talmud, in a creative reading of the Hebrew of Psalm 68:17, offer that a divine voice chastised two mountains—Carmel and Tabor—for seeking judgment of Mount Sinai. The voice warns the mountains, "You are all blemished in comparison with Sinai."[32] When we compare ourselves to an impossible ideal, be it mountain or body, we will discover that we are all blemished. Our bodies, impermanent and vulnerable, will inevitably break and bend. While some of us may be considered fit to step behind the veil today, we may not be fit tomorrow.

Illness, injury, aging, chosen body modification—whatever the reason, the clay that is our bodies does not keep its shape. It cracks, sags, reforms, and shatters.

The Talmudic discussion continues, drawing a comparison between *gibben* (גבן, the Hebrew word for "hunchback" in Lev 21:20) and *gabnunim* (גבנים, the Hebrew word for "peaks" in Ps 68:17). Rabbi Ashi concludes, "If a man is arrogant, he is blemished."[33] Even if our bodies are considered fit today, our arrogance in that fact would render us unfit for this holy service. Humility, not arrogance, must be central to our approach to bodies deemed qualified. We must remember the impermanence of these embodied qualifications. It is our spiritual qualifications, our humility, that will ultimately bring us closer to the Holy One, whether or not we qualify to step behind the veil.

*Alex Weissman*

## Priestly Purity and Sacred Donations (22:1-9)

Leviticus 22 begins with the responsibility that priests bear when they consume the sacred foods that the people of Israel offer. The text states that no priest may partake of the sacred donations while in a state of ritual impurity—whether through skin affliction, genital discharge, corpse contact, seminal emission, or contact with impure animals or

32. b. Meg 29a.
33. Ibid.

²²:¹The Lᴏʀᴅ spoke to Moses, saying: ²Direct Aaron and his sons to deal carefully with the sacred donations of the people of Israel, which they dedicate to me, so that they may not profane my holy name; I am the Lᴏʀᴅ. ³Say to them: If anyone among all your offspring throughout your generations comes near the sacred donations, which the people of Israel dedicate to the Lᴏʀᴅ, while he is in a state of uncleanness, that person shall be cut off from my presence: I am the Lᴏʀᴅ. ⁴No one of Aaron's offspring who has a leprous disease or suffers a discharge may eat of the sacred donations until he is clean. Whoever touches anything made unclean by a corpse or a man who has had an emission of semen, ⁵and whoever touches any swarming thing by which he may be made unclean or any human being by whom he may be made unclean— whatever his uncleanness may be— ⁶the person who touches any such shall be unclean until evening and shall not eat of the sacred donations unless he has washed his body in water. ⁷When the sun sets he shall be clean; and afterward he may eat of the sacred donations, for they are his food. ⁸That which died or was torn by wild animals he shall not eat, becoming unclean by it: I am the Lᴏʀᴅ. ⁹They shall keep my charge, so that they may not incur guilt and die in the sanctuary for having profaned it: I am the Lᴏʀᴅ; I sanctify them.

persons. Any priest who eats sanctified foods while impure is to be cut off from YHVH's presence.

While on the surface it makes sense that priests should not consume sanctified foods while in a state of impurity, there are additional messages embedded in the wording of the text. Leviticus 22:2 provides the introduction for verses 1-9 with rather convoluted wording. The Hebrew syntax of this verse is usually construed as difficult, and translations transpose the middle phrase to the end, treating it as a parenthetical clause. Thus, NJPS: "Instruct Aaron and his sons to be scrupulous about the sacred donations that the Israelite people consecrate to Me, lest they profane My holy name, Mine the Lᴏʀᴅ's." In this translation, the participle מקדשים refers to the sacred donations. But, there is no reason why this verse cannot be translated in a more direct way: "Instruct Aaron and his sons to be scrupulous about the sacred donations of the Israelite people; they should not desecrate my holy name which they sanctify for me, I am YHVH." Thus, it is the people and priests, not the donation, that sanctify the name of God.

## Priestly Household and Sacred Donations (22:10-16)

The next section in Leviticus 22 defines the members of a priest's household by presenting who is eligible and ineligible to partake of the sanctified foods. Priestly privilege is made most apparent by access to sanctified food. Males of the priestly lineage who are in a state of ritual purity consume the most holy foods that constitute the cereal offerings, the purification offerings, and the guilt offerings. Numbers 18:8-20 specifies what sacred foods may be eaten by the sons and daughters of the priest, as long as they are in a state of ritual purity. These include the elevation offerings and the first fruit donations.

The members of the priestly household include the males of priestly lineage, the wives of priests, daughters who are not married, daughters who are widowed or divorced with no children to support them, and slaves who have been purchased or born within the household. Guests, hired laborers, daughters who are married outside of the priestly family, and daughters who have children to support them are excluded. Saul Olyan has noted that male slaves are ineligible to eat the most holy foods, so it is not enough to be a male in the household. Those who partake in the sacred meals are those who are dependent on the priest. "The priest's special holiness is, in a symbolic sense, extended to his dependents—with the exception of his sons who possess it in their own right—to allow them to partake of the holy foods, since they need to eat and the holy foods are what the priests receive as their due."[34] Regarding the position of the slave, Olyan notes that "he is subject to the same ritual requirements as his master and has access to ritual privileges, but solely as an extension of his master's person, not in his own right. Paradoxically, the slave's apparent privilege at first blush really stems from the extent of his debasement."[35] Olyan's point is important because he highlights the intersectionality of social class and status. A slave may have access to food that is denied to free men and women in the community, but at the cost of his freedom.

## Sacrificial Offerings and Perfect Bodies (22:17-25)

Leviticus 22:17-25 addresses blemishes on animals that preclude them from serving as sacrificial offerings. The lists of blemishes for animals and

---

34. Saul Olyan, *Rites and Rank: Hierarchy in Biblical Representations of Cult* (Princeton: Princeton University Press, 2000), 32.
35. Ibid., 96.

¹⁰No lay person shall eat of the sacred donations. No bound or hired servant of the priest shall eat of the sacred donations; ¹¹but if a priest acquires anyone by purchase, the person may eat of them; and those that are born in his house may eat of his food. ¹²If a priest's daughter marries a layman, she shall not eat of the offering of the sacred donations; ¹³but if a priest's daughter is widowed or divorced, without offspring, and returns to her father's house, as in her youth, she may eat of her father's food. No lay person shall eat of it. ¹⁴If a man eats of the sacred donation unintentionally, he shall add one-fifth of its value to it, and give the sacred donation to the priest. ¹⁵No one shall profane the sacred donations of the people of Israel, which they offer to the Lᴏʀᴅ, ¹⁶causing them to bear guilt requiring a guilt offering, by eating their sacred donations: for I am the Lᴏʀᴅ; I sanctify them.

¹⁷The Lᴏʀᴅ spoke to Moses, saying: ¹⁸Speak to Aaron and his sons and all the people of Israel and say to them: When anyone of the house of Israel or of the aliens residing in Israel presents

priests that render them ineligible to participate in sacred rites are parallel but not identical. The H source defines P's use of תמים ("without blemish," v. 19) by listing a series of defects (מום) that disqualify an animal from use as an offering. According to Leviticus 22:22-24, defects include any animal that is blind, injured, maimed, oozing, scarred, or scabbed or whose testicles are bruised, crushed, torn, or cut. In addition, an animal cannot have extended or contracted limbs unless it is being used for a freewill offering.

Leviticus 22:24 prohibits the use of animals as offerings if they have wounded or mutilated testicles. There are a few points that merit discussion of this verse. The text uses four different words to describe "defective" testicles. Scholars are not in agreement about the meaning of these terms. It is possible that the words refer to both congenital conditions and injuries, on the one hand, and to castration, on the other. Elaine Adler Goodfriend suggests that the four terms may correlate with four forms of castration that are utilized. The first two terms may refer to methods that involve the cutting off of blood to the testicles by means of an elastic band or clamp, so that the testicles atrophy; the third term may refer to the separation of the testes from the body by means of a clamp; and the final term may refer to surgical removal.[36] For Goodfriend, then, the issue is castration and not necessarily deformities.

---

36. Elaine Adler Goodfriend, "Leviticus 22:24: A Prohibition of Gelding," in *Current Issues in Priestly and Related Literature: The Legacy of Jacob Milgrom and Beyond*, ed. Roy Gane and Ada Taggar-Cohen (Atlanta: SBL Press, 2015), 76–77.

an offering, whether in payment of a vow or as a freewill offering that is offered to the Lord as a burnt offering, [19]to be acceptable in your behalf it shall be a male without blemish, of the cattle or the sheep or the goats. [20]You shall not offer anything that has a blemish, for it will not be acceptable in your behalf.

[21]When anyone offers a sacrifice of well-being to the Lord, in fulfillment of a vow or as a freewill offering, from the herd or from the flock, to be acceptable it must be perfect; there shall be no blemish in it. [22]Anything blind, or injured, or maimed, or having a discharge or an itch or scabs—these you shall not offer to the Lord or put any of them on the altar as offerings by fire to the Lord. [23]An ox or a lamb that has a limb too long or too short you may present for a freewill offering; but it will not be accepted for a vow. [24]Any animal that has its testicles bruised or crushed or torn or cut, you shall not offer to the Lord; such you shall not do within your land, [25]nor shall you accept any such animals from a foreigner to offer as food to your God; since they are mutilated, with a blemish in them, they shall not be accepted in your behalf.

The other significant confusion in verse 24 regards the last clause: "you shall not do such a thing in your land." The question is: what should not be done? Does the text ban offering up animals with damaged or removed testicles or does the text ban castration in general? NJPS reads: "You shall not offer to the Lord anything [with its testes] bruised or crushed or torn or cut. You shall have no such practices in your own land." KJV reads: "Ye shall not offer unto the Lord that which is bruised, or crushed, or broken, or cut; neither shall ye make any offering thereof in your land." Early Jewish interpreters understood the text as a general ban on castration, and this has been the dominant reading in Jewish tradition; if the point of the phrase is not to offer up the animals, then the clause is superfluous.

## Protecting the Newborn (22:26-33)

Leviticus 22:27-28 prohibits a newborn from the herd or flock from being separated from its mother for seven days. On the eighth day, the newborn may be offered for sacrifice. Additionally, a member of the herd or flock may not be sacrificed on the same day as its offspring. Leviticus 22:27 is usually interpreted as deriving from a humanitarian concern, that a newborn not be separated from its mother. Newborn cattle and sheep are still suckling at eight days, however, so it is more likely that the prohibition against separating the mother and offspring for seven days

*Lev 22:26-33*

²⁶The Lᴏʀᴅ spoke to Moses, saying: ²⁷When an ox or a sheep or a goat is born, it shall remain seven days with its mother, and from the eighth day on it shall be acceptable as the Lᴏʀᴅ's offering by fire. ²⁸But you shall not slaughter, from the herd or the flock, an animal with its young on the same day. ²⁹When you sacrifice a thanksgiving offering to the Lᴏʀᴅ, you shall sacrifice it so that it may be acceptable in your behalf. ³⁰It shall be eaten on the same day; you shall not leave any of it until morning: I am the Lᴏʀᴅ.

³¹Thus you shall keep my commandments and observe them: I am the Lᴏʀᴅ. ³²You shall not profane my holy name, that I may be sanctified among the people of Israel: I am the Lᴏʀᴅ; I sanctify you, ³³I who brought you out of the land of Egypt to be your God: I am the Lᴏʀᴅ.

has symbolic significance. Perhaps the eighth-day release functioned as a symbolic parallel to separating a boy from his mother on the eighth day for circumcision.

### Compassion for Animals?

The use value that animals have for human beings was weighed against the intrinsic needs of each animal in the Torah's moral calculus, and human beings were required to allow animals to meet their most basic needs. For example, a newborn animal could not be separated from its mother until the eighth day (Lev 22:26). The question of whether these needs should be ascribed primarily to individual animals or to species is, however, not always clear, and both possibilities are reflected in the interpretations given to various rules. For example, there is a well-known debate between Maimonides and Nachmanides about the prohibition against sacrificing an animal and its parent on the same day (Lev 22:28) and the mitsvah to send the mother bird away when taking the eggs or chicks (Deut 22:6-7). Maimonides declared that the reason was to avoid causing suffering to individual animals, because "the love and the tenderness of a mother for her child is not consequent upon reason, but upon the activity of the imaginative faculty, which is found in most animals just as it is found in humankind" (*Guide for the Perplexed*, 3.48). Nachmanides, however, rejects Maimonides's reasoning and expounds several other reasons, including that the Torah forbids doing anything that would

> "uproot" (or have the appearance of uprooting) an entire species, such as killing parent and child together (commentary at Deut 22:6). The debate between Maimonides and Nachmanides parallels contemporary debates between animal rights activists and environmentalists.[37]
>
> *David Seidenberg*

Leviticus 22:28, which forbids an animal from the herd or flock to be sacrificed on the same day as its offspring, is also puzzling. Nobuyoshi Kiuchi, along with many ancient and modern interpreters, believes that an offerer should exhibit a "tender and considerate attitude" toward the animals.[38] Erhard Gerstenberger, influenced by the injunction not to boil a kid in its mother's milk (Exod 23:19), argues that the prohibition was limited to a mother and its male offspring.[39] The problem with this reading is that the Hebrew uses the masculine to describe the parent. NRSV translates verse 28: "But you shall not slaughter, from the herd or the flock, an animal with its young on the same day." A more literal translation reads: "But you shall not slaughter, from the oxen or the flock, him and his offspring (or son) on the same day." The appearance of the term שׁוֹר for bull or ox is odd, given that Leviticus generally uses gender-neutral language for cattle.[40] The assertion that a mother and child are implied in this verse may be influenced by the prior verse, but it is not clear in and of itself. In fact, we have seen that female animals were rarely used for sacrifices. Whatever the meaning behind this verse, we should be wary of imposing assumptions about the mother and child noted in verse 27. The text is just as likely referring to a father and son. If so, the prohibition may point symbolically to the male concern with progeny.

37. See David Seidenberg, "Animal Rights in the Jewish Tradition" in *Encyclopedia of Religion and Nature*, vol. 1 (London: Bloomsbury, 2005), 64–66, and *Kabbalah and Ecology: God's Image in the More-Than-Human World* (Cambridge: Cambridge University Press, 2017), chap. 5.

38. Kiuchi, *Leviticus*, 410.

39. Gerstenberger, *Leviticus*, 331. So too Samuel E. Balentine, *Leviticus* (Louisville: Westminster John Knox, 2002), 171, and many ancient interpreters.

40. Contra Naphtali Meshel, *The "Grammar" of Sacrifice: A Generativist Study of the Israelite Sacrificial System in the Priestly Writings* (Oxford: Oxford University Press, 2014), 52.

## TRANSLATION MATTERS

As noted above, the syntax of Leviticus 22:2 is difficult. My proposed translation is: "Instruct Aaron and his sons to be scrupulous about the sacred donations of the Israelite people; they should not desecrate my holy name which they sanctify for me, I am YHVH." Thus, it is the people and the priests, not the donations, that sanctify the name of God. Desecration of the name is inextricably linked to the people's potential and charge to sanctify God. Israel (including both priests and lay community) has the power both to expand and to contract God's holiness. Leviticus 22:32 expresses the same dynamic between sanctification or desecration and the role of the people and of God. Leviticus 22:32 offers a summary statement following God's admonition to observe all of the commandments. It presents H theology in unambiguous language. The people of Israel have the power to desecrate God's name, that is, to diminish an aspect of God's holiness, but that desecration inhibits God's ability to make God's self holy among the people of Israel and, in turn, diminishes Israel's holiness, since it is God who is ultimately their source of holiness.[41] Leviticus 21–22 in particular focuses on the role of the priests in negotiating these complex dynamics,[42] while Leviticus 18–20 concentrates on the role of the community.

41. The same theology is expressed in Lev 22:9, where desecration and sanctification are mentioned together.

42. Kiuchi (*Leviticus*, 404) rightly notes that "if the people abstain from uncleanness and present their offerings, the mediating priest can undermine the very act of offering sacrifices by profaning them."

# Leviticus 23:1–25:55

# *Sacred Time, Space, Speech, and Land*

The Pentateuch presents a number of festival calendars, almost all of which include the three pilgrimage festivals as attested in Exodus 23:14-17.

> Three times in the year you shall hold a festival for me. You shall observe the *festival of unleavened bread*; as I commanded you, you shall eat unleavened bread for seven days at the appointed time in the month of Abib, for in it you came out of Egypt. No one shall appear before me empty-handed. You shall observe the *festival of harvest*, of the first fruits of your labor, of what you sow in the field. You shall observe the *festival of ingathering* at the end of the year, when you gather in from the field the fruit of your labor. Three times in the year all your males shall appear before the Lord God. (NRSV, italics mine)

Leviticus 23 presents seven sacred times, only two of which are pilgrimage festivals. The sacred calendar in this chapter, which belongs to the work of the Holiness Legislation, directs attention to the role of the laypeople and to the concept of refraining from work. This is in contrast to the P calendar, which appears in Numbers 28–29[1] and which focuses

---

1. Among biblical scholars, there is still much debate regarding the chronology of Lev 23 and Num 28–29. Christophe Nihan ("Israel's Festival Calendars in Leviticus 23, Numbers 28–29 and the Formation of 'Priestly' Literature," in *The Books of Leviticus and Numbers*, ed. Thomas Romer, BETL 215 [Leuven: Peeters, 2008], 228–29) argues that Num 28–29 does not belong to P or H and comes from yet another post-H source.

on the sacrifices required at each sacred time. Leviticus 23 attempts to reconcile the ancient traditions of the pilgrimage holidays (Exod 23:14-17; 34:18-24) with the notion of a set calendar in which the first and seventh months are most important (see Ezek 45).

## Sabbath Innovations and the New Moon (23:1-3)

Leviticus 23 begins with brief introductory remarks (vv. 1-2) followed by the commandment to observe the Sabbath (v. 3). The Jewish medieval commentator Bahya ben Asher wrote: "Know that the Sabbath commandment is the primary commandment given to Israel before the giving of the Law and that it is the (central) principle of the faith, as weighty as all the rest of the commandments combined."[2] H's version of the Sabbath commandment focuses on the concept of rest or cessation. Exodus 31:15 and 35:2 use similar language, stating that work may be done for six days but that the seventh day is a day of Shabbat ("cessation"). Exodus also indicates that a violation of the law results in the death penalty. In contrast, Leviticus 23 replaces the death penalty with a call for a holy convocation, asserting that the Sabbath belongs to God and is to be observed in all of the settlements (v. 3).

The word שבת ("Sabbath") is used three times in Leviticus 23:3. The ideas of cessation—of honoring the day as belonging to God—and of the importance of lay practice outside the priestly domain are typical for H. In fact, Alan Cooper and Bernard Goldstein note that in P there is no commandment to cease working on the Sabbath; P legislates only special Sabbath sacrifices.[3] According to Israel Knohl, all the Sabbath passages in the Torah belong to H, except for Genesis 2:1-3 and Numbers 28:9-10.[4] Cooper and Goldstein argue that those two texts, as well as Exodus 20:8-11, belong to H's redactional work. They come to this conclusion by positing that the term מועדים ("appointed time," Lev 23:44) never designates the Sabbath for P and that P calculated all of its special days according to astronomical observations. For example, the priestly festival calendar in Numbers 28 begins with daily offerings, then Sabbath

---

2. Bahya is commenting on Exod 31:13, which prioritizes Sabbath observance over the building of the tabernacle.

3. Alan Cooper and Bernard R. Goldstein, "The Development of the Priestly Calendars (I): The Daily Sacrifice and the Sabbath," *HUCA* 74 (2003), 14–20.

4. Israel Knohl, *The Sanctuary of Silence: The Priestly Torah and the Holiness School* (Winona Lake, IN: Eisenbrauns, 2007), 14–19.

23:1The LORD spoke to Moses, saying: 2Speak to the people of Israel and say to them: These are the appointed festivals of the LORD that you shall proclaim as holy convocations, my appointed festivals.

3Six days shall work be done; but the seventh day is a sabbath of complete rest, a holy convocation; you shall do no work: it is a sabbath to the LORD throughout your settlements.

offerings, and finally with new moon offerings. Sabbath and new moon offerings fall under the category of מועדים because they are calculated according to astronomical observations, specifically the cycle of the moon. For P, Sabbath signified the full moon, just as ראשי חדשיכם ("heads of your months") marked the new moon.

H's innovation would thus be to conflate P's full moon "appointed time" (מועד) with H's concept of a seven-day weekly cycle in which the seventh day is called Shabbat ("cessation," "rest," "Sabbath"). This shift is emphasized in Leviticus 23 several times. Verses 2-3 introduce all of the מועדים, identifying the first one as the Sabbath, which is defined as the seventh day of the weekly cycle; thus, the category of מועדים is expanded to include a Sabbath on the seventh day. Verse 4, which may have been the original opening to this unit, presents a second introduction of מועדים as the festivals of the year. In verses 37-38, מועדים are again defined as Sabbaths. In fact, to some extent, Leviticus 23 redefines all of the festival days or מועדים as Sabbath days insofar as Shabbat and מקרא קדש ("holy convocation") are conflated. In summary, H essentially turns a sacrificial festival related to the moon into a weekly day of rest, a practice that would come to define Jewish in the postexilic period.

From a postbiblical perspective, Ron H. Feldman notes that rabbinic traditions claimed that the determination of the new moon was to be made through rabbinic rulings, while the Sabbath came every seven days, independent of human calculation. Feldman asserts that "this dual move—to make what is cultural natural, and naturalize what is cultural—conspires to decrease the importance of the natural world."[5]

From a feminist perspective, this shift raises interesting questions. On the one hand, H's innovation dissolves the full moon cultic observance

---

5. Ron H. Feldman, "'On Your New Moons': The Feminist Transformation of the Jewish New Moon Festival (1)," *Journal of Women and Religion* 19 (2001): 26–53.

and replaces it with an artificial weekly construct. One can only imagine what a full moon celebration might have signified for women and their monthly menstrual cycles. On the other hand, the full moon offerings were not associated with a day of rest. Like the daily offerings, the offerings for the full moon and new moon did not entail any participation by the community at large. These days were not marked as holy convocations.

b. Taanit 1:6 states that it is acceptable for women to refrain from working on the new moon. In Pirkei deRabbi Eliezer 45, a midrash suggests that the new moon was given to women as a reward for refusing to hand over their gold and jewelry for the making of the golden calf. These early associations between women and the new moon provided the impetus among Jewish feminists to reclaim the new moon, that is, Rosh Hodesh, as a legitimate Jewish sacred day for women. For several decades now, Jewish women have gathered on the evening of the new moon, creating new rituals and prayers, talking about issues particular to Jewish women, and cultivating strong ties among small communities of Jewish women. In some circles, celebrating the cycle of the moon is connected to the monthly rhythm of women's bodies. Contemporary Rosh Hodesh literature advocates for a more embodied Judaism, one in which nature is celebrated rather than domesticated.[6]

## Sacred Times of Spring and Autumn (23:4-44)

The first festival of the year begins in the spring at twilight on the fourteenth day of the first month, with a Passover offering for YHVH (Lev 23:4-5), and then the Festival of Unleavened Bread begins on the fifteenth day of the month (v. 6). Unleavened bread is to be eaten for seven days, and participants are to bring sacrificial gifts on each day. In addition, the first and seventh days are declared as sacred proclamations (מקרא קדש) during which work is forbidden (v. 7). H calls the Festival of Unleavened Bread a pilgrimage holiday (חג).

After the first Sabbath following the Festival of Unleavened Bread, a sheaf of new barley is offered to God along with the stipulated burnt

6. For additional information about this Jewish women's celebration, see Susan Berrin, ed., *Celebrating the New Moon: A Rosh Chodesh Anthology* (Northvale, NJ: Jason Aronson, 1996), especially the essay by Arlene Agus, "Examining Rosh Chodesh: An Analysis of the Holiday and Its Textual Sources," 3–12; Penina V. Adelman, *Miriam's Well: Rituals for Jewish Women Around the Year* (New York: Biblio Press, 1990).

4These are the appointed festivals of the Lord, the holy convocations, which you shall celebrate at the time appointed for them. 5In the first month, on the fourteenth day of the month, at twilight, there shall be a passover offering to the Lord, 6and on the fifteenth day of the same month is the festival of unleavened bread to the Lord; seven days you shall eat unleavened bread. 7On the first day you shall have a holy convocation; you shall not work at your occupations. 8For seven days you shall present the Lord's offerings by fire; on the seventh day there shall be a holy convocation: you shall not work at your occupations.

9The Lord spoke to Moses: 10Speak to the people of Israel and say to them: When you enter the land that I am giving you and you reap its harvest, you shall bring the sheaf of the first fruits of your harvest to the priest. 11He shall raise the sheaf before the Lord, that you may find acceptance; on the day after the sabbath the priest shall raise it. 12On the day when you raise the sheaf, you shall offer a lamb a year old, without blemish, as a burnt offering to the Lord. 13And the grain offering with it shall be two-tenths of an ephah of choice flour mixed with oil, an offering by fire of pleasing odor to the Lord; and the drink offering with it shall be of wine, one-fourth of a hin. 14You shall eat no bread or parched grain or fresh ears until that very day, until you have brought the offering of your God: it is a statute forever throughout your generations in all your settlements.

15And from the day after the sabbath, from the day on which you bring the sheaf of the elevation offering, you

offering and libations (v. 9). This sacred time is the offering of the First Fruits (see Lev 2:14-16). The community may eat of the new harvest only after the first grains are offered to YHVH. On the day after the Sabbath following the First Fruits, seven weeks are to be counted, and on the fiftieth day another grain offering, consisting of two loaves of baked leavened bread (see Lev 2:11-12), is brought to the priests along with an array of offerings, including burnt offerings, a purification offering, and well-being offerings (vv. 15-20). The loaves of bread, which are holy for YHVH, go to the priests for eating (v. 20). This day is also called a sacred time and includes cessation from work (v. 21).

Israel Knohl, following a number of other commentators, argues that these grain offerings originated in ancient popular religious practices. Knohl notes that H adds a few significant elements to the ancient practice: "The sheafs are waved on the stalk, as a symbol of the flourishing grain. . . . The wave offering of the two loaves is brought at the end of seven weeks of harvest, and the combination of leavened loaves with shall count off seven weeks; they shall be complete. [16]You shall count until the day after the seventh sabbath, fifty days; then you shall present an offering of new grain to the Lord. [17]You shall bring from your settlements two loaves of bread as an elevation offering, each made of two-tenths of an ephah; they shall be of choice flour, baked with leaven, as first fruits to the Lord. [18]You shall present with the bread seven lambs a year old without blemish, one young bull, and two rams; they shall be a burnt offering to the Lord, along with their grain offering and their drink offerings, an offering by fire of pleasing odor to the Lord. [19]You shall also offer one male goat for a sin offering, and two male lambs a year old as a sacrifice of well-being. [20]The priest shall raise them with the bread of the first fruits as an elevation offering before the Lord, together with the two lambs; they shall be holy to the Lord for the priest. [21]On that same day you shall make proclamation; you shall hold a holy convocation; you shall not work at your occupations. This is a statute forever in all your settlements throughout your generations.

[22]When you reap the harvest of your land, you shall not reap to the very edges of your field, or gather the gleanings of your harvest; you shall leave them for the poor and for the alien: I am the Lord your God.

a sacrifice of well-being provides evidence that this ritual is intended as a thanksgiving for the bounties of the field."[7] Knohl also notes that, according to P (see Num 28–29 and Lev 2:11-16), these grain offerings were voluntary but that, in H, these practices were incorporated into the official practices. Knohl suggests that the prohibition of eating from the harvest before a first part has been offered to God is part of H's appreciation of "the Lord's jurisdiction over the land and its bounty, an idea that lies at the foundation of the HS (Holiness School) sabbatical year and jubilee legislation as well."[8] As a seeming side note, the text contains a reminder that as the harvest is reaped, some of the harvest must be left for the poor and the גר ("alien" in v. 22).

On the first day of the seventh month, another sacred proclamation is commemorated with loud blasts and the cessation of work, along with an אשה ("fire" in v. 25, NRSV, or "gift") offering for YHVH. Then the

7. Knohl, *Sanctuary of Silence*, 25.
8. Ibid., 26–27.

²³The LORD spoke to Moses, saying: ²⁴Speak to the people of Israel, saying: In the seventh month, on the first day of the month, you shall observe a day of complete rest, a holy convocation commemorated with trumpet blasts. ²⁵You shall not work at your occupations; and you shall present the LORD's offering by fire.

²⁶The LORD spoke to Moses, saying: ²⁷Now, the tenth day of this seventh month is the day of atonement; it shall be a holy convocation for you: you shall deny yourselves and present the LORD's offering by fire; ²⁸and you shall do no work during that entire day; for it is a day of atonement, to make atonement on your behalf before the LORD your God. ²⁹For anyone who does not practice self-denial during that entire day shall be cut off from the people.

³⁰And anyone who does any work during that entire day, such a one I will destroy from the midst of the people. ³¹You shall do no work: it is a statute forever throughout your generations in all your settlements. ³²It shall be to you a sabbath of complete rest, and you shall deny yourselves; on the ninth day of the month at evening, from evening to evening you shall keep your sabbath.

³³The LORD spoke to Moses, saying: ³⁴Speak to the people of Israel, saying: On the fifteenth day of this seventh month, and lasting seven days, there shall be the festival of booths to the LORD. ³⁵The first day shall be a holy convocation; you shall not work at your occupations. ³⁶Seven days you shall present the LORD's offerings by fire; on the eighth day you shall observe a holy convocation and present the LORD's

Day of Purification comes on the tenth day of the month. Like the other festivals, it calls for a sacred proclamation and a cessation from work.

On the fifteenth day of the month, just five days after the Day of Purification, comes the Festival of Booths. The festival is also called a pilgrimage (חג). The festival lasts for seven days with offerings each day, and a sacred proclamation is declared along with cessation of work for the first and eighth days. An addition to the text elaborates on festival practices that include bringing a variety of branches and rejoicing while living in booths for the week to remind the Israelites of the time when they were made to live in booths after deliverance from Egyptian oppression (vv. 40-43).

Baruch Schwartz argues that this priestly calendar communicates one central idea: there are certain days that belong to YHVH, certain days during which the deity receives additional offerings and the community refrains from work in order not to disrupt YHVH's sacred moment. In fact, Schwartz claims that it is only in this priestly tradition that the offerings by fire; it is a solemn assembly; you shall not work at your occupations.

[37]These are the appointed festivals of the Lord, which you shall celebrate as times of holy convocation, for presenting to the Lord offerings by fire—burnt offerings and grain offerings, sacrifices and drink offerings, each on its proper day—[38]apart from the sabbaths of the Lord, and apart from your gifts, and apart from all your votive offerings, and apart from all your freewill offerings, which you give to the Lord.

[39]Now, the fifteenth day of the seventh month, when you have gathered in the produce of the land, you shall keep the festival of the Lord, lasting seven days; a complete rest on the first day, and a complete rest on the eighth day. [40]On the first day you shall take the fruit of majestic trees, branches of palm trees, boughs of leafy trees, and willows of the brook; and you shall rejoice before the Lord your God for seven days. [41]You shall keep it as a festival to the Lord seven days in the year; you shall keep it in the seventh month as a statute forever throughout your generations. [42]You shall live in booths for seven days; all that are citizens in Israel shall live in booths, [43]so that your generations may know that I made the people of Israel live in booths when I brought them out of the land of Egypt: I am the Lord your God.

[44]Thus Moses declared to the people of Israel the appointed festivals of the Lord.

---

holidays are "sacred," belonging to God.[9] From this perspective, the role of the people is to stay out of the way, to make space for God to have moments of time.

Leviticus 23 is the basis from which the traditional Jewish holiday calendar is derived. Passover (conflated with the Festival of Unleavened Bread) begins on the fourteenth day of the month of Nissan. On the second day of Passover, it is customary to count forty-nine days with a blessing that announces each day, and then the holiday of Shavuot (Weeks) comes on the fiftieth day. Over time, Shavuot has become a more central holiday that commemorates the receiving of the Torah on Mount Sinai.[10] The first day of the seventh month marks the New Year, Rosh Hashanah, followed by Yom Kippur and then Sukkot (Booths).

---

9. Baruch J. Schwartz, "Miqra' Qodesh and the Structure of Leviticus 23," in *Purity, Holiness, and Identity in Judaism and Christianity: Essays in Memory of Susan Haber*, ed. Carl S. Ehrlich, Anders Runesson, and Eileen Schuller (Tübingen: Mohr Siebeck, 2013), 11–24.

10. In Christian liturgical calendars, Easter corresponds with Passover, and Pentecost with Shavuot. In Acts 2, Luke describes a gathering of "devout Jews from every nation under heaven" to celebrate Shavuot in Jerusalem as the setting for the coming of the Holy Spirit at Pentecost.

It is difficult to ascertain what role women played in the biblical festivals. Frankly, the biblical calendar of Leviticus 23 gives us little information about the roles of the lay community apart from bringing offerings and refraining from work on sacred days. Evaluating the role of women in the observance of holidays in Judaism is complex because the halachic (legal) traditions are not consistent and because women's activities are generally not dictated; they emerge from day-to-day activities. m. Kiddushin 1.7 exempts women from all positive time-bound commandments but makes exceptions to the rule. So women are required to eat matzah, to drink four cups of wine, and to eat bitter herbs during the Passover Seder, but they are exempt from hearing the blowing of the shofar on Rosh Hashanah or from dwelling in sukkahs during Sukkot.[11] In non-halachic Jewish communities, men and women participate equally in the ritual practices that have evolved for the holidays. In addition, there is a blossoming of new rituals that seek to integrate women's experiences more fully.[12]

## Tabernacle Miscellanea (24:1-9)

Leviticus 24 addresses a number of seemingly disparate topics, beginning with laws regarding the lampstands, laws regarding the showbread, a brief narrative about blasphemy, and finally the *talion* laws ("an eye for an eye"). While the topics are distinct, they move the reader from the most inward part of the sanctuary out to the camp and then outside of the camp. This chapter exemplifies H's ongoing concern with traditional priestly matters as well as teachings unique to H.

The chapter begins with regulations regarding two items that reside in the outer section of the inner sanctum, that is, in front of the curtain behind which the ark and the divine presence dwell. The first item is the lampstand (vv. 1-4). The community is required to provide the priests with the finest olive oil so that a light may be burnt regularly by Aaron (and presumably the high priests that succeed him) from evening until night. Judaism has held a longstanding tradition that there must be an "eternal" light over the synagogue ark that houses the synagogue's

---

11. For an excellent analysis of women's exemption from Sukkot practices, see Marjorie Lehman, "The Gendered Rhetoric of Sukkah Observance," *JQR* 96 (2006): 309–35.

12. Feminist Passover Haggadahs began emerging in the 1980s, and now a woman can find a ritual for almost every significant lifecycle event. For examples of many of these rituals, see https://ritualwell.org.

²⁴:¹The Lᴏʀᴅ spoke to Moses, saying: ²Command the people of Israel to bring you pure oil of beaten olives for the lamp, that a light may be kept burning regularly. ³Aaron shall set it up in the tent of meeting, outside the curtain of the covenant, to burn from evening to morning before the Lᴏʀᴅ regularly; it shall be a statute forever throughout your generations. ⁴He shall set up the lamps on the lampstand of pure gold before the Lᴏʀᴅ regularly.

⁵You shall take choice flour, and bake twelve loaves of it; two-tenths of an ephah shall be in each loaf. ⁶You shall place them in two rows, six in a row, on the table of pure gold. ⁷You shall put pure frankincense with each row, to be a token offering for the bread, as an offering by fire to the Lᴏʀᴅ. ⁸Every sabbath day Aaron shall set them in order before the Lᴏʀᴅ regularly as a commitment of the people of Israel, as a covenant forever. ⁹They shall be for Aaron and his descendants, who shall eat them in a holy place, for they are most holy portions for him from the offerings by fire to the Lᴏʀᴅ, a perpetual due.

Torah scrolls.[13] While the context of Leviticus, by specifying a light from evening until morning, understands תמיד as "regularly" (vv. 2, 3, and 4, NRSV), Jewish tradition comes to understand תמיד as "always" or "continuously." Finally, the lights are to be set on the lampstand of pure gold.[14]

The next topic is the showbread (vv. 5-9). Twelve loaves of bread are baked with semolina flour and set on a gold table before the curtain behind which God's presence resides. The twelve loaves are set in two rows of six each Sabbath. Frankincense is burned beside the loaves and this incense offering is the symbolic offering to God, since the priests would consume the sacred bread within the holy precincts. In standard meal offerings brought by the laity, frankincense would accompany the grain as an offering to God.

## Desecrating the Divine Name (24:10-23)

Leviticus 24:10 abruptly introduces a narrative, the only narrative in H. Without transition, we move from a description of the most sacred space to a narrative about a fight between two men in the camp. One man is of

13. Similarly, some Christian churches maintain an "eternal" light beside the tabernacle where the consecrated communion hosts are kept.

14. The same practice is found in Exod 27:20-21, and the description of the actual lampstand is in Exod 25:31-39.

*Lev 24:10-23*

[10]A man whose mother was an Israelite and whose father was an Egyptian came out among the people of Israel; and the Israelite woman's son and a certain Israelite began fighting in the camp. [11]The Israelite woman's son blasphemed the Name in a curse. And they brought him to Moses—now his mother's name was Shelomith, daughter of Dibri, of the tribe of Dan—[12]and they put him in custody, until the decision of the LORD should be made clear to them.

[13]The LORD said to Moses, saying: [14]Take the blasphemer outside the camp; and let all who were within hearing lay their hands on his head, and let the whole congregation stone him. [15]And speak to the people of Israel, saying: Anyone who curses God shall bear the sin. [16]One who blasphemes the name of the LORD shall be put to death; the whole congregation shall stone the blasphemer. Aliens as well as citizens, when they blaspheme the Name, shall be put to death. [17]Anyone who kills a human being shall be put to death. [18]Anyone who kills an animal shall make restitution for it, life for life. [19]Anyone who maims another shall suffer the same injury in return: [20]fracture for fracture, eye for eye, tooth for tooth; the injury inflicted is the injury to be suffered. [21]One who kills an animal shall make restitution for it; but one who kills a human being shall be put to death. [22]You shall have one law for the alien and for the citizen: for I am the LORD your God. [23]Moses spoke thus to the people of Israel; and they took the blasphemer outside the camp, and stoned him to death.

mixed parentage (mother is Israelite and father is Egyptian), and one man has two Israelite parents. Verse 11 tells us in a parenthetical comment that the mother's name was Shlomit, the daughter of Dibri, from the tribe of Dan. The Bible gives us no information about Dibri or Shlomit, although rabbinic Midrash fills in the story. According to one account, the son of Shlomit was setting up his tent within the tribe of Dan in the Israelite camp. The Danites chased him off, arguing that tribal allotments are set by patrilineal descent. The son of Shlomit took his case to Moses and Moses rejected his claim.[15] The rabbis cast Shlomit in a negative light, describing her as a promiscuous gossip. As a counter-reading to these negative portrayals of Shlomit and her son, Wendy Zierler offers her own creative interpretation:

> But given the context of Israelite enslavement in Egypt, is it not possible that Shelomit, like so many African American slaves who were raped and impregnated by their masters, might have been abused and used by a slavemaster or overseer, and that is how she came to give birth to the son of an Egyptian man?

15. Sifra Parashat Emor 14.

According to this reading, Shelomit bat Divri was a struggling ex-slave and single mother, who labored against all odds to raise her son and shield him from the prejudices of the surrounding community. Alas, the son—whom the text presents as a בֵּן, a "son" or "boy," rather than an אִישׁ, a "man," hinting, perhaps, at his not-yet or barely emergent manhood—went out of his mother's tent and discovered that the world around him was not what he expected. He saw that he was a second-class citizen in a society of former second-class citizens, that he was not wanted among his would-be brethren. His mother may have attempted to counter and to diffuse his youthful anger when it flared. Befitting her name, Shelomit—from *shalom*, "peace"—she may have tried on any number of occasions to bring peace and calm and to shore up her son's bifurcated identity.[16]

Baruch Schwartz suggests that the narrative in Leviticus 24:10-23 focuses on a character of mixed parentage "in order to establish the legal principle that the desecration of YHVH's name by definition is a capital offense, whether performed by an Israelite or a גֵּר. The Bible's principle of patrilineal descent would consider such a person Egyptian rather than Israelite."[17] John E. Hartley offers a similar position and suggests that the details regarding the mother's name and her family credentials are provided to make it clear that the offender is indeed part Israelite.[18] The man's position in the camp is uncertain because, according to Numbers 2:34, the camp was organized by tribe and, within each tribe, according to the father's house. This observation has led a number of scholars to argue that this man lived in the camp of the mixed multitude[19] but that he entered into the Israelite camp.

Alternatively, Jacob Milgrom, quoting Shaye Cohen, suggests that the child of an Israelite woman would have lived with the mother's clan, provided the father also had joined the woman's clan. The son would have lived with his mother's clan but would not have had any rights to inheritance, which was determined by patrilineal descent. The man's association with the tribe of Dan adds additional points against him because the tribe of Dan is often associated with apostasy in biblical narratives.[20]

---

16. Wendy Zierler, "A Tribute to the Blasphemer's Mother: Shelomit, Daughter of Divri," http://thetorah.com/a-tribute-to-the-blasphemers-mother-shelomit-daughter-of-divri/.

17. Baruch Schwartz, "Leviticus," in *The Jewish Study Bible*, ed. Adele Berlin and Marc Zvi Brettler (Oxford: Oxford University Press, 2004), 254.

18. John E. Hartley, *Leviticus*, WBC 4 (Waco, TX: Word Books, 1992), 408.

19. See Exod 12:38, which describes a mixed crowd that left Egypt with the Israelites.

20. Jacob Milgrom, *Leviticus 23–27*, AB 3B (New York: Doubleday, 2001), 2107. See Judg 18; 1 Kgs 12.

The insertion of a brief narrative, the only narrative in H, indicates that the writers wanted to communicate an essential theological concept, which could not be communicated through legislation alone. As we will see, the message embedded in this narrative empowers the community of worshipers in a rather unprecedented manner and raises important questions about where power resides in H's theology.

The meaning of the words קלל ("blasphemed" in v. 11) and נקב ("curse" in v. 11) and their syntactic relationship have remained a topic of great dispute among commentators from the earliest postbiblical times to the present. There is no consensus on the meaning of these words and how they relate to one another. Interpretations include the following: "He blasphemed the Name and then cursed the Name"; "He invoked the Name to curse the Name";[21] and "He pronounced the Name in a disdainful manner."[22]

These interpretations are derived from and have been debated by the Targum, early rabbinic sources, medieval commentators, and modern Jewish and Christian biblicists. It appears that already among the earliest generations of interpreters, there was a lot of disagreement. A series of articles in *Vetus Testamentum* from the 1960s to recent years gives a broad range of interpretations.[23] So, to the myriad possibilities I will add yet another—beginning with a look at the key terms קלל and נקב and then setting those concepts into H's theological framework.

## Disrespecting YHVH

The verbal form of the root קלל appears twice in this passage, in verses 11 and 15. In the first instance, Shlomit's son does something to the name and then acts as the agent of the verb קלל, without a direct object:

ויקב בן־האשה הישראלית את־השם ויקלל

The root קלל is strongly associated with the concept of cursing. Cursing is generally understood to be the invocation of divine power to affect a

---

21. b. Sanh 56a.

22. Jacob Weingreen, "The Case of the Blasphemer (Leviticus XXIV, 10ff)," *VT* 22 (1972): 118–23, reads the verb as an adverbial modification.

23. H. Mittwoch, "The Story of the Blasphemer Seen in a Wider Context," *VT* 15 (1965): 386–89; Weingreen, "The Case of the Blasphemer," 118–23; J. B. Gabel and C. B. Wheeler, "The Redactor's Hand in the Blasphemy Pericope of Leviticus Xxiv," *VT* 30 (1980): 227–29; Dennis H. Livingston, "The Crime of Leviticus Xxiv 11," *VT* 36 (1986): 352–54; Rodney R. Hutton, "Narrative in Leviticus : The Case of the Blaspheming Son (Lev 24,10-23)," *Zeitschrift Für Altorientalische Und Biblische Rechtsgeschichte/Journal for Ancient Near Eastern and Biblical Law* 3 (1997): 145–63.

person or group for ill. The primary use of this verb occurs, however, in contexts of social relationships and status issues. For example, in Genesis 16:4, the use of the verb indicates the perceived change in status between Sarah and Hagar. In Judges 9:27, the Shechemites disrespect Avimelech and lower his status in the public eye. Nehemiah engages in a series of shaming acts with the men of Jerusalem to establish his authority regarding intermarriage policies (Neh 13:25).[24] And in Leviticus 19:14, a person who disrespects a person who cannot hear is exploiting the victim's vulnerability. The common thread in all of these cases is that the root קלל indicates a stance of disrespect that impacts the social order. The most egregious form of disrespect is against one's parents. In Leviticus 20:9, the punishment for cursing a father or mother is the death penalty; Proverbs 20:20 suggests a similar fate in more metaphorical language.[25]

Biblical evidence regarding use of this term suggests that Shlomit's son was belittling or disrespecting God but not cursing God. The difference between the concept of cursing and disrespecting is significant: no curse can have power without God's oversight; that is, a curse works because a power greater than the individual is invoked. Therefore, a person cannot curse YHVH because there is no greater power in H's theology to enforce the harm indicated by the curse.

Thus, Shlomit's son was neither invoking God's name to effect a curse nor cursing God. His action somehow resulted in his disrespecting God and potentially impacting the status of God vis-à-vis the community of witnesses to the fight. In other words, the man did something, according to verse 11, that led to belittling the name.

### Breaching YHVH's Domain

The second key term in Leviticus 24:11, נקב ("blaspheme"), appears again in the chapter, in legislation indicating that anyone who commits the act of נקב against the divine space will be put to death by stoning (vv. 15–16). Clearly, נקב is a greater offense than is קלל ("curse") when directed to YHVH. The term נקב has two meanings, both of which are operative in verses 15–16: to pierce (as a splinter pierces the palm of a hand)[26] and to designate or "summon by name" (as in Isa 62:2 and Amos 6:1). In Leviticus 24:15–16, therefore, one could argue on the philological

---

24. See also 1 Sam 18:23; 2 Sam 19:44; Jer 15:10; and Eccl 10:2.
25. See also Ezek 22:7.
26. See 2 Kgs 18:2//Isa 36:6; Hab 3:14; Hag 1:6; and Job 40:24, 26.

evidence alone that the man has either simply invoked the name or has somehow "pierced" the name.

In the broader context of the history of the ban on the pronunciation of the divine name in postbiblical Judaism, I would argue that Leviticus 24 is an important pivotal text, because it introduces constraints on the name that we do not find in other source traditions.[27] The concern is not simply with the utterance of the divine name in any context (as it becomes in Judaism); it is a particular kind of utterance that somehow penetrates into the divine sphere.

Simeon Chavel juxtaposes Leviticus 24 with the Nadav and Avihu narrative (Lev 10:1-3) under the rubric of apostasy narratives at Sinai.[28] Chavel argues that the man's offense was cursing God and that the offender intentionally attempted to attack God in some way that was similar to murder. I agree that it is helpful to juxtapose the incident involving Nadav and Avihu with the episode about Shlomit's son, but I do not see either as apostasy narratives. Juxtaposing these two narratives does highlight the contrast between P's focus on holy space as the meeting place for the divine-human encounter and H's concern with the use of speech as an arena by which any Israelite (even a half-Israelite) might encounter God. Both of these narratives are about challenges to a healthy divine-human relationship of holiness and to the proper roles of both partners in this relationship. Holiness implies separation and distinction. The role of the priests in P is to maintain boundaries to ensure God's כבוד remains within the sanctuary, not to join God's realm by offering themselves up as sacrifices. According to H, the role of Israel and those who have joined its community (the גר or "stranger," for example) is to act righteously by following the laws, and that includes not penetrating the name. In both cases, Nadav and Avihu and the son of Shlomit bat Divri go too far, even though Nadav and Avihu may have done it with good intentions (if we accept Philo's interpretation) and the son of Shlomit with malice. Going where one should not obfuscates the holiness

---

27. m. Yoma 6:2 indicates that the name of God, the Tetragrammaton, could be pronounced only by the high priest in the holy of holies on the Day of Atonement. b. Kid 71a explains that YHVH is to be pronounced as Adonai and not as it is written. Septuagint translations of the Tetragrammaton also reveal the practice of replacing YHVH with Adonai. The Lachish letters use the Tetragrammaton in correspondence, however, suggesting that the ban on pronunciation occurred sometime after the destruction of the First Temple.

28. Milgrom, *Leviticus 23–27*, 2141. Milgrom cites a paper that Chavel wrote in a class for Milgrom.

relationship. In any case, Shlomit bat Divri is left bereft of a son, either living with her husband in a no-man's-land within the Israelite camp or widowed and living with the Danites. As is the case with other biblical texts, like the abduction of Dinah in Genesis 34, the text shows no more concern with the fate of the woman after her narrative role is completed.

The seemingly misplaced narrative in Leviticus 24:10-23 serves to enforce the theological arguments embedded in H's legal material. Just as the name can be desecrated by certain actions, so the name can be penetrated by inappropriate utterance. In both cases, the name is vulnerable to some extent—in one case, through Israel's actions and, in the other, through speech. While P locates the place of connection in the sancta, H locates it in the name.

Unfortunately, this powerful theological message uses an individual on the margins of society and thus vulnerable to serve as the victim of the story. Or as Julián Andrés González Holguin writes: "He [the son of Shelomit] is a victim of impossible demands that a closed community places upon the marginalized individuals who live on its fringes and of severely biased attitude—that the deity seems to share in the story—towards such individuals."[29] Holguin compares Shelomit's son to a 1996 case of a documented resident who had lived in the United States since the age of ten. After leaving the country for business, the young man could not return to his home because he inadvertently misspoke about his citizenship status. By the time he clarified his responses, immigration officials refused to allow him to enter the country because he had falsely claimed to be a citizen of the United States. González Holguin concludes that "those who cross the border from outside are viewed with suspicion no matter how hard they try to blend in and can be targeted for life-shattering expulsion when their knowledge of local culture proves insufficient to prevent them from making an innocent mistake."[30]

## Sabbath for the Land (25:1-7)

Leviticus 25 addresses land use, land ownership, and debt. This chapter addresses class and ethnicity and opens the door for consideration of the intersectionality of identities as portrayed in the Holiness Legislation. Leviticus 25 takes note of several problems that are still quite relevant in

29. Julián Andrés González Holguin, "Leviticus 24:10-23: An Outsider Perspective," *HS* 56 (2015): 99.

30. Ibid., 102.

**Lev 25:1-7**

25:1The LORD spoke to Moses on Mount Sinai, saying: 2Speak to the people of Israel and say to them: When you enter the land that I am giving you, the land shall observe a sabbath for the LORD. 3Six years you shall sow your field, and six years you shall prune your vineyard, and gather in their yield; 4but in the seventh year there shall be a sabbath of complete rest for the land, a sabbath for the LORD: you shall not sow your field or prune your vineyard. 5You shall not reap the aftergrowth of your harvest or gather the grapes of your unpruned vine: it shall be a year of complete rest for the land. 6You may eat what the land yields during its sabbath—you, your male and female slaves, your hired and your bound laborers who live with you; 7for your livestock also, and for the wild animals in your land all its yield shall be for food.

our age, and the text offers radical solutions to those challenges. Some of those solutions have been applied in our contemporary period. For example, Jubilee 2000, made up of a coalition of organizations and countries, rallied to promote debt forgiveness for the world's poorest nations.[31]

In Leviticus 25, references to "land rights" indicate two different things: the Israelite right to land and the land's own right for rest and health. The chapter begins with an announcement that, when the people settle into the land of Israel, the land itself will claim a sabbatical year of rest (vv. 1-2). As a consequence, the work of the agricultural community must come to a stop every seventh year (vv. 3-5). During the seventh year, the community may eat whatever the land produces on its own (v. 6).[32] One of the extraordinary points of these opening verses is that the Sabbath year is a year of rest for the land, not for the community. The land is allowed to do what it would normally do without human intervention, and people must depend on what is naturally produced to

31. See David Lazonby, "Applying the Jubilee to Contemporary Socio-Economic and Environmental Issues," *Journal of European Baptist Studies* 16 (2016): 30–50, for a number of connections between Leviticus 25 and contemporary challenges of human trafficking, over-farming, and accumulation of wealth.

32. There is plenty of scholarship on the literary and historical relationship among Lev 25:1-7; Exod 23:10-11; and Deut 15:1-18. See, for example, Adrian Schenker, "The Biblical Legislation on the Release of Slaves: The Road from Exodus to Leviticus," *JSOT* 78 (1998): 23–41; and Jeffrey Stackert, "The Sabbath of the Land in the Holiness Legislation: Combining Priestly and Non-Priestly Perspectives," *CBQ* 73 (2011): 239–50; and John Sietze Bergsma, *The Jubilee from Leviticus to Qumran: A History of Interpretation*, VTSup 115 (Leiden: Brill, 2007).

sustain themselves or, as Nihan puts it regarding the average Israelite, "his condition is identical to that of the landless."[33]

The members of the Israelite household are referred to as "you," male slaves, female slaves, hired laborers, and residents who live in the household, as well as domesticated animals and all other animals. The list in Leviticus 25:6 is not randomly ordered; the landed Israelite owner (and presumably his family) comes first and the animals come last. Male and female slaves (the only category in which gender is specified) are listed immediately after Israelites and are followed by hired laborers and alien residents. The commentary that follows will explore the status of each of these groups.

### The Jubilee Reset (25:8-24)

After a sequence of seven sabbatical years, on the Day of Purification, a public call is sounded to mark the beginning of the Yovel or Jubilee Year, during which the community calls for a דרור ("release"; "liberty" in v. 10), so that all Israelites must return to their ancestral land allotments and to their families.[34] The Jubilee Year, like the sabbatical years, is a year of rest for the land; it is designated holy, a reminder that the land belongs to God (v. 12). The fact that the Jubilee is called on the Day of Purification is akin to an absolute reset button. The sanctuary is thoroughly cleansed from impurities, while property allocations are returned to their original allotments.

Verses 13-17 describe the process by which sales and purchases of land are to be transacted between Jubilee years. The text mandates that any sale of land must take account of the number of years that the buyer will have access to the land. So, for example, the purchase of land in year three should cost more than the sale of land in the thirty-fifth year. An interesting aspect of this text is that it uses the Hebrew terminology for "buy"

---

33. Christophe Nihan, *From Priestly Torah to Pentateuch: A Study in the Composition of the Book of Leviticus*, FAT 25 (Tübingin: Mohr Siebeck, 2007), 524.

34. The concept of a "release" or דרור comes from similar practices in Mesopotamia, where kings would call for righteousness, forgiving debts, and releasing slaves upon ascension to the throne. See Moshe Weinfeld, *Social Justice in Ancient Israel and in the Ancient Near East* (Jerusalem: Magnes Press, 1995) for a detailed discussion of the practices in Mesopotamia and Egypt; more recently, Bergsma, *The Jubilee from Leviticus to Qumran*, 19–36.

⁸You shall count off seven weeks of years, seven times seven years, so that the period of seven weeks of years gives forty-nine years. ⁹Then you shall have the trumpet sounded loud; on the tenth day of the seventh month—on the day of atonement—you shall have the trumpet sounded throughout all your land. ¹⁰And you shall hallow the fiftieth year and you shall proclaim liberty throughout the land to all its inhabitants. It shall be a jubilee for you: you shall return, every one of you, to your property and every one of you to your family. ¹¹That fiftieth year shall be a jubilee for you: you shall not sow, or reap the aftergrowth, or harvest the unpruned vines. ¹²For it is a jubilee; it shall be holy to you: you shall eat only what the field itself produces.

¹³In this year of jubilee you shall return, every one of you, to your property. ¹⁴When you make a sale to your neighbor or buy from your neighbor, you shall not cheat one another. ¹⁵When you buy from your neighbor, you shall pay only for the number of years since the jubilee; the seller shall charge you only for the remaining crop years. ¹⁶If the years are more, you shall increase the price, and if the years are fewer, you shall diminish the price; for it is a certain number of harvests that are being sold to you. ¹⁷You shall not cheat one another, but you shall fear your God; for I am the Lord your God.

¹⁸You shall observe my statutes and faithfully keep my ordinances, so that you may live on the land securely. ¹⁹The land will yield its fruit, and you will eat your fill and live on it securely. ²⁰Should you ask, "What shall we eat in the seventh year, if we may not sow or gather in our crop?" ²¹I will order my blessing for you in the sixth year, so that it will yield a crop for three years. ²²When you sow in the eighth year, you will be eating from the old crop; until the ninth year, when its produce comes in, you shall eat the old. ²³The land shall not be sold in perpetuity, for the land is mine; with me you are but aliens and tenants. ²⁴Throughout the land that you hold, you shall provide for the redemption of the land.

and "sell," when, in fact, "buyers" are really only leasing the land for a designated number of years. Thus, someone can lease a neighbor's land to increase his agricultural capacity, but he cannot keep the land indefinitely; ultimately, in the Jubilee Year, it goes back to the original owner.

The text takes an additional step: the owners of the land are not even owners; they too are living on land that ultimately belongs to God (v. 23). There is only one property owner (God) and that owner approves sublets, but only for limited periods of time. As the owner of the land, God is also responsible for the land's wellbeing and upkeep; thus the sabbatical years!

## Destitution and Dignity (25:25-55)

The second half of chapter 25 addresses four stages of impoverishment and landlessness. The first case (vv. 25-28) describes a landowner who must sell his land to pay off debts. In this case, ideally a close relative should redeem the land from the purchaser. Baruch Levine argues that one of the innovations of the Jubilee text is not only concern for redeeming tribal lands but concern for individuals as well.

> Chapter 25 guarantees the rights of individual landowners in contrast to the more ancient system of *ge'ullah*, "redemption," that sought to retain ancestral land within the clan. According to that system, the redeemer, a relative within the clan, gained title to the land he had redeemed out of his own resources, for preventing loss of land to the clan as a whole was deemed more important than protecting the rights of any individual owner. Chapter 25 represents a significant adaptation of the ancient system of redemption. The redeemer from the same clan was commanded to restore the land to its original owner, as concern shifts from the clan to the individual owner.[35]

If there is no redeemer and the impoverished seller is in a stronger financial position, then he should buy his land back at a prorated sale price. This means that the original purchaser never really owns the land but has access to the land for agricultural purposes until it is redeemed or until the Jubilee Year comes. The text leaves a number of questions unanswered. For example, is it possible that the seller and his family actually remain on the land although they do not have access to the fields? If the household leaves the property, what is the fate of the members of the household? The text uses the term אִישׁ ("man," NRSV) to describe the landowner, but what if a woman is the landowner? Does she have the same rights of redemption? V. N. N. Mtshiselwa writes:

> Poverty affects both men and women, and not just one's "brother" as H presupposes in verse 25. Thus, one can assume that the section on "Loss of land because of poverty (vv. 25–28)" particularly H's v. 25 in its present form would not enjoy an affirmative reception among women in both post-exilic Yehud and post-apartheid South Africa. From an

---

35. Baruch Levine, *Leviticus: A JPS Torah Commentary* (Philadelphia: Jewish Publication Society of America, 1989), 168. So too Jacob Milgrom, "The Land Redeemer and the Jubilee," in *Fortunate the Eyes That See: Essays in Honor of David Noel Freedman in Celebration of His Seventieth Birthday*, ed. Astrid B. Beck, Andrew H. Bartelt, Paul R. Raabe, and Chris A. Franke (Grand Rapids: Eerdmans, 1995), 66–69.

*Lev 25:25-55*

²⁵If anyone of your kin falls into difficulty and sells a piece of property, then the next of kin shall come and redeem what the relative has sold. ²⁶If the person has no one to redeem it, but then prospers and finds sufficient means to do so, ²⁷the years since its sale shall be computed and the difference shall be refunded to the person to whom it was sold, and the property shall be returned. ²⁸But if there are not sufficient means to recover it, what was sold shall remain with the purchaser until the year of jubilee; in the jubilee it shall be released, and the property shall be returned.

²⁹If anyone sells a dwelling house in a walled city, it may be redeemed until a year has elapsed since its sale; the right of redemption shall be one year. ³⁰If it is not redeemed before a full year has elapsed, a house that is in a walled city shall pass in perpetuity to the purchaser, throughout the generations; it shall not be released in the jubilee. ³¹But houses in villages that have no walls around them shall be classed as open country; they may be redeemed, and they shall be released in the jubilee. ³²As for the cities of the Levites, the Levites shall forever have the right of redemption of the houses in the cities belonging to them. ³³Such property as may be redeemed from the Levites—houses sold in a city belonging to them—shall be released in the jubilee; because the houses in the cities of the Levites are their possession among the people of Israel. ³⁴But the open land around their cities may not

African liberationist perspective, the most compelling response by H to the challenge of poverty and landlessness should have been a gender sensitive one.³⁶

The second case (vv. 35-38) is more difficult to interpret because of the use of technical terminology in verse 35. A comparison of the NRSV and NJPS translations reveals the issues:

> If any of your kin fall into difficulty and become dependent on you, you shall support them; they shall live with you as though resident aliens. (NRSV)

> If your kinsman, being in straits, comes under your authority, and you hold him as though a resident alien, let him live by your side. (NJPS)

36. Ndikho Mtshiselwa, "Reading Ruth 4 and Leviticus 25:8-55 in the Light of the Landless and Poor Women in South Africa: A Conversation with Fernando F. Segovia and Ernesto 'Che' Guevara," *HTS Theologiese Studies/Theological Studies* 72 (2016): a3140.

be sold; for that is their possession for all time.

³⁵If any of your kin fall into difficulty and become dependent on you, you shall support them; they shall live with you as though resident aliens. ³⁶Do not take interest in advance or otherwise make a profit from them, but fear your God; let them live with you. ³⁷You shall not lend them your money at interest taken in advance, or provide them food at a profit. ³⁸I am the LORD your God, who brought you out of the land of Egypt, to give you the land of Canaan, to be your God.

³⁹If any who are dependent on you become so impoverished that they sell themselves to you, you shall not make them serve as slaves. ⁴⁰They shall remain with you as hired or bound laborers. They shall serve with you until the year of the jubilee. ⁴¹Then they and their children with them shall be free from your authority; they shall go back to their own family and return to their ancestral property. ⁴²For they are my servants, whom I brought out of the land of Egypt; they shall not be sold as slaves are sold. ⁴³You shall not rule over them with harshness, but shall fear your God. ⁴⁴As for the male and female slaves whom you may have, it is from the nations around you that you may acquire male and female slaves. ⁴⁵You may also acquire them from among the aliens residing with you, and from their families that are with you, who have been born in your land; and they may be your property. ⁴⁶You may keep them as a possession for your children after you, for them to inherit as property. These you may

The NRSV reads the protasis or the "if" clause as ending at "dependent on you," while the NJPS reads the protasis through "resident alien." In other words, there is a disagreement about the condition and status of the person in dire straits, and there is disagreement regarding the obligation of the addressee.

Another point of uncertainty has to do with the term גר ותושב ("resident aliens," v. 35 in NRSV). Most scholars take these two terms as a hendiadys, where תושב serves as an adjective for גר, thus leading to the common translation of "resident alien." תושב never appears independently of another term; the other common pairing is שכיר ותושב. If we take these two terms together as a hendiadys, the common translation is "resident hireling" (v. 40). Milgrom argues that a resident hireling is not like a day laborer but rather a long-term employee who lives with the landowner's family and receives room and board.³⁷

37. Milgrom, *Leviticus 23–27*, 2221.

treat as slaves, but as for your fellow Israelites, no one shall rule over the other with harshness.

[47]If resident aliens among you prosper, and if any of your kin fall into difficulty with one of them and sell themselves to an alien, or to a branch of the alien's family, [48]after they have sold themselves they shall have the right of redemption; one of their brothers may redeem them, [49]or their uncle or their uncle's son may redeem them, or anyone of their family who is of their own flesh may redeem them; or if they prosper they may redeem themselves. [50]They shall compute with the purchaser the total from the year when they sold themselves to the alien until the jubilee year; the price of the sale shall be applied to the number of years:

the time they were with the owner shall be rated as the time of a hired laborer. [51]If many years remain, they shall pay for their redemption in proportion to the purchase price; [52]and if few years remain until the jubilee year, they shall compute thus: according to the years involved they shall make payment for their redemption. [53]As a laborer hired by the year they shall be under the alien's authority, who shall not, however, rule with harshness over them in your sight. [54]And if they have not been redeemed in any of these ways, they and their children with them shall go free in the jubilee year. [55]For to me the people of Israel are servants; they are my servants whom I brought out from the land of Egypt: I am the LORD your God.

Another point of disagreement has to do with the phrase: "You shall support him" (NRSV),[38] or "He comes under your authority" (NJPS).[39] Milgrom describes the situation in verses 35-38 as follows: "This time when he defaults on his loan, he forfeits all his lands, but still owing on his loan, he becomes a 'tenant farmer' for the creditor. Technically, he has lost his land but the produce is still his. It amortizes his loan since he pays no interest. In a sense, he rents the land from the creditor."[40] Milgrom rejects the view that the debtor enters into the household of the creditor, who is responsible for supporting the debtor and his family. Adrian Schenker suggests that this law indicates that "if your brother becomes poor and cannot maintain himself with you, then you shall relieve him: a stranger and a sojourner, he shall live with you."[41] In

38. So too Hartley, *Leviticus*, 440; and Nihan, *From Priestly Torah to Pentateuch*, 531.
39. So too Milgrom, *Leviticus 23–27*, 2206.
40. Ibid., 2204–5.
41. Schenker, "The Biblical Legislation," 29.

other words, Schenker suggests that this legislation enables Israelites to migrate to new lands within Israel, and then when such a person comes onto the addressee's land, the addressee should accept him as one would an alien or a sojourner. More recently, Yoram Mayshar has contributed a new interpretation. First, he argues that the term תושב in H refers to a rent-paying tenant farmer. By contrast, he argues, the phrase שכיר ותושב should not be taken as a hendiadys but rather as two economic categories of farming dependents who are not slaves. He argues that the תושב ("tenant") would have had a superior social status to the שכיר ("employee"). Both categories represent free but dependent individuals. Finally, Mayshar argues that these tenants and employees could be Israelites or non-Israelites.[42]

Bruce Wells argues that, contrary to Milgrom's claim that the debtor remains on his own lands and pays off the debt, the debtor enters into an antichretic pledge arrangement. There are essentially two ways that a debtor can set aside collateral when taking a loan: hypothecary pledges, which are kept by the debtor until he defaults on his loan; and possessory pledges, which are kept by the creditor for the term of the loan. Wells argues that verses 35-38 describe a particular type of possessory pledge, an antichretic pledge, in which the debtor provides labor rather than interest on the loan. The debtor cannot continue to live on his own lands because he has sold them off to others. Wells notes that this arrangement can benefit the creditor who might actually make a greater profit on rental income than interest. This arrangement may also benefit the debtor who immediately begins paying back the principal rather than making interest payments.[43]

The importance of Wells's position is that most other scholars assume that the point of every law in Leviticus 25 is to encourage a spirit of generosity and to alleviate the exploitation of the poor. Wells suggests that verses 35-38 may financially benefit the creditor to the detriment of the debtor because the latter is under the authority of the creditor. "Creditors in this position sought to maintain a balance between keeping their pledges reasonably fit for work and spending as little as possible on them."[44] The creditor could work the debtor as hard as he chose. Wells

---

42. Yoram Mayshar, "Who Was the *Toshav*?," *JBL* 133 (2014): 225–46.

43. Bruce Wells, "The Quasi-Alien in Leviticus 25," in *The Foreigner and the Law: Perspective from the Hebrew Bible and the Ancient Near East*, ed. R. Achenbach, Rainer Albertz, and J. Wöhrle, BZAR 16 (Weisbaden: Harrassowitz, 2011), 135–55.

44. Ibid., 149.

suggests that the ban on setting interest makes the text seem generous but that the reality of the situation may have been dire for the debtor.

The final two cases involve an Israelite who chooses to "sell himself" or "is sold" to another Israelite (in the third case) or to a non-Israelite (in the fourth scenario) because he no longer has any means to pay off debts or manage his own land. In one interpretation, the paterfamilias sells himself in order to support his family. This interpretation assumes that this debt-slave is really treated as an employee. The second interpretation holds that an Israelite is sold by another Israelite, perhaps against his will. In this case, the fate of the family is unclear. Verse 55 admonishes the community to remember that the Israelites are God's servants (or slaves) and thus cannot serve as slaves to any person. The text says that at the Jubilee, the sold man will be released along with his sons, but what about female debt-slaves? The text is silent on this issue. The ambiguous status of female debt-slaves or even of female landowners is reflected in today's world. As the Housing and Land Rights Network has noted:

> Land in particular is important for women because they depend on it for food, nutrition, and income security. Endowing women with land empowers them economically and strengthens their ability to challenge social and political gender inequalities. Women worldwide play a central role in ensuring family food security. They also produce goods and provide services to earn income for the family, as both primary and secondary income earners. Yet, the majority of the world's women are resource poor. Hunger is chronic among women and children in many women-headed households. The reason: they lack access and control over land including village common lands and forests. It is critical for women, who live in rural areas and depend on agriculture and related activities for survival, to gain access to, and control over land and to usufruct rights on village common lands and forests.[45]

A recent report from the United Nations Human Rights Division confirms these claims that there are clear "interlinkages between adequate housing and violence against women, forced evictions, homelessness, property, privatization, inheritance and access to land, the impact of cultural and social norms and multiple discrimination." The report lists categories of women who are particularly vulnerable to loss of land:

> Victims of domestic violence, widowed, elderly, divorced or separated women, female-headed households, women forcibly separated from

45. http://hlrn.org.in/womens-rights.

their children, women victims of forced evictions, indigenous and tribal women, women with disabilities and women in conflict/post-conflict situations, women from ethnic and national minorities, including refugees, migrant women workers, women from descent- and work-based communities, domestic women workers, sex workers, and lesbian and transgender women. The testimonies from recent regional consultations have highlighted additional groups of women who can be particularly vulnerable to violations of their right to adequate housing including Roma/traveller women, women who have become widows as a result of HIV/AIDS, and young women—particularly young homeless women.[46]

Thus, a key question about Leviticus 25 is what it envisions as justice. While the text addresses socio-economic inequalities, it does not address the particular vulnerabilities of women in any way. The focus of the text is on Israelite landowners and their rights when they fall on hard times. The text does not offer any protections for the poor in urban settings. And finally, the text does not seem to advocate for closing the gap between wealthier and poorer landowners; instead, Leviticus 25 concerns itself with maintaining the status quo as God had determined. Not every tribe had equal access to arable lands. Some tribes received much larger portions of land than others. Clans and families within tribal allotments in rich, arable soil would inevitably amass greater wealth from Jubilee to Jubilee. While lands had to be returned to the original owners at the Jubilee, the profits from amassed lands would remain with the buyers and creditors. Leviticus teaches that no Israelite actually owns land and that the community ultimately receives its land from God, but it does not say that all Israelites receive an equal portion. This stands in stark contrast to other biblical texts that call out for justice and righteousness; for example, Zechariah 7:9-10, which states: "Thus says the Lord of hosts: Render true judgments, show kindness and mercy to one another; do not oppress the widow, the orphan, the alien, or the poor; and do not devise evil in your hearts against one another."[47] Leviticus 25 never uses the terms "justice" or "righteousness."

---

46. United Nations Economic and Social Council, "Women and Adequate Housing: Report by the Special Rapporteur on Adequate Housing as a Component of the Right to an Adequate Standard of Living, and on the Right to Non-Discrimination" (February 27, 2006), pars. 29–30, https://www.nuigalway.ie/media/housinglawrightsandpolicy/files/undocs/-UN-Doc.-E:CN.4:2006:118.pdf.

47. See also, for example, Jer 7:5-6; Ezek 18.

On the other hand, the legislation in Leviticus 25 does address the dangers of exploitation and attempts to put in place a system to alleviate potential exploitation of Israelite landowners. The text also benefits the land, ensuring that no land is ever overworked. Leviticus 25 does reveal an awareness of the complex relationship among people, animals, the produce of the land, and the land itself; this appreciation becomes even more evident in Leviticus 26.

# Leviticus 26:1-46

# *Eco-Friendly Blessings and Curses of Chaos*

L eviticus 26 functions as the epilogue following a body of law.[1]
Each of the three major bodies of law in the Torah ends with
a list of blessings and curses—blessings for fulfillment of the law and
curses for failing to observe it. This kind of epilogue was typical in ancient Near Eastern vassal treaties and law codes and biblical literature
was consistent with the convention of the times.

Since this epilogue form was common in the ancient Near East, it is
not surprising to find a range of similar expressions among the blessings
and curses in Leviticus 26 and Deuteronomy 28–29, as well as in ancient
Near Eastern documents. In a few cases, Leviticus and Deuteronomy use
terms that appear nowhere else in the Bible, though frequently they use
different vocabulary to convey similar images. For example, both books
refer to "skies of iron and land of bronze"; additionally, both use similar
language for diseases and similar imagery regarding eating the flesh of

1. See Baruch A. Levine, "The Epilogue to the Holiness Code: A Priestly Statement
on the Destiny of Israel," in *Judaic Perspectives on Ancient Israel*, ed. Jacob Neusner,
Baruch A. Levine, and Ernest S. Frerichs (Philadelphia: Fortress, 1987), 9–34 for a
discussion of rare and unusual terms in this chapter.

children and the coming of rains. Interestingly, a great number of rare terms and phrases from Leviticus 26 also appear in the book of Ezekiel. This is not surprising given the many connections between the two books.

In reference to "When I break your staff of bread, ten women shall bake your bread in a single oven" (Lev 26:26), Baruch Levine notes a bilingual statuary inscription, written in Aramaic and Akkadian, from Tell Fekherye in northeast Syria. Line 22 of the Aramaic reads: "May one hundred women bake bread in a single oven, but let them not fill it!" The Akkadian reads: "May one hundred baking women not even fill a single oven!"[2] These similarities suggest that much of the language in Leviticus 26 is formulaic, and thus the language departs a great deal from Holiness Legislation language.

Having said this, while the epilogue in Leviticus 26 shares the same function and similar formulaic language as Deuteronomy 28–29 (and to a lesser extent Exodus 23:20-33), each epilogue has its own defining features. The typical pattern is first to offer blessings as rewards for covenant obedience and then a list of curses that will result from disobedience. While Leviticus 26 follows that pattern, it also modifies it so that the curses come in stages, each stage corresponding to a different expression of Israel's disobedience. Israel's failure to obey God results in a series of punishments (v. 18); then Israel's coldness or contrariness results in another series of punishments (v. 21); then another set of curses is presented when the people refuse to accept admonishment (vv. 23-24); a final set of punishments is presented as God becomes cold or contrary to Israel (vv. 27-28). While the epilogue in Deuteronomy 27 begins with an exhortation to the people to make the right decision, Leviticus 26:3 and 14 present the decision to obey or disobey the commandments as a moral choice with clear consequences. That moral choice is, however, dynamic: Israel might choose obedience and experience rewards for that choice (vv. 3-13) but then change course and experience penalties for disobedience (vv. 14-39).

## The Good News (26:1-13)

Leviticus 26:3-13 notes positive consequences for obeying the law. This section presents a concise yet holistic picture of an ideal world, beginning with the promise of rains and agricultural bounty. Verse 4

---

2. Levine, *Leviticus* Excursus 11, p. 278, where he cites Jonas C. Greenfield and Aaron Shaffer, "Notes on the Curse Formulae of the Tell Fekherye Inscription," *RB* 92 (1985): 47–59.

*Lev 26:1-13*

²⁶ᐟ¹You shall make for yourselves no idols and erect no carved images or pillars, and you shall not place figured stones in your land, to worship at them; for I am the Lord your God. ²You shall keep my sabbaths and reverence my sanctuary: I am the Lord.

³If you follow my statutes and keep my commandments and observe them faithfully, ⁴I will give you your rains in their season, and the land shall yield its produce, and the trees of the field shall yield their fruit. ⁵Your threshing shall overtake the vintage, and the vintage shall overtake the sowing; you shall eat your bread to the full, and live securely in your land. ⁶And I will grant peace in the land, and you shall lie down, and no one shall make you afraid; I will remove dangerous animals from the land, and no

sword shall go through your land. ⁷You shall give chase to your enemies, and they shall fall before you by the sword. ⁸Five of you shall give chase to a hundred, and a hundred of you shall give chase to ten thousand; your enemies shall fall before you by the sword. ⁹I will look with favor upon you and make you fruitful and multiply you; and I will maintain my covenant with you ¹⁰You shall eat old grain long stored, and you shall have to clear out the old to make way for the new. ¹¹I will place my dwelling in your midst, and I shall not abhor you. ¹²And I will walk among you, and will be your God, and you shall be my people. ¹³I am the Lord your God who brought you out of the land of Egypt, to be their slaves no more; I have broken the bars of your yoke and made you walk erect.

describes what the earth produces while verse 5 focuses on the human work necessary in separating chaff from wheat, cultivating a vineyard, and sowing seeds. The result is an environment where the land and the people live in a symbiotic relationship, or as the text puts it: "you will dwell in your land with peace of mind" (v. 5, translation mine). In addition, there is a promise of peace, which is defined in verse 6 as the absence of sword and wild animals; in other words, no external predators, whether human or animal, will threaten the biome.[3] In this ideal environment, God promises that the community will thrive and that God will uphold the covenant (v. 9).

At the pinnacle of blessings is God's actual presence among the community, which is expressed with the terms מִשְׁכָּנִי ("my dwelling" in v. 11)

---

3. Some scholars argue that v. 6 addresses two distinct promises. First, peace in the land equals the absence of civil unrest, and second, the verse promises no threat from the outside. See, for example, Jacob Milgrom, *Leviticus 23–27*, AB 3B (New York: Doubleday, 2001), 2295–96.

and מתהלך ("walk among you" in v. 12). Jacob Milgrom argues that H transforms P's משכן from a physical dwelling place to a generalized term for God's presence; thus, משכני and מתהלך are one and the same: a promise of God's presence everywhere in the community.[4] As I have suggested elsewhere,[5] I disagree with Milgrom's assertion that H's use of technical priestly terminology is only metaphorical; instead I would suggest a both/and proposition. Leviticus 26:12 both affirms God's presence in dedicated holy space and extends this concept so that God is not restricted to the holy place. What is unusual about this verse is the phrase "I will walk among you," which is highly anthropomorphic language and which resembles non-priestly texts like Genesis 5:22 in which God walks with Enoch (also Gen 2:24; 6:9; and 7:1). That concept is extraordinary in that it acknowledges God's presence within the sanctuary, but it also describes a God who "walks" with the people of Israel, just as Enoch, Noah, and Abraham (Gen 5:22, 24; 6:9; and 7:1) first walked with God. While H does anthropomorphize God in comparison to P (see Israel Knohl), the characteristic of God walking about with people is generally associated with J texts. The blessings conclude with the formal covenant oath "You will be my people and I will be your God" and a reference to when YHVH brought the people out from Egyptian bondage (v. 13).

The ideal world depicted in Leviticus 26 is internally focused and is essentially about food, progeny, and a sense of security and safety. Furthermore, instead of focusing (as many priestly texts do) on hierarchies of social status, gender, and states of holiness, the most important quality of the ideal world of Leviticus 26 is that the land, domesticated animals, people, and God all live together in harmony. The complex priestly cult provides a mechanism to reach for that ideal. The ideal agricultural community, while certainly not the Garden of Eden, shares with the Garden of Eden and with J's view of ideal highland farming a number of features. The Garden of Eden is situated in arable land, and the role of humans is to work the land with a certainty that the land will produce its bounty. Leviticus 26 promises that God will walk (התהלך) among the people of Israel, just as God walks (התהלך) through the Gar-

---

4. Ibid., 2299–2301.

5. S. Tamar Kamionkowski, "Did the Priests Have a 'Name' Theology?," in *The Bible and Its World, Rabbinic Literature and Jewish Law and Jewish Thought*, vol. 1 of *'Iggud—Selected Essays in Jewish Studies*, ed. Baruch Schwartz, Abraham Melamed, and Aharon Shemesh (Jerusalem: Proceedings of the Fourteenth World Congress of Jewish Studies, 2008), 21–38.

den of Eden (Gen 3:8). I am not suggesting that this priestly writer was intentionally calling to mind the Garden of Eden but that the priestly writer does present a world that is not radically different. This view is also presented in Ezekiel 34:25-28:

> I will make with them a covenant of peace and banish wild animals from the land, so that they may live in the wild and sleep in the woods securely. I will make them and the region around my hill a blessing; and I will send down the showers in their season; they shall be showers of blessing. The trees of the field shall yield their fruit, and the earth shall yield its increase. They shall be secure on their soil; and they shall know that I am the LORD, when I break the bars of their yoke, and save them from the hands of those who enslaved them. They shall no more be plunder for the nations, nor shall the animals of the land devour them; they shall live in safety, and no one shall make them afraid.

The most significant difference between Leviticus 26 and Ezekiel's vision, on the one hand, and the J Garden of Eden story, on the other, lies with God's relationship to the natural world. As Theodore Hiebert has written regarding the J view,

> J views the world of nature as a single metaphysical reality, the central and defining feature of which is adama, arable land. Nature's constituent parts, the earth and soil and its various forms of life—plant, animal, human—are distinct features of the same organic system, sharing a common essence derived from the soil. Even the character and activity of J's deity are narrated largely in terms of this same metaphysical realm.[6]

In contrast to J's view of God in Genesis 2 as deeply connected to nature, Leviticus 26 and Ezekiel 43 portray God as separate from nature.

The beauty of this vision is even more apparent when we compare it to Deuteronomy 28:10, which states, "All the peoples of the earth shall see that you are called by the name of the LORD, and they shall be afraid of you," and Deuteronomy 28:12b-13a, which declares, "You will lend to many nations, but you will not borrow. The LORD will make you the head, and not the tail; you shall be only at the top, and not at the bottom." Deuteronomy includes the common trope of power and strength with respect to Israel's standing among the nations, while Leviticus 26 focuses on internal harmony.

---

6. Theodore Hiebert, *The Yahwist's Landscape: Nature and Religion in Early Israel* (Oxford: Oxford University Press, 1996), 65.

### The Curses in Judaism

According to Leviticus 26, the rights of the land, embodied in the laws of the Sabbatical or Shmitah Year, take precedence over the needs of people, for "the land must enjoy her Sabbaths" (Lev 26:34, 43). This chapter describes six curses that will come, one after the other, if the people of Israel do not let the land rest on the Sabbatical Year. These curses describe the unraveling of the relationship between the people and the land, marked by who eats what or whom. The thread of this progression is woven in and out with other threads, but here is what it looks like when we isolate it: (1) "you will sow your seed for emptiness, for your enemies will eat it" (v. 16); (2) "you will completely use your strength for emptiness, and your land will not give her produce and the tree of the land will not give his fruit" (v. 20); (3) "I will send out against you the animal of the field and she will make you childless and cut off your animals and diminish you" (v. 22); (4) "you will be gathered [i.e., like a harvest] into your cities . . . and I will break the staff of bread against you . . . you will eat, and you will not be satisfied" (v. 26); (5) "you will eat the flesh of your sons and your daughters' flesh you will eat" (v. 29); (6) "you will be lost in the nations and the land of your enemies will eat you" (v. 38). In the third curse, the animals, who should have been allowed to share the Sabbatical Year produce from the land alongside the people, instead take the people themselves as their due, while in the fifth, it is the people who eat their own children. Because the Jewish people was in exile for so long, the last curse, that "the land will eat you," does not sound like the worst one; because we love our children, it is the fifth that sounds the worst. But symbolically, if the land eats us, this represents the final step: a complete reversal of the right relationship between people and land.[7]

*David Seidenberg*

## The Bad News (26:14-46)

The result of a failed system is a natural world that has essentially turned into stone or, more literally, iron and copper (v. 19), a world devoid of life and the potential for life. In that world wild animals over-run the community, killing people and destroying domesticated ani-

---

7. See David Seidenberg, "Shmitah: The Purpose of Sinai" in Ellen F. Davis, *Scripture, Culture, and Agriculture: An Agrarian Reading of the Bible* (New York: Cambridge University Press, 2009), 99–100.

¹⁴But if you will not obey me, and do not observe all these commandments, ¹⁵if you spurn my statutes, and abhor my ordinances, so that you will not observe all my commandments, and you break my covenant, ¹⁶I in turn will do this to you: I will bring terror on you; consumption and fever that waste the eyes and cause life to pine away. You shall sow your seed in vain, for your enemies shall eat it. ¹⁷I will set my face against you, and you shall be struck down by your enemies; your foes shall rule over you, and you shall flee though no one pursues you. ¹⁸And if in spite of this you will not obey me, I will continue to punish you sevenfold for your sins. ¹⁹I will break your proud glory, and I will make your sky like iron and your earth like copper. ²⁰Your strength shall be spent to no purpose: your land shall not yield its produce, and the trees of the land shall not yield their fruit.

²¹If you continue hostile to me, and will not obey me, I will continue to plague you sevenfold for your sins. ²²I will let loose wild animals against you, and they shall bereave you of your children and destroy your livestock; they shall make you few in number, and your roads shall be deserted.

²³If in spite of these punishments you have not turned back to me, but

mals (v. 22). There will be an increase in swords and pestilence with a constant diminishing of resources (vv. 23-25), so that "ten women bake . . . in a single oven," and even then there will barely be enough bread to go around (v. 25).[8] Conditions will deteriorate until starvation leads to massive deaths, survivors scatter, and the land becomes utterly desolate. Ironically, in this picture, the writer asserts good news: despite the distress that people and domestic animals will experience as a result of disobedience, the land will get its sabbatical rest.

Most scholars believe that the descriptions of increased anxiety and constant terror in Leviticus 26:14-33 are later additions to the text that reflect the actual experiences of the exiled survivors. There is also general agreement that the promise of a restored covenant (vv. 40-45) also reflects later additions.[9]

---

8. Carol Meyers observes that the text refers to women not only as bread bakers but also as those who control the allocation of food portions, thus revealing a source of power for women in the household. "Lev 26:26 Women as Bread Bakers," in *Women in Scripture: A Dictionary of Named and Unnamed Women in the Hebrew Bible, The Apocryphal/Deuterocanonical Books and the New Testament*, ed. Carol Meyers, Toni Craven, and Ross S. Kraemer (Boston: Houghton Mifflin, 2000), 213–14.

9. See Levine, "The Epilogue to the Holiness Code," 9–34.

continue hostile to me, ²⁴then I too will continue hostile to you: I myself will strike you sevenfold for your sins. ²⁵I will bring the sword against you, executing vengeance for the covenant; and if you withdraw within your cities, I will send pestilence among you, and you shall be delivered into enemy hands. ²⁶When I break your staff of bread, ten women shall bake your bread in a single oven, and they shall dole out your bread by weight; and though you eat, you shall not be satisfied.

²⁷But if, despite this, you disobey me, and continue hostile to me, ²⁸I will continue hostile to you in fury; I in turn will punish you myself sevenfold for your sins. ²⁹You shall eat the flesh of your sons, and you shall eat the flesh of your daughters. ³⁰I will destroy your high places and cut down your incense altars; I will heap your carcasses on the carcasses of your idols. I will abhor you. ³¹I will lay your cities waste, will make your sanctuaries desolate, and I will not smell your pleasing odors. ³²I will devastate the land, so that your enemies who come to settle in it shall be appalled at it. ³³And you will scatter among the nations, and I will unsheathe the sword against you; your land shall be a desolation, and your cities a waste.

³⁴Then the land shall enjoy its sabbath years as long as it lies desolate, while you are in the land of your enemies; then the land shall rest, and enjoy its sabbath years. ³⁵As long as it lies desolate, it shall have the rest it did not have on your sabbaths when you were living on it. ³⁶And as for those of you who survive, I will send faintness into their hearts in the lands of their enemies; the sound of a driven leaf shall put them to flight, and they shall flee as one flees from the sword, and they shall fall though no one pursues. ³⁷They shall stumble over one another, as if to escape a sword, though no one pursues; and you shall have no power to stand against your enemies. ³⁸You shall perish among the nations, and the land of your enemies shall devour you. ³⁹And those of you who survive shall languish in the land of your enemies because of their iniquities; also they shall languish because of the iniquities of their ancestors.

⁴⁰But if they confess their iniquity and the iniquity of their ancestors, in that they committed treachery against me and, moreover, that they continued hostile to me—⁴¹so that I, in turn, continued hostile to them and brought them into the land of their enemies; if then their uncircumcised heart is humbled and they make amends for their iniquity, ⁴²then will I remember my covenant with Jacob; I will remember also my covenant with Isaac and also my covenant with Abraham, and I will remember the land. ⁴³For the land shall be deserted by them, and enjoy its sabbath years by lying desolate without them, while they shall make amends for their iniquity, because they dared to spurn my ordinances, and they abhorred my statutes. ⁴⁴Yet for all that, when they are in the land

of their enemies, I will not spurn them, or abhor them so as to destroy them utterly and break my covenant with them; for I am the LORD their God; ⁴⁵but I will remember in their favor the covenant with their ancestors whom I brought out of the land of Egypt in the sight of the nations, to be their God; I am the LORD.

⁴⁶These are the statutes and ordinances and laws that the LORD established between himself and the people of Israel on Mount Sinai through Moses.

# Leviticus 27:1-34

# *How Much Is a Woman Really Worth?*

## An Appendix

Leviticus 26 offers a poetic and powerful conclusion to the book of Leviticus, with an articulation of the blessings or curses that will fall on the people of Israel as a consequence of the choices they make; so it is somewhat surprising and curious that there follows one additional chapter that is neither theologically profound nor beautiful in its articulation. The topic of Leviticus 27 is about taking back vows made to God. Some scholars suggest that the placement of this chapter after Leviticus 26 works well because Leviticus 26 focuses on what God vows to us, and Leviticus 27 focuses on what the people vow to God. This is a superficial connection, however, since Leviticus 27 is actually about getting out of vows, not fulfilling them. Scholars have also noted that this final chapter alludes to the laws of the Jubilee, so the material in Leviticus 27 had to be placed after Leviticus 25. Nonetheless, it is likely that this material was added to the book of Leviticus as an appendix of sorts.

## The Commodification of People and Status (27:1-8)

Leviticus 27:1-8 has little to commend it from a feminist perspective, except to affirm that, in the patriarchal environment in which these texts were composed, men were considered to be of greater worth than

*Lev 27:1-8*

²⁷:¹The Lᴏʀᴅ spoke to Moses, saying: ²Speak to the people of Israel and say to them: When a person makes an explicit vow to the Lord concerning the equivalent for a human being, ³the equivalent for a male shall be: from twenty to sixty years of age the equivalent shall be fifty shekels of silver by the sanctuary shekel. ⁴If the person is a female, the equivalent is thirty shekels. ⁵If the age is from five to twenty years of age, the equivalent is twenty shekels for a male and ten shekels for a female. ⁶If the age is from one month to five years, the equivalent for a male is five shekels of silver, and for a female the equivalent is three shekels of silver. ⁷And if the person is sixty years old or over, then the equivalent for a male is fifteen shekels, and for a female ten shekels. ⁸If any cannot afford the equivalent, they shall be brought before the priest and the priest shall assess them; the priest shall assess them according to what each one making a vow can afford.

women. Behind verses 1-8 lies an assumption that a person could pledge him- or herself, or a member of one's family, to full-time service to God. Such is the case with the vow that Jephthah makes to God in Judges 11 and Hannah's promise that she would devote her son to a life of service in 1 Samuel 1. While Jephthah's vow involved the actual slaughter of his daughter, the priestly writings substitute donations of actual people with donations in shekels (money). Verses 1-8 set out the monetary value of different people by age and biological sex for the purposes of substituting a payment in place of a person. Adult males from twenty to sixty years old are valued at fifty shekels while adult females of the same age are valued at thirty shekels. From five to twenty years old, males are valued at twenty shekels while females are valued at ten. A male infant up to five years old is worth five shekels, and baby girls are worth three shekels. Finally, males over sixty years old are valued at fifteen shekels and women at ten shekels. Some scholars have argued that these amounts represent a small fortune and would have been very difficult to pay. The high expense may have served as a deterrent from having individuals make frivolous vows.[1]

Many commentaries have been eager to point out that the shekel designations do not measure a human being's intrinsic worth but rather their

---

1. Gordon Wenham has argued that the price was set according to the prices in the slave market; "Leviticus 27:2-8 and the Price of Slaves," *ZAW* 90 (1978): 264–65.

monetary value as laborers.[2] I find this distinction unconvincing and meaningless. The value of different kinds of skills and jobs is socially determined just as a human being's worth is subjective and determined by a host of social, economic, and cultural factors. It is not accurate to assume that a male worker is more productive than a female worker, especially if the labor involves work for the official cult in textiles, bread making, and supervision of administrative units. A female is worth less in this chapter because the society in which this text was produced reflected and further inscribed status to gender. As Judith Romney Wegner has noted: "Women occupied with childbearing and nurturing would have less time to devote to their 'economic' labor at spindle or loom. Then, as now, the facts of life produced a differential in the biblical equivalent of male and female wages!"[3]

Carol Meyers suggests that women's importance in the economy of ancient Israel was acknowledged and is reflected in the monetary assessments. Meyers considers the female percentage of the combined value of a male and female in each group. She notes that women are placed at the lowest valuation between the ages of five and twenty, during childbearing age and the risks attendant with high infant/mother mortality. She also notes that the difference between males and females over sixty years old is the smallest because a man is less productive in his physical labors while a woman can still be productive in domestic responsibilities.[4] Her arguments are compelling and yet, were a child to be given to the priests as payment of a vow, that child would offer a lifetime of service and thus be of more value than a forty-year-old male. Meyers's thesis works if we assume that a value is placed on a person based on her or his economic productivity at the age at which the vow is made.

It is interesting to note that the valuations are set by only two factors: age and biological sex. The text does not use the words "men" and "women," but rather "male" and "female." There are no distinctions between social classes, between skill sets, between free people and slaves, between Israelites and non-Israelites.

2. Samuel E. Balentine, *Leviticus* (Louisville: Westminster John Knox, 2002), 208–9.

3. Judith Romney Wegner, "Leviticus," in *The Women's Bible Commentary*, ed. Carol A. Newsom and Sharon H. Ringe (Louisville: Westminster John Knox, 1992), 43.

4. Carol Meyers, "Procreation, Production and Protection: Male-Female Balance in Early Israel," *JAAR* 51 (1983): 569–93, esp. 584–87.

## Consecrating Animals and Homes (27:9-15)

Leviticus 27:9-15 addresses gifts of animals and houses to God. A person might bring an animal to the priests to serve as an offering to God. According to Leviticus 27, once that promise of a gift has been made, the animal belongs to YHVH; that is, the animal is considered holy. Even if one should find a more appealing animal to offer, the better animal cannot be substituted because the first animal belongs to YHVH. If someone attempts to substitute another animal, the individual has essentially promised both animals and so both animals become the property of YHVH. The same principle holds for "impure" animals, that is, animals that cannot be offered as sacrifices but that can be used for other purposes. The difference is that a nonsacrificial animal can be redeemed by paying a fine of 20 percent of the animal's value.

Saul Olyan argues that this process of redemption, whether of nonsacrificial animals or of property or persons, is a form of legitimate profanation. Legitimate profanation, he argues, is expressed in Leviticus 27 via the mechanism of vows and redemption. "Legitimate profanation, according to Leviticus 27, is therefore mainly a mechanism to undo a vow."[5] When one vows land, animals, or houses to God, that vow makes the thing holy. To bring it back to the profane, it can be redeemed with the addition of a fifth of its value. Olyan contrasts such legitimate profanation (redemption of vows) with illegitimate profanation. For example, when unqualified people eat sacred food, that sacred food is polluted, or when a priest's daughter engages in unsanctioned sexual activity, the priest's holiness status is profaned.[6]

## Consecrating Land (27:16-25)

The consecration of land, that is, gifting land to YHVH, is more complicated than gifting animals or property because the laws of the Jubilee must be taken into account. Verses 16-25 address two different cases: the gifting of land by someone who owns the land according to the laws of inheritance and the gifting of land by someone who has purchased the land for the term of a Jubilee. The value of gifted or consecrated land is established by "its seed requirements" (v. 16). It is not clear if

---

5. Saul Olyan, *Rites and Rank: Hierarchy in Biblical Representations of Cult* (Princeton: Princeton University Press, 2000), 26.

6. For example, see Lev 19:12; 20:3; 22:31-32.

9If it concerns an animal that may be brought as an offering to the LORD, any such that may be given to the LORD shall be holy. 10Another shall not be exchanged or substituted for it, either good for bad or bad for good; and if one animal is substituted for another, both that one and its substitute shall be holy. 11If it concerns any unclean animal that may not be brought as an offering to the LORD the animal shall be presented before the priest. 12The priest shall assess it: whether good or bad, according to the assessment of the priest, so it shall be. 13But if it is to be redeemed, one-fifth must be added to the assessment.

14If a person consecrates a house to the LORD, the priest shall assess it: whether good or bad, as the priest assesses it, so it shall stand. 15And if the one who consecrates the house wishes to redeem it, one-fifth shall be added to its assessed value, and it shall revert to the original owner.

16If a person consecrates to the LORD any inherited landholding, its assessment shall be in accordance with its seed requirements: fifty shekels of silver to a homer of barley seed. 17If the person consecrates the field as of the year of jubilee, that assessment shall stand; 18but if the field is consecrated after the jubilee, the priest shall compute the price for it according to the years that remain until the year of jubilee, and the assessment shall be

seed requirement refers to a land's expected annual produce or if seed requirement indicates the size of the fields and the amount of seed that could be planted.[7] Most commentators argue that the reference is to the size of land or, as Timothy M. Willis has stated, "The valuation is a reflection of the cost of the investment, not an estimate of any profits the land might provide."[8]

In the first case, if a landowner wishes to gift his land to YHVH immediately following a Jubilee Year, the value of the land is assessed based on its seed requirements multiplied by forty-nine, the number of years until the land reverts back to the original landowner. If the landowner

---

7. Nobuyoshi Kiuchi (*Leviticus*, ApOTC 3 [Nottingham: Inter-Varsity Press, 2007], 499) claims that the property's value is based on the amount of the barley produced. Both Baruch Levine (*Leviticus: A JPS Torah Commentary* [Philadelphia: Jewish Publication Society of America, 1989], 196) and Jacob Milgrom (*Leviticus 23–27*, AB 3B [New York: Doubleday, 2001], 2383) argue that seed requirement, fifty shekels of silver for a homer of barley seed, refers to the size of the arable land. Both commentators cite parallel designations from Mesopotamian sources. So too John E. Hartley, *Leviticus*, WBC 4 (Waco, TX: Word Books, 1992), 482.

8. Timothy M. Willis, *Leviticus*, AOTC (Nashville: Abingdon, 2009), 233.

reduced. ¹⁹And if the one who consecrates the field wishes to redeem it, then one-fifth shall be added to its assessed value, and it shall revert to the original owner; ²⁰but if the field is not redeemed, or if it has been sold to someone else, it shall no longer be redeemable. ²¹But when the field is released in the jubilee, it shall be holy to the LORD as a devoted field; it becomes the priest's holding. ²²If someone consecrates to the LORD a field that has been purchased, which is not a part of the inherited landholding, ²³the priest shall compute for it the proportionate assessment up to the year of jubilee, and the assessment shall be paid as of that day, a sacred donation to the LORD. ²⁴In the year of jubilee the field shall return to the one from whom it was bought, whose holding the land is. ²⁵All assessments shall be by the sanctuary shekel: twenty gerahs shall make a shekel.

wishes to redeem the land, the landowner must pay the assessed value in addition to a twenty percent fine. Verses 22-24 describe a similar process for a person who wishes to consecrate purchased lands. The difference is that in the Jubilee Year the land reverts back to the original owner.

Essentially, according to Leviticus 25, all the land ultimately belongs to YHVH, but each tribe has an allotment that is permanently leased by YHVH. When a landowner consecrates her or his land to YHVH, that person is turning over the land for use by the priests in service to YHVH. The crux of this section of Leviticus 27 appears in verses 20-21. NRSV translates verse 20 as "but if the field is not redeemed or if it has been sold to someone else, it is not redeemable." NJPS translates the same verse as "but if he does not redeem the land, and the land is sold to another, it shall no longer be redeemable." According the NRSV, if one of two conditions exist—either the land is not redeemed or the land is sold—then the laws of the Jubilee releasing the property to its original owners no longer apply. NJPS, however, interprets the verse to indicate that both conditions must exist: both the owner does not redeem the land and the land is sold to another. Presumably, if the owner does not redeem the land before the Jubilee, the land would automatically return to the landowner in the fiftieth year, so the NRSV translation does not make sense. Who would sell the land in such a manner that it would no longer belong to the designated inheritors?

Baruch Levine argues that "the sense must be, therefore, that the priesthood sold the land when it became apparent that its donor did not intend to redeem it. Once this occurred, the donor lost his right to redeem it,

ever." Levine argues that the release of lands back to the original owners during the Jubilee does not apply to consecrated lands.[9] Nobuyoshi
Kiuchi posits that perhaps the landowner sells land to another buyer
while also having consecrated the lands to YHVH: "Perhaps an owner
comes to consider his dedication of a field an unwise move. Then he
seeks some way to recover some value from his loss. He sells the field
to another without informing the buyer that the field has been consecrated to YHWH. The penalty for employing this conniving tactic is the
owner's loss of that land."[10] It is also possible that the priests chose to sell
the land before it was redeemed by the original owner. Jacob Milgrom
argues that the owner consecrates the land after having sold it, knowing
that the buyer has full use of the land until the Jubilee but that the land
goes to YHVH at the release. For Milgrom, the sanctuary had no priority
over landowners, and the priestly principle that any land can become
the sole property of the sanctuary only if it is given by the landowner
was a critique of "indentured land being swallowed up by avaricious
creditors" as reflected in the prophetic writings of the eighth century.[11]

## Firstlings, Proscriptions, Tithes (27:26-34)

Leviticus 27:26-33 offer a series of miscellaneous laws that are connected by the general theme: if God already owns something, it cannot be used for a vow or be redeemed. Exodus 13:2 commands that all
firstlings must be consecrated to God, so Leviticus 27:26-27 comments
that firstlings can never be used in vows because they do not belong to
the people in the first place.[12] Verses 28-29 state that anything that has
been devoted to God cannot be ransomed. The challenge in these verses
focuses on the term חרם ("devoted" in NRSV v. 28; or "proscribed" in NJP).
Gordon J. Wenham says that the חרם is more solemn than a vow and that
only leaders would have had the authority to declare such a proscrip-
tion.[13] Milgrom accepts Ephraim Stern's definition that it is "consecration

---

9. Levine, *Leviticus*, 196–97.

10. Kiuchi, *Leviticus*, 483. So too Raymond Westbrook, *Property and the Family in Biblical Law* (Sheffield: Sheffield Academic, 1991), 56.

11. Milgrom, *Leviticus 23–27*, 2383–85.

12. Biblical texts on the firstlings are contradictory. Deut 15:20 legislates that the meat of the firstlings actually belongs to the owner and his family.

13. Gordon J. Wenham, *The Book of Leviticus* (Grand Rapids: Eerdmans, 1979), 341.

²⁶A firstling of animals, however, which as a firstling belongs to the Lᴏʀᴅ, cannot be consecrated by anyone; whether ox or sheep, it is the Lᴏʀᴅ's. ²⁷If it is an unclean animal, it shall be ransomed at its assessment, with one-fifth added; if it is not redeemed, it shall be sold at its assessment.

²⁸Nothing that a person owns that has been devoted to destruction for the Lᴏʀᴅ, be it human or animal, or inherited landholding, may be sold or redeemed; every devoted thing is most holy to the Lᴏʀᴅ. ²⁹No human beings who have been devoted to destruction can be ransomed; they shall be put to death.

³⁰All tithes from the land, whether the seed from the ground or the fruit from the tree, are the Lᴏʀᴅ's; they are holy to the Lᴏʀᴅ. ³¹If persons wish to redeem any of their tithes, they must add one-fifth to them. ³²All tithes of herd and flock, every tenth one that passes under the shepherd's staff, shall be holy to the Lᴏʀᴅ. ³³Let no one inquire whether it is good or bad, or make substitution for it; if one makes substitution for it, then both it and the substitute shall be holy and cannot be redeemed.

³⁴These are the commandments that the Lᴏʀᴅ gave Moses for the people of Israel on Mount Sinai.

through destruction."[14] A person who has been proscribed by a court is to be put to death, and enemy lands that were devoted to God were to be utterly destroyed. Verses 30-33 exclude tithes from items that may be used in making vows. In other words, using the same item as a tithe and as a vow is double-dipping!

Leviticus 27:34 brings the book of Leviticus to a close with a simple statement that YHVH commanded all the material set forth to Moses at Mount Sinai. A similar conclusion is found in Leviticus 26:46; most scholars believe that the concluding statement in Leviticus 26 was the book's original ending and that the concluding statement in Leviticus 27 serves to connect this appendix to the rest of the book.

14. Milgrom, *Leviticus 23–27*, 2391.

# Postscript

As I reflect on years of immersion with Leviticus, feelings arise before thought. The book of Leviticus feels as much a mystery to me today as it did many years ago. Now that I have finished the commentary, I feel that I may be ready to begin studying it again.

This book of the Hebrew Bible continues to be elusive because it is so foreign to the modern mind. As a feminist who is mindful of the power of the hegemonic voice in shaping our perceptions of everything in this world, I have some concern about the power of the commentator's voice in defining the reader's experience of the text. So my advice to students of Leviticus is to read the text with an open and curious mind, to be both judgmental and nonjudgmental, to read many commentaries without giving up your own authority, and to let yourself relish in the multiplicity of interpretations. As a famous rabbinic dictum states: אלו ואלו דברי אלהים חיים, "These and those are the words of the living God" (b. Eruvin 13b).

# Works Cited

Abusch, Tzvi. *Mesopotamian Witchcraft: Toward a History and Understanding of Babylonian Witchcraft Beliefs and Literature*. Ancient Magic and Divination 5. Leiden: Brill, 2002.

Adams, Carol J. *The Sexual Politics of Meat: A Feminist-Vegetarian Critical Theory*. New York: Bloomsbury Academic, 2015.

Adelman, Penina V. *Miriam's Well: Rituals for Jewish Women Around the Year*. New York: Biblio Press, 1990.

Ademiluka, Solomon Olusola. "Prophetic Intervention in Eighth-Century Israel: A Recipe for Socio-Economic Recovery in Africa." *Uma: Journal of Philosophy and Religious Studies* 2 (2007): 24–37.

Amundson, Ron, and Akira Ruddle-Miyamoto. "A Wholesome Horror: The Stigmas of Leprosy in 19th Century Hawaii." *Disability Studies Quarterly* 30 (2010). http://dsq-sds.org/article/view/1270.

Anderson, Gary A. "Sacrifice and Sacrificial Offerings (OT)." *ABD* (1992), 5:870–86.

Asher-Greve, Julia M. "Mesopotamian Concepts of the Gendered Body." In *Gender and the Body in the Ancient Mediterranean*, edited by Maria Wyke, 8–37. Oxford: Blackwell Publishers, 1998.

Austin, J. L. *How to Do Things with Words*. Cambridge, MA: Harvard University Press, 1962.

Baden, Joel S., and Candida R. Moss. "The Origin and Intepretation of Sara'at in Leviticus 13–14." *JBL* 130 (2011): 643–62.

Bahrani, Zainab. *Women of Babylon: Gender and Representation in Mesopotamia*. London: Routledge, 2001.

Baker, Cynthia M. *Rebuilding the House of Israel: Architectures of Gender in Jewish Antiquity*. Stanford, CA: Stanford University Press, 2002.

Balentine, Samuel E. *Leviticus*. Louisville: Westminster John Knox Press, 2002.

Barber, Elizabeth Wayland. *Women's Work: The First 20,000 Years; Women, Cloth and Society in Early Times*. New York: Norton, 1996.

Bark, Franziska. " 'Listen Your Way in with Your Mouth': A Reading of Leviticus." *Judaism* 48 (1999): 198–208.

Barton, John. *Reading the Old Testament: Method in Biblical Study*. Rev. and enl. ed. Louisville: Westminster John Knox, 1996.

Baumgarten, Joseph M. "A Fragment on Fetal Life and Pregnancy in 4Q270." In *Pomegranates and Golden Bells: Studies in Biblical, Jewish, and Near Eastern Ritual, Law, and Literature in Honor of Jacob Milgrom*, edited by David P. Wright et al., 445. Winona Lake, IN: Eisenbrauns, 1995.

Baynton, Douglas C. "Disability and the Justification of Inequality in American History." In *New Disability History: American Perspectives*, edited by Paul K. Longmore and Lauri Umansky, 33–57. New York: New York University Press, 2001.

Bender, Claudia. *Die Sprache des Textilen: Untersuchungen zu Kleidung und Textilien im Alten Testament*. BWANT 177. Stuttgart: Kohlhammer, 2008.

Benetti-McQuoid, Jessica, and Krisanne Bursik. "Individual Differences in Experiences of and Responses to Guilt and Shame: Examining the Lenses of Gender and Gender Role." *Sex Roles* 53 (2005): 133–42.

Bergen, Wesley J. *Reading Ritual: Leviticus in Postmodern Culture*. LHB/OTS 417. London: T&T Clark, 2005.

Bergsma, John Sietze. *The Jubilee from Leviticus to Qumran: A History of Interpretation*. VTSup 115. Leiden: Brill, 2007.

Berrin, Susan, ed. *Celebrating the New Moon: A Rosh Chodesh Anthology*. Northvale, NJ: Jason Aronson, 1996.

Bibb, Bryan D. *Ritual Words and Narrative Worlds in the Book of Leviticus*. LHB/OTS 480. London: T&T Clark, 2009.

Blenkinsopp, Joseph. "An Assessment of the Alleged Pre-Exilic Date of the Priestly Material in the Pentateuch." *ZAW* 108 (1996): 495–518.

Boer, Roland. *The Sacred Economy of Ancient Israel*. LAI. Louisville: Westminster John Knox, 2015.

Bouloubasis, Victoria. "Women Butchers and Farmers Are Growing in Number, Especially in North Carolina." *Indy Week*. October 5, 2016. http://www.indyweek.com/indyweek/women-butchers-and-farmers-are-growing-in-number-especially-in-north-carolina/Content?oid=507291.

Boyarin, Daniel. "Are There Any Jews in 'The History of Sexuality'?" *Journal of the History of Sexuality* 5 (1994): 333–55.

Brenner, Athalya. "Gender in Prophecy, Magic and Priesthood: From Sumer to Ancient Israel." In *Embroidered Garments: Priests and Gender in Biblical Israel*, edited by Deborah W. Rooke, 3–18. Sheffield: Sheffield Phoenix, 2009.

———. "On Incest." In *A Feminist Companion to Exodus to Deuteronomy*, edited by Athalya Brenner, 113–38. FCB 6 Sheffield: Sheffield Academic, 1994; repr. 2001.

Brumberg-Kraus, Jonathan D. "Meat Eating and Jewish Identity: Ritualization of the Priestly 'Torah of Beast and Fowl' (Lev 11:46) in Rabbinic Judaism and Medieval Kabbalah." *AJSR* 24 (1999): 227–62.

Buckley, Thomas, and Alma Gottlieb. *Blood Magic: The Anthropology of Menstruation*. Berkeley: University of California Press, 1988.

Budin, Stephanie Lynn. *The Myth of Sacred Prostitution in Antiquity*. Cambridge: Cambridge University Press, 2008.

Burnside, Jonathan. "At Wisdom's Table: How Narrative Shapes the Biblical Food Laws and Their Social Function." *JBL* 135 (2016): 223–45.

Chevannes, Barry. "Rastafari: Toward a New Approach." *New West Indian Guide* 64 (1990): 127–48.

Cohn, Naftali S. "Domestic Women: Constructing and Deconstructing a Gender Stereotype in the Mishnah." In *From Antiquity to the Postmodern World: Contemporary Jewish Studies in Canada*, edited by Daniel Maoz and Andrea Gondos, 38–61. Newcastle upon Tyne: Cambridge Scholars Publishing, 2011.

Collins, Billie Jean. "Pigs at the Gate: Hittite Pig Sacrifice in Its Eastern Mediterranean Context." *JANER* 6 (2006): 155–88.

Cooper, Alan, and Bernard R. Goldstein. "The Development of the Priestly Calendars (I): The Daily Sacrifice and the Sabbath." *HUCA* 74 (2003): 1–20.

Cooper, Howard. "Some Thoughts on 'Scapegoating' and Its Origins in Leviticus 16." *European Judaism* 41 (2008): 112–19.

Coppes, Leonard J. "עני." In *TWOT*, edited by R. Laird Harris et al., 683–84. Chicago: Moody Publisher, 1980.

Davis, Ellen. *Scripture, Culture, and Agriculture: An Agrarian Reading of the Bible*. Cambridge: Cambridge University Press, 2009.

Day, John. *Molech: A God of Human Sacrifice in the Old Testament*. University of Cambridge Oriental Publications 41. New York: Cambridge University Press, 1989.

de Shong Meader, Betty. *Inanna, Lady of the Largest Heart: Poems of the Sumerian High Priestess Enheduanna*. Austin: University of Texas Press, 2000.

Destro, Adriana, and Mauro Pesce. "The Ritual for the Leper in Leviticus 14." In *Ancient Israel: The Old Testament in Its Social Context*, edited by Philip F. Esler, 66–77. Minneapolis: Fortress, 2006.

Douglas, Mary. "Atonement in Leviticus." *JSQ* 1 (1993): 109–30.

———. "The Forbidden Animals in Leviticus." *JSOT* 59 (1993): 3–23.

———. *In the Wilderness: The Doctrine of Defilement in the Book of Numbers*. JSOTSup, 158. Sheffield: JSOT Press, 1993.

———. *Leviticus as Literature*. Oxford: Oxford University Press, 1999.

———. *Purity and Danger: An Analysis of Concepts of Pollution and Taboo*. London: Routledge, 2003.

———. *Thinking in Circles: An Essay on Ring Composition*. New Haven: Yale University Press, 2007.

Ebeling, Jennie. "Women's Daily Life in Bronze Age Canaan." In *Women in Antiquity: Real Women Across the Ancient World*, edited by Stephanie Lynn Budin and Jean Macintosh Turfa, 465–76. New York: Routledge, 2016.

Eilberg-Schwartz, Howard. "Creation and Classification in Judaism: From Priestly to Rabbinic Conceptions." *History of Religions* 26 (1987): 357–81.

———. "The Problem of the Body for the People of the Book." In *Reading Bibles, Writing Bodies: Identity and the Book*, edited by Timothy K. Beal and David M. Gunn, 34–55. London: Routledge, 1997.

———. *The Savage in Judaism: An Anthropology of Israelite Religion and Ancient Judaism*. Bloomington: Indiana University Press, 1990.

Eisenberg, Evan. *The Ecology of Eden: An Inquiry into the Dream of Paradise and a New Vision of Our Role in Nature*. New York: Vintage Press, 1999.

Ellens, Deborah L. "Leviticus 15: Contrasting Conceptual Associations regarding Women." In *Reading the Hebrew Bible for a New Millennium*, edited by W. Kim et al., vol. 2, 131–36, 138–41. Harrisburg, PA: Trinity Press International, 2000.

———. "Menstrual Impurity and Innovation in Leviticus 15." In *Wholly Woman, Holy Blood: A Feminist Critique of Purity and Impurity*, edited by Judith A. Herbert, Judith Ann Johnson, and Anne-Marie Korte, 29–44. Harrisburg, PA: Trinity Press International, 2003.

———. *Women in the Sex Texts of Leviticus and Deuteronomy: A Comparative Conceptual Analysis*. LHB/OTS 458. London: T&T Clark, 2008.

Elliger, Karl. *Leviticus*. HAT 1/4. Tübingen: C. B. Mohr [Siebeck], 1966.

Erbele-Küster, Dorothea. *Körper und Geschlecht: Studien zur Anthropologie von Leviticus 12 und 15*. WMANT 121. Neukirchen-Vluyn: Neukirchener Verlag, 2008.

Eskenazi, Tamar Cohn. "VaYikra." In *The Torah: A Women's Commentary*, edited by Tamara Cohn Eskenazi and Andrea L. Weiss, 568–86. New York: URJ Press, 2008.

Feder, Yitzhaq. "Contagion and Cognition: Bodily Experience and the Conceptualization of Pollution (tum'ah) in the Hebrew Bible." *JNES* 72 (2013): 151–67.

———. "On Kuppuru, Kipper and Etymological Sins That Cannot Be Wiped Away." *VT* 60 (2010): 535–45.

Feinstein, Eve Levavi. *Sexual Pollution in the Hebrew Bible*. Oxford: Oxford University Press, 2014.

Feldman, Ron H. "'On Your New Moons': The Feminist Transformation of the Jewish New Moon Festival (1)." *Journal of Women and Religion* 19 (2001): 26–53.

Feuchtwang, Stephan. *Popular Religion in China: The Imperial Metaphor*. Richmond, Surrey: Curzon, 2001.

Finkelstein, Jacob J. "The Ox That Gored." *Transactions of the American Philosophical Society* 71 (1981): 1–89.

Fleming, Daniel E. "The Biblical Tradition of Anointing Priests." *JBL* 117 (1998): 401–14.

———. *Time at Emar: The Cultic Calendar and the Rituals from the Diviner's Archive.* Winona Lake, IN: Eisenbrauns, 2000.

Fonrobert, Charlotte Elisheva. "Bodily Perfection in the Sanctuary." In *Torah Queeries: Weekly Commentaries on the Hebrew Bible*, edited by Gregg Drinkwater, Joshua Lesser, and David Schneer, 123–28. New York: New York University Press, 2009.

———. "Gender Identity in Halakhic Discourse." In *Jewish Women: A Comprehensive Historical Encyclopedia*. March 1, 2009. *Jewish Women's Archive*. http://jwa.org/encyclopedia/article/gender-identity-in-halakhic-discourse.

———. *Menstrual Purity: Rabbinic and Christian Reconstructions of Biblical Gender.* Stanford, CA: Stanford University Press, 2002.

Fox, Everett. *The Five Books of Moses: Genesis, Exodus, Leviticus, Numbers, Deuteronomy: A New Translation with Introductions, Commentary, and Notes.* New York: Schocken Books, 1997.

Fried, Lisbeth S. "Another View on P'kudei." In *The Torah: A Women's Commentary*, edited by Tamara Cohn Eskenazi and Andrea L. Weiss, 560. New York: URJ Press, 2008.

Friedman, Susan Stanford. "Creativity and the Childbirth Metaphor: Gender Difference in Literary Discourse." *Feminist Studies* 13 (1987): 49–82.

Frymer-Kensky, Tikva. "Pollution, Purification, and Purgation in Biblical Israel." In *The Word of the Lord Shall Go Forth: Essays in Honor of David Noel Freedman in Celebration of His Sixtieth Birthday*, edited by Carol L. Meyers and M. O'Connor, 399–414. ASOR. Winona Lake, IN: Eisenbrauns, 1983. Reprinted in Tikva Frymer-Kensky, *Studies in Biblical and Feminist Criticism*, 329–50. Philadelphia: Jewish Publication Society of America, 2006.

Gabel, J. B., and C. B. Wheeler. "The Redactor's Hand in the Blasphemy Pericope of Leviticus XXIV." *VT* 30 (1980): 227–29.

Gafney, Wilda C. *Womanist Midrash: A Reintroduction to the Women of the Torah and the Throne.* Louisville: Westminster John Knox, 2017.

Gane, Roy. *Cult and Character: Purification Offerings, Day of Atonement, and Theodicy.* Winona Lake, IN: Eisenbrauns, 2005.

Geller, Myron S. "Woman Is Eligible to Testify." Committee on Jewish Law and Standards of the Rabbinical Assembly. HM 35:14.2001a. https://www.rabbinicalassembly.org/sites/default/files/public/halakhah/teshuvot/19912000/geller_womenedut.pdf.

Geller, Stephen A. "Blood Cult: Toward a Literary Theology of the Priestly Work of the Pentateuch." *Prooftexts* 12 (1992): 97–124.

———. "The God of the Covenant." In *One God or Many? Concepts of Divinity in the Ancient World*, edited by Barbara Nevling Porter, 273–319. Transactions of the Casco Bay Assyriological Institute 1. Chebeague, ME: Casco Bay Assyriological Institute, 2000.

———. *Sacred Enigmas: Literary Religion in the Hebrew Bible.* New York: Routledge, 1996.

Gerstenberger, Erhard. *Leviticus*. OTL. Louisville: Westminster John Knox, 1996.

Gevaryahu, Gilad J. "Ketovet Ka'aka (Leviticus 19:28): Tattooing or Branding?" *JBQ* 38 (2010): 13–20.

Gilchrest, Eric. "For the Wages of Sin Is . . . Banishment: An Unexplored Substitutionary Motif in Leviticus 16 and the Ritual of the Scapegoat." *EvQ* 85 (2003): 36–51.

Gilligan, Carol. *In a Different Voice: Psychological Theory and Women's Development.* Cambridge, MA: Harvard University Press, 1982.

Goldstein, Elizabeth W. *Impurity and Gender in the Hebrew Bible*. Lanham, MD: Rowman & Littlefield, 2015.

Goodfriend, Elaine Adler. "Leviticus 22:24: A Prohibition of Gelding." In *Current Issues in Priestly and Related Literature: The Legacy of Jacob Milgrom and Beyond,* edited by Roy Gane and Ada Taggar-Cohen, 67–92. Atlanta: SBL Press, 2015.

Goossaert, Vincent. "Chinese Religion: Popular Religion." In *Encyclopedia of Religion,* edited by L. Jones, 1613–21. Detroit: Macmillan Reference USA, 2005.

Graham, Ruth. "A Female Butcher on Beef, Death Threats, and Why Women Are Better at the Job." *The Grindstone.* May 14, 2012. http://www.thegrind stone.com/2012/05/14/office-politics/kari-underly-range-female-butcher -career-152/2/#ixzz4aTbGlJ00.

Greenberg, Moshe. "The Etymology of *niddah* (Menstrual) Impurity." In *Solving Riddles and Untying Knots: Biblical, Epigraphic and Semitic Studies in Honor of Jonas C. Greenfield,* edited by Ziony Zevit et al., 69–77. Winona Lake, IN: Eisenbrauns, 1995.

Greenfield, Jonas C., and Aaron Shaffer. "Notes on the Curse Formulae of the Tell Fekherye Inscription." *RB* 92 (1985): 47–59.

Grey, Mary. *Redeeming the Dream: Feminism, Redemption and Christian Tradition.* London: SPCK, 1989.

Gruber, Mayer I. "Women in the Cult According to the Priestly Code." In *Judaic Perspectives on Ancient Israel,* edited by Jacob Neusner, Baruch A. Levine, and Ernest S. Frerichs, 35–48. Philadelphia: Fortress, 1987.

Hamori, Esther. *Women's Divination in Biblical Literature: Prophecy, Necromancy and Other Arts of Knowledge.* ABRL. New Haven: Yale University Press, 2015.

Haran, Menahem. "Behind the Scenes of History: Determining the Date of the Priestly Source." *JBL* 100 (1981): 321–33.

———. "The Priestly Image of the Tabernacle." *HUCA* 36 (1965): 191–226.

———. *Temples and Temple-Service in Ancient Israel: An Inquiry into the Character of Cult Phenomena and the Historical Setting of the Priestly School.* Oxford: Oxford University Press, 1978.

Harris, Maurice D. *Leviticus: You Have No Idea.* Eugene, OR: Cascade Books, 2013.

Hartley, John E. *Leviticus*. WBC 4. Waco, TX: Word Books, 1992.

Hawley, Lance. "The Agenda of Priestly Taxonomy: The Conceptualization of טמא and שקץ in Leviticus 11." *CBQ* 77 (2015): 231–49.

Heider, George C. *The Cult of Molek: A Reassessment.* JSOTSup 43. Sheffield: JSOT Press, 1985.

Herman, Judith, and Linda Hirschman. "Father-Daughter Incest." *Signs* 2 (1977): 735–56.

Hiebert, Theodore. *The Yahwist's Landscape: Nature and Religion in Early Israel.* Oxford: Oxford University Press, 1996.

Hill, Kim, and A. Magdalena Hurtado. "Hunter-Gatherers of the New World." *American Scientist* 77 (1989): 436–43.

Holguín, Julián Andrés González. "Leviticus 24:10-23: An Outsider Perspective." *HS* 56 (2015): 89–102.

Honeyman, A. M. "The Salting of Shechem." *VT* 3 (1953): 192–95.

Houston, Walter J. "Towards an Integrated Reading of the Dietary Laws of Leviticus." In *The Book of Leviticus: Composition and Reception,* edited by Rolf Rendtorff, Robert A. Kugler, and Sarah Smith Bartel, 142–61. Leiden: Brill, 2003.

Hulse, E. V. "The Nature of Biblical 'Leprosy' and the Use of Alternative Medical Terms in Modern Translations of the Bible." *PEQ* 107 (1975): 87–105.

Hurowitz, Victor. "The Priestly Account of Building the Tabernacle." *JAOS* (1985): 21–30.

Hurvitz, Avi. "Dating the Priestly Source in Light of the Historical Study of Biblical Hebrew: A Century of Wellhausen." *ZAW* 100 (1988): 88–100.

———. "The Evidence of Language in Dating the Priestly Code: A Linguistic Study in Technical Idioms and Terminology." *RB* 81 (1974): 24–56.

———. "On the Usage of the Priestly Term עדה in Biblical Literature." *Tarbiz* 40 (1970–1971): 261–67 [Hebrew].

Hüttermann, Aloys. *The Ecological Message of the Torah: Knowledge, Concepts and Laws which Made Survival in a Land of Milk and Honey Possible.* Gainesville: University Press of Florida, 1999.

Hutton, Rodney R. "Narrative in Leviticus: The Case of the Blaspheming Son (Lev 24,10-23)." *Zeitschrift Für Altorientalische Und Biblische Rechtsgeschichte/ Journal for Ancient Near Eastern and Biblical Law* 3 (1997): 145–63.

Jacoby, Mario. *Shame and the Origins of Self-Esteem: A Jungian Approach.* Translated by Douglas Whitcher. London: Routledge, 1994; repr. 2003.

Janowski, Bernd. "Azazel עזאזל." In *Dictionary of Deities and Demons in the Bible,* edited by Karel van der Toorn, Bob Becking, and Pieter W. van der Horst, 128–31. 2nd rev. ed. Leiden: Brill and Grand Rapids, MI: Eerdmans, 1999.

Joosten, Jan. "La non-mention de la fille en Lévitique 18: exercice sur la rhétorique du Code de Sainteté." *ETR* 75 (2000): 415–20.

———. *People and Land in the Holiness Code: An Exegetical Study of the Ideational Framework of the Law in Leviticus 17–26.* VTSup 67. Leiden: Brill, 1996.

Joseph, Norma Baumel. "Introduction." *Nashim* 5 (2002): 7–13.

Kalimi, Isaac. "The Day of Atonement in the Late Second Temple Period: Sadducees' High Priests, Pharisees' Norms, and Qumranites' Calendar(s)." *Review of Rabbinic Judaism* 14 (2011): 71–91.

Kamionkowski, S. Tamar. "Breaking Through the Binaries: A Case Study of Ezekiel 16." In *The Feminist Companion to the Latter Prophets*, edited by Athalya Brenner, 170–85. FCB 8, 2nd ser. Sheffield: Sheffield Academic, 2002.

———. "Did the Priests Have a 'Name' Theology?" In *The Bible and Its World, Rabbinic Literature and Jewish Law and Jewish Thought*. Vol. 1 of *'Iggud: Selected Essays in Jewish Studies*, edited by Baruch Schwartz, Abraham Melamed, and Aharon Shemesh, 21–28. Jerusalem: Proceedings of the Fourteenth World Congress of Jewish Studies, 2008.

———. "The Erotics of Pilgrimage: A Fresh Look at Psalms 84 and 63." In *Gazing on the Deep: Ancient Near Eastern, Biblical, and Jewish Studies in Honor of Tzvi Abusch*, edited by Jeffrey Stackert, Barbara Nevling Porter, and David P. Wright, 467–78. Bethesda, MD: CDL Press, 2010.

———. "Nadav and Avihu and Dietary Laws: A Case of Action and Reaction." In *Torah Queeries: Weekly Commentaries on the Hebrew Bible*, edited by Gregg Drinkwater, Joshua Lesser, and David Schneer, 135–39. New York: New York University Press, 2009.

———. "Will the Real Miriam Please Stand Up." http://thetorah.com/will-the-real -miriam-please-stand-up/.

Kaufmann, Yehezkel. *The Religion of Israel: From Its Beginnings to the Babylonian Exile*. Translated by Moshe Greenberg. Chicago: University of Chicago Press, 1960.

Kazen, Thomas. "Dirt and Disgust: Body and Morality in Biblical Purity Laws." In *Perspectives on Purity and Purification in the Bible*, edited by Baruch S. Schwartz, Naftali S. Meshel, Jeffrey Stackert, and David P. Wright, 43–64. LHB/OTS 474. New York: T&T Clark, 2008.

Kirschner, Robert. "The Rabbinic and Philonic Exegesis of the Nadab and Abihu Incident (Lev. 10:1-6)." *JQR* 73 (1984): 375–93.

Kiuchi, Nobuyoshi. *Leviticus*. ApOTC 3. Nottingham: Inter-Varsity Press Academic, 2007.

———. *The Purification Offering in the Priestly Literature: Its Meaning and Function*. Sheffield: Sheffield Academic, 1987.

———. *A Study of Ḥāṭā' and Ḥaṭṭā't in Leviticus 4–5*. FAT 2. Tübingen: Mohr Siebeck, 2003.

Klawans, Jonathan. *Impurity and Sin in Ancient Judaism*. Oxford: Oxford University Press, 2000.

———. *Purity, Sacrifice, and the Temple: Symbolism and Supersessionism in the Study of Ancient Judaism*. Oxford: Oxford University Press, 2006.

Kline, Moshe. "'The Editor Was Nodding': A Reading of Leviticus 19 in Memory of Mary Douglas." *JHebS* 8 (2008): 1–59.

———. "Structure Is Theology: The Composition of Leviticus." In *Current Issues in Priestly and Related Literature: The Legacy of Jacob Milgrom and Beyond*, edited by Roy Gane and Ada Taggar-Cohen, 225–64. Atlanta: SBL Press, 2015.

Klingbeil, Gerald A. "Ritual Time in Leviticus 8 with Special Reference to the Seven Day Period in the Old Testament." *ZAW* 109 (1997): 500–513.

Knohl, Israel. *The Sanctuary of Silence: The Priestly Torah and the Holiness School.* Winona Lake, IN: Eisenbrauns, 2007.

Kohlberg, Lawrence. "The Claim to Moral Adequacy of a Highest Stage of Moral Judgment." *The Journal of Philosophy* 70 (1973): 630–46.

———. "Education, Moral Development and Faith." *Journal of Moral Education* 4 (1974): 5–16.

Kraemer, David C. *Jewish Eating and Identity Through the Ages.* London: Routledge, 2007.

Kriger, Diane. *Sex Rewarded, Sex Punished: A Study of the Status "Female Slave" in Early Jewish Law.* Boston: Academic Studies Press, 2011.

Kugel, James L. "On Hidden Hatred and Open Reproach: Early Exegesis of Leviticus 19:17." *HTR* 80 (1987): 43–61.

Lacks, Roslyn. *Woman and Judaism: Myth, History, and Struggle.* Garden City, NY: Doubleday, 1980.

Lazonby, David. "Applying the Jubilee to Contemporary Socio-Economic and Environmental Issues." *Journal of European Baptist Studies* 16 (2016): 30–50.

Leavitt, Gregory C. "Tylor vs. Westermarck: Explaining the Incest Taboo." *Sociology Mind* 3 (2013): 45–51.

Lehman, Marjorie. "The Gendered Rhetoric of Sukkah Observance." *JQR* 96 (2006): 309–35.

Leick, Gwendolyn. *Sex and Eroticism in Mesopotamian Literature.* London and New York: Routledge, 1994.

Leuchter, Mark. "The Politics of Ritual Rhetoric : A Proposed Sociopolitical Context for the Redaction of Leviticus 1–16." *VT* 60 (2010): 345–65.

Levin, Mordechai Zvi. "Hallalah (Profaned) / חללה." *Beit Mikra: Journal for the Study of the Bible and Its World* 29 (1984): 180–81 [Hebrew].

Levine, Baruch A. "The Epilogue to the Holiness Code: A Priestly Statement on the Destiny of Israel." In *Judaic Perspectives on Ancient Israel*, edited by Jacob Neusner, Baruch A. Levine, and Ernest S. Frerichs, 9–34. Philadelphia: Fortress, 1987.

———. *In the Presence of the Lord: A Study of Cult and Some Cultic Terms in Ancient Israel.* SJLA 5. Leiden: Brill, 1974.

———. *Leviticus: A JPS Torah Commentary.* Philadelphia: Jewish Publication Society of America, 1989.

Lings, K. Renato. "The 'Lyings' of a Woman: Male-Male Incest in Leviticus 18.22?" *Theology & Sexuality* 15 (2009): 231–50.

Lipka, Hilary B. *Sexual Transgression in the Hebrew Bible.* Sheffield: Sheffield Phoenix, 2006.

Liss, Hanna. "Ritual Purity and the Construction of Identity: The Literary Function of the Laws of Purity in the Book of Leviticus." In *The Books of Leviticus and Numbers*, edited by Thomas Romer, 329–54. BETL 215. Leuven: Peeters, 2008.

Livingston, Dennis H. "The Crime of Leviticus Xxiv 11." *VT* 36 (1986): 352–54.

Macht, David Israel. "A Scientific Appreciation of Leviticus 12:1-5." *JBL* 52 (1933): 253–60.

Macy, Gary, William T. Ditewig, and Phyllis Zagano. *Women Deacons: Past, Present, Future*. Mahwah, NJ: Paulist, 2011.

Magonet, Jonathan. " 'But If It Is a Girl She Is Unclean for Twice Seven Days . . .': The Riddle of Leviticus 12.5." In *Reading Leviticus: A Conversation with Mary Douglas*, edited by John F. A. Sawyer, 144–52. LHB/OTS 277. Sheffield: Sheffield Academic, 1996.

———. "The Structure and Meaning of Leviticus 19." *HAR* 7 (1983): 151–67.

Malul, Meir. "אִישׁ עִתִּי (Leviticus 16:21): A Marginal Person." *JBL* 128 (2009): 437–42.

Marsman, Hennie J. *Women in Ugarit and Israel: Their Social and Religious Position in the Context of the Ancient Near East*. Leiden: Brill, 2003.

Mayshar, Yoram. "Who Was the *Toshav*?" *JBL* 133 (2014): 225–46.

McClenney-Sadler, Madeline Gay. "Cry Witch! The Embers Still Burn." In *Pregnant Passion: Gender, Sex, and Violence in the Bible*, edited by Cheryl A. Kirk-Duggan, 117–41. Atlanta: SBL Press, 2003.

———. *Recovering Daughter's Nakedness: A Formal Analysis of Israelite Kinship Terminology and the Internal Logic of Leviticus 18*. LHM/OTS 476. New York: T&T Clark, 2007.

Meacham, Tirzah Z. "The Missing Daughter: Leviticus 18 and 20." *ZAW* 109 (1997): 254–59.

Melcher, Sarah J. "Blemish and Perfection of the Body in the Priestly Literature and Deuteronomy." *Journal of Religion, Disability & Health* 16 (2012): 1–15.

Mendes-Flohr, Paul. *Love, Accusative and Dative: Reflections on Leviticus 19:18*. The B.G. Rudolph Lectures in Judaic Studies. Syracuse, NY: Syracuse University Press, 2007.

Meshel, Naphtali. "Food for Thought: Systems of Categorization in Leviticus 11." *HTR* 101 (2008): 203–29.

———. *The "Grammar" of Sacrifice: A Generativist Study of the Israelite Sacrificial System in the Priestly Writings*. Oxford: Oxford University Press, 2014.

Meyer-Rochow, Victor Benno. "Food Taboos: Their Origins and Purposes." *Journal of Ethnobiology and Ethnomedicine* 5, no. 18 (2009), http://www.ethnobiomed.com/content/5/1/18.

Meyers, Carol L. "Having Their Space and Eating There Too: Bread Production and Female Power in Ancient Israelite Households." *Nashim* 5 (2002): 14–44.

———. "In the Household and Beyond: The Social World of Israelite Women." *ST* 63 (2009): 19–41.

———. "Lev 26:26 Women as Bread Bakers." In *Women In Scripture: A Dictionary of Named and Unnamed Women in the Hebrew Bible, The Apocryphal/Deuterocanonical Books and the New Testament*, edited by Carol Meyers, Toni Craven, and Ross S. Kraemer, 213–14. Boston: Houghton Mifflin, 2000.

———. "Procreation, Production, and Protection: Male-Female Balance in Early Israel." *JAAR* 51 (1983): 569–93.

Michalowski, Piotr. "Carminative Magic: Towards an Understanding of Sumerian Poetics," *ZA* 71 (1981): 1–18.

Milgrom, Jacob. "The Changing Concept of Holiness in the Pentateuchal Codes with Emphasis on Leviticus 19." In *Reading Leviticus: A Conversation with Mary Douglas*, edited by John F. A. Sawyer, 65–75. Sheffield: Sheffield Academic, 1996.

———. "Ethics and Ritual: The Foundations of the Biblical Dietary Laws." In *Religion and Law: Biblical-Judaic and Islamic Perspectives*, edited by Edwin Firmage, Bernard G. Weiss, and John W. Welch, 159–91. Winona Lake, IN: Eisenbrauns, 1990.

———. "Israel's Sanctuary: The Priestly 'Picture of Dorian-Gray,'" *RB* 83 (1976): 390–99.

———. "The Land Redeemer and the Jubilee." In *Fortunate the Eyes That See: Essays in Honor of David Noel Freedman in Celebration of His Seventieth Birthday*, edited by Astrid B. Beck, Andrew H. Bartelt, Paul R. Raabe, and Chris A. Franke, 66–69. Grand Rapids: Eerdmans, 1995.

———. *Leviticus 1–16*. AB 3. New York: Doubleday, 1991.

———. *Leviticus 17–22*. AB 3A. New York: Doubleday, 2000.

———. *Leviticus 23–27*. AB 3B. New York: Doubleday, 2001.

———. *Leviticus: A Book of Ritual and Ethics; A Continental Commentary*. Minneapolis: Fortress, 2004.

Miller, William Ian. *The Anatomy of Disgust*. Cambridge: Harvard University Press, 1997.

Miron, Ayala. "Nagu'a: Touched by the Divine." In *Torah Queeries: Weekly Commentaries on the Hebrew Bible*, edited by Gregg Drinkwater, Joshua Lesser, and David Shneer, 140–44. New York: New York University Press, 2009.

Mittwoch, H. "The Story of the Blasphemer Seen in a Wider Context." *VT* 15 (1965): 386–89.

Moskala, Jiří. "Categorization and Evaluation of Different Kinds of Interpretation of the Laws of Clean and Unclean Animals in Leviticus 11." *BR* 46 (2001): 5–41.

Mtshiselwa, Ndikho. "Reading Ruth 4 and Leviticus 25:8-55 in the Light of the Landless and Poor Women in South Africa: A Conversation with Fernando F. Segovia and Ernesto 'Che' Guevara." *HTS Teologiese Studies/Theological Studies* 72 (2016), a3140.

Murrell, N. Samuel. "Woman as Source of Evil and Contaminant in Rastafarianism: Championing Hebrew Patriarchy and Oppression with Lev 12." *Proceedings: East Great Lakes and Midwest Biblical Societies* 13 (1993): 191–209.

Neudecker, Reinhard. "'You Shall Love Your Neighbor as Yourself—I am the Lord' (Lev 19, 18) in Jewish Interpretation." *Bib* 73 (1992): 496–517.

Nihan, Christophe. *From Priestly Torah to Pentateuch: A Study in the Composition of the Book of Leviticus*. FAT 25. Tübingen: Mohr Siebeck, 2007.

———. "Israel's Festival Calendars in Leviticus 23, Numbers 28–29 and the Formation of 'Priestly' Literature." In *The Books of Leviticus and Numbers*, edited by Thomas Romer, 177–232. BETL 215. Leuven: Peeters, 2008.

Ogunyemi, Biodun. "Beyond the Security Threats." *The National Scholar: A Publication of the Academic Staff Union of Universities* (ASUU) 9 (2012): 36–37.

Oju, E. "Nigerians Have Stolen N7.9 Trillion." *Daily Times, Nigeria* (2013): 6.

Olanisebe, Samson O. "Laws of *Tzara'at* in Leviticus 13–14 and Medical Leprosy Compared." *JBQ* 42 (2014): 121–27.

Olaniyi, A. A. "The dal in Exodus 30:15 and Poverty Alleviation in Nigeria." *ASUU Journal of Humanities: A Journal of Research and Development* 2 (2012): 129–40.

Olyan, Saul M. " 'And with a Male You Shall Not Lie the Lying down of a Woman': On the Meaning and Significance of Leviticus 18:22 and 20:13." *Journal of the History of Sexuality* 5 (1994): 179–206.

———. *Disability in the Hebrew Bible: Interpreting Mental and Physical Differences.* Cambridge: Cambridge University Press, 2008.

———. *Rites and Rank: Hierarchy in Biblical Representations of Cult.* Princeton: Princeton University Press, 2000.

Overholt, Thomas. "1 Sam 28:7-25 Medium of Endor." In *Women in Scripture: A Dictionary of Named and Unnamed Women in the Hebrew Bible, The Apocryphal/ Deuterocanonical Books and the New Testament*, edited by Carol Meyers, Toni Craven, and Ross S. Kraemer, 244–45. Boston: Houghton Mifflin, 2000.

Peck, Alice, ed. *Godliness: Finding the Sacred in Housekeeping.* Woodstock, VT: Skylights Path Publishing, 2007.

Philip, Tarja S. "Gender Matters: Priestly Writing on Impurity." In *Embroidered Garments: Priests and Gender in Biblical Israel*, edited by Deborah W. Rooke, 40–59. Sheffield: Sheffield Phoenix, 2009.

———. *Menstruation and Childbirth in the Bible: Fertility and Impurity.* StBibLit 88. New York: Lang, 2006.

Pigott, Susan M. "Leviticus." In *The IVP's Women's Bible Commentary*, edited by Catherine Clark Kroeger and Mary J. Evans, 50–69. Downers Grove, IL: Intervarsity Press, 2002.

Radner, Janet. "Contemporary Reflection on Vayikra." In *The Torah: A Women's Commentary*, edited by Tamara Cohn Eskenazi and Andrea L. Weiss, 589. New York: URJ Press, 2008.

Ramban. *Commentary on the Torah.* Translated by Charles B. Chavel. New York: Shiloh, 1974.

Raphael, Rebecca. *Biblical Corpora: Representations of Disability in Hebrew Biblical Literature.* LHB/OTS 445. London: T&T Clark, 2008.

Rattray, Susan. "Marriage Rules, Kinship Terms and Family Structure in the Bible." In *Society of Biblical Literature 1987 Seminar Papers*, 537–44. Atlanta: Scholars Press, 1987.

Reid, Barbara E. *Taking up the Cross: New Testament Interpretations through Latina and Feminist Eyes.* Minneapolis: Fortress, 2007.

Rendtorff, Rolf. "Another Prolegomenon to Leviticus 17:11." In *Pomegranates and Golden Bells: Studies in Biblical Jewish and Near Eastern Ritual, Law and Literature in Honor of Jacob Milgrom*, edited by David P. Wright, David Noel Freedman, and Avi Hurvitz, 23–28. Winona Lake, IN: Eisenbrauns, 1995.

Rooke, Deborah W. "The Bare Facts: Gender and Nakedness in Leviticus 18." In *A Question of Sex? Gender and Difference in the Hebrew Bible and Beyond*, edited by Deborah W. Rooke, 20–38. HBM 14. Sheffield: Sheffield Phoenix, 2009.

———. "Breeches of the Covenant: Gender, Garments and the Priesthood." In *Embroidered Garments: Priests and Gender in Biblical Israel*, edited by Deborah W. Rooke, 19–37. Sheffield: Sheffield Phoenix, 2009.

Rosenblum, Jordan D. *Food and Identity in Early Rabbinic Judaism*. Cambridge: Cambridge University Press, 2010.

Rosenberg, Michael. "The Conflation of Purity and Prohibition: An Interpretation of Leviticus 18:19." *HTR* 107 (2014): 447–69.

Rosenstock, Bruce. "Incest, Nakedness, and Holiness: Biblical Israel at the Limits of Culture." *JSQ* 16 (2009): 333–62.

Rosenzweig, Franz. *The Star of Redemption*. Translated by William Hallo. New York: Holt, Rinehart and Winston, 1973.

Ruane, Nicole J. "Bathing, Status and Gender in Priestly Ritual." In *A Question of Sex? Gender and Difference in the Hebrew Bible and Beyond*, edited by Deborah W. Rooke, 66–81. HBM 14. Sheffield: Sheffield Phoenix, 2009.

———. "Pigs, Purity, and Patrilineality: The Multiparity of Swine and Its Problems for Biblical Ritual and Gender Construction." *JBL* 134 (2015): 489–504.

———. *Sacrifice and Gender in Biblical Law*. Cambridge: Cambridge University Press, 2013.

Ruddick, Sara. *Maternal Thinking: Towards a Politics of Peace*. London: Women's Press, 1990.

Rushton, Kathleen P. *The Parable of the Woman in Childbirth of John 16:21: A Metaphor for the Death and Glorification of Jesus*. Lewiston: Mellen, 2011.

Sacks, Jonathan. *Covenant and Conversation: A Weekly Reading of the Jewish Bible; Leviticus: The Book of Holiness*. Covenant and Conversation. Jerusalem: Koren Publishers, 2015.

Satlow, Michael L. " 'They Abused Him Like a Woman': Homoeroticism, Gender Blurring, and the Rabbis in Late Antiquity." *Journal of the History of Sexuality* 4 (1994): 1–25.

Sawyer, John F. A., ed. *Reading Leviticus: A Conversation with Mary Douglas*. Sheffield: Sheffield Academic, 1996.

Schearing, Linda S. "Double Time . . . Double Trouble? Gender, Sin, and Leviticus 12." In *The Book of Leviticus: Composition and Reception*, edited by Rolf Rendtorff, Robert A. Kugler, and Sarah Smith Bartel, 429–50. Leiden: Brill, 2003.

Schenker, Adrian. "The Biblical Legislation on the Release of Slaves: The Road from Exodus to Leviticus." *JSOT* 78 (1998): 23–41.

———. "What Connects the Incest Prohibitions with the Other Prohibitions Listed in Leviticus 18 and 20?" In *The Book of Leviticus: Composition and Reception*, edited by Rolf Rendtorff, Robert A. Kugler, and Sarah Smith Bartel, 162–85. Leiden: Brill, 2003.

Schipper, Jeremy, and Jeffrey Stackert. "Blemishes, Camouflage and Sanctuary Service: The Priestly Deity and His Attendants." *Hebrew Bible and Ancient Israel: Bodies and Religion* 4 (2013): 458–78.

Schüssler Fiorenza, Elisabeth. *Jesus: Miriam's Child, Sophia's Prophet: Critical Issues in Feminist Christology.* New York: Continuum, 1995.

Schwartz, Baruch J. "Israel's Holiness: The Torah Traditions." In *Purity and Holiness: The Heritage of Leviticus,* edited by Marcel Poorthius and Joshua Schwartz, 47–59. Jewish and Christian Perspectives 2. Leiden: Brill, 2000.

———. *The Holiness Legislation: Studies in the Priestly Code.* Jerusalem: Magnes Press, 1999 [Hebrew].

———. "Leviticus." In *The Jewish Study Bible,* edited by Adele Berlin and Marc Zvi Brettler. Oxford: Oxford University Press, 2004.

———. "Leviticus." In *The New Interpreter's Bible,* edited by Beverly Roberts Gaventa and David Petersen, 57–82. Nashville: Abingdon, 2010.

———. "A Literary Study of the Slave-Girl Pericope: Leviticus 19:20-22." *Scripta Hierosolymitana* 31 (1986): 241–55.

———. "Miqra' Qodesh and the Structure of Leviticus 23." In *Purity, Holiness, and Identity in Judaism and Christianity: Essays in Memory of Susan Haber,* edited by Carl S. Ehrlich, Anders Runesson, and Eileen Schuller, 11–24. Tübingen: Mohr Siebeck, 2013.

———. "The Priestly Account of the Theophany and Lawgiving at Sinai." In *Texts, Temples and Traditions: A Tribute to Menahem Haran,* edited by Michael V. Fox et al., 103–34. Winona Lake, IN: Eisenbrauns, 1996.

———. "'Profane' Slaughter and the Integrity of the Priestly Code." *HUCA* 67 (1996): 15–42.

———. "The Prohibitions Concerning the 'Eating' of Blood in Leviticus 17." In *Priesthood and Cult in Ancient Israel,* edited by Gary A. Anderson and Saul M. Olyan, 34–66. JSOTSup 125. Sheffield: JSOT Press, 1991.

Schwartz, Regina. "Joseph's Bones and the Resurrection of the Text: Remembering in the Bible." *PMLA* 103 (1988): 114–24.

Seidenberg, David. "Animal Rights in the Jewish Tradition." In *Encyclopedia of Religion and Nature.* Vol. 1. London: Bloomsbury, 2005.

———. "Brit Taharah: Reconstructing the Covenantal Body of the Jew." *Sh'ma* 25/486 (January 20, 1995).

———. *Kabbalah and Ecology: God's Image in the More-Than-Human World.* Cambridge: Cambridge University Press, 2016.

———. "Kashroots: An Eco-History of the Kosher Laws." *The Jew and the Carrot: Jews, Food, and Contemporary Issues.* November 21, 2008. www.jcarrot.org/kashroots-an-eco-history-of-the-kosher-laws; revised on NeoHasid.org, September 2009, www.neohasid.org/torah/kashroots.

Sered, Susan Starr. "Food and Holiness: Cooking as a Sacred Act among Middle Eastern Jewish Women." *Anthropological Quarterly* 61 (1988): 129–39.

———. *Women as Ritual Experts: The Religious Lives of Elderly Jewish Women in Jerusalem.* Oxford: Oxford University Press, 1996.

Shapiro, James. *Evolution: A View from the 21st Century*. Upper Saddle River, NJ: FT Press, 2011.

Shectman, Sarah. "The Social Status of Priestly and Levite Women." In *Levites and Priests in Biblical History and Tradition*, edited by Mark A. Leuchter and Jeremy M. Hutton, 83–99. Atlanta: SBL Press, 2011.

———. *Women in the Pentateuch: A Feminist and Source-Critical Analysis*. HBM 23. Sheffield: Sheffield Phoenix, 2009.

Sherwin-White, A.N. *Roman Citizenship*. Oxford: Oxford University Press, 1979.

Sherwood, Yvonne. *The Prostitute and the Prophet: Hosea's Marriage in Literary-Theoretical Perspective*. JSOTSup 212. Sheffield: JSOT Press, 1996.

Shorter, Edward. *Women's Bodies: A Social History of Women's Encounter with Health, Ill-Health and Medicine*. New Brunswick, NJ: Transaction Press, 1997.

Sklar, Jay. "Sin and Impurity: Atoned or Purified? Yes!" In *Perspectives on Purity and Purification in the Bible*, edited by Baruch J. Schwartz, David P. Wright, Jeffrey Stackert, and Naphtali S. Meshel, 18–31. LHB/OTS 474. New York: T&T Clark, 2008.

———. *Sin, Impurity, Sacrifice, Atonement: The Priestly Conceptions*. HBM 2. Sheffield: Sheffield Academic, 2005.

Stackert, Jeffrey. "The Sabbath of the Land in the Holiness Legislation: Combining Priestly and Non-Priestly Perspectives." *CBQ* 73 (2011): 239–50.

Steinert, Ulrike. "Fluids, Rivers and Vessels: Metaphors and Body Concepts in Mesopotamian Gynecological Texts." *Journal des Médecines Cunéiformes* 22 (2013): 1–23.

Stevens, Paul. "'Leviticus Thinking' and the Rhetoric of Early Modern Colonialism." *Culture* 35 (1993): 441–61.

Stewart, David Tabb. "Does the Priestly Purity Code Domesticate Women?" In *Perspectives on Purity and Purification in the Bible*, edited by Pamela Barmash, Shachar Pinsker, and Rick Painter, *HS* 50 (2009): 65–73.

———. "Leviticus." In *The Queer Bible Commentary*, edited by Deryn Guest, Robert Goss, and Mona West, 77–104. London: SCM Press, 2015.

———. "Leviticus 19 as Mini-Torah." In *Current Issues in Priestly and Related Literature: The Legacy of Jacob Milgrom and Beyond*, edited by Roy E. Gane and Ada Taggar-Cohen, 299–334. Atlanta: SBL Press, 2015.

———. "Parturient's Ritual for a Girl: The Puzzle of Double Pollution." In *Hermeneutics, Gender and Biblical Law*, edited by Athalya Brenner and F. Rachel Magdalene, 65–73. Sheffield: Sheffield Phoenix, forthcoming.

Stiebert, Johanna. *First-Degree Incest and the Hebrew Bible: Sex in the City*. LHB/OTS 596. Bloomsbury: T&T Clark, 2016.

———. *Fathers and Daughters in the Hebrew Bible*. Oxford: Oxford University Press, 2013.

———. "Human Conception in Antiquity: The Hebrew Bible in Context." *Theology & Sexuality* 16 (2010): 209–27.

Stigers, Harold G. "גּר." In *TWOT*, edited by R. Laird Harris et al., 155–56. Chicago: Moody Press, 1980.

Sun, Henry T. C. *An Investigation of the Compositional History of the So-Called Holiness School: Leviticus 17–26.* PhD diss., Claremont Graduate School, Claremont, CA, 1990.

Teubal, Savina. *Sarah the Priestess: The First Matriarch of Genesis.* Athens, OH: Swallow Press, 1984.

Van Dyke Parunak, H. "Transitional Techniques in the Bible." *JBL* 102 (1983): 541.

Walsh, Jerome T. "Leviticus 18:22 and 20:13: Who Is Doing What to Whom?" *JBL* 120 (2001): 201–9.

Walzer, Michael. *Exodus and Revolution.* New York: Basic Books, 1985.

Watts, James W. *Leviticus 1–10.* HCOT. Leuven: Peeters, 2013.

———. *Ritual and Rhetoric in Leviticus: From Sacrifice to Scripture.* Cambridge: Cambridge University Press, 2007.

Wegner, Judith Romney. " 'Coming Before the Lord': The Exclusion of Women from the Public Domain of the Israelite Priestly Cult." In *The Book of Leviticus: Composition and Reception,* edited by Rolf Rendtorff, Robert A. Kugler, and Sarah Smith Bartel. Leiden: Brill, 2003.

———. "Leviticus." In *The Women's Bible Commentary,* edited by Carol A. Newsom and Sharon H. Ringe, 36–44. Louisville: Westminster John Knox, 1992.

Weinfeld, Moshe. *The Worship of Molech and of the Queen of Heaven and Its Background.* Butzon & Bercker, 1972.

———. *Social Justice in Ancient Israel and in the Ancient Near East.* Jerusalem: The Magnes Press, 1995.

Weingreen, Jacob. "The Case of the Blasphemer (Leviticus XXIV 10 Ff.)." *VT* 22 (1972): 118–23.

Weisberg, Dvora E. "Post-biblical Interpretations: VaYikra." In *The Torah: A Women's Commentary,* edited by Tamara Cohn Eskenazi and Andrea L. Weiss, 588–89. New York: URJ Press, 2008.

Weller, Robert P. *Unities and Diversities in Chinese Religion.* Seattle: University of Washington Press, 1987.

Wellhausen, Julius. *Prolegomena to the History of Israel.* Translated by J. S. Black and A. Menzies. Eugene, OR: Wipf and Stock, 2003.

Wells, Bruce. "The Quasi-Alien in Leviticus 25." In *The Foreigner and the Law: Perspective from the Hebrew Bible and the Ancient Near East,* edited by R. Achenbach, Rainer Albertz, and J. Wöhrle, 135–55. BZAR 16. Weisbaden: Harrassowitz, 2011.

Wenham, Gordon J. *The Book of Leviticus.* Grand Rapids: Eerdmans, 1979.

———. "Leviticus 27:2-8 and the Price of Slaves." *ZAW* 90 (1978): 264–65.

———. "Why Does Sexual Intercourse Defile (Lev 15,18)?" *ZAW* 95 (1983): 432–34.

Westbrook, Raymond. *Property and the Family in Biblical Law.* Sheffield: Sheffield Academic, 1991.

Westbrook, Raymond, and Theodore J. Lewis. "Who Led the Scapegoat in Leviticus 16:21?" *JBL* 127 (2008): 417–22.

Westenholz, Joan Goodnick. "Tamar, *Qedesa*, *Qadistu*, and Sacred Prostitution in Mesopotamia." *HTR* 82 (1989): 245–65.

Whitekettle, Richard. "Levitical Thought and the Female Reproductive Cycle: Wombs, Wellsprings, and the Primeval World." *VT* 46 (1996): 376–91.

———. "Leviticus 15.18 Reconsidered: Chiasm, Spatial Structure and the Body." *JSOT* 49 (1991): 31–45.

Willis, Timothy M. *Leviticus*. AOTC. Nashville: Abingdon, 2009.

Wolf, Arthur P. "Gods, Ghosts, and Ancestors." In *Religion and Ritual in Chinese Society*, edited by A. P. Wolf, 131–82. Stanford, CA: Stanford University Press, 1974.

Wong, Sonia K. "Gendering Nakedness (ערוה) and Sexual Policing: A Cross-Cultural Perspective," a session paper presented at the annual meeting of the Society of Biblical Literature, San Antonio, TX (November 2016).

———. "The Notion of כפר in the Book of Leviticus and Chinese Popular Religion." In *Leviticus and Numbers*, edited by Athalya Brenner and Archie Chi Chung Lee, 77–96. Minneapolis: Fortress, 2013.

Wright, Christopher J. H. "Leviticus." In *New Bible Commentary*, edited by G. J. Wenham et al., 121–57. Nottingham: Inter-Varsity Press, 1994.

Wright, David P. *Disposal of Impurity: Elimination Rites in the Bible and in Hittite and Mesopotamian Literature*. Atlanta: Scholars Press, 1987.

———. "The Gesture of Hand Placement in the Hebrew Bible and in Hittite Literature." *JAOS* 106 (1986): 433–46.

———. "Holiness in Leviticus and Beyond: Differing Perspectives." *Int* 53 (1999): 351–64.

———. "Observations on the Ethical Foundations of the Biblical Dietary Laws: A Response to Jacob Milgrom." In *Religion and Law: Biblical-Judaic And Islamic Perspectives*, edited by Edwin Firmage, Bernard G. Weiss, and John W. Welch, 193–98. Winona Lake, IN: Eisenbrauns, 1990.

———. "The Spectrum of Priestly Impurity." In *Priesthood and Cult in Ancient Israel*, edited by Gary A. Anderson and Saul M. Olyan, 150–81. JSOTSup 125. Sheffield: JSOT Press, 1991.

———. "Unclean and Clean (OT)." *ABD* 6:729–41.

Zevit, Ziony. "Converging Lines of Evidence Bearing on the Date of P." *ZAW* 94 (2013): 263–75.

Zierler, Wendy. "A Tribute to the Blasphemer's Mother: Shelomit, Daughter of Divri." http://thetorah.com/a-tribute-to-the-blasphemers-mother-shelomit-daughter-of-divri/.

Ziskind, Jonathan R. "The Missing Daughter in Leviticus XVIII." *VT* 46 (1996): 125–30.

Zornberg, Aviva Gottlieb. *Genesis: The Beginning of Desire*. Lincoln: University of Nebraska Press, 1995.

# Index of Scripture References and Other Ancient Writings

# Index of Subjects

## General Editor

Barbara E. Reid, OP, is a Dominican Sister of Grand Rapids, Michigan. She holds a PhD in biblical studies from The Catholic University of America and is professor of New Testament studies at Catholic Theological Union, Chicago. Her most recent publications are *Wisdom's Feast: An Invitation to Feminist Interpretation of the Scriptures* (2016) and *Abiding Word: Sunday Reflections on Year A, B, C* (3 vols.; 2011, 2012, 2013). She served as vice president and academic dean at CTU from 2009 to 2018 and as president of the Catholic Biblical Association in 2014–2015.

## Volume Editor

Lauress Wilkins Lawrence is an African-American Hebrew Bible scholar. She holds an AB from Smith College, and an MDiv and PhD from Boston University. She is the author of *The Book of Lamentations and the Social World of Judah in the Neo-Babylonian Era* (Gorgias Press, 2010). Previously on the Religious Studies faculty at Regis College in Weston, Massachusetts, she now balances her time as an independent scholar with her work in philanthropy in Maine.

## Author

Tamar Kamionkowski is professor of biblical studies at the Reconstructionist Rabbinical College outside of Philadelphia, where she has also served as the vice president for academic affairs and dean of the college. She currently serves as the cochair for the Jewish Interpretation of the Bible section of the Society for Biblical Literature. She is the author of *Gender Reversal and Cosmic Chaos: Studies in the Book of Ezekiel* (Sheffield Academic, 2003) and coeditor of *Bodies, Embodiment and Theology of the Hebrew Scriptures* (T&T Clark, 2010). She holds a BA from Oberlin College, an MTS from Harvard Divinity School, and a PhD in Near Eastern and Judaic studies from Brandeis University.